TRAMPS
AND
TRADE-UNION TRAVELERS

TRAMPS
AND
TRADE-UNION TRAVELERS

Internal Migration and Organized Labor in Gilded-Age America, 1870–1900

KIM MOODY

Haymarket Books
Chicago, Illinois

Published in 2019 by
Haymarket Books
P.O. Box 180165
Chicago, IL 60618
773-583-7884
www.haymarketbooks.org
info@haymarketbooks.org

ISBN: 978-1-60846-755-6

Distributed to the trade in the US through Consortium Book Sales and Distribution (www.cbsd.com) and internationally through Ingram Publisher Services International (www.ingramcontent.com).

This book was published with the generous support of Lannan Foundation and Wallace Action Fund.

Special discounts are available for bulk purchases by organizations and institutions. Please call 773-583-7884 or email info@haymarketbooks.org for more information.

Cover photograph courtesy of the San Diego Railroad Museum Library.
Cover design by Eric Kerl.

Printed in Canada by union labor.

Library of Congress Cataloging-in-Publication data is available.

10 9 8 7 6 5 4 3 2 1

CONTENTS

CONTENTS

PREFACE

THIS BOOK will argue that high levels of internal migration in Gilded-Age America undermined the stability and growth of trade unions and labor-based parties. Most of the traditional "American exceptionalist" arguments that assert a lack of class consciousness among American workers will be challenged. Significant weight will be given to the racial, ethnic, and gender divisions within the American working class as a source of relative organizational weakness. As archival sources reveal, however, despite their divisions, workers of all ethnic and racial groups drawn into wage-labor in the Gilded Age often displayed high levels of class consciousness and political radicalism through their actions, organizations, and hundreds of weekly labor papers. They also showed an awareness of the problems of frequent migration, or "tramping," in building stable organizations. Driven by the tumultuous conditions of uneven industrialization, millions of people migrated from state to state, countryside to city, and city to city at rates far higher than in Europe. A detailed analysis of the statistics on migration, work-related traveling, and union membership trends shows that this created a high level of membership turnover in the major organizations of the day—the American Federation of Labor and the Knights of Labor. Confronted in the 1880s with the highest level of migration in the period, the Knights of Labor saw rapid growth turn into continuous decline. The more stable craft unions also saw significant membership loss to migration through an ineffective traveling-card system. The organizational weakness that resulted undermined efforts by American workers to build independent labor-based parties in the 1880s and 1890s. "Pure and simple" unionism would triumph by the end of the century despite the existence of a significant socialist minority in organized labor.

ACKNOWLEDGMENTS

First I want to thank my thesis supervisors in the Department of American and Canadian Studies at the University of Nottingham, John Ashworth, Peter Ling, and Christopher Phelps, whose criticisms, suggestions, and encouragement have been invaluable. Many others in the department have also helped me over various intellectual, technical, and administrative hurdles. Through their many comments, my fellow postgraduate students have also been a source of commentary and encouragement from a variety of perspectives.

I am grateful for the financial assistance from the Arts and Humanities Research Council for both my time in the doctoral program and for a research training support grant, which made possible the research and completion of my doctoral studies. I was fortunate to receive a great deal of help from a number of archivists and librarians.

Special thanks to the following: David Hays at the University of Colorado–Boulder Archives; Julie Herrada of the Labadie Collection at the University of Michigan–Ann Arbor; the staff of the Tamiment Library at New York University; and the librarians at the New York Public Library Newspaper and Microfilm Department in the Schwarzman Building and the Science, Industry, and Business Library. Thanks also to the staff of Haymarket Books who helped me through the publication process.

For the love, encouragement, and patience of my partner, Sheila Cohen, my enduring thanks.

INTRODUCTION

Migration and movement, mobility and motion characterized identity in Victorian America. A country in transition was also in transit.
—Thomas J. Schlereth[1]

I N AUGUST 1879, Robert Louis Stevenson, the Scottish writer then at the outset of a career that would later bring him fame with *Treasure Island* and *Dr. Jekyll and Mr. Hyde*, crossed the United States by train. In an essay titled "Across the Plains," he described his journey in some detail. When he boarded a train in Ogden, Utah, he found himself among the mostly working-class "emigrants" seeking a better life in the far West, divided into three passenger cars: the Chinese in one car, women and children (presumably white) in another, and white males in the car he occupied. This division was in some ways a metaphor for the society taking shape. With the exception of "one German family and a knot of Cornish miners . . . the rest were all American born" and "they came from every quarter of that Continent." He saw them as fugitives who spoke of a "hope that moves ever westward." Yet, "as we continued to steam westward toward the land of gold, we were continually passing other emigrant trains upon the journey east" whose disillusioned passengers advised the westbound migrants to "Come back!"[2]

The great teller of tales had witnessed a small piece of a gigantic drama of humanity fleeing one circumstance in hopes of a better one, often to find the metaphoric "gold" they sought in the West to be but a thin gilding, a gilding which hid the grimmer reality of wage labor much like the age itself that Mark Twain and Charles Dudley Warner called "gilded."[3] This book will argue that this geographic mobility, or internal migration—the movement of people back and forth across the land, deemed so worthy of remark by Stevenson in his American travels—is a crucial, if largely neglected, factor in determining the relative weakness of organized labor in Gilded-Age America. The working class of the late nineteenth-century United States was, so to speak, formed on the run. While migration was a feature of early class formation in other countries as well, the size, scale, and rapidity of this constant migration in the late nineteenth-century United States far outstripped that of any European country.

It was, to be sure, the wealth and power of industry and city that drew these "emigrants" in many directions across the vast continent that contained the United

States. But for the majority of those who were now becoming wageworkers, it was a time of trial and turmoil. The difficulties were easier on average for the native-born than the immigrant, the "old" immigrants than the "new," the skilled than the un-skilled, the white than the black or Chinese, and the man than the woman, but were still hard traveling anyway for most people who lived from payday to payday. The condition of wage labor was new for many, an experience radically different from the self-employment of the farm, peasant plot, or artisan's shop, where master and journeyman had once worked side by side. By 1879, the "boss" was typically no longer someone the employee knew personally, but a man, increasingly part of an impersonal corporation, possessed of enormous financial and material wealth and now known as a "capitalist."

These two emerging social classes were creating one another. Without labor there was no capital, as almost anyone could have told you at the beginning of the Gilded Age. Similarly, the same people would have agreed that without capital to build the railroads, factories, and machinery, there would be no work for the wage earner. This relationship, however, was anything but equal. For one thing, the wealth created was in no way distributed equally, a fact that was becoming increasingly obvious to most.

Thus, as the workers saw it, at the heart of this new relationship there was an implicit conflict over how to divide the wealth, which the labor theory of value—a widely held belief—told the workers they had created.

But that wasn't all. The labor market in which the wageworker sought work was uncertain, highly competitive, and—with great consequence—movable. The new "labor-saving" machinery seemed to make the work harder and more precar-ious. The capitalist employer had the power to hire and fire and, hence, to com-mand. The term "wage slave" came to capture the condition resulting from this new authority often vested in the arbitrary realm of the "foreman's empire" with its brutal "drive system."[4] Yet the formation of a new permanent wage-earning class in the United States was not simply a national process. The labor markets of the US might be local, regional, or national, but the workforce was drawn from around the world where huge numbers of peasants, farm laborers, and even wageworkers were being displaced.

As in the Old World, the built-in conflict of class formation and relations gave rise to new working-class organizations with which to fight this contest on and off the job: labor unions of various sorts, eight-hour leagues, weekly labor newspapers, cooperative enterprises, mutual-aid societies, and political organizations and parties, among others. Yet in the United States, the unions and political organizations in particular appeared weak in relation to their European cousins. Trade unions arose in the 1860s, but for the most part they collapsed in the depression of the 1870s. The Knights of Labor galloped onto the scene in the first half of the 1880s, soared to three-quarters of a million members in the midst of the Great Upheaval of 1886, helped to launch the most promising movement for independent working-class political action in the period, and then from 1887 onward the Knights declined steadily. The trade unions that came together to form the American Federation of Labor in 1886 survived but grew slowly until the turn of the twentieth century. The trend was very different from Britain, where union membership nearly tripled between 1889 and 1899, and from Germany, where union membership increased fivefold even under Bismarck's antisocialist laws and faster still after these laws lapsed in 1890.[5]

What inhibited the growth of labor organization that made the development of class conflict in the United States seem so different from that in the other major industrial nations of the period? This book will contend that historians of working-class developments in the United States would do well to pay greater attention to the observation of Howard P. Chudacoff: "With a spacious continent before him, the American had an especial opportunity to migrate. No account of the country's development can evade the continuous population movement which has settled the land, dissolved the frontier, and filled the cities."[6] Chudacoff is among the historians and social scientists who have taken notice of the unusual geographic mobility of the American population in the late nineteenth century. Few, however, have investigated its extent, and almost none have analyzed its impact on working-class organizations. This book will attempt to do just that.

Traditional "Exceptionalist" Explanations

Conventional explanations for the relative weakness of labor in the US have typically sought to find something essential in the American character resistant to collective class action. Werner Sombart set the tone and much of the content of the various exceptionalist explanations in *Why Is There No Socialism in the United States?*, published in 1906. Sombart argued that American workers lacked the class consciousness common to German workers. Essentially, the reasons he gave for this were that workers in the US, regardless of where they came from, experienced a prosperity unknown in Europe; had access to free or cheap land that provided an escape from permanent wage labor; and frequently experienced upward social mobility. In addition, he made the structural argument that the US political system with its cross-class two-party "monopoly" and electoral barriers made the formation of alternative parties difficult. Two decades later, Selig Perlman added to this body of analysis the notion that American workers possessed "job consciousness" rather than class consciousness.

These views have been frequently challenged over time. While this book cannot recite the full arguments against Sombart, Perlman, and those who have followed in their footsteps, a few examples and comments are relevant. To Sombart's question of why there is no socialism in the US, Aristide Zolberg observed, "It should be noted . . . that the question might have been equally asked of Britain, the homeland of industrial capitalism, where workers at the time still voted mostly Liberal."[7] Furthermore, my own research into primary sources reveals widespread support among American workers for labor-based third parties throughout the Gilded Age. As we will see, American workers were not less receptive to class politics in this period.

Sombart's arguments about the structural political barriers to an independent party emerging in the United States have been similarly undermined by Robin Archer in his analysis. Archer notes that the single-member first-past-the-post electoral system does pose disadvantages to alternative parties compared to proportional representation, but that "before 1900 no European country used proportional representation for national elections, and no large European country used it before the end of the First World War. Thus, these obstacles, far from being unique to the United States, were actually the norm."[8]

Furthermore, in the nineteenth century, state-level politics were much more critical to the interests of labor, as well as being more electorally accessible to alternative parties. As Gary Gerstle has pointed out, it was at this level that most economic and developmental policies were formulated and carried out and social, educational, and even moral legislation were passed as well.[9] This was so much so that as Selig Perlman noted upon the founding of the American Federation of Labor in 1886, "The legislative interests of labor were for the most part given into the care of the state federations of labor."[10] Neville Kirk makes a similar point about the importance of the AFL's state federations of labor, which he termed "the 'crucial agencies' for political action."[11]

Indeed, the most basic function of the state federations organized during this period was legislation at the state level. As a history of the Illinois State Federation of Labor, founded in 1884, argued, "It is in the legislative functions of the State Federation of Labor that its essential character lies." Article 2 of its 1885 constitution states, "The objects of this Association are the encouragement and formation of trade and labor organizations and to secure legislation favorable to the interests of the industrial classes."[12] Not only did state federations seek legislation at the state level, but as Theda Skocpol shows, they also differed from the antistate voluntarist positions taken by the national AFL and its leader Samuel Gompers on key issues. For example, while Gompers and the national federation officially opposed winning the eight-hour work day through legislation, the state federations routinely fought for such legislation at the state level.[13] The focus on state and local politics opened the way for a role for alternative-party efforts throughout the Gilded Age.

As to the possibility of an alternative party establishing a foothold in urban America, Robin Archer points to a practical strategy used by alternative parties at state and local levels in the "balance of power" approach to legislative elections, in which a minority party can block with others to pass or bar legislation. While the labor and populist parties of the Gilded Age could seldom capture an entire state legislature, much less the US House of Representatives, they could and at times did elect enough representatives to hold the balance of power in the state legislature. As Gerald Friedman has pointed out, "Working-class political leverage was enhanced in the 1880s by special, and transient, circumstances. The close balance between the political parties made even small groups of voters crucial in elections."[14]

Following the rise of Republican domination in elections with the "system of 1896," this strategy became more difficult.

This approach was practiced in Detroit with the formation of the Independent Labor Party in 1882, backed by the city's trade unions and Knights of Labor. As Richard Oestreicher put it, "The emergence of the Independent Labor Party in a balance of power role confirmed activists' expectations of rising working class power."[15] Similarly, in Troy, New York, into the 1880s, as Daniel Walkowitz writes, "Since the mid-sixties, when the Working Men's Party demonstrated that it held the balance of power in local elections, the Democrats had chosen candidates who could win labor endorsement."[16] When scattered remnants of the 1886–1887 labor-party movement in Illinois attempted to form the Union Labor Party to launch a statewide slate, the *Chicago Times* speculated, wrongly as it turned out, that it "may develop sufficient strength to hold the balance of power."[17]

In fact, this was the strategy of the United Labor Parties in 1886–1888 and the proposed labor-Populist alliance of 1893–1894.[18] Frank K. Foster, former Knight and editor of the Boston-based *Labor Leader*, optimistically predicted just before the 1894 elections "that the Populists will hold the balance of power in the coming United States Senate."[19] This tactic had been used by Charles Stewart Parnell and his Irish Home Rule Party in the British Parliament and was well known in US labor circles. It was also employed by Australia's new Labour Party in the 1890s and the British Labour Party after 1906. Even in the US, at the height of the labor-party movement of the 1880s, the Washington lobbyist of the Knights of Labor called for the formation of a "Parnell party."[20]

Oddly enough, Sombart himself allowed that America's electoral system was no absolute deterrent to a socialist party when he wrote, "If it really were possible to unite the broad sections of the working population . . . no election machine, however complicated, and no monopoly of major parties, however longstanding, would halt such a triumphant march." Presumably, the barrier to such unified action lay in the lack of socialist consciousness. Yet he even predicted that "in the next generation socialism in America will very probably experience the greatest possible expansion of its appeal."[21] Thus in the end, America's political system does not seem the barrier to a labor or socialist party that Sombart spent so much time explaining.

Of course, since the triumph of the Republican Party in the 1860 election, no alternative party has succeeded in becoming a permanent or second party. Yet, at least until the realignment of the 1930s, alternative parties were a permanent part of the American party system. In his famous 1933 address to the Mississippi Valley Historical Association, John D. Hicks argued for what has become the generally accepted role of alternative parties. He told his fellow historians, "It is a fact, easily demonstrated, that at least for the last hundred years one formidable third party has succeeded another with bewildering rapidity." These parties, he argued, reflected dissatisfaction with the two major parties and affected both presidential election outcomes and influenced "important national policies"[22]—that is, when alternative parties are not dismissed altogether.

More recently, Mark Voss-Hubbard has argued that during "the party period" from the 1830s to the 1896 election, there was always a deep antiparty sentiment in the US, and much policy formation in US history came from the actions of socially rooted voluntary associations, including trade unions, farmers' organizations, and mutual-aid societies. He writes, "Third party dissent almost always traced its lineage to some broader social movement, manifest in a matrix of extrapartisan voluntary reform organizations."[23] This well describes the working-class efforts at independent political action launched by the Knights of Labor, trade unions, state federations of labor, and local trade and labor assemblies during the Gilded Age. The argument that will be made in this book, particularly in chapter 5, is that it was ultimately the very weakness of these labor organizations that undermined the various efforts and proposals for an alternative labor or populist party. This in turn was in large part a consequence of the continuous migration and geographic mobility of the working class in formation in this period.

Most of Sombart's arguments, however, dealt with what he saw as the root causes of the lack of class consciousness he ascribed to American workers: prosperity, free or cheap land, and social mobility. The idea that the relatively higher living standards of US workers explained their alleged lack of class consciousness is here again refuted by Archer's comparison with Australian workers who did found a labor party in 1891 despite their relative prosperity. Archer writes, "The trouble for the prosperity thesis is that this was also true of Australia. Indeed, in the second half of the nineteenth century, Australia was the most prosperous country in the world—more prosperous than the United States."[24] The whole idea that relative prosperity undermines class consciousness is dubious, not least because the uneven world of the late nineteenth century contained many relative income inequalities between industrial nations, most of which did see the formation of mass socialist parties. For another, in the US, as in Germany and Britain during these years, it was generally the better-paid skilled workers who organized unions, launched labor-based parties, and sometimes embraced socialism. What is more, any contentment that might be presumed to come with the increase in real wages in this period, as shown in the widely cited figures produced by Stanley Lebergott for workers "when working,"[25] would have been frequently canceled out by irregular work, technological displacement, wage cuts, and other economic realities of the Gilded Age.

Contrary to the notion that much of the migration in this decade was for "homesteading" in the West, migration throughout the US in the 1880s was largely an urban affair—a fact that is important to understanding the growth and collapse of the Knights of Labor. Nationally, urban population grew by 57 percent from 1880 to 1890, almost three times the natural growth rate of 20 percent, or by 7.5 million people. This is twice the rate of national population growth and four times that of the rural population, which at 14 percent was below the natural growth rate, indicating significant rural out-migration. Subtracting for a 20 percent natural growth rate in this decade, some 6 million people, *net*, entered US cities from elsewhere. Thus, urban turnover probably numbered from 12 to 15 million for the decade, at least two-thirds—or about eight to ten million—of them of working age when the entire nonagricultural workforce numbered 10.9 million by 1890.[26]

The notion that free or cheap land in the West provided a "safety-valve" for eastern workers was long ago put to rest. Fred Shannon, for example, pointed out that most of the land had already gone to corporate interests and speculators and that, in any case, the major trend in the late nineteenth century was not the movement of industrial workers to the land but rather the movement of farmers to the factories and cities. As he put it, "It is a fact too apparent to require much argument that the population movement, from 1860 to the end of the century, was preponderatingly from the farm to the city, rather than the reverse." Thus, "for every city laborer who took up farming, twenty farmers flocked to the city."[27] Those workers who migrated to the West "had exchanged drudgery in an Eastern factory for equally ill-paid drudgery (considering living costs) in a Western factory or mine," he wrote.[28]

The limits of movement to farming in the West were recognized at the time by many of those in the labor movement. For example, the *Iron Molders' Journal* stated as early as 1877, "The number of mechanics that become successful farmers is comparatively few."[29] In 1885, Knights of Labor leader Terence Powderly told his members, "The real facts in the case, plainly stated, are that very few men who have lived any length of time in the city or town have enough money laid by to even defray the expenses of themselves and families to the land."[30] Matters grew even worse by the 1890s, when migration into the mountain and Pacific states of the West dropped by nearly 40 percent from the level of the 1880s, while the Great Plains states saw net out-migration due to drought, with a loss of 86,700 people. Migration into the industrializing Midwest east of the Mississippi, on the other hand, grew by 50 percent in the 1890s.[31] As labor journalist John Swinton observed in his 1894 book,

Striking for Life, "A man cannot now, as formerly he could, squat upon or pre-empt his quarter section of 160 acres anywhere between the Cinnamon River and the Yellowstone, between the Father of Waters and the Rocky Mountains, between those mountains and the Pacific Ocean. The free lands of other years are fenced in."[32]

Social mobility—the reality or prospect of advancement up the ladder of occupations and income—is another oft-cited suspect for the undermining of class consciousness. Sombart went so far as to argue that mobility "to the top or almost to the top" was open to "a far from insignificant number of ordinary workers."[33] In a way this is an odd argument, as the overwhelming social trend of the era was not up the ladder from manual work, but precisely into permanent wage labor, a condition that almost everyone viewed as a step down into dependence. Even for skilled workers, as David Montgomery argues, "the rhetoric of the labor movement stressed the downward movement of the mechanic's social status."[34]

Few of the more recent investigations into social mobility in the late nineteenth century would go as far as Sombart in seeing elevation to the "top" as likely. There are, nevertheless, problems with the manner in which many of these studies have attempted to show more modest upward mobility. For example, Stephan Thernstrom's classic study placed the border of mobility between unskilled or skilled "manual" labor and "low white collar" employment.[35] Similarly, Chudacoff drew the line most often at "manual" versus "non-manual" or between skilled workers and clerical workers.[36] As Michael Katz put it in his critique of this sort of category, "The choice of occupational classification predetermines the patterns of social stratification and social mobility that the historian will find."[37]

Many who crossed this nonmanual or white-collar frontier, however, continued to behave and think like other wageworkers. Telegraph operators and store clerks, for example, flooded the Knights of Labor, and when that collapsed, they went on to organize craft unions, continuing to see themselves as wageworkers—and exploited ones at that.[38] In other words, this distinction does not indicate elevation from working-class status. In any case, it was not so much upward mobility that Gilded-Age workers sought. As John Bodnar found in his study of immigrant workers in Pennsylvania, most were "less interested in mobility than in security."[39] For most of the millions of people who poured into wage labor in these years, and indeed, traveled far and wide to find such work, significant upward social mobility was neither a goal nor a possibility. As Howard Chudacoff, who also emphasized security as more important than mobility, put it, "People move upward and downward but seldom far."[40]

Selig Perlman and "Job Consciousness"

In his 1928 book, *A Theory of the Labor Movement*, Selig Perlman, a former student of John R. Commons's, argues that what American workers had instead of class consciousness was "job consciousness." Perlman saw the positive evidence of this job consciousness in the "working rules" or "shop rules" commonly practiced by American unions in order to gain "job control." Early in the book, he states, "Labor's own 'home grown' ideology is disclosed only through a study of the 'working rules' of labor's own 'institutions'—that is, the trade unions."[41] Perlman's own comparative analysis, however, undermines any alleged uniqueness of American labor consciousness. For one thing, he equated class consciousness with socialist ideas, which he said are common to British trade unionists, albeit from religious roots. Yet British trade unionists, he argued, were ardent practitioners of the same "working rules" he attributed to American unions. He wrote, "Working rules of the English unions, which they hammered out in the struggle for decent living standards and a modicum of security and shop freedom, were clung to, regardless of their effect on output or even on ability to compete in the international market."[42] The job-control unionism practiced in Britain was, he wrote, "just unionism." Or later, he said, "Unionism and the striving for shop control are identical."[43] Thus, it would seem the basis of American labor's "home grown" ideology had become or at least was becoming an international norm.

Perlman also wrote of the employer's ability "to carry his own individualistic competitive spirit into the ranks of his employees."[44] To this he attributed a supposed special degree of individualism to American workers. Yet when he looks at what he calls "economic group psychology," presumably something like consciousness, he concludes the opposite. His argument is put in the language of the mainstream marginalist economics of the time, whereby jobs become "opportunities," but the consequences of his argument are clear. Writing of the manual workers, Perlman says, "*The group then asserts its collective ownership over the whole amount of opportunity*" (italics in original) and then proceeds to share it out "on the basis of a 'common rule.'" This "collective disposal of opportunity" is "as natural to the manual group as '*laissez-faire*' is to the business man."[45] Thus, the "home grown" ideology of the industrial worker is a collective one in opposition to the individualist views of the capitalist class. The study of work or shop rules has led inevitably to the conclusion of opposing class ideologies and values. Thus, Perlman's own analysis leads to the conclusion that job-control unionism and job consciousness do not necessarily negate class consciousness.

In the final analysis, the traditional explanations for US labor's alleged lack of class consciousness, its exceptionalism, and the failure to produce a lasting labor-based party assume or assert what needs to be demonstrated: that US workers in the nineteenth century lacked class consciousness. All the explanations that are supposed to have affected consciousness—prosperity, free land, job consciousness, social mobility—describe the causes of this assumed or asserted lack of class consciousness rather than the state of consciousness itself. The implied argument is that the lack of class consciousness can be derived from the failure to form an independent working-class party. No party, no class consciousness. The lack of such a socialist or labor-based party is, in turn, explained by the lack of class consciousness. No class consciousness, no party. The argument is circular and does not actually tell us much about the consciousness of Gilded-Age workers at all. This is all the more remarkable in light of the documentary evidence of class consciousness in testimony before congressional hearings of the time, in union convention proceedings, in countless contemporary reports, in the memoirs of labor activists, and in the weekly labor press of the period. In the final analysis, these arguments do not explain or even address American labor's relative organizational weakness in the late nineteenth century. As Sean Wilentz summarized the problem, "The history of American class consciousness is not so much studied and written about as it is written off from the start."[46]

Other "Factors": The State and the Power of Capital

The factor underlying labor's relative weakness that this book seeks to focus attention on is the high degree of internal migration that made the process of class formation in the US uneven. There are, however, other major factors that are more plausible than the traditional exceptionalist arguments in analyzing American labor's weakness. Primary among these are the extent of state repression against labor through the use of the military and court injunctions; the growing power of the new capitalist class in relationship to the state and civil society, as well as to labor; and the competition and conflict of the racial, ethnic, and gender groups within this working class in formation. The argument here is that these factors did hold power, if in varying degrees and extent, but that increased attentiveness to geographic mobility will help to enhance our understanding of why their effect was so compelling. This section will examine the question of state intervention and its relationship to the unique power of America's rising industrial and financial capitalist class.

One recent school of analysis sees state repression as key to organized labor's weakness. For example, in a 2010 symposium conducted by the journal *Labor History*, Robert Goldstein takes several historians to task for underestimating the negative influence of state violence against strikers. To be sure, violence against union activists was widespread in Gilded-Age America, but some perspective on this is needed.

Goldstein's major quantitative figure in support of this thesis is that the state militias or National Guard intervened in strikes some 250 times between 1873 and 1937.[47] Looking specifically at the Gilded Age, Jerry Cooper, the leading expert on military intervention in labor disputes, states that the number of National Guard interventions between 1877 and 1900 was "at least one hundred and fifty times to deal with industrial disputes." Yet between 1881 and 1900 alone there were some 22,000 strikes, so that all these state interventions would not have affected even one percent of strikes. According to Cooper, 118 of these took place between 1885 and 1895, during which period there were 14,214 strikes.[48] Thus, once again, less than 1 percent of strikes in these years of high, often bitter strike activity were affected. With some ups and downs, the trajectory of strike activity was upward, and well above the level of other industrial nations, indicating that state repression did not stifle labor resistance to the new regime of capital.

In terms of timing, David Montgomery sees these state interventions as rising only toward the end of our period during the mid- to late 1890s and "rising more often than ever before between 1900 and 1922," after our period.[49] Interventions by federal troops were actually rare, with only eleven instances between 1877 and 1900. Three of these occurred during the violent railroad strike of 1877, six during the 1890s, and only two in the 1880s, one of which was to suppress anti-Chinese "disorders" by white workers in Seattle in 1885–1886.[50] Thus, it seems clear that state and federal military interventions cannot explain the general weakness of organized labor, much less the decline of the Knights of Labor in the 1880s. Interventions by local police forces or private armed groups were certainly more common, but also less effective.[51]

Much the same can be said concerning the closely related role of the law and the courts. As many historians have demonstrated, the legal atmosphere of the Gilded Age was rooted in the rights of private property and highly antagonistic to organized labor.[52] But as with direct military interventions by the state, those by the courts in the form of injunctions against strikes were not frequent enough to explain or restrain the behavior of organized workers for most of this period. While there were 924 federal and state injunctions from 1880 to 1920, there were almost 52,000 strikes. Furthermore, according to Edwin Witte's detailed account, only 28 of these federal and state injunctions were issued in the 1880s and 122 during the 1890s. William Forbath offers a higher estimate with 105 injunctions in the 1880s, 410 in the 1890s, and 850 in the first decade of the twentieth century. Even allowing for a large number of unreported injunctions issued by courts below the national and state levels, they still would have affected only a tiny percentage of all strikes in these years. In any case, the highpoint of injunctions came after the turn of the century.[53]

It can be argued that both military interventions and court actions had a demonstration effect, particularly when used against a high-profile strike such as Pullman in 1894. The impact on strike activity, however, was not large. The average number of strikes per year dropped only very slightly from 1896 to 1900 following the Pullman boycott, while the number of strikers actually increased somewhat. After 1900, even as the number of injunctions increased, the number of strikes and strikers both soared.[54] As Currie and Ferrie argue, "The legal environment had little effect on aggregate-level strike activity." Witte drew the same conclusion.[55] It is more likely that both military and court interventions had an impact on the political thinking of many labor leaders, particularly after the defeat of the Pullman boycott in 1894, as both William Forbath and Leon Fink have argued, pushing some toward "pure and simple" unionism, with its rejection of socialist politics in favor of "non-partisanship" in elections and an embrace of the capitalist market, and others toward industrial unionism or even socialism toward the end of our period.[56]

Nevertheless, since the use of federal or National Guard troops, local police, and court injunctions in labor disputes were almost always at the instigation of the struck employers, it seems that the questions of repression and legal environment are better subsumed in the rising power of the new industrial and financial capitalist class and its relation to the state rather than in America's rather minimalist state, at least in comparison to those in Europe. For, unlike the state apparatuses of most other industrial nations of the time, the rising power of capital outstripped the development of America's uniquely complex state, and during this period capital came to dominate Congress and most state legislatures through its influence in both major parties, its use of money in elections, its control of the daily mass media, and its mobilization of massive lobbying machines.

As historian Nelson Lichtenstein writes of the unbalanced relative power of capital and state in the late nineteenth century,

> In sharp contrast to their counterparts in Britain or Germany, American businessmen had presided over economic institutions that were of both continental scope and vast revenue long before the rise of a powerful state or the emergence of overt class politics. In every other capitalist nation, a strong bureaucratic state either preceded or emerged simultaneously with the appearance of the multidivisional firm, but this pattern was inverted in the United States.[57]

Whether one considers the federal government "weak" or not, for most of this period the US lacked the type of permanent, professional civil service common to Britain and Germany (Prussia) and as of 1890 possessed a standing army and navy of fewer than 40,000, compared to 420,000 for Britain, 504,000 for Germany, and 542,000 for France.[58] The US national state was dwarfed by the rise of the business behemoths of the era. Looking at the railroads, the first of the giant corporations, Alfred D. Chandler pointed out, "No [US] public enterprise, either, came close to the railroad in size and complexity of operation." In 1891, he reports, the US Post Office, by far the largest federal employer, employed 95,440 people, while the Pennsylvania Railroad alone employed 110,000.[59] As Theodore Roosevelt wrote with something of the hyperbole one might expect from him, "In no other country . . . was such power held by the men who had gained these fortunes . . . The power of the mighty industrial overlords had increased with giants' strides . . . the government [was] practically impotent."[60]

Though America's entrepreneurs and "robber barons" had no hesitation in demanding and taking favors from the various levels of government, including huge land grants, protective tariffs, and yes, the occasional use of the state militia (National Guard) or even federal troops to break strikes, they almost never accepted serious regulation until the very end of this period. When, for example, states passed eight-hour laws in the 1870s under pressure from labor, employers simply ignored them without consequence.[61] In the 1880s, employers similarly ignored state arbitration laws passed under union pressure.[62] When various academic experts and government commissions proposed state-sponsored labor arbitration in the 1890s, businesses, as well as some labor leaders, vetoed the idea.[63] The power that derived from the ever-increasing scale of capital and business organization in relation to the decentralized state apparatus facilitated the dominance of state legislatures, courts, and even Congress by representatives of capital, allowing Gilded-Age entrepreneurs to do as they pleased more often than not even when public opinion was wary.

What is more, quite independently of state action, the vast wealth the growing corporations accumulated meant they could often outlast striking workers who had no state benefits and at best limited strike funds or savings to fall back on. Of course, they could also hire a small army of Pinkertons to help break strikes, but more often than not time alone could foil a strike. The monthlong 1883 strike of telegraph operators against Jay Gould's Western Union is a clear example. No troops or police were required to defeat this nationwide strike by skilled workers who could not be easily replaced, but who had no strike fund and little in the way of savings.[64] It is worth remembering, too, that in addition to the many thousands of failed strikes over this period, between 1886 and 1900 employers conducted lockouts at 9,228 establishments involving 375,954 workers, well over half of which were successful.[65] The unique aggressiveness attributed to American business in this period was extremely well financed and seldom restrained by the state, over which large-scale business exercised increasing control, nor was it in need of state help in all but the largest labor conflicts.

None of this is to say the power of the capitalist class in formation was omnipotent. Overall more strikes were won than lost, nor did all lockouts bring victory for the employer. As Herbert Gutman pointed out, in midsize industrial cities, middle-class and small-business people often sided with labor against the local capitalist, at least in the earlier years of the Gilded Age.[66] Nevertheless, it was a power that "increased with giant strides" over these years, a power that was independent of and in many ways superior to that of America's dispersed, underfunded, and understaffed state. All of this makes capital in the US unique among the developed nations of the period and makes the independent power of capital a major factor in the relative weakness of organized labor.

Other "Factors": Gender, Race, and Ethnicity

If the power of capital in the US was concentrated in a relatively small, mostly stable, and ethnically, linguistically, and culturally homogeneous layer of society, the American working class of the late nineteenth and early twentieth century was famously diverse and divided along the lines of gender, race, and ethnicity, as well as religion, national identity, and language. For historians these divisions have represented something different from Europe in their extent and centrality to American society.

Race, ethnicity, and gender, therefore, are among the most compelling accepted explanations for American labor's weaknesses and woes.

Victorian gender relations and attitudes did indeed hinder unionization, as the patriarchal family structures and ideology led male unionists to exclude women in many cases. In addition to the widespread notion that women belonged in the home, as Ileen DeVault argues, craft identities were highly gendered, and the concept of "'manliness' was a defining feature of craft unionism." This included, of course, the idea of the man as the breadwinner of the family wage.[67] Women composed 15 percent of the workforce in 1880 and 18 percent by 1900. In that year almost a million and a half women were classified as non-farm manual workers, mostly factory operatives, almost as many as in domestic service.[68] Yet, in New York State, the Industrial Commission reported that only about 4 percent of women workers belonged to unions.[69] Despite their exclusion from many craft unions, women played an important role in the labor movement of the period both as community activists and union members. The Knights of Labor claimed fifty thousand to sixty thousand women members at its height in 1886 and included key women leaders such as Elizabeth Rodgers and Leonora Barry.[70] Women were admitted to a number of craft unions such as the Typographers, Telegraphers, Cigar Makers, Boot and Shoe Workers, Garment Workers, and Tailors, but a study conducted shortly after the turn of the century reported, "These two industries, cigar making and the manufacture of clothing, are practically the only ones in this country in which women have been organized in large numbers." Even there, moreover, women were subordinate within the union. For example, the same study stated that in the United Garment Workers, with almost a third of its twenty-five thousand members women, the "guiding power is exerted by a small group of men," and "women have had little if any influence."[71] Symbolic of the problem was the fact that there were only two women delegates at the AFL's 1891 convention and, judging by names, only one out of ninety-three delegates in 1893.[72]

There is no doubt that this patriarchal ideology and practice limited the growth of organized labor in late nineteenth-century America. Yet sexism and patriarchy were hardly unique to the US. In 1875, Henry Broadhurst, secretary of Britain's Trade Union Congress, explained that one purpose of trade unionism was "to bring about a condition . . . where wives and daughters would be in their proper sphere at home." And indeed, despite some gains with the rise of the "new unionism" in Britain from 1888 through the 1890s, on the eve of the First World War, historian Mary Davis reports, "90 per cent of all trade unionists were men and 90 per cent of women workers remained unorganized."[73]

What *was* unique to the United States was the racial and ethnic composition of the emerging Gilded-Age working class. Unlike the more or less culturally and linguistically homogeneous capitalist class, the working class that took shape in this period in the United States was not only ethnically and racially diverse, but it also saw a major part of its growth come from abroad. None of the other major Western industrializing nations of this era saw levels of immigration comparable to that of the United States, where over twelve million people entered the country from abroad, in net terms contributing about 15 percent to population growth. Indeed, Britain and Germany saw large-scale emigration in this period, while France's population was frozen at thirty-eight to thirty-nine million from the 1870s to the First World War.[74] While Britain, France, and Germany had their ethnic minorities, none came close to the size and proportion of the foreign-born and their offspring, who composed a third of the US population by 1890 and in the industrial northeast and Midwest nearly half the population by that time. The Irish in Britain, certainly one of the largest ethnic minorities in any European country, by contrast, amounted to just over 3 percent of the UK's population by the 1880s.[75] Nor, as we shall see, did these minorities move around those nations to any degree comparable to that in the US.

The literature on race and ethnicity is too vast to review here. Furthermore, it is strewn with debates about the relative importance and even the meaning of race and ethnicity, which cannot possibly be resolved in this book. There are, however, two aspects of this that relate strongly to this work and without which the impact of migration cannot be fully understood. The first is that the Gilded-Age working class was not merely a diverse workforce, but a social class in formation composed of many differing and changing occupations and skill levels, as well as members of the class engaged in the reproduction of the class, and those losing and seeking employment.

Capitalism in Gilded-Age America created not only giant machine-driven factories but also strings of sweat shops, gangs of day laborers, armies of the jobless, growing numbers of underpaid home workers, and countless unpaid homemakers. Second, to a greater extent than in most other industrializing countries at the time, this varied and layered class formation was "racialized" into a hierarchy of labor often sorted out in the "foreman's empire" or by alleged "scientific" race theories, as David Roediger and Elizabeth Esch, as well as Sanford M. Jacoby, have shown. Not only did workers of different races and nationalities compete for jobs, housing, education, and political influence, but as black or immigrant workers entered the labor market or workplace anew, they found themselves slotted into work according to some preconceived notion of their racial or ethnic fitness. This, too, contributed to the power of capital over labor and made unity among workers difficult.[76]

Work-based racial hierarchies were, in part, a consequence of the legacy of slavery, but also of the failure of Reconstruction and the consequent rising tide of racism throughout American society that symbolically culminated nationally in the 1896 Supreme Court decision in *Plessy v. Ferguson* that legalized segregation. "Race-thinking," as David Roediger calls it, had become universal. As Roediger summarized it,

> National and even transnational dynamics ultimately also accounted for the survival of race-thinking generally and, in important ways, for the failure of anti-racist struggles in the South itself. Northern and Midwestern racism, anti-Chinese agitation, energized settler colonialism, and by the turn of the century, imperial war all contributed to a landscape in which white supremacy was shared across the lines of political party and of region.

Race-thinking and the idea of racial hierarchies were applied to immigrants as well, although their eventual assimilation would take a different tack than the continually delayed integration of African Americans. At the time, however, this allowed meatpacking tycoon Philip Armour to state what other capitalists also advised, namely to "keep the races and nationalities apart after working hours and to foment suspicion, rivalry, and even enmity among such groups."[77]

In their studies of African American workers, Sterling Spero and Abram Harris, as well as Philip Foner, agree with W. E. B. DuBois that racial tolerance and efforts at inclusion, if seldom equality, in the labor movement with regard to African American workers reached its high point in the 1880s in the Knights of Labor and the early AFL. However, a clear turning point came in the mid-1890s when the AFL admitted the International Association of Machinists (1895) and the Boilermakers and Iron Ship Builders Union (1896) despite their well-known policies of racial exclusion.[78] DuBois found that by 1902, forty-three trade unions had no black members. There were at that time about 120 trade unions, so presumably many did still admit black workers. Concerning those that did admit African Americans, however, Foner relates that "Du Bois found, too, that in some AF of L affiliates Negro membership had declined from 1890 to 1900, the decade in which the policy of Negro-white unity had retrogressed." By 1902, DuBois calculated that there were only 41,000 black union members out a total of 1.2 million, or less than 5 percent of all union members—fewer than the 60,000 black workers who had joined the Knights of Labor alone a decade and a half earlier.[79] Thus, race, like gender and ethnicity, was an indisputably rising factor in limiting the growth of working-class organizations in the Gilded Age.

The South: Deflected Migration, Different Development

The South, here defined as the eleven former Confederate states plus Kentucky, followed a very different path on matters of race, class formation, urbanization, and economic development. It is almost universally agreed that the Old South did not follow the pattern of development experienced to one degree or another by the rest of the country. C. Vann Woodward provided the classic observations of both the relative lack of urbanization and industrialization despite all the efforts of "New South" promoters. By 1900 the south central region of the US had an urban population of only 11.1 percent, while the north central region reached 30.6 percent. From this he concluded that despite some urban growth, "The sum total of urbanization in the South was comparatively unimportant." On the South's failure to industrialize to anywhere near the extent of the North, he wrote,

> The abundance of natural resources and industrial opportunities was widely advertised and the desperate need of an industrialized and diversified economy was acknowledged, but in spite of thirty years of intensive propaganda and effort the South remained largely a raw-material economy, with attendant penalties of low wages, lack of opportunity, and poverty.[80]

Woodward attributed this to the South's colonial position as a supplier of raw materials and to relatively high freight rates for southern goods, efforts by northern industry to block southern development, and the low incomes of the region that made it a poor market.[81] Since that time, a debate over the causes of the South's economic backwardness has taken somewhat different directions. Here I will look at two major, often counterposed explanations.

Economic historian Gavin Wright locates the roots of southern backwardness primarily in the region's separate and low-wage labor market. The separation was rooted in the older east-west migratory routes of labor, trade, and investment established under slavery and in the dependence on the price of cotton, which dominated the southern economy even more in the postbellum era. Low wages were a function of this separation, as well as falling cotton prices and labor-intensive production. The low wages, in turn, discouraged the use of new technology in both agriculture and industry and, hence, development itself. What is central to his argument is the existence of a true labor market.[82]

This analysis and, indeed, most neoclassical analyzes, have been challenged by other writers who argue that backwardness was rooted in the social system of labor in the postwar South. John Wiener, for example, argues that sharecropping and tenancy in the South composed a system of "bound" labor based in debt peonage in which mobility was restricted. The fact of widespread debt peonage and tenancy is hardly disputable. Yet, as noted above, Wright cited a number of studies that demonstrated considerable migration within the South by both blacks and whites. In response, Wiener argues that "the movement of tenants among landlords preserved the system's repressive nature as long as the debt moved with the tenant, as typically it did. Movement alone does not, therefore, disprove the existence of debt peonage."[83]

Yet, Wright comes close to contradicting himself later in *Old South, New South*, where he argues, "For poor farmers and laborers, the only way to establish creditworthiness was to stay in one locality and develop a track record of reliability."[84] There were, to be sure, farm laborers in the South who, as Robert Zieger points out, "typically moved from farm to farm, rarely establishing roots in one location." But even these, he argues, hoped to eventually establish "a favorable tenant or cropping agreement with a landowner."[85]

Wright is nevertheless correct in the sense that there was a labor market in the South, but it did not include most of the rural population. A true capitalist labor market consists of wage earners who do not possess their own capital. As Wiener writes,

> Unlike the true agricultural proletarian, the Southern share tenant working on "thirds and fourths" claimed his portion of the product not only on the basis of his labor but also as possessor of part of the instruments of production: the Southern share tenant provided his own tools and draft animals; the Northern agricultural wage worker, "freed" of possession of the means of production, provided only his labor.[86]

To this, it must be added that sharecroppers and tenants did not receive a wage at all. In other words, a large section of the total workforce of the South were not wage earners in the capitalist sense. If most had been wageworkers, surely the exodus from the low-wage South to the higher-wage North would have been much greater. This, in turn, might have encouraged greater mechanization and development. Clearly, neither of these things happened. The post–Civil War South was a contradictory social system, combining precapitalist and capitalist forms of labor that discouraged industrial and urban development.

The consequence of this distinctly different pattern of development is highly relevant to this thesis in that it meant that the South, as a low-wage, labor-intensive region, could not compete with the North for the huge influx of immigrants or the flow of internal migrants to higher-wage areas. Efforts to induce or even contract for immigrants to the Mississippi Delta, for example, failed due to the rigidity of the tenant system.[87] Low wages and the relative lack of industry, on the other hand, discouraged footloose "floaters" and "tramps" from the North, as well as skilled workers from seeking work in most of the South. The outcome of this deflection of migration was to compress and concentrate the flows of immigration and internal migration through the northern half of the country, intensifying problems of competition between native and foreign-born workers, as well as between black and white.

The second consequence was the virtual segregation of the vast majority of African Americans from the industrializing, urbanizing processes of the North and West. Throughout the period, 90 percent of the African American population remained in the South.[38] This meant that the proportion of African American workers in the North and West was very small. One indication of this is the relative percentage of blacks in northern cities compared to southern cities. So for example, in 1900, 56.6 percent of Charleston's population was African American, while that of Birmingham was 43 percent, Atlanta 39.8 percent, Richmond 37.9 percent, and New Orleans 27.1 percent. The population of New York and Chicago, on the other hand, comprised only 1.8 percent blacks each, while Cleveland had 1.6 percent and Detroit 1.4 percent in 1900.[89] The small size of the black population in almost all northern and western cities in this period meant these communities did not have the social weight or power that black communities in Richmond and New Orleans had, where African Americans played an important role in the labor movement. This, along with exclusion and discrimination, inhibited their ability to play a major role in organized labor in most of the North and West, with notable exceptions.

The analysis in this work focuses on those regions where industrialization, urbanization, and working-class formation were most advanced and geographic mobility most developed. To put it simply, too few people crossed the Mason-Dixon Line permanently in either direction to impact the overall patterns of internal migration analyzed in this book. While the South had an enormous impact on race relations, the weakness of organized labor, the politics of the country as a whole in the Gilded Age and after, and its distinctive development, migratory patterns, and history, make any detailed analysis of the region beyond the scope of this study.

The Ascending Arc of Opposition to Organized Labor

State repression, racial and ethnic divisions, and the presence of urban political machines are among the most frequently cited causes of organized labor's relative weakness *and* political conservatism in the Gilded Age and Progressive Era by more recent scholars. Looking at the long period from 1870 to the early twentieth century, these analytical summaries of the forces of opposition to organized labor's development appear valid. Nevertheless, it is important to specify the timing and periodicity of these three forms of opposition to the growth, power, and political independence of organized labor in our period. The argument here is that in each case there is, in fact, an ascending arc of opposition in which each of these factors plays an increasing role over time. As we saw above, in the case of court injunctions against strikes, this is well documented in the works of Witte, Forbath, and Currie and Ferrie, where the number of injunctions rose in each decade, with the least frequency in the 1880s.[90]

The same holds true for military interventions. As both Cooper and Montgomery show, both federal and state military intervention grew only after the mid-1880s, and then more rapidly in the 1890s.[91] Additionally, as we saw above as well, racism and racial exclusion by the unions grew from the relatively racially and ethnically inclusive period of the 1880s to the increasingly exclusive practice after the mid-1890s. This applies particularly to the Knights of Labor, who were composed of all the major ethnic and racial groups of the 1880s, except the Chinese. As with the rise of injunctions and military interventions, the impact of racism and anti-immigrant practices on unions rises from the early to mid-1890s and is strongest of all in the early twentieth century.

Finally, there is the contention by Werner Sombart, Martin Shefter, Ira Katznelson, and others that the rise of urban political machines, particularly Democratic Party organizations, with their dense presence in working-class neighborhoods, foreclosed the possibility of independent political action by organized labor.[92] The limits and impact of urban Democratic machines will be discussed in detail in chapter 5. Here, however, it is worth noting that, as with the other forces of opposition to labor organization, the development of urban Democratic Party machines also saw a rise in their development and effectiveness, in this case even more uneven in our period and beyond. Steven Erie, in his detailed analysis of eight Irish-led urban Democratic Party organizations, argues that the amount of patronage during the period of machine growth was small and that "party bosses had to husband *scarce* resources." In fact, in per capita terms in the cities with the strongest Irish Democratic organizations, city expenditures actually fell by 43 percent from 1880 to 1900. Furthermore, during the Gilded Age, these party organizations did not incorporate other ethnic groups into these party organizations, while during their formative years, "the urban Irish working class grew increasingly militant and alienated from the early machines in the 1870s and 1880s." In addition, the existing urban "machines" would virtually collapse during the depression of the 1890s. In fact, it was only in the early twentieth century that these urban machines acquired the patronage resources and citywide coherence we associate with "the machine."[93] Brown and Halaby also conclude that there were very few citywide machines of the Tammany type before the turn of the century.[94] In short, as we will see in chapter 5, the institutions that were supposed to absorb the ethnic working class and immunize them from alternative-party activity were not yet strong enough to consistently accomplish this during the Gilded Age. As with state repression and racial and ethnic division, their power and ability to frustrate the growth of unions and their ability to deflect independent political action only rose with time and then only after the turn of the century and then never absolutely.

Among the conclusions to be drawn from the rising trajectory of these three oft-cited forces of opposition undermining organized labor is that none of these, even taken together, can explain the rapid decline of the Knights of Labor in the mid-1880s, which in turn brought down the strongest efforts at working-class independent political action of the period. While the three forces of opposition can explain the failure of unions to grow in the 1890s, they must share even this with the deep depression of that decade. As will be argued below, it is far more likely that the rise of these factors affected the ideology of much of the labor leadership after 1894 even more than the organizational state of the labor movement did.

The "Missing Factor"

While the difficulties of building effective labor organizations created by the power of capital on the one hand and the divisions within the US working class on the other have been well recognized, analyzed, and developed by late twentieth- and early twenty-first-century historians and social scientists, the effects of internal migration on the ability of workers to build stable organizations have not—even where the fact of geographic mobility has been acknowledged. Geographic mobility is, therefore, the "missing factor." The purpose of this book is not to dismiss or demote all of the recognized and plausible causes of labor weakness discussed above, but to introduce the dynamics of internal migration into our understanding of the unevenness of class formation and organization in the Gilded Age. While the focus of this book will be on the impact of geographic mobility, it is important to view that mobility in relation to these other critical factors. The growing power of accumulated capital as it expanded rapidly and moved westward was itself the major cause of internal migration in the Gilded Age. Capital's magnetic ability to draw millions from Europe, Asia, and America's farms across the continent could only mean a workforce on the move. The clash of races and nationalities was intensified by this very motion into and across the country and into growing urban centers, where they had to compete for jobs, housing, education, and space. It was in these churning centers of accumulated capital and their built environment that the drama of organized labor's rise, fall, and revival occurred with the greatest intensity in this period. Thus, internal migration is not only the missing piece in the puzzle of American class *formation* but also a cause and consequence of these other underlying forces of class *disruption*.

As this suggests, internal migration itself has underlying causes that form an important part of the analysis in this book. These are the economic forces behind the "push" and "pull" factors of migration theory as pioneered by E. G. Ravenstein in the late nineteenth century and elaborated and modified in the twentieth and early twenty-first centuries.[95] These "push-pull" forces were rooted not only in industrialization in the US, but also in changes in the international economy, above all the crisis of agriculture in much of Europe. Thus, the major underlying forces behind immigration and migration were and are today recognized by most analysts as predominantly economic in nature—the major exception being war, which was not the leading variable in the particular period in question, the Gilded Age.

At the same time, immigration and internal migration were not random. There was a structure to immigrant integration and movement. During the Gilded Age, the "old" immigrant groups (Germans, Irish, British, and Scandinavians) remained close to 90 percent of the foreign-born population—more if their American-born offspring are included. African American migration from the South was minimal, and even the "new" immigrants from eastern and southern Europe did not surpass the older European groups until after the mid-1890s, by which time the number of immigrants had dropped significantly as a result of the depression of that decade. Indeed, the contribution of all foreign-born workers to the growth of the labor force fell from 30 percent in the 1880s to 10 percent in the 1890s.[96]

Additionally, the vast majority of those arriving in the US in these years moved into and between cities, and while the turmoil and alienation of life in a new city, itself still half-formed, was a daunting experience, most European immigrants knew where they were going before crossing the Atlantic. By the Gilded Age, communities of the older immigrant groups were well established in most cities, despite the high turnover of population.[97] These provided not only a destination for those new to the US, but also a refuge for those on the move from city to city. Furthermore, Oscar Handlin notes that as "the newcomers took pains early to seek out those whom experience made their brothers; and to organize each others' support, they created a great variety of formal and informal institutions."[98] Like trade unions, these often ethnically based benevolent and mutual-aid societies were meant to mitigate the negative effects of industrialization and urbanization and were part of the often contradictory process of class formation.[99]

It was the "old" foreign-born that also composed a large part of the labor movement of the Gilded Age. For example, the Illinois Bureau of Labor Statistics reported that in 1886, while 44 percent of the Knights of Labor in Illinois were native-born (some of immigrant parents, no doubt), Germans formed 18 percent of the membership, the Irish 14 percent, British 7 percent, and Scandinavians 6 percent, a total of 45 percent, with the newer groups from eastern and southern Europe, those whose nationality could not be determined, and presumably the small number of African American workers together amounting to merely 12 percent of the total. For the trade unions, the concentration of older immigrant groups was even more extreme, with Germans amounting to 30 percent of union members, the Irish 17 percent, Scandinavians 11 percent, the British about 9 percent, the native-born Americans 20 percent, and the rest either new immigrants or those of indeterminate nationality. As the Illinois report noted, no attempt was made to ascertain "the parentage of those born in this country," so that in ethnic terms the weight of the older immigrant groups was certainly much greater in that second generation immigrants outnumbered the foreign-born by 1890.[100]

What these figures for the Knights of Labor and the trade unions of Illinois reveal is that, unlike race in many cases, ethnicity or nationality per se was not a barrier to participation in the central organizations of the working class in this period, at least among the "old" immigrant ethnic groups. This did not mean a lack of prejudice or of conflict born of competition for space in the overcrowded cities or for jobs in the ever-changing labor markets, and to be sure, some unions would discriminate against the newer arrivals, as they did against African Americans or the Chinese. It did mean, however, that the process of class formation had a certain structure in its mainly urban setting—a structure of ethnicities and languages that, by the 1880s at least, was familiar to many caught in the process of permanent wage labor.

What tied these various groups together was the increasingly common experience of wage labor. Jobs, occupations, and skill levels, of course, differed often for different groups, as we have seen, but dependence on the oft-interrupted wage, subjugation of one's will to that of the impersonal employer, and adjustment to a rigid time schedule that had nothing to do with nature's rhythms or traditional work habits were common, and widely resented, experiences. This common experience and perceptions and interpretations of it composed an essential part of class consciousness throughout this period. Class outlook was never absent from Gilded-Age America; what was missing was coherence generated by stable organization.

Methods and Structure

The underlying methodological framework of my research and analysis is a version of Marxism rooted in the analysis of capital accumulation in *Capital*, in which class is understood in relational terms, as developed above all by E. P. Thompson. This relationship is defined by three conditions: workers are "free" of the means of production and must sell their labor power in a competitive market; they are exploited in the sense that they produce more value than is required for their maintenance and reproduction; and capital and its overseers have a relationship to them that is "purely despotic."[101] This phrase is Marx's and refers to the fact that private property in industrial capitalism granted the owner absolute command over the workforce. In the US in this period this was often exercised through "the long accumulated prerogatives regarding hiring, firing, and disciplining workers that were termed the 'foreman's empire' at the time."[102] Of course, this despotism was resisted as often as not, and herein lay one of the roots of conflict in this era.

Thus, the two major classes that arose in this period in the US created one another in a relationship that was inherently unequal and conflictual. This conflict began in the production process, but necessarily spread throughout society and became politicized. It is a historical process of class formation in motion, socially and geographically in which, as E. P. Thompson has argued for England, the working class was itself a participant. As he famously put it, "The working class did not rise like the sun at an appointed time. It was present at its own making." Nevertheless, there also comes a point, always hard to identify, when, as Thompson says of the English working class around 1832, "the working class was no longer in the making but (in its Chartist form) already made."[103] Although it is hard to put a date on it, the process that more or less made the working class distinct in social being and consciousness in the United States was a long one that occurred most clearly in the wake of the great railroad strike of 1877, which awakened both capital and labor to the reality of class conflict. The context of capital accumulation was also in motion, technologically as well as geographically, commodifying more and more aspects of social life. Thus there came a point, somewhere in the second half of the Gilded Age in the US, where capital's appropriation of increasing aspects of daily life imposed limits on how working-class people could shape their daily lives. This did not reduce class conflict or consciousness but tended to limit some activities and create others. We will see some of this later in the discussion in chapter 1 of how a working-class "culture of opposition" changed in the 1890s.

This book also reflects the influence of the "new labor history" and "new urban history" that arose in the 1960s and 1970s, as well as the focus on race and gender, sometimes associated with "whiteness" studies since the late 1980s. The major contribution of writers in these "new" modes of historical analysis was a focus on the local and particular, and the integration of the insights of the social sciences and their greater use of quantitative evidence with the tools of the historian. As Stephan Thernstrom, a leading figure in the "new urban history," wrote, "Quantitative evidence plays a greater role in both types of literature than in their traditional counterparts."[104] Its focus on the social and quantifiable differentiated it from the earlier emphasis on political and institutional aspects of history. This is particularly clear in the differences between the labor histories of John R. Commons and those who followed in his tracks on the one hand and the writings of new labor historians such as Herbert Gutman, David Montgomery, Leon Fink, David Brody, and Melvyn Dubofsky. Since then, authors such a David Roediger, Noel Ignatiev, Jacqueline Jones, Robin D. G. Kelley, and countless others have increased our attention to the subtleties of race, gender, and national identity.[105] In addition, I have attempted to integrate the insights of internal migration theory pioneered by E. G. Ravenstein in the 1880s and since refined and enriched by such writers as Oscar Handlin, Everett Lee, Guido Dorigo and Waldo Tobler, and J. Trent Alexander and Annemarie Steidl,

among others.[106] The effort to position these different insights of demographic social history within the framework of labor history and draw out its implications is,
I believe, itself something "new." In addition, in line with an increasing emphasis by
scholars on the international context of American development, I have attempted
within the limits of space allowed to point to the international economic dynamics
in which mass immigration and internal migration occurred, as well as presenting
an international comparative dimension particularly in relation to Britain.

Methodologically, this book is shaped with appreciation of Thompson's warn-
ing that "historical knowledge must always fall short of positive proof (of the kinds
appropriate to experimental science)."[107] There is, however, evidence and argument.

That internal migration in the United States was massive during the Gilded
Age on a scale unknown in any other industrial nation of the time is fairly easy to
demonstrate. That this migration followed a pattern that correlates strongly with
the decline of the Knights of Labor and the ups and downs and leaky nature of
the trade-union traveling-card system in use at the time will also be demonstrated.
Throughout, primary sources have provided a mass of information supporting the
importance and impact of geographical mobility on organized labor. In the end,
however, there is no mathematical "proof" that links these trends to the relative
weakness of organized labor directly to internal migration in the US in this period—only evidence and argument. The bulk of the evidence and the manner in
which they are tied together in the arguments are meant to establish an integral
and direct connection.

While this book draws on the secondary work of many historians and social
scientists, it is also informed by new findings in primary sources held in archives
and libraries that highlight the reality of internal migration, its recognition by people at the time, and the impact it had on the many working-class organizations
of the Gilded Age. These primary sources include congressional testimony, trade-
union publications, the weekly labor press of the era, the convention proceedings
of various labor organizations, contemporary government reports and academic
studies, memoirs and autobiographies of activists, and miscellaneous materials
written and published by individuals during the period that is the focus of this
book. Most have been found in the archives and libraries in the United States I
visited on two research trips in 2013 and 2014, as listed in the acknowledgments.
Others have been located on internet sources such as the invaluable Hathi Trust
website and US government sites. Many of these rich seams of primary material
have been mined by historians before in pursuit of different lines of inquiry, but my
focus on extracting evidence of the importance of internal migration and its impact
on labor organization is, as far as I can tell, unique.

This book is meant to explore the hypothesis that geographic mobility undermined the major efforts to construct unions and labor-based parties in the US

during the Gilded Age. To this end, the book is divided into six chapters that attempt to capture this flow of evidence and argumentation. Chapter 1 will present evidence for the existence, extent, and content of class consciousness, drawing heavily on the archival materials in order to demonstrate that the classical explanations of American "exceptionalism" are basically hollow. Chapter 2 will look at the works of various labor and social historians, critically noting the absence of attempts to link geographical mobility with the weakness of the labor organizations and parties of the era. Following this, the chapter will discuss the extent of internal migration in the US and the forces underlying its uniquely high levels in comparison with those in Britain and Europe generally. Chapter 3 draws on primary sources to show that key groups of workers were well aware of the extent of migration and the problems it posed for them. Chapter 4 will make the case for the impact of this migration on labor organization, revealing both high levels of membership turnover and the ineffectiveness of the trade-union traveling-card system that resulted from high levels of "tramping" in search of work and better pay. Chapter 5 will examine the three major efforts at independent political action by labor during this period, rooting their failure in the union weakness brought on by constant migration, among other factors. Finally, the conclusion will look at what the Knights of Labor might have done to minimize the impact of migration on high member turnover, summarize the major arguments of the thesis, and look at its relevance to the massive global labor migrations of our own time.

In summary, the traditional arguments for American exceptionalism implied in Sombart's famous question, *Why is there no socialism in the United States?*, or even its less demanding cousin, Why is there no labor party?, fail to explain the unsustainability of labor's efforts at independent political action. Above all, the arguments focused on relative or absolute prosperity, access to free or cheap land, or social mobility do not hold up well, and in the end assume a lack of class consciousness that needs to be demonstrated. The proposition that higher incidence of state repression in the US compared to most other industrial countries falls apart on its relative infrequency compared to the number and growth of strikes and class conflict throughout the period. Far more credible are those analyses focusing on the power of capital and the many divisions of gender, race, and ethnicity. To these compelling explanations for the relative weakness of American labor and the unevenness of consciousness, this analysis adds and integrates the highly disruptive impact of geographical mobility on working-class efforts to construct mass, sustainable organizations capable of breaking through the business-dominated politics of the Gilded Age.

Chapter 1

CLASS FORMATION AND CONSCIOUSNESS IN GILDED-AGE AMERICA

The process of class formation is always and everywhere
difficult. In no way does it resemble a victory march.
—**Michelle Perrot**[1]

We cannot overlook the fact that at the present time
the relations subsisting between capitalists and laborers
are those of war, and intense conflict of interests.
—**Bureau of Labor Statistics of the State of
California,** *Fifth Biennial Report,* **1893**[2]

Whereas a struggle is going on in all the nations of the
civilized world, between the oppressors and the oppressed
of all countries, a struggle between capital and labor,
which must grow in intensity from year to year.
—**Preamble to the Constitution of the American
Federation of Labor, adopted 1886**[3]

LIKE CLASS formation, class consciousness necessarily takes shape in the context of the changes in society itself that occur over time. The rise of industrial capitalism in the decades following the US Civil War saw not only the formation of new social classes but also changes in the way those who belonged to these rising classes viewed the world and each other. Measuring class consciousness or even defining it with much precision is, however, a difficult task. The place to start, perhaps, is to specify what it is not. Above all, class consciousness cannot be measured or defined in terms of simple dualities: "false" versus "revolutionary" consciousness; Lenin's later abandoned dichotomy between "trade union" and "political" consciousness; or the oft-cited "in itself" versus that "for itself" duality, wrongly attributed to Marx.[4] Nor is it valid to equate class consciousness with socialist ideology or politics, which evolve over time, if at all, as both Sombart and Perlman do. To do this, as Thompson argues, is "to disclose class-consciousness, not as it is, but as it ought to be."[5] Even granting that class consciousness must have some clear content, simple dualities or fixed ideological equations cannot define the perceptions of society and sets of related values and views that compose a class consciousness in formation that, like social classes themselves, takes shape over time.

Here class consciousness will be defined as E. P. Thompson defined it. Class is first of all a "historical relationship," in this case the relations of production, which "must always be embodied in real people and in a real context." Thus, "class happens when some men, as a result of common experiences (inherited or shared), feel and articulate the identity of their interests as between themselves, and against other men whose interests are different from (and usually opposed to) theirs."[6] That is, there are two dimensions to this basic class consciousness: a general identity of wageworkers as a class in formation, and the perception of the emerging capitalist class or employers as different and opposed to the interests of the working class. This is the view of class consciousness taken here, and it will be argued that this sort of consciousness emerged in the US between 1870 and the 1880s and was sustained despite organizational and political changes into the twentieth century.

Class consciousness arises and is shaped through experience. As Thompson puts it, "experience is a necessary middle term between social being and social consciousness."[7] In the broadest terms, for the Gilded Age, this experience involved what Schneirov described as the transition "from a self-employed or free labor mode of production to a capitalist one"—namely, to wage labor and the degradation of work that went with it.[8] The transition from the self-employment of the artisan to the wage labor of the majority of manual workers and an increasing number of service workers necessarily had an impact on those who became wage laborers, regardless of their previous modes of labor or nationality. Their experience in the maelstrom of the postbellum industrial revolution was not unlike that of the English working class in its earlier transition to industrial society described by Thompson.

Experience, however, runs up against what the Italian Marxist Antonio Gramsci called "common sense"—not "the obvious" or "sensible," as American or British usage often implies, but a "traditional conception of the world." Class consciousness in this view is always contradictory to one extent or another.[9] Certainly many in the working class of the Gilded Age accepted much of this sort of common sense: the patriarchal family, degrees of racism, religion, and the sanctity of the republic as it existed in the US.

Gramsci provided an enriched explanation for this in the concept of hegemony, or "the 'spontaneous' consent given by the great masses of the population to the general direction imposed on social life by the dominant fundamental group." This consent, however, does not imply agreement and is never total so that a "state coercive power" is required at times to discipline "those groups who do not 'consent' either actively or passively."[10] Certainly this dialectic between consent and repression describes events in both early nineteenth-century England and late nineteenth-century America.

Nevertheless, while the notion of hegemony gives us a glimpse of the contest of values and views that must have affected the minds of working-class people, it has limits. As Leon Fink argued in a debate with those who would deny the existence of oppositional culture in the working class of the Gilded Age, "But if hegemony theory might best be restricted to a textured civil society (which differs from a slave regime, in that consent is a real issue), it also might be better applied to the absence, rather than the presence, of protest."[11] For working-class protest in just about every conceivable form was present throughout the Gilded Age on a massive scale, indicating the limits of capitalist "hegemony."

Thus, class consciousness arose first as "an identity of interest" among wage-workers in opposition to the newly emerging industrial capitalists, but not as a commonly held consistent ideology. Rather, in Gilded-Age America, this class consciousness contained both shared goals and competing ideas for how to deal with the new state of permanent wage labor and the industrial capitalist class that was imposing it, much as it had earlier in Britain. While becoming aware of basic class differences between labor, now defined as wage labor, and capital, now seen not just as accumulated wealth or factory and equipment but also as a distinct class of people, this new consciousness clung to old ideas such as the Victorian family, distinct racial characteristics, and republicanism, but in a new context that required modification or challenges to some of these. As Leon Fink suggests, these traditional ideas sometimes provided both the means of legitimizing opposition and alternatives (for example, the cooperative commonwealth) as well as sources of division and confusion. But they did not prevent the growth of the movement or sufficiently explain its eventual demise in the case of the Knights of Labor.[12]

The enormous changes in circumstance and experience necessarily brought shared changes in the language and, hence, new ways of viewing "labor." As Bruce Laurie described this transition,

> Recognizably modern words and economic institutions replaced older ones. No one spoke of artisans, mechanics, or even master craftsmen by the closing decades of the nineteenth century: these terms went the way of the wooden plow, the keelboat, and the journeyman shoemaker's lap stone. Indeed, wage workers did not refer to themselves as journeymen any longer. Distinctions of skill endured and even sharpened, but manual employees thought of themselves as workers, just as employers became manufacturers or businessmen.[13]

Indeed, the very word "labor" was transformed in meaning from its earlier "free labor" connotation as a fluid state in which one moved from employee to master to "labor" as a permanent class of wage earners. As Sarah Watts put it, by the late nineteenth century, "the term *labor* had come to denote a distinct class of wage workers, separated by the growth of workers' neighborhoods, widened by the 'alien' ways of immigrants, and distanced by the growing inequities of economic distribution."[14] The term that was most commonly used to describe this new social reality was "wageworker." Michael Kazin is mistaken when he argues that the word most used in the rhetoric of the Knights of Labor was "producer."[15] While this was the general definition of who might join the Knights, even the preamble and declaration of principles of the Knights refers to the "laborer," the "toiler," the "industrial classes," and only once to the "producing masses."[16] Indeed, officially for one to become a member, he or she "must be, or must have been at some time, a wage-worker," according to Knights grand secretary Robert Layton, although like so many of the Knights' "rules," this was no doubt frequently violated.[17]

Throughout the trade-union and labor press of the time, the words that appeared over and over were "worker," "wage worker," "laborer," "workingmen," "working classes," "working class," "industrial classes," "laboring classes," and "wage-slave." This last term received a vigorous defense in the pages of the Knights of Labor's *Journal of United Labor* in 1883 when a member criticized the use of "wage-slave" "in speaking of the condition of the toiler." In an editorial, the journal replied that "the term is not mis-applied however harsh it may sound."[18] While "proletariat" was not much used in the US, it is interesting that one of the most popular Knights of Labor songs in the 1880s was precisely the "Song of the Proletaire: Dedicated to the Wage Workers of the World."[19]

The "labor question," as it was then called, became one of the dominant economic and social concerns of the nation in the years following the Civil War, on a par with the tariff and the currency. It was sparked by the economic turmoil of the era, but as Rosanne Currarino writes in *The Labor Question in America*, "Most of all, though, it was linked to the increasing number of permanent wage workers and the declining number of independent, self-employed producers." By the end of the Civil War, she notes, "there were now 2.5 wage workers for every self-employed man."[20] By 1870 in Pennsylvania, 65–75 percent of the economically active population worked for someone else, while in Massachusetts it was already 75–85 percent.[21] And 1870 was, of course, just at the beginning of the process.

What Some Observers Thought About Class

All of this was widely recognized at the time. Looking at the social wreckage of the long depression that began in 1873, economist David Wells observed in mid-1877 that with lands in the West "exhausted" or sold, the "American laborer without capital" could no longer, as was previously the case, "raise himself from the position of laborer, dependent on others for employment to the position of capitalist." As the changes Wells saw commenced, he wrote, "The United States will have entered upon a new social order of things; an order of things similar to what exists in the more densely populated countries of the Old World, in which the tendency is for a man born a laborer, working for hire, to never be anything but a laborer."[22]

Wells had, in effect, announced the death of the old "free labor" ideology that saw wage labor as merely temporary and advancement out of the wage-earing class open to all but the lazy or incompetent. Only two years later, the Ohio Bureau of Labor Statistics drew the same conclusion, noting that the "rapid concentration of capital, the massing of machinery in immense workshops" had led to "the destruction of the possibility of the workman becoming his own employer."[23] Writing in 1889, by which time the scale of industry, finance, and commerce were clear to all, economist Richard T. Ely put the arrival of permanent wage labor in simple numerical terms: "Every railroad president necessitates the existence of several thousand wage-receivers; every bank president presumes clerks, book-keepers, and others in subordinate positions; every merchant of wealth requires numerous salaried employés. By no human possibility can this be otherwise."[24]

Wells and Ely were not alone in observing the rise of a class of permanent wageworkers. Currarino notes that "by the late 1870s, as testimony before a House subcommittee shows, some ordinary Americans feared that the era of the small proprietary producer was ending and that they were now fated permanently to live as wage workers."[25] This was the first in a series of congressional hearings on the topic of the "relations of labor and capital" throughout this period. Scarcely six years later, in hearings before a Senate committee, other observers described the change in relations between the workers and their employers that accompanied the growth of permanent wage labor. Herbert Newton, an Episcopal minister from Long Island, told the Senate committee in 1883:

> The factory system is a new feudalism, in which the master rarely deals directly with his hands. Superintendents, managers, and "bosses" stand between him and them. He does not know them; they do not know him. The old common feeling is disappearing.[26]

In a similar vein, the editor of a New York newspaper, which he described as "the organ of the manufacturers," told the Senate of the way workers and employers viewed each other:

> There has been a very thorough change in that respect within the last ten or fifteen years. The old confidential relation between the American employer and his employees has ceased to exist. They look at each other now more or

less as enemies, at least in certain branches of business. Each party thinks the other his enemy.[27]

Thomas Miller, general manager of the Atlas Works in Pittsburgh, blamed this social distance on the unions. He told the Senate, "I don't think they have been so friendly since the unions have been established as they were before. The employers are inclined to treat the men as an organization and not as individuals. They do not have that personal sympathy that they had before with each individual workingman."[28]

What Wageworkers Thought About Class

Our concern here, of course, is primarily with the consciousness of the workers themselves. There are no "opinion polls" to consult, so we cannot be sure just how deeply into the working class this new consciousness penetrated. Here, David Montgomery provides a critical argument for focusing on the activist layer of the class. He writes,

> Both "history from the bottom up" and the common fixation on great leaders have obscured the decisive role of those whom twentieth-century syndicalists have called the "militant minority": the men and women who endeavored to weld their workmates and neighbors into a self-aware and purposeful working class.[29]

What is clear is that those in the "militant minority" or the somewhat larger activist layer of this class in formation saw the changes in the nature of labor described by Wells in very similar terms. For example, as Knights of Labor activist George McNeill put it in the 1887 book he edited, "Under the present system of wages for laborers, and profits upon labor for capitalists, the natural tendency is toward the establishment of permanent classes; the wage-receiving class becoming more and more permanent."[30]

The 1883 Senate hearings, labor conventions, trade-union journals, and the labor press of the time provide a wealth of evidence of a strong awareness of class and class conflict. Looking first at testimony before the Senate committee in 1883, we find many workers ready to describe the situation of their class. Writing of the conflict of classes in a letter to the committee, a self-described "workman" said, "The investigation which you are prosecuting makes very plain at least two facts. First, that the 'irrepressible conflict' between liberty and slavery is still on, and will yield no settlement but that of justice. Second, the problem of the times is pre-eminently that of capital and labor."[31]

Discussing the new relationship between employer and worker, a brass worker testified,

> Well, I remember that fourteen years ago the workmen and the foremen and the boss were all as one family; it was just as easy and free to speak to the boss

as any one else, but now the boss is superior, and the men all go to the super-intendent or to the foreman; but we would not think of looking the foreman in the face now any more than we would the boss.

The average hand growing up in the shop now would not think of speak-ing to the boss, would not presume to recognize him, nor the boss would not recognize him either.[32]

When asked what he thought the feelings of the laborers were toward capital, telegraph operator and member of the Knights of Labor John McClelland said, "There is a generally unfriendly feeling, brought about by the conditions which have been enforced upon them by capital." When asked how the "workingmen feel towards the people who employ you," a tailor replied, "They hate the bosses and the foremen more than the bosses, and that feeling is deep."[33]

In the same 1883 hearings, Senator James George of Mississippi inquired of Frank Foster, a member of the International Typographical Union and the Knights of Labor, about "social intercourse" between laborers and capitalists. Foster replied that it was "the exception" and went on to say that "we are rapidly developing classes in society as well as in the industrial world, and that these classes are becom-ing more and more fixed . . . The walls are being erected higher and higher."[34] Asked to speculate on the causes of strikes, Foster spoke of "the hardness of temper that exists between the different classes."[35] Robert Layton, cited above, put the growing conflict and the recognition of the employers "as a class" in more moderate terms: "I find in the first place that in nearly every instance the relation between employed and employers, with a few honorable exceptions, is not of that cordial nature it should be. I find that the mere idea of organization on the part of the laboring men is repugnant to the manufacturers and employers as a class."[36]

P. H. McLogan, a printer representing the Chicago Trades Assembly, offered the committee a critique of the notion of class harmony:

It is an old saying that the interests of capital and labor are identical, but we have got to look at it in this way, that the interests of capital and labor are not identical at all in this sense. For instance, capital wants to get labor just as cheap as he can, and labor, on the contrary, wants to get as much wages as it can. Now, how you can get those interests identical I cannot conceive.[37]

Expressing the sense of exploitation held by many workers, telegraph operator John McClelland told the Senate committee, "I mean to say, taking all the wealth that is created for the company by its operators, and by all the men whom it uses for the production of that wealth, of that product the employees received as their share about one tenth, and capital receives the rest." Citing the introduction of improved technology or an automatic system—that is, capital accumulation—McClelland went on to state, "The advantages at present are tending all to the benefit of the capitalist and to the detriment of the employee."[38]

In the same hearings, even so conservative a labor leader as John Jarrett of the Amalgamated Association of Iron and Steel Workers, while noting that relations between employers and employees in the West were "as a rule, very favorable," went on to say, "But I believe the tendency of manufacturers in this country, as a rule, has been to grow more autocratic with their men, to draw farther apart from them; they will not affiliate with the men; they will not talk to them as they ought to."[39]

The official trade-union journals, as well as reports to annual conventions, often expressed similar sentiments. As early as 1878, the *Iron Molders' Journal* carried the following lesson in class definition:

> "We are all workingmen" is a remark very often made by capitalists of all shades and grades. With some, it is pure ignorance. Others make the assertion with a view to confuse and perplex the conception as to the true meaning of "workingmen." A workingman proper, is a person whose only means of existence is his own labor—consequently would have no existence without it—and whose interest lies only in the elevation of useful labor.[40]

A few years later, the *Iron Molders' Journal*, reporting on the outcome of the national election in 1884, noted that "the elections are over, but there is no alteration in the relationship of labor and capital. Labor is still slave and capital is still master."[41] In both cases, labor is seen as a class with common interests and not merely as a trade or craft. It would seem that job consciousness and class consciousness are not mutually exclusive.

In 1886, in the face of an accelerated employers' offensive, the *Iron Molders' Journal* editorialized about the need for a federation of all trades that would make it "impossible for any combination of capital to crush out any individual trade organization." It went on to say,

> Now it is needless to assert that in the past the working classes, partly by reason of their isolation and partly their ignorance, have been at the mercy of the so-called upper classes, still the glaring anomalies of the present social system often pass for sound political economy, and those who neither "toil nor spin" are counted public benefactors, while the producer is but little better than a slave.[42]

A letter to the Knights of Labor's *Journal of United Labor* put this relationship in rather stronger terms: "The reason we know that the present industrial system is wrong is because capital, when it wants to, can starve labor, and the only time it takes its brutal hands off the throat of labor is when it suits its own interests best."[43] At the Knights of Labor's 1882 General Assembly, Grand Statistician Theodore

Cuno reported the members' reactions to the less than cordial system of wage labor. Many replied to his survey as follows, to use only a few examples: "tyrannical and oppressive"; "treat us like slaves"; "treated the same as any other piece of machinery"; and "harsh and exacting"—with the words "tyrannical" and "slave" being most frequent. A few reported that treatment was "fair," others that it had improved once the workers had organized and the employers "are forced to treat their employees well."[44]

An 1886 article in the *Journal of United Labor* expressed views on exploitation similar to that of the telegraph operator quoted above:

> Wealth has increased three times as fast as the number of producers, and it looks to the average workman that they ought to have more of "that pile," especially as other people who do not labor with their hands are getting more of it. They see palaces and millionaires increasing and know where the bulk of it is going—know by bitter experience that they are getting a very small share of it.[45]

The fact that such views appeared in official union publications indicates that they were representative of a significant portion of the membership, even if not a majority.

The independent labor press also frequently reported strong sentiments about the formation of a permanent wage-earning class and its conflict with capital. In 1881, the Chicago-based *Progressive Age*, describing itself as "A Weekly Paper Devoted to the Interests of the Industrial Classes," wrote that "the workers form a class to themselves, and are generally considered, even by themselves, as inferior to those persons who live upon the interest of their money, by means of a profession, or by traffic."[46] A letter to the Denver-based *Labor Enquirer* asked "what is the future of my class?" and went on to argue, "For the wageworkers do constitute a class, and a hereditary class, notwithstanding all assertions to the contrary."[47] In November 1885, the *Labor Leaf* reported that, despite the ethnic diversity of the Detroit workforce, "the class lines . . . have been drawn to a large extent."[48] A year earlier, the *Labor Leaf* reprinted a statement from the Furniture Workers Union to the effect that "society at present is composed of classes whose interests are highly antagonistic."[49]

That activists, leaders, and journals of such mainstream craft unions as the Iron Molders, Typographers, and Iron and Steel Workers saw class conflict as a reality and expressed it in those terms—much like the generally more radical weekly labor press or the Knights of Labor—indicates that basic class consciousness and the recognition of class conflict were indeed widespread. Even as "pure and simple" unionism was beginning to take shape, this perception of class differences and opposition remained fundamental to the outlook of most labor activists and leaders. The 1881 preamble to the constitution of the craft union–dominated Federation of

Organized Trades and Labor Unions had opened with the statement, "Whereas a struggle is going on in all the nations of the civilized world, between the oppressors and the oppressed of all countries, a struggle between capital and labor, which must grow in intensity from year to year." When the American Federation of Labor was formed in 1886, the delegates voted unanimously to make this the preamble to the new organization's constitution.[50] Thus, class conflict was widely accepted as a consequence of industrial capitalism, though the conclusions one drew from that were more controversial. Perhaps the ultimate testimony to the pervasiveness of this working-class consciousness came from the labor leader who most wished it had not existed at all. Toward the end of his autobiography, onetime grand master workman of the Knights of Labor Terence V. Powderly complained, "Perhaps the day will come when people will stop talking about 'classes' in this country."[51]

A "Subculture of Opposition"

To get a clearer idea of the degree to which class relations were understood not only vertically, as in the conflict between capital and labor, but also horizontally, encompassing all wageworkers, we turn to the concept of a "subculture of opposition" developed by Richard Oestreicher. First, however, it is necessary to examine what composes the core of a working-class culture.

Citing Raymond Williams, E. P. Thompson wrote of working-class culture, "As contrasted with middle class ideas of individualism or (at best) of service . . . 'what is properly meant by "working-class culture" . . . is the basic collective idea, and the institutions, manners, habits of thought and the intentions which proceed from this.'"[52] David Montgomery describes this rejection of individualism as it occurred in the US during the Gilded Age and beyond and gives us an idea of how the experience of industrial change and growth affected the larger class and its diverse elements:

> Although the personal bondings of families, migrant groups, young wage-earning women, craftsmen, strikers, voters, and rioters defined people's loyalties in different and often conflicting ways, all attachments were rooted in the shared presumption that individualism was appropriate only for the prosperous and wellborn.[53]

This sense of difference from those above—the employers, the wealthy, the capitalists—along with the many "institutions" that both sprang from it and helped to develop it, were major building blocks of class consciousness in Gilded-Age America that connected the "militant minority" to the rest of the class.

The differences in class world views were not limited to collectivist or mutualist versus individualist values. They involved conflicting and competing views of the role of labor and capital in society. Noting the development of class consciousness within the English working class by the 1830s, Thompson described the "dividing-line" between middle class and working class, thought as "alternative notions of political economy."[54] This was certainly the case during the Gilded Age in the United States.

Throughout this era and beyond, most working-class people clung to a generalized labor theory of value in which they, not capital, were the creators of wealth. This view was spread in more concrete forms within the activist core of the working class by widely read home-grown publicists such as Ira Stewart, John Swinton, George O'Neill, Joseph Labadie, and Henry George, among others, as well as through the labor press.

Capital, for its part, fought hard to convince society that it was *they*, the capitalists, who really produced wealth through their own abstinence—an argument not likely to convince many workers in light of the ostentatious lifestyles of many Gilded-Age capitalists. In this they were nonetheless supported by the older school of economists such as Henry Carey and Edward Atkinson, who upheld the Ricardian wage-fund theory that wages came from capital as a result of the abstinence of the capitalist.[55] Beginning in the 1870s with the development of the new marginalist economics, capital was further aided in this virtuous self-image. The British economist William Stanley Jevons's famous statement, "I hold labor to be essentially variable, so that its value must be determined by the value of the product, not the value of the product by that of the labor," must have come as a liberating message for capital and was soon spread by American economists such as John Bates Clark.[56] Against both the old Ricardian and Malthusian orthodoxy as well as the new marginalism, labor spokesmen opposed to the tyranny of supply and demand and the market fought not only for the eight-hour day and higher wages, but also for legislation on child labor, contract labor, and convict labor, and often the nationalization of railroads, the telegraph, and the mines.

As we will see in chapter 5, in the mid-1890s significant majorities of the members of most of the larger trade unions would endorse the "political program" of Britain's reform socialist Independent Labour Party in referendums held by AFL affiliates.[57] Political class consciousness and conflict was not limited to workplace or trade union–based issues or initiatives. As Montgomery shows, the fight over housing and its regulation was central to working-class issues in urban centers where the majority of workers were also renters. In his 1886 United Labor Party campaign for mayor of New York, Henry George's daily campaign publications began, "We are wage-workers and renters."[58] In a similar vein, Francis Couvares analyzes how class cultural views led to political conflict over the content and practice of leisure in the Gilded Age and beyond.[59] Indeed, throughout the Gilded Age and into the twentieth century, such major ideological concepts as the work ethic, republicanism in its democratic form, religion, morality, and even "law and order" continued to be contested terrain between labor and capital.[60]

Richard Oestreicher proposes a "subculture of opposition" as a way to understand both the content and institutions that characterized class consciousness. Writing of Detroit, he states, "The subculture defined itself by its opposition to employers, to great wealth, and to existing industrial conditions, not by a clear ideology."[61] In a brief summary of the institutions of Detroit's subculture of opposition in the 1880s, Oestreicher writes,

> A growing list of producers' cooperatives including a shoe factory, a cooperage, and an iron foundry appealed to workers to invest their savings and to buy cooperative goods. By 1886, the movement included a weekly labor press in both English and German, a workers' militia (The Detroit Rifles), regular debates in the Dialectical Union, a theatre group, singing societies, and almost nightly social or educational events.[62]

In fact, there were two weekly English-language labor papers during these years: the *Detroit Unionist*, with a claimed circulation of almost three thousand a week, and the *Labor Leaf*, which set a goal of ten thousand a week, though it probably didn't reach it.[63] In addition, Detroit had its own Independent Labor Party from 1882 through 1886. Strikes and demonstrations, sometimes involving thousands, were not unusual and typically received widespread support. The growing subculture radiated out from a core of a few hundred activists to perhaps ten thousand, when family and friends are included, to the thousands more who joined the trade unions and the Knights of Labor at one time or another. Turnover was large so that the estimated five thousand Knights as of 1886 was certainly an undercount of how many passed through that organization and were touched by this culture. Mass parades, successful boycotts, popular lectures, labor papers, and electoral action all provided ways of participating that went beyond the activist core.[64]

That this working-class culture combated the "received culture" of the middle and upper classes of Detroit and, indeed, of the nation was central to its growth. As Oestreicher puts it, "These core values of cooperation, mutual trust, equality, and mutual assistance constituted the beginnings of the emerging working-class subculture. They conflicted with native middle-class values of competition, individualism, and personal success."[65]

Despite ethnic tensions, Detroit's movement was multi-ethnic and was "grounded in the mutualism and democratic traditions of each of its ethnic working-class fragments."[66] It was, as Oestreicher emphasizes over and over, an oppositional culture that had to be made by its participants in the manner in which E. P. Thompson described class formation.

Detroit's working-class subculture was by no means exceptional. A reading of Knights of Labor leader Joseph Buchanan's autobiography reveals the same cluster of institutions and collectivist sentiments in Denver: the reading room, lectures, a local independent socialist group that drew hundreds to its events, a workers' rifle club, mass social events, trade unions, citywide trades council, boycotts, efforts at independent political action, mass parades with the singing of "Storm the Fort Ye Knights of Labor," Buchanan's own weekly labor paper, the *Labor Enquirer*, and a culture of mutualism and collectivism.[67] David Brundage, in his history of working-class Denver, argued that this collectivist culture actually had its origins in the various ethnic societies of the 1870s and early 1880s, which acted as "a kind of incubator for the values the labor movement would soon uphold."[68] This reminds us that while ethnic differences and organizations could divide workers under certain circumstances, these ethnic societies served as building blocks for the broader labor movement of Denver.

Schneirov's description of Chicago's labor culture is substantially the same, only on a larger scale. Chicago's *Progressive Age*, one of a number of labor papers in that city, for example, claimed a circulation of twenty thousand and was supported by the entire union movement. Chicago, of course, was the center of the May 1, 1886, eight-hour strike, when eighty thousand workers marched through the city. During that year at the height of the "Great Upheaval," some eighty-eight thousand workers went on strike in Chicago. As a result of these events, writes Schneirov, "There can be little doubt that capital-labor conflict, labor organization, and the awareness of class issues assumed a far more pervasive role than ever before in Chicago."[69] As Peter Rachleff has shown, this same "culture of opposition" reached into the African American community of Richmond, Virginia, where Knights District Assembly 92 was organized by the preexisting activist layer of black Richmond, who led the many African American fraternal and mutual-aid societies. For a time, District Assembly 92 worked in unity with the white District Assembly 84.[70]

The 1880s were undoubtedly the high point of the culture of opposition described by Oestreicher. Just how many working-class people were influenced by this subculture is hard to say, but it certainly reached far beyond the static figures of trade-union or Knights membership. As we will see in a subsequent chapter, the turnover of membership in the Knights of Labor was huge even before its collapse. Bruce Laurie estimates that "two to three million people passed through its portals between the early 1870s and the mid-1890s."[71] Most trade unions also saw significant levels of turnover, as well as large numbers of traveling members who were often not included in the official count. It is not inconceivable that as many as three million workers passed through or stayed in a union or the Knights of Labor in the 1880s alone, forming a major part of the industrial workforce that grew from 5,011,000 in 1880 to 7,051,000 by the end of the decade. Overlapping but stretching this further were nonworking family members and all of those who, with some sense of class solidarity, observed a union boycott, marched in a parade, read a labor paper, or otherwise had contact with the subculture of opposition created and sustained by the activist minority.

Even the subculture, however, could not have been as widespread and influential as it was for much of the Gilded Age, had its own values and ideas not struck a chord with the broader ranks of the working class, including many nonunion workers. Indeed, as Oestreicher writes, "A substantial proportion of the nonunionized workers were neither opposed to unionism nor indifferent to it. While unable or afraid to organize, they sympathized with union doctrines."[72]

Indeed, this class conscious subculture of opposition was national in scope. Insofar as organization and activity reflected consciousness, the spread and diversity of these indicate that this "culture of opposition" was, indeed, widespread by the 1880s. These efforts included local and national unions; local trades councils; the largely German Central Labor Unions; the Federation of Trades and Labor Organizations (as of 1886 the American Federation of Labor); the Knights of Labor; the eight-hour leagues; the labor press; various cooperative efforts; mutual-aid societies; national boycotts; clubs; labor libraries; and the independent labor parties that swept across the US in 1886–1887, including an attempt to form a national labor party. That not all of these efforts were successful in the long run does not negate the obvious desire for independent class organization. The forces that undermined both the Knights and the labor-party efforts will be examined in a subsequent chapter. Here it is, perhaps, permissible to reverse the circular argument that no party means no consciousness to say that efforts toward such a party, as well as other class-wide institutions, must reveal some level of class consciousness that reached beyond the activist core.

The Eight-Hour Movement

Another indicator of widespread class consciousness was the movement for the eight-hour workday. In the late nineteenth century, the eight-hour day was not simply a trade-union demand but an idea that drew in vast numbers of working people both union and nonunion, skilled and unskilled, black and white, and virtually all the ethnic groups that composed the Gilded-Age working class. It is best understood as a social movement for a class-wide demand in which unions and other labor organizations played a leading role. Like most social movements it had its ups and downs, but the persistence and popularity of the eight-hour day as a class-wide objective is one more piece of evidence of a broad class consciousness that developed from the Civil War years into the twentieth century. The methods of winning it varied, moving from legislation to direct action with a crescendo on May 1, 1886, and the months following. But even after the setbacks that followed, eight hours persisted as a universal goal for working people into the twentieth century.

In their highly detailed account of the movement for shorter hours, Roediger and Foner write, "While instances of eight-hour agitation occurred much earlier, the emergence of a movement for the eight-hour day dates from the Civil War period." And "by 1866 eight-hour organizations thrived across the nation." It was a movement rooted in earlier antislavery struggles and the enormous sense of possibilities brought on by the victory of the North and the end of chattel slavery.[73]

The leading theorist of this movement was Ira Steward, a machinist and union activist from Boston. His theory argued that shortening the workday would lead to higher needs as workers experienced the time to educate themselves, which would in turn lead to demands for higher wages. In this way, shorter hours would lead to higher wages. Steward recognized exploitation and sought to diminish it through shorter hours of work. As Commons and Andrews put it, "Steward saw the increasing elevation of labor and the general absorption of capital through increased wages at the expense of capital." Further, they argue, "Steward's doctrine, like that of his greater contemporary, Karl Marx, is explicitly a 'class-conscious,' or perhaps wage-conscious doctrine." Thus, in the political struggle for eight hours, as Steward himself put it, "The eight-hour system will make a coalition between ignorant labor and selfish capital on election day, impossible." Commons and Andrews credit this initial period of agitation along with the new pressures of capital accumulation as leading to "the class conscious period of the sixties and seventies when the common interests of all wage-earning labor as such, regardless of skill, privilege, or power of organization became the watchword of labor."[74]

The experience that Thompson refers to in shaping class consciousness is also an intellectual experience, and Steward's ideas propagated not only by him but also by associates such as George McNeill, George Gunton, and F. A. Sorge, a correspondent of Marx's, provided one of the key theoretical alternatives to mainstream capitalist thought, particularly in the realm of political economy. As Montgomery put it, the working-class advocates of the eight-hour day "had to substitute a political economy of the working class for the utilitarian economics of the [Republican] Radicals."[75] Steward explicitly took on such mainstream pro-employer economists as Edward Atkinson. In addition, while almost all wageworkers favored a shorter workday, almost all employers opposed it. This debate, therefore, underlined this class difference and was a factor in giving the new class consciousness of the Gilded Age some specific content.

So widely accepted was Steward's basic theory that even Samuel Gompers quoted him before the Industrial Commission in 1899. Steward's theory even became a semiofficial doctrine of organized labor and was propagated into the new century by works done by McNeill for the AFL.[76]

As the 1880s opened, the eight-hour demand became even more central. As Frank Foster told the Senate committee in 1883, "One of our most pressing needs, we think, as a class is shorter hours of labor in all the industrial pursuits of the country."[77] Disillusioned with the ineffective eight-hour laws of the 1870s, however, the movement turned toward direct action. The movement for shorter hours reached a climax in the mid-1880s with the May 1, 1886, mass strike for eight hours. Roediger and Foner say that perhaps four hundred thousand participated. Furthermore, virtually all ethnic groups were involved in one city or another.[78] Many nevertheless considered it a failure, including Knights of Labor general master workman Terence Powderly. And indeed, following the Haymarket disaster, employers around the country took the opportunity to accelerate an organized counterattack against those who had won shorter hours. Even as the employers sought to push back this movement, in 1888 the AFL turned to a plan to have major unions lead the movement by striking for eight hours. The carpenters were chosen to make the fight in 1890, a plan that drew many socialists who had been Knights as well into the AFL unions. The carpenters won eight hours for thousands of building trades workers. Backed by the AFL, other strikes followed by other building trades workers in 1891 and with the massive general strike of black and white longshore workers in New Orleans in 1892. The miners, who were to strike next, however, proved unable to do so, and the plan was abandoned by 1894, after which unions fought separately for reduced hours.[79]

Yet the eight-hour demand remained a central goal of the entire movement through the 1890s and into the new century. In 1899, for example, United Mine Workers president John Mitchell testified before the Industrial Commission that one of the principles of his union was "to uncompromisingly demand that eight hours shall constitute a day's work." Further, he stated that they had won the eight-hour day in Pennsylvania, Ohio, Indiana, and Illinois.[80] More generally, in 1902–1903, reduction of hours was listed as a demand for 588,200 strikers compared to 387,505 who only demanded increased wages.[81] Ira Steward's argument that shorter hours would bring higher wages was still being stated at the end of the 1890s. Also testifying before the Industrial Commission, D. F. Kennedy, an AFL organizer, stated, "The short workday trades always get the biggest wages, and they get the biggest wages as a result of the shortening of the hours."[82]

Looking back on the general movement for shorter hours, even Samuel Gompers told the Industrial Commission in 1899, "I have no hesitancy in expressing my conviction that the movement of 1886 resulted in a reduction of fully 1 hour's labor of the working people of the United States."[83] Overall, the Industrial Commission concluded in its 1901 report, "The general drift of opinion among American trade unionists is strongly in the direction of emphasizing the importance of a shorter work day."[84] Thus, this central class-wide goal continued to hold universal appeal for workers into the early twentieth century.

A Gilded-Age Social Media: The Labor Press

All of these strands of class consciousness and organization were tied together and developed by a network of dozens of official trade-union journals and hundreds of local weekly labor papers that exchanged news items, economic analysis, political ideas, and labor-market information. E. P. Thompson gives considerable weight to the ability of early nineteenth-century artisans and wageworkers to read and to the materials they read. He sees the early 1830s when working-class radical papers such as the *Poor Man's Guardian*, the *Gorgon*, and the *Trades Newspaper* broke from the middle-class Radicals, a political current that fought for political liberties and opposed government corruption, as a key moment in the development of class consciousness in England.[85] Benedict Anderson argues that it was largely the "printer-journalist" who produced the hundreds of newspapers of early America that "emerged as the key to North American communications and community intellectual life," which in turn developed the identity as "Americans."[86] So it was in terms of class consciousness with the union "printer-journalists" of the Gilded Age who produced the hundreds of weekly labor papers—printers such as Joseph Buchanan, Frank K. Foster, Joseph Labadie, Joseph McDonnell, and John Swinton, to name but a few.

More recently, in the light of the growth of internet social media, scholars have noted that nineteenth-century periodicals took on a network character often for specific social or cultural groups in the US and internationally.[87] The labor press of the Gilded Age, through its overlapping circulation, press association, and crisscrossing web of editors, certainly played this networking role for the labor movement in the US, aided by widespread literacy. Literacy rates were fairly high by the Gilded Age. For native-born whites they rose from a little over 90 percent in 1880 to 94 percent in 1900, while for foreign-born whites it was about 87 percent for the period. Even African Americans, who had been denied literacy under slavery, saw their literacy rate rise from 30 percent in 1880 to 55 percent by 1900.[88] Thus, the labor press was able to play an important role in creating class consciousness by contesting the "received culture" of capital's daily press throughout this period.

Expressing the solidifying role of the labor press in the language of the building trades, in 1881 the Chicago-based *Progressive Age*, backed by that city's Trade and Labor Council, described the function of this emerging network of newspapers: "The labor press is to the labor movement what plaster is to the wall of brick—without it no substantial or enduring edifice can be reared."[89] According to Commons et al., from 1863 to 1873 there had been 120 labor papers.[90] A January 1885 article by Richard Hinton in the *North American Review* revealed the growth of the labor press by the mid-1880s:

> There are nearly four hundred weeklies that are in sympathy with the labor organizations in some one or all of their methods. Recently a large number of these papers have formed a "Labor Press Association." They do not use the wires as yet, but by a judicious use of the mails are able to supply one another with a great deal of interesting news, much of it of value as

showing the condition of labor, the places where the market is crowded, or the trades in which men are needed. All this has grown out of a feeling that the ordinary press is hostile and presents the action of labor from the point of antagonism.[91]

Expressing the importance that even craft unions saw in the independent labor press, in December 1885 the *Iron Molders' Journal* strongly recommended this emerging journalistic network to its members:

Within the past five years there has sprung up a class of papers known and recognized as labor papers. These have been issued owing to the necessities of the hour, that labor might give expression to the injustice being done it . . . Every labor paper in the country should receive the hearty support of the workingmen where such a paper exists.[92]

Most of these papers, while independently published and edited, were supported by local unions, trades councils, and local and district assemblies of the Knights of Labor. Henry George's paper, the *Standard*, for example, reported how the *Ohio Valley Budget*, which he called "the first labor paper started in Wheeling [West Virginia] has just put in a new press, the money for which was raised by the trades unions of the valley."[93] The Knights of Labor's *Journal of United Labor* frequently printed a list of local labor papers and urged members to "Support Your Own Papers."[94]

This extensive network of weekly papers even received international attention. A French study of the US labor press cited in the *Patterson Labor Standard* in 1888 stated that there were in 1887 some eight hundred labor papers, perhaps two-thirds of them supported by local Knights of Labor groups.[95] In the report they wrote on their "tour" of the US labor movement in 1886, Eleanor Marx and Edward Aveling were much impressed by the "purely working class journalism" they found in the US labor press, which they compared to "the meagre list of journals of this kind to be found in England."[96] Some papers, such as *John Swinton's Paper* from New York, the *National Labor Tribune* out of Pittsburgh, and the *Labor Enquirer* published in Denver, achieved substantial national distribution. For example, the *Chicago Boycotter* reported that "John Swinton's Paper is having an immense circulation and doing yeoman service in the cause of labor."[97]

The network quality of the labor press was indicated by attempts to form press associations mentioned by Hinton. In 1886 economist Richard T. Ely reported, "Some twenty labor papers have formed an associated labor press, and each paper furnishes all the others with labor items gathered in its own locality."[98] The Associated Labor Press circulated news from various cities and regions to papers across the country. In February 1885, the *Haverhill Laborer* reported that Associated Labor Press had now established an advertising department to help affiliated papers secure advertising. It also offered discounts for those subscribing to two or more papers.[99] At the 1886 Richmond convention of the Knights of Labor, "the editors of labor papers and other newspaper men who are delegates to the convention at Richmond" met "to form a new labor bureau, through which authentic information with regard to labor matters can be transmitted to the country." Frank Foster of the *Haverhill Laborer* was chosen secretary.[100] As he was also involved in the Associated Labor Press, it seems this "bureau" must have been for Knights of Labor local papers.

No one has attempted an estimate of the overall circulation of the labor press at its height in the mid-1880s, but we know that the local circulation of many of these papers was substantial, although far less than the mainstream daily press. In addition to the "immense" circulation of Swinton's paper, the *Chicago Boycotter* claimed a circulation of ten thousand, while a New York paper called the *Boycotter* said it printed twenty-five thousand of each issue.[101] The Chicago-based *Progressive Age* had a circulation of twenty thousand in 1882, the *Detroit Unionist* claimed almost three thousand copies a week that same year, while in 1885 the *Labor Leaf* set a goal of ten thousand a week.[102] In 1885, the *Laborer*, edited by Frank Foster of Haverhill, Massachusetts, also predicted it would reach a circulation of ten thousand by late 1886.[103] Given four hundred to eight hundred such papers existed in 1886 with an average circulation of perhaps five thousand, it is not inconceivable that between two million and four million copies circulated each week across the country. This would have reached far beyond union membership even at its height in 1886 and into an industrial workforce that numbered about six million at that time. Such an impressive communications network would have both reflected and helped to form and solidify a broad class consciousness.

As mostly products of "printer-journalists," labor papers often depended on the energies of their editors. Joseph Buchanan, editor of the Denver *Labor Enquirer*, attested to this when he wrote in his autobiography, "I labored sixteen to twenty hours a day—Sundays included."[104] Even this was not always enough, so that labor papers often had a short life. Yet, this was not much different from other periodicals of the era, which averaged about four years.[105] More important for the life of a labor paper was the state of the labor movement itself. In their introduction to volume 9 of *A Documentary History of American Industrial Society*, editors John R. Commons and John B. Andrews wrote, "The rise and fall of a labor movement is marked by the rise and fall of the labor press."[106]

The fate of one of the most popular labor papers of the 1880s, *John Swinton's Paper*, provides an example of this. In the final issue of his paper, published on August 21, 1887, Swinton provided a brief history of its growth and final demise that no doubt applied to many of the labor papers of the era. He traced the rise and fall of the paper's circulation, growing from 2,500 at the end of the first year of publication in 1883 to

5,000 in the next year, while in 1885 "it bounded along for six months with the bounding labor movement," reaching 10,000 at the beginning of 1886. As the labor movement and above all the Knights grew in 1886, his circulation reached "ten thousand or twice ten." "But sometime after that, several things happened, one after another, which handicapped the labor movement, and also, to speak of an infinitely lesser evil, crippled this paper." Among those things were Knights leader Terence Powderly's "circular of doom against the advancing eight-hour movement; the [Knights'] forty days 'halt' in the organization of new Assemblies" in May 1886, lost strikes, and capital's counter-offensive. He listed several cities where circulation had collapsed rapidly.[107] In effect he had described some of the causes of the collapse of the Knights of Labor itself. Thus, like the labor-party movement of 1886–1887, the labor press suffered from the rapid decline of the Knights of Labor in 1887–1888. The French study cited above reported that by 1888 the number of such papers had fallen to 150.[108]

That this press survived or even revived as trade unions grew in the 1890s, however, was indicated by the tribute to the continued existence of many labor papers and the formation of new ones, when in 1893 the Boston-based *Labor Leader*, edited by Frank K. Foster, reported that in addition to some forty journals published by trade unions, there were still 150 papers "which should be ranked as part of the labor press."[109] In 1898 the *Pueblo Courier*, the labor paper in Pueblo, Colorado, and for a time the "official" paper of the radical Western Labor Union, editorialized that "the labor press of the United States during the past fifteen years has rendered service to the cause of labor that has born much fruit and has left seed sown that will ripen later on." The *Courier* went on to note, "But for all we have lost in the field of labor journalism there is still left considerable of the labor press to look out for and keep watch for labor's interests."[110] Some of the older labor papers survived into the twentieth century. John P. McDonnell's influential *Labor Standard* only went under with his death in 1908, while the *National Labor Tribune* was still listed in the *American Labor Press Directory* in 1925.[111]

Frustrated by the increasing ability of the daily press to overshadow the weekly labor press, A. L. Strauss noted in January 1895 in the *American Federationist* that "Capital's Weapon is the Press" and proposed that "a daily paper be started in the largest cities of the United States under the auspices of the Federation of Labor." "A daily labor press," he continued, "would prove the greatest organizer and educator that can be obtained for labor's cause," leading, he argued, to "an early emancipation from the present cruel system of wage slavery."[112] While a daily labor press never materialized, the survival of the independent labor press into the early twentieth century is attested to by the annual praise lavished on it by Samuel Gompers in his reports to the AFL conventions. As late as 1907, he told the delegates to the AFL convention, "I cannot adequately express my own appreciation and the deep obligation I feel that our fellow workers owe to the magnificent labor press of

America." He added, "The influence of the labor press is even as wide if not wider outside our own ranks than is generally known or acknowledged."[113]

Although perhaps diminished in numbers, the labor press was a central piece of the working-class "culture of opposition" that survived into the early twentieth century. It provides not only the evidence for a developing class consciousness throughout the Gilded Age, but also was, in fact, a major shaper of that consciousness and much of its content. One finds there not only news, but political advocacy, international labor developments, and the ideas of Ira Steward and the many nameless autodidacts who rejected the wage-fund theory, the inevitability of supply and demand, the authority of capital over the lives of the wage-earning class, and indeed for many the wage-system itself.

Working-Class Culture in the 1890s

The standard narrative of labor's development in the 1890s was that of a "rightward drift," the emergence of "prudential" unionism in the AFL, and the dominance of "pure and simple" unionism.[114] With the decline of the Knights, much of the visible "culture of opposition" described by Oestreicher also declined or altered by the end of the 1880s. Yet, as even Oestreicher argues in his conclusion, "Despite that destruction [of the Knights], the events of the 1880s left a legacy. Even without the framework of a unifying organization like the Knights of Labor, the memories of the 1880s were repeatedly sufficient to bring workers into the streets in the 1890s." Perhaps even more important, he wrote, "The cooperative work traditions, the spirit of mutuality that lay at the heart of the subculture of opposition continued."[115] It is this set of class values, after all, that defines much of the heart of working-class consciousness, as well as the difference with both middle-class and capitalist consciousness with their emphasis on individualism and "survival of the fittest."

Despite the changing organizational framework that followed the collapse of the Knights after 1888 and the momentary slump in strike activity, it is more useful to understand "the nearly two decades of the most severe and sustained labor conflict in American history" that ran from the mass railroad strikes of 1877 to the 1894 Pullman strike as a single period, as Schneirov, Stromquist, and Salvatore argue.[116] For one thing, though the Knights and some of the institutions that accompanied them had seemed to disappear by 1890, there was a certain continuity as a new wave of efforts at industrial and multigrade unionism took hold with the rise of the National Union of Brewers (1886), the United Mine Workers (1890), the Western Federation of Miners (1893), the American Railway Union (1893), the United Garment Workers (1895), and the Boot and Shoe Workers (1895), with the surviving Knights' national trade districts and local assemblies providing much of the initial membership for these new unions.[117]

Thus, the picture of the more or less complete domination of organized labor in the 1890s by pure and simple craft unions needs modification. As Laurie argues concerning the depiction of "craft" unionism,

> The historical literature which continues to depict the AFL as a club of Yankee and first- and second-generation Old Stock (Irish and German) immigrants plying skilled trades. The ethnicity of the federation men is not in dispute; their social pedigree, however, was not so lofty as we have been led to believe. The confusion stems in part from equating craft unionism with craftsmen—that is, from conflating a jurisdictional term with a social category. All AFL units were called "craft" unions but were not confined to skilled workmen. Unions of unskilled hod carriers and street railway workers were attached to the federation along with societies of semi-skilled factory hands from a range of industries. In an occupational sense the federation was more diverse than has been appreciated.[118]

Not only that, but sometimes these craft unions used their power directly to aid the less skilled to organize. If the Knights' culture of opposition seemed to fade in Detroit by the 1890s, about seventy miles to the south in Toledo, Ohio, a new culture of opposition and class action arose as that city's AFL unions gained strength. As the 1890s unfolded and the Knights continued to decline, Toledo's Central Labor Union was transformed in a process repeated in many cities after the decline of the Knights.

From an organization of fifteen or sixteen locals with 1,500 members in 1891, it grew to one of fifty locals and 5,000 members in 1897, representing at least a quarter of the industrial workforce in this small industrial city. As Gregory Zieren writes,

> The determination with which the mainly skilled craft locals of the Toledo Central Labor Union (CLU) utilized the boycott to promote unionization campaigns of the less-skilled calls into question the traditional picture of the American Federation of Labor as the preserve of a selfish "aristocracy of labor."[119]

Among the people whom these craft unionists helped to organize in the 1890s were laundry workers, teamsters, bartenders and waitresses, streetcar employees, and hod carriers.[120] Certainly what Zieren describes reflects an enduring, if evolved, class consciousness and culture of opposition by no means limited to Toledo. Thus, the Homestead strike of 1892 saw a high level of solidarity among both union and nonunion workers, as well as immigrants and native-born strikers. The 2,400 nonunion workers voted to strike in solidarity, while the 600 eastern Europeans among them elected a representative to the advisory committee that ran the strike.[121]

Similarly, during the Pullman boycott and strike in 1894, "there was an outpouring of solidarity from the entire city of Chicago."[122]

Aside from many instances of solidarity, with the number of sympathy strikes growing nationally in the early 1890s,[123] a strong tendency toward industrial or multigrade unionism arose in the late 1880s and 1890s even among some older craft unions, indicative of more than "job consciousness" or pure and simple unionism. This was seen not only in the formation of the United Mine Workers, the Western Federation of Miners, the American Railway Union, and the United Garment Workers in the 1890s noted above, but also in the expansion of membership to semiskilled and even unskilled workers by the Machinists, Iron Molders, and the Iron and Steel Workers.

Indeed, by some of the most common measures of class consciousness, most of the 1890s were even more divided by class and class conflict. Despite the deep depression that unfolded in 1893, the level of strike activity surpassed that of the 1880s, averaging over fourteen hundred strikes per year, a level previously reached only in 1886 and 1887. In 1894, over half a million workers went on strike, more than in any previous year for which there are statistics. These included not only the massive Pullman strike but also strikes of over 100,000 coal miners and 2,500 textile workers, all of whom were organized along industrial rather than craft lines.[124]

At the same time, the 1890s saw the rise of socialism in the labor movement beyond and outside the Socialist Labor Party in the wake of the Pullman strike, replacing the somewhat incoherent radicalism of the Knights, as well as anarchism, as the major opponent of pure and simple unionism. Laurie argues, "As the 1880s drew to a close, German- and English-speaking radicals entered locals of national and international unions affiliated with the AFL."[125] This trend continued into the new century. Melvyn Dubofsky summarized it for the first decade or so of the twentieth century when he wrote,

> Not only was socialism making substantial inroads among American workers, especially in such large core unions as the United Mine Workers, the International Association of Machinists, and the United Brewery Workers, but city centrals and state federations of labor also flooded AFL headquarters with petitions and letters demanding the creation of an American labor party.[126]

And if the labor press of the Gilded Age declined as the new century arrived, it nevertheless survived and was to a considerable extent supplemented by the national and local socialist press, which increased from about 100 weeklies or monthlies in 1903 to 323 papers and periodicals by 1912.[127]

The 1890s would see a more "political" bifurcation within the labor movement with the rise of socialist influence, the brief attraction of Populism, and the eventual but continuously challenged domination of pure and simple ideology. The high-profile strikes at New Orleans (1892), Homestead (1892), Coeur d'Alene (1892), and Pullman (1894) had an impact on the political debate within the AFL, moving some leaders to embrace what Laurie calls "prudential" unionism or out-right "pure and simple" unionism, which included a worsening practice toward African American workers, particularly after 1897 as DuBois found,[128] while others were drawn to socialism or industrial unionism or both. Thus, between 1893 and 1894, another effort was made to push labor toward the formation of an independent party through an alliance with the Populists based on the "political program" of Britain's Independent Labour Party. This idea was supported by the American Railway Union and the Western Federation of Miners, but the debate around it mostly took place within the AFL, where in a referendum members of affiliated unions voted overwhelmingly in favor of this social democratic program—perhaps the closest thing we have to a political opinion poll in that period. The details of this debate will be looked at in a later chapter, but what they reveal is not a clear victory for pure and simple unionism, but a strong continuation of class consciousness among both leaders and the ranks.

To a certain extent, the movement as it arose after the mid-1890s saw a new generation of leaders and activists replace those who had led the upheavals of 1877 and 1886–1887. Eugene V. Debs, Big Bill Haywood, Emma Goldman, and Florence Kelley are obvious examples—men and women who might have experienced the 1886 upheaval but were not among its leaders. This generational change was perhaps even more the case among socialists. Writing of the decline of the anarchist International Working People's Association (IWPA) and the Socialist Labor Party (SLP) in Chicago's labor movement and its replacement among the radical activists by the Socialist Party, Bruce C. Nelson wrote,

> At the turn of the century, the Socialist Party became the linear descendent of the SLP and the IWPA. In 1901 [Thomas] Morgan wrote to his friend Henry Demarest Lloyd: "The local Socialist movement has changed personnel. The foreign element is submerged by the American inflow. Nearly all the actives are young American enthusiasts."[129]

Leon Fink's profile of sixty well-known socialist leaders of the first two decades of the twentieth century found that, in 1900, 70 percent were "no more than thirty two years of age." Eugene Debs, the best known of them, was considered an "elder" at forty-five.[130]

In addition to a generational change and a larger role for American-born workers in the socialist movement, the ethnic composition of the working class itself began to change in the second half of the 1890s, as the wave of "new" immigrants from eastern and southern Europe increased. For most of the Gilded Age, it was a working class in formation in which German, Irish, British, and Scandinavian workers came to outnumber those born in the US. The immigration that would fill the ranks of the unskilled and semiskilled in the 1890s and the first decade of the new century brought new cultures and languages as the class was once more reshaped. Some of these workers would enter the new industrial unions in min- ing and garment making. A smaller cohort would enter the socialist movement through the Foreign Language Federations of the new Socialist Party of America or be swept up in the mass strikes led by the Industrial Workers of the World.[131] The second half the 1890s was a period of transition from the older ethnic composition to this transformed working class and the labor movement it would help shape.

The basic observations about social classes and their differences, however, had not changed by the end of the Gilded Age. David Montgomery's statement that for working-class people "the shared presumption that individualism was appropriate only for the prosperous and wellborn" was, after all, a statement about the whole period from the Civil War to the early 1920s. Sarah Watts, in an argument for the eventual hegemony of capitalist ideology over labor, nevertheless states, "Between 1880 and 1910, the variety of working class ethnic values, religious beliefs, and class consciousness socially distanced workers from employers." Some scholars would stretch this to the end of World War II.[132] In its 1899–1900 hearings, the Indus- trial Commission was still asking about the formation of permanent classes. When asked if the "large combinations of capital" would not "make two classes, a capital- istic class and a laboring class," Jacob Schonfarber, a member of the remnant of the Knights of Labor, replied, "I think it has already done so, and I think it is increas- ing. In other words, I think the opportunity for rising from the ranks of labor to the ranks of the employers has largely gone."[133] When asked the same question, D. F. Kennedy, an organizer for the AFL in Indiana and probably a pure and simple unionist admitted, "Well, I rather guess that is the tendency."[134]

The rejection of capital's competitive values had not changed for most. Testify- ing before the Industrial Commission in 1899, Horace Eaton of the Boot and Shoe Workers was asked, "Has the competitive system, in your opinion, been a blessing or a curse to the workingmen?" He replied, "I should say a curse."[135] In other words, class consciousness did not die in the 1890s or even in the first decade or two of the twentieth century, but the ideas that dominated the 1870s and 1880s, such as greenbackism, cooperation, anarchism, and Lassallean socialism, were replaced by a more politicized contest within the labor movement between modern socialism in both its reform and revolutionary variants, to some extent reflecting the emerging split throughout the world socialist movement, as well as revolutionary syndicalism and pure and simple unionism. At the same time, the rise of the United Mine Work- ers, the Western Federation of Miners, the Amalgamated Clothing Workers, and the International Ladies' Garment Workers, as well as the IWW, brought industrial unionism in various forms to the first decade of the twentieth century.

Even within the craft unions, the assumption that everyone embraced a conservative pure and simple outlook has been challenged. Jeffrey Haydu, in his comparative analysis of British and American skilled workers, while pointing out that machinists' resistance usually occurred "along sectional lines," went on to argue, "This picture of factory politics in the 1890s might suggest that engineers and machinists were uniformly conservative. They were not. Distinct minorities in both the ASE [Amalgamated Society of Engineers] and the IAM endorsed socialism and supported the organization of less skilled workers."[136]

By the early twentieth century, socialists controlled about a third of the votes at AFL conventions.[137] As Dubofsky argues, even the mainstream unions rejected the individualism and competition of the dominant capitalist ideology. He writes, "Trade unions, no matter how conservative many may have appeared, practiced solidarity and sought to repeal the 'natural' laws of the Marketplace."[138]

To be sure, there were changes in a good deal of the visible aspects of working-class culture. The balls, picnics, workers' theater, and parades became less common not only as the Knights declined but also as recreation and entertainment became increasingly commercialized with the rise of professional baseball, amusement parks, vaudeville, and burlesque in the late 1890s. Massive May Day assemblies and mass strike parades, however, survived into the twentieth century. A similar process occurred in Britain, where football became professional, seaside resorts became accessible to skilled workers, and the music hall attracted working-class audiences at about the same time without altering class consciousness.[139] The working class in both countries had passed the phase where it simply "made itself as much as it was made," as Thompson put it, to one in which capitalism increasingly shaped daily life as it already had the workplace, or as he put it, "the working class is no longer in the making, but has been made."[140] In fact, the decline of the labor balls and picnics of the 1880s was part of a larger change in the political culture of the US alongside the rise of commercialized entertainment and recreation. As R. Hal Williams points out in his history of the "critical" election of 1896, the "military style" of election mobilization with its mass torchlight parades and picnics that had characterized major elections from the time of Jackson "lasted roughly through the 1880s." After that it was replaced by the more professional type of voter mobilization through "educational" materials, party organization, and fund-raising among the business elite.[141] Nevertheless, neither the underlying culture of opposition within the activist layer nor the collectivist values of the majority described above by Montgomery, Oestreicher, Rodgers, and Watts disappeared.

In important ways, however, the mid- to late 1890s were a turning point, as Schneirov, Stromquist, and Salvatore have argued, both capital and labor reconsidered their strategies toward one another in the light of the disruptive and costly struggles at Homestead, the central competitive coalfields, Coeur d'Alene, and Pullman on the one hand, and the increasing rise of the giant corporation on the other.[142] This was indicated on labor's side in part by the ultimate defeat of the "political program" in 1894, the admission of the International Association of Machinists to the AFL in 1895 despite its continued exclusion of African American workers by ritual, and the turn toward institutionalized collective bargaining that not only characterized the rise of pure and simple unionism but was also the increasing practice of most unions. As we will see in a subsequent chapter, organized labor would become more institutionalized in the late 1890s and, no doubt, the culture of opposition would be altered. The defeat of Populism, the realignment election of 1896, the intensification of segregation and disenfranchisement of African Americans in the South, the turn toward extracontinental imperialism in 1898, and the vast corporate merger movement at the turn of the century all contributed to another change in the economic and political atmosphere as the nineteenth century came to an end.

Nevertheless, if throughout the Gilded Age (and beyond) there was sufficient class consciousness to launch or fight for labor parties, publish and read the labor press, create the often dense network of working-class institutions that characterized most cities for a part of the Gilded Age, and launch industrial unions whose membership potentially equaled that of the craft unions for a time, then the explanation for the limits and failures of these initiatives must lie elsewhere than in an alleged absence of such consciousness. Nor did this radical working-class culture end with the Gilded Age.

Shelton Stromquist summarized the new "culture of opposition" that would arise in the early twentieth century as the working class was once again transformed:

> In time a revolt of unskilled immigrant laborers and a revived general union movement, with support of socialists and radical allies, would make its own claims to the legacy of 1894. In a wave of strikes beginning at McKees Rocks in 1909 and cresting in the Patterson silk shops and the Colorado coal fields in 1913–14, a new immigrant working class constituted itself and in so doing asserted a class perspective that echoed the producerism of the Pullman strike and belied the reformers' dreams of social harmony.[143]

Indeed, the turn of the century opened with an upsurge of strikes and union growth greater than that of 1886. A million and a half workers flooded into unions or created new ones in the first four years of the new century, while the number of strikes rose from 1,779, involving four hundred thousand workers in 1900, to 3,494 strikes with over half a million strikers in 1903.[144] In the middle of this upsurge, the Socialist Party of America was formed, followed four years later by the revolutionary syndicalist Industrial Workers of the World. The content of class consciousness may have changed in both radical and conservative ways, but it did not disappear. If, then, class consciousness was sufficiently strong to explain all that has been described above, the answer to labor's failure to form an independent labor or mass socialist party during the Gilded Age must lie elsewhere.

The central argument of this book is that the high level of internal migration in this period undermined the stability and growth of labor organizations that in turn frustrated efforts at independent working-class political action, not a lack of class consciousness, however uneven that may have been. It is this migration that is the "missing factor" in virtually all analyzes of this question. Chapter 2 will examine the literature covering labor organization and patterns of migration in this period and then turn to the extent of internal migration and the underlying forces that created it.

Chapter 2

THE MISSING FACTOR: INTERNAL MIGRATION

That which strikes us most . . . is not so much the large number
of persons of foreign birth, than the great mobility of the
native Americans. They are greater wanderers, less tied to
home associations, than are the inhabitants of Europe.

E. G. Ravenstein, 1889[145]

I T IS not surprising that Ernst Ravenstein, the pioneer of internal migration theory, should have noticed this difference in his 1889 comparative study of internal migration in Europe and North America, where not even Canada came close to the US in the percentage of "wanderers" in the 1880s.[146] Nearly six million people crossed state borders into just twelve states between 1870 and 1900, while perhaps twice as many migrated within those states. As Ravenstein put it in his 1885 work, the vast majority of these migrants were those "in search of work of a more remunerative or attractive kind than that afforded by the place of their birth."[147] They were more or less evenly divided between men and women and, no doubt, most simply sought a new permanent home.[148] Within this great migration, however, were those who traveled more regularly. They were more likely to be male and young. The boardinghouse was often the temporary home, while the train was the means of transport from one job and temporary residence to another. Even those who had a more or less permanent home and family often took to the roads and rails to seek better wages and conditions elsewhere. And like Ravenstein, most were aware of this constant movement as a fact of life in Gilded-Age America.

Yet, internal migration has been the missing factor in explaining the relative weakness of organized labor in the Gilded Age. Two of the best-documented social trends of the Gilded Age were the movement of masses of people across the continent and into the cities on the one hand, and the rise of industrial conflict and efforts to organize unions on the other. Nevertheless, whether pluralist, institutionalist, or Marxist, historians have failed to put the two together as a problem for the growth and stability of labor organizations and their political efforts. Instead, for years many labor historians have followed John R. Commons in seeing in these two trends only the spread of unions across the country and their efforts to form national organizations in hope of controlling labor markets. Commons wrote of the years following the Civil War, "Pre-eminently, it was the period of nationalization in the American labor movement. Back of it all lay the nationalization of the economic life of the country."[149] The possibility that this "nationalization" might have disrupted or limited union organization was seldom entertained.

The idea that geographic mobility might have been a problem was noted by John B. Anderson, however, who in his contribution to John R. Commons's *History of Labour in the United States* observed that the unions of the late nineteenth century "were scattered over a wider territory than had ever been organized." After explaining that the depression of the 1870s had wiped out many unions, he remarked simply, "The great West, too, was still drawing off the more energetic members of unions."[150] Unfortunately, there was no development of this idea or even examples. In his 1928 work on the theory of the labor movement, Selig Perlman (one of Commons's best-known disciples), also mentioned lack of a "settled" wage-earning class as a factor in what he saw as low class consciousness. Intriguingly, he writes of the "great mass of wage earners," and notes, "However, many of these do not stay in a given industry for life, but keep moving from industry to industry and from locality to locality, in search for better working conditions."[151] Here, too, this provocative thought was dropped, never to be pursued. Norman Ware's 1929 classic history of late nineteenth-century labor makes no mention of this issue despite the huge turnover of membership experienced by the Knights of Labor.[152] The subsequent works of Perlman and Philip Taft also ignore this problem.[153]

Writing in the 1950s, about the same time as Taft, Lloyd Ulman placed the formation of national unions squarely in the movement of population westward and the mobility of labor. He wrote, "The extension of the railway net, the increasing industrialization and urbanization of the country (one concomitant of which was the movement of the 'country mechanic' to the larger labor centers), and the westward movement of the frontier (the boom town phenomenon) made for increased mobility." This motion "was of greater concern to the labor movement in that period than it has been in recent times." Ulman's analysis is too complex to be spelled out here, but though it occasionally refers to problems that arise due to migration, it follows Commons in basically explaining the growth and relative success of the national governance of unions. As far as it goes, it is fairly convincing. But the idea that the very same migration and the forces underlying it might be an explanation for the limited success of unions in this period is not pursued.[154]

Beginning in the 1960s, a new generation of labor historians revolutionized the writing of US labor history. Following the works of British historians E. P. Thompson and Eric Hobsbawm, such American writers as Herbert Gutman,

David Montgomery, David Brody, Barbara Wertheimer, Melvyn Dubofsky, Leon Fink, and others abandoned the institutional focus of the Commons school for a detailed look at working-class communities, culture, and work in what became known as the "new labor history." The importance of this new approach to labor history can hardly be exaggerated. No matter how critical one may be of this or that interpretation or conclusion, subsequent historians have been freed to pursue these new lines of research further precisely because they stand on the shoulders of the first wave of "new labor historians."

A review of the entire literature of the "new" labor historians is not possible in this book. Although the fact of migration is often recognized in many works, with notable exceptions it is almost never explored in detail. David Montgomery, in his monumental *Fall of the House of Labor*, for example, writes, "Labor and especially immigrant labor proved to be responsive to every upsurge in demand and also very mobile geographically," but despite the enormous contribution in the detail of working-class life found in Montgomery's work, he only describes where immigrants were concentrated.[155] In their biography of John L. Lewis, Melvyn Dubofsky and Warren Van Tine observe, concerning Lewis's early life, "Perhaps the most typical feature of working class life was spatial mobility; families seldom remained permanently in the same home or neighborhood and moved in amazing numbers from city to city and state to state."[156] As the bulk of the biography deals with Lewis's career in the twentieth century, there is no real development from this observation.

One of the most intriguing observations by a "new" labor historian concerning working-class migration came from Herbert Gutman. In his classic essay "Work, Culture, and Society in Industrializing America" he argued that "aspirations and expectations interpret experience and thereby help shape behavior." Citing the example of the New England mill "girls" of the early nineteenth century, who seldom engaged in collective action, and the immigrant workers of the later nineteenth and early twentieth centuries who planned to return to their homeland, he wrote, "Men as well as women who expect to spend only a few years as factory workers have little incentive to join unions."[157] More recently, Mark Wyman has elaborated the question of return migration in *Round-Trip to America*, where he presents a great deal of data and analysis of those immigrants who returned to the "old country" either by intention or from disillusion. As with Gutman's examples, however, most are from the early twentieth century when the rates of return were much higher than during the Gilded Age.[158] Looking at long swings of immigration, Kuznets and Rubin argued, "Thus, for 1878–1897, gross immigration was 4.36 million per decade, and departures .074 million. The ratio is about 17 per cent, compared with a similar ratio of well over 30 per cent for the immigrant-emigrant flow in the long swing of 1897–1918 or the even higher ratio for 1918–1932."[159]

Seventeen percent, of course, is a significant proportion of those who arrived in the US during the Gilded Age. But as Wyman's figures show, the groups with the highest rates of return were the "new" immigrants of the early twentieth century, notably Italians, Hungarians, and other eastern Europeans. The rates of return for the "old" immigrant groups that composed a majority of the ranks of organized labor in the US during the Gilded Age were much lower.[160] John Bodnar's study of immigrant workers in Steelton, Pennsylvania, reveals the same pattern.[161] One might also question whether or not even the intended emigrant might not have joined a union, if the opportunity arose, precisely to increase his or her nest egg upon return. As most of the new immigrants were unskilled, their membership would have been limited to the few unions, such as the United Mine Workers, that did recruit among these groups in the 1890s and afterward.[162] Wyman makes note of this, but in addition remarks, "In fact many [returnees] had participated in American labor movements that challenged the capitalist order."[163] Still, the leavers were part of the multidirectional waves of internal migration, and it is fair to say, as Gutman argued, that intention played a role in their decisions about joining labor or political organizations in the US, though one we cannot measure. Furthermore, Gutman, building on David Brody's work on the steelworkers, actually underlined the role of returning immigrants (and hence, migration in general) in weakening steelworker unionism in the first decade of the twentieth century by pointing to the fact that the First World War "blocked the traditional route of overseas outward mobility," contributing to the role of eastern European immigrants in the 1919 steel strike.[164] Indeed, departures dropped by over half after 1915, while internal migration declined for most of the US during the decade of 1910–1920, contributing to the overall strike wave of 1919–1921 and underlining Gutman's point as well as reinforcing the argument of this book.[165]

By the 1980s a second generation of labor historians such as Bruce Laurie, Richard Schneirov, Shelton Stromquist, Daniel Walkowitz, Kim Voss, Alice Kessler-Harris, Robin D. G. Kelley, and David Roediger, to mention only a few, picked up the banner of the "new labor history," deepening our understanding of working-class life further. With some exceptions, however, the matter of internal migration still received little attention. Bruce Laurie's important and sweeping history of labor in the nineteenth century, for example, mentions the migration from farm to city, but not its impact on the ability of workers to unionize.[166] Granted that book indexes are often incomplete, a perusal of the indexes of ten books from both generations of the "new labor history" dealing with Gilded-Age labor nevertheless revealed that only two, both by Montgomery, had any reference to "migration," "mobility," or "geographic mobility." The outstanding exception to this among the second-generation new labor historians is Shelton Stromquist, whose *A Generation of Boomers* contains a complex and subtle discussion and analysis of the effects of geographic mobility on the solidarity, class consciousness, and militancy of railroad workers in the second half of the nineteenth century. Stromquist also provides us with a powerful analytical tool, to be explained below, in what he calls the "moving frontier of labor scarcity."[167]

The literature on the high residential turnover rates of Gilded-Age cities, written mostly in the 1960s and 1970s, provides a sweeping view of the vast movement of people of different classes into and out of the cities of the late nineteenth-century United States. Like most of the labor history works, however, it seldom connects this to problems of worker organization. In his 1964 book, *Poverty and Progress*, Stephan Thernstrom simply speculates about the unskilled transient workers, or "floaters," as they were known: "Members of this floating group naturally had no capacity to act in concert against an employer or to assert themselves politically; stable organization based on a consciousness of common grievances was obviously impossible."[168] This is certainly an overstatement even about unskilled "floaters," but, in any case, is not developed or defended.

While more recent literature by historians of the US West has revealed much about the patterns of migration,[169] there is virtually no effort to link this to the volatile life of unions in the West. Patricia Nelson Limerick's *The Legacy of Conquest* provides an excellent overview of the complex patterns of migration and settlement, both industrial and human, of the West. Yet her brief description of miners' unions in the West, particularly the Butte Miners' Union, the Western Federation of Miners, and the Industrial Workers of the World, is simply the standard tale of growing unions and a few high-profile strikes crushed by employers and the state.[170]

In his book on western hard-rock mining, which includes an extensive discussion of migration, Mark Wyman does offer some paragraphs on the impact of geographic mobility on union organization. He notes, "Mobility could spread unionism, but it also presented enormous hurdles for any organized movement seeking a better world." He cites the example of a local miners' union in California.[171] Yet, despite a lengthy discussion and analysis of the Western Federation of Miners and the Industrial Workers of the World, this suggestive idea is not pursued. In Wyman's subsequent book about transient agricultural workers, we again get a useful discussion of the IWW in the West, but virtually no mention of the impact, positive or negative, of migration or turnover.[172]

Rodman Paul, another well-known historian of the West, also offers a teaser on the effects of migration via disaccumulation when the famous Comstock lode went dry: "After Comstock's big mines failed, the leadership of unionism passed to Butte, the new capital of western mining, and for years Butte was hailed as 'the Gibraltar of unionism.'"[173] What happened to the union leaders and members who left the Comstock? Did Butte actually draw on those leaders and activists? Was the transition from the Comstock to Butte smooth or problematic? We are not told.

One could go on with examples, but the fact is that, with some notable exceptions, we are left with either an absence of discussion or analysis of migration as a barrier to unionization, or suggestive propositions that remain undeveloped. Migration remains the missing factor. Yet, as we will see in the coming chapters, the leaders and activists of the time were acutely aware of the problems of migration and "tramping." To begin the process of establishing migration as an important element in the relative weakness of labor organizations and working-class political efforts in Gilded-Age America, I will look at the scale and major streams of immigration and internal migration, along with a comparison with Britain and an examination of the underlying forces pulling and pushing population, industry, and wageworkers in the heat of industrial revolution and upheaval from 1870 to 1900.

Migration in Broad Strokes

The story of internal migration in the US begins in the world economy of the late nineteenth century. Commencing in the 1870s, two major developments swept most of the industrializing world. The first, Eric Hobsbawm argues, was a major slump in profit rates—not necessarily the amount of profits, but their rate of return on investment. This underlay a recurring series of depressions throughout this period as well as the second major trend, an international crisis in agriculture. "Agriculture," Hobsbawm wrote, "was the most spectacular victim of this decline in profits." With characteristic understatement, he wrote, "The decades of depression were not a good time in which to be a farmer in any country involved in the world market."[174] This crisis set off waves of emigration from the "old worlds" of Europe and Asia, and even from the "new world" nations of Mexico and Canada, to the United States. In 1881 alone, 125,450 Canadians entered the US, along with 325 Mexicans— this latter figure certainly a drastic undercount.[175] Altogether net immigration for the Gilded Age amounted to 9,296,000 people. Of course, of the 3,364,000 leavers, many stayed awhile, so their impact on labor markets and internal migration counts as well. As Kuznets and Rubin point out, this figure for leavers includes nonimmigrants who would not have stayed in any case.[176] In this way, at least ten million people were added to the streams of internal migration crisscrossing the continent.

This inflow reached its high point in the 1880s, which accounted for 44 percent of the immigration of this period.

To get an idea of the size of this movement within the US, we will look at the net decade-to-decade interstate migration into the Northeast, Midwest, and West of the US from 1870 through 1900. Table 1 shows the movement into or out of each major region. It also shows that migration differed from decade to decade. In general, interstate migration, like immigration, moved in inverse relationship to the major depressions of the era, 1873–1877 and 1893–1897. A shorter and shallower depression in 1883–1885 meant that most of that decade saw relative growth and greater migration in the most industrial regions of the country. This indicates, as internal migration theory emphasizes, and as examples of trade-union tramping and traveling show, that people are more likely to migrate when they are fairly sure there is an opportunity for improvement elsewhere. It should be borne in mind that migration *within* these states from farm to city or city to city was, if anything, on an even larger scale as industrialization and urbanization drew people from rural areas and smaller towns to the growing large cities, particularly in the Midwest. Furthermore, because the census is taken over ten-year periods, it will miss an enormous amount of movement within the decade. For example, migratory workers joining the annual harvest labor force each year will be caught by the census taker only once, if at all, yet they will have migrated at least ten times. Similarly, the migrant craftsman with his union traveling card may well have ended up at home by the time the census taker arrived. Thus, the number of migrations is far greater than the number of migrants recorded in the census.

Table 1. Net Intercensal/Interstate Migration: Northeast, Midwest, West

Region	1870s	1880s	1890s
Northeast	265,300	1,235,500	1,573,000
East North Central	28,300	398,200	597,400*
West North Central	868,900	1,080,500	−86,700*
Mountain	189,900	299,900	196,400
Pacific	197,300	505,500	296,100
Total	1,549,700	3,519,600	2,576,200

* Gains in East North Central and losses in West North Central in the 1890s were due in part to net migration from Kansas, Nebraska, and North Dakota as a result of extreme drought.
Source: US Census Bureau, *Historical Statistics of the United States: Colonial Times to 1970*, pt. 1 (Washington, DC: US Government Printing Office, 1975), 93–95.

Another aspect of this high level of internal migration that made union organizing more difficult than in many other countries was the ethnic turnover that accompanied the movement of people in and out of cities and states. Table 2 shows that there was inward movement of large numbers of the foreign-born alongside of a significant out-migration by native-born people in the major industrial states of the East and Midwest. The 1880s were the high point of immigration in the Gilded Age, with over 5.5 million immigrants entering the country in that decade. As Simon Kuznets and Ernest Rubin noted in their study of immigration,

The flow of people from abroad added millions of workers, consumers, and family heads to the population of this country. This movement directly affected the size and structure of the country's population and had far-reaching influences through the chain-reaction of internal migration and economic mobility which it stimulated.[177]

In other words, immigration pushed internal migration and continually altered the population across the country. A majority of these immigrants were or became working class, and their motion as well as that of those they replaced in the key industrial states rendered unionization a constant problem often enhanced by ethnic conflict and competition.

Table 2. In-Migration and Out-Migration in Major Industrial States of the East and Midwest Regions, 1880–1890 (Thousands)

State	Native-Born Whites	Foreign-Born
Ohio	−96.7	+133.4
Indiana	−120.4	+29.9
Illinois	−170.7	+332.6
Michigan	−19.7	+193.2
Wisconsin	−75.6	+176.3
Total Midwest	−483.1	+865.4
New York	−146.4	+532.0
Pennsylvania	−70.0	+334.3
Massachusetts	+31.9	+259.3
Total East	+194.5	+1,126.6

Source: US Census Bureau, Historical Statistics of the United States: Colonial Times to 1970, pt. 1 (Washington, DC: US Government Printing Office, 1975), 93–94.

In the wake of the Civil War and early Reconstruction, there was significant migration of newly emancipated African Americans within the South. According to Eric Foner, there was a sizable migration into the cities of that region. Foner writes, "Between 1865 and 1870, the black population of the South's ten largest cities doubled." Lack of employment and de facto segregation in shantytowns in these cities, however, meant that "the urban migration slowed dramatically after 1870 and the proportion of Southern blacks living in cities stabilized at around 9 percent."[178] Thus, during the Gilded Age, the South represents a different pattern from the rest of the country in which all states of the Old South, except Texas and Florida, saw net out-migration, some of it to other states of the South, while the presence of the foreign-born was far lower than in all the other regions. During this period, nine of the former states of the Confederacy, excluding Texas and Florida, saw a net emigration of 871,000 people. Some 641,800 African Americans left southern states, with 236,600 going to Texas, Arkansas, Florida, Oklahoma, and Virginia combined, while others disappear from the net figures in other southern states. One example of movement from the Deep South to the upper South is to be found in the thousands of African Americans who migrated from the agricultural and mining regions of Alabama, Virginia, and North Carolina to the coalfields of West Virginia and Kentucky in the 1880s and 1890s.[179] Just under three hundred thousand African Americans entered northern and midwestern states over this entire period, which is one reason why the black population of northern cities remained so small throughout the Gilded Age.[180] Whether moving north or west, their movement was no doubt due to the failure and betrayal of Reconstruction, the continued agricultural backwardness and low wages of the older parts of the region, and the intensification of antiblack violence.

Overall, by the census counts more than seven and a half million people, many of whom had recently entered the country, moved from one state to another during this thirty-year period. Here, as elsewhere in this study, timing is important. Internal migration, like immigration, reached its high point in the 1880s in the wake of accelerated industrialization and urbanization. Looking at the Midwest, net migration into the region rose from 897,200 between 1870 and 1880 to 1,478,700 between 1880 and 1890, then fell to 510,700 by 1900. Some of that of the 1890s was actually eastward migration from Kansas and Nebraska to Iowa and even farther eastward as agriculture on the Great Plains collapsed due to drought west of the ninety-eighth meridian.[181] The West saw a rising, then falling, rate of internal migration similar to that of the Midwest, though involving fewer people.[182] Net migration from 1870 through 1900 accounted for 18.3 percent of population growth in these five census regions. Unfortunately, interstate migration figures by decade conceal a great deal of movement within states and decades.

Another great stream of migration flowed from country and small town to burgeoning urban centers across the United States, with the proportion of the population living in urban areas in the US increasing from 6,217,000 or 20 percent of total population in 1860 to 30,583,411 or 40 percent in 1900.[183] The growth of cities across the Midwest in this period, of course, was largely a function of industrialization. The proportion of residents originally from another state is even higher for cities than for states, indicating that much of the migration was to cities rather than farms. Conrad Taeuber has shown that throughout the Gilded Age, the percentage of a city's population not born in the state where the city is located was higher in newer cities west of Pennsylvania. For example, in 1870, 30 percent of the population of Baltimore and 47 percent of New York was from another state, while the proportion in Chicago was 70 percent and in San Francisco 74 percent. The proportion of out-of-state migrants would decline somewhat over the period to 1900 but remain significantly higher in the more western cities. In line with this, Taeuber observed that "the mush-rooming of cities on the frontier is one of the unique features in the history of the peopling of the United States."[184] Much of this was accomplished at the edges of the frontier by the advance of the railroad and the huge workforce it brought with it. As Shelton Stromquist argues, the railroads "provided the logic and the means for estab-lishing networks of urban settlement that implanted the nuclei of a class-stratified society in advance of agricultural settlement."[185] In other words, urban development and class formation led the general path of migration to the West.

It has been fairly standard to see the growth of urban population as simply a move from country to city. As Edward Kirkland, put it, "The startling accessions of population came from two migrations: one from the country to the city and the other from abroad."[186] In fact, the flow of population from region to region was accompanied by migration from city to city where population turnover was high throughout this period. Measured by "persistence rates"—that is, the percentage of people who remained in the same city from one decade to another—Stephan Thernstrom gives the following figures:

- 1870–1880: Waltham, Massachusetts, and Poughkeepsie, New York, 50 percent; San Francisco, 48 percent.
- 1880–1890: Boston, 64 percent; Omaha, 44 percent; and Los Angeles, 50 percent.[187]

Olivier Zunz puts the persistence rates for Detroit's native-born population between 28 percent and 37 percent from 1888 to 1900. For Polish residents the average rates are higher, between 45 percent to 69 percent in different neighbor-hoods.[188] Robert Tank puts Denver's persistence rate at a very low 37 percent from 1870 to 1880.[189] In his study of the Pennsylvania mill town of Steelton, John Bod-nar states "that between 1880 and 1888 about one-half the population of Steelton either died or moved elsewhere."[190] In most cases more people left between decades than stayed. The vast majority of these leavers were wageworkers, many of them unskilled, according to Thernstrom.[191]

The actual flow of people into and out of the cities, however, was far greater than the persistence rates imply. Looking at the actual volume of in-migration into Boston, the city with the highest recorded persistence rate, Thernstrom explained, "The actual volume of movement into Boston during the 1880s was approximately twelve times larger than the estimated net in-migration, because huge numbers were leaving the city at the same time huge numbers of others were entering." He esti-mates that as many a 1.5 million people moved in and out of Boston in the 1880s.[192] Indeed, an earlier essay by Thernstrom and Peter Knights concluded that "the typ-ical urban migrant went not to one city but to three or four (or perhaps a dozen) in the course of his wanderings."[193] In other words, the country-to-city migration common to most analyses tells us only part of the story of the vast movement of people around the United States and into its cities in the late nineteenth century.

Even the transformation of the far West was largely an urban affair during the Gilded Age. By the beginning of this period, as agriculture spread west, Clarence Danhoff argues, it had "emerged entirely from its earlier self-sufficiency into a maturely capitalistic, profit-seeking, and market-focused system."[194] Borrowing the term "central place cities" from the field of geography, Robert Higgs wrote, "Commercial agriculture like that in the American West could only operate with the aid of hundreds of almost uniformly scattered central place cities."[195] Mining, too, of course, contributed to urbanization in the West.

Certainly, in this era many workers made individual decisions to migrate. Indeed, as Daniel Rodgers argues, one "act of rebellion" against the increasingly strict discipline of factory work "was to quit." Thus, the high workforce turnover of the era was in part due to efforts to flee the "foreman's empire," at least when work was available elsewhere. But much of this turnover resulted from the widespread irregular or "part-year" work that was common throughout the period. Rodgers cites a Pennsylvania miner who had changed jobs five times in 1885 who said, "If I had stopped at one place, I should not have worked half of my time."[196] What might have appeared to be simply an individual choice to move on was not always voluntary in any real sense.

Employment and Unemployment in Gilded-Age America

Employment and unemployment in the Gilded Age were radically different from that of most of the twentieth century. On the one hand, full-time employment was far rarer. Much employment was based in "part-year" operations and production, as it was called at the time. This stemmed from the fact that, even beyond pursuits normally considered seasonal in nature, such as construction and farm labor, many industries in the late nineteenth century did not operate on a year-round basis, as would be normal for most of the twentieth century.[197] Even steel companies preferred to shut down when orders were slow rather than running at a slower speed.[198] In their study of part-year operation, Jeremy Atack, Fred Bateman, and Robert Margo state, "Substantial numbers of establishments (for example, nearly 40 percent in 1880) were 'part-year,'" most of it due to "differences in months of operation, not hours per day or days per month." In fact, as they point out using census data, part-year operations increased from 26–29 percent in 1870 to 38–40 percent in 1880, once again underlining the acceleration of volatility in the 1880s. An 1886 survey of eighty-five thousand workers by the Illinois Bureau of Labor Statistics found that 65 percent worked fewer than forty weeks a year. Larger capital-intensive, urban-based firms were less likely to operate part-year, although the example of steel production above indicates some large firms operated only part-year. Monthly wages were higher at part-year firms, but annual income was lower than in full-year companies due to periods of unemployment.[199]

One consequence of this was occasional unemployment and lost income for a time, even during growth periods, unless other work could be found. The fact of potentially lower annual income was clearly an incentive to seek other work to fill in the lost time or to change jobs altogether. Thus, the nature of unemployment was different in the late nineteenth century than it was for most of the twentieth century, in that there was, as one study put it, "greater emphasis on higher incidence of job loss rather than longer times spent out of work."[200] Speaking of the early nineteenth century, in the heat of Britain's industrial revolution, E. P. Thompson made a similar point about employment. He wrote that "the very notion of regularity of employment—at one place of work over a number of years for regular hours and at a standard wage—is an anachronistic notion, imposed by 20th-century experience upon 19th-century realities."[201] What this meant was that workers in late nineteenth-century America were likely to seek serial employment, like those in early nineteenth-century England, often by traveling.

So, for example, the US commissioner of labor's 1889 survey of sixty railroad systems found that the average worker was employed by the surveyed companies only 147 days a year. Railroad workers were notorious travelers, so it is certain that they sought employment in a number of railroad companies or systems in order to fill in the year as much as possible, making it clear that serial employment was a norm among railroad workers, as among many other occupations. So startling were the results that the commissioner wrote, "I do not remember having seen this feature, the tendency of labor to migration, brought out statistically on such an extended scale before. This constitutes a new phase of the labor question."[202]

Similarly, Commons's study of workers in the meatpacking industry showed that while hourly wages for "floormen," a skilled job, ran $0.40 an hour for most years, both weekly hours and the percentage of potential full-time work fluctuated. These workers reached 76 percent full-time equivalent in only two years between 1888 and 1904 and in most years averaged between 58 percent and 66 percent equivalent of full-time work.[203] Joseph Buchanan, writing in the *Labor Enquirer* in 1883, put an ironic spin on this when he wrote of employment in Denver: "If it were not for the continual changing of employees, which prevents the same men being idle all the time, death from starvation would ere this have cut down the city's population."[204]

All this motion involved a constant turnover of the workforce. Sanford Jacoby reports turnover rates for a variety of manufacturers ranging from 7 percent to 15 percent a month in the early years of the twentieth century.[205] Indicating that turnover was high in the 1880s, Thomas Livermore, an agent of the Amoskeag cotton mills in Manchester, New Hampshire, told the Senate in 1883 that "each month we have about 10 percent of our people leave."[206] In the same year, a Woonsocket, Rhode Island, textile employer told a state commission,

> It is almost universally said by those unacquainted with factory populations, that they possess as roving a disposition as the Tartars. This fact is, it is a very large calculation as far as my experience goes, to suppose that one-eighth of a factory village remove in the course of a year. They go, it is true, where they can get the best wages, but few remove because they are fond of changing their location.[207]

The Knights of Labor's erstwhile general master workman Terence Powderly wrote in his autobiography, "What is now called the turnover in the working force of shop and factory was in early days welcomed by employers, for the new men were engaged at lower wage levels than the displaced workers occupied."[208] This opportunity for the employers nonetheless also created continuous openings for those in the migratory queue. For some workers it was even seen as a relief from drudgery. Recalling her days as a mill worker, Cornelia Parker wrote that to "the factory girl, it saves her life, like as not. Praise be the labor turnover."[209]

Irregular employment and high turnover were not aberrations in the rise of industrial capitalism but the means by which it became viable in Gilded-Age America. Just as E. P. Thompson argued against F. A. Hayek's and T. S. Ashton's picture of the smooth ascent of the factory system by pointing to the rise of irregular outwork that "multiplied" as a result of "*steam and the factory*,"[210] so it was that industrial capitalism in the United States required what today would be called a "flexible" workforce in order to minimize labor costs. It is precisely part-year work, the turnover, the fluctuation, and the alternating waves of migration by different people, that fed capital accumulation *and* undermined stable labor organization. To establish this high degree of internal migration and geographic mobility as a major factor in the relative weakness of US labor organizations in this period, it is appropriate to compare the degree of such population movement with other industrial countries.

Comparing Trade Union and Internal Migration in the US and UK, 1870–1900

The most obvious comparison is that of the United Kingdom and the United States during the late nineteenth century. For one thing, both were industrial nations by the late nineteenth century that shared the "free market" model of capitalism more than most other industrial nations. Furthermore, many of the craft unions in the US were consciously modeled on those in Britain.[211] While there were also many differences, the aspect of development that will be looked at in terms of this analysis is the level of internal migration. For additional comparison, some references to migration in Germany will be made as well.

Looking first at the development of the unions, it was in the wake of the "new unionism," which brought in some two hundred thousand members in one year (1889–1890), that most British trade unions, including craft unions, grew strong enough and embraced enough of the working class to eventually form the British Labour Party in 1906.[212] The development of unions in the US in this period saw more extreme ups and downs in the 1870s and 1880s, as well as slower growth in the 1890s. Table 3 shows the relative size and growth of British and American union membership in the 1890s. The course of union development in the two countries was significantly different. The "Great Upheaval" in the US came in the mid-1880s when the exponential growth of the Knights of Labor brought total union membership to 1.2 million in 1886. Within two years, however, membership had shrunk to 700,825 as the Knights rapidly declined.[213] This was still slightly ahead of the UK in absolute numbers. Yet, as table 3 shows, within a year British unions had pulled well ahead in the wake of the new unionism, so that in absolute terms, on average American union membership was just a little over half that of British unions over the entire decade. Perhaps even more telling, as table 4 shows, was the gap in the proportion of workers belonging to unions, with Britain's union density being more than twice that of the US by the end of the decade.

Table 3. Trade Union Membership in the US and UK, and
US Percent of UK, 1889–1900 (Thousands)

Country	1889	1890	1891	1892	1893	1894	1895	1896	1897	1898	1899
UK	679	871	1109	1576	1559	1530	1504	1608	1731	1752	1911
US	718	822	857	796	805	873	700	617	620	710	831
% UK	106%	94%	77%	51%	52%	57%	46%	38%	36%	41%	48%

Source: Ken Coates and Tony Topham, *The Making of the Labour Movement: The Formation of the Transport & General Workers' Union, 1870–1922* (Nottingham, UK: Spokesman, 1994), 127; Gerald Friedman, "Historical Statistics: New Estimates of Union Membership in the United States, 1880–1914," *Historical Methods: A Journal of Quantitative and Interdisciplinary History* 32, no. 2 (1999): 78.

One reason for the relative stability of British unions was the early acceptance of unions by employers. As Eric Hobsbawm wrote, it was in "the 1860s and 1870s that formal mechanisms to smooth labor relations were discovered to be desirable from a business point of view."[214] This would not happen in the US even partially until the end of the nineteenth century. Clearly, American unions were significantly weaker in numbers of members and the proportion of the workforce they organized in the 1890s than their British counterparts. To a large extent, this difference can be attributed to the relative stages of economic development of the two countries, with the US going through a highly volatile period of rapid industrialization and urbanization and Britain's economy slowing down and stabilizing.

Table 4. Average Industrial Employment (Thousands)
and Union Density, US and UK, 1891, 1899

	1891	1899
Employment*		
UK	8,370	9,650**
US	7,051	9,414
Union Density		
UK	19 percent	20 percent
US	11 percent	9 percent

* Includes: Mining, manufacturing, construction, and transport.
** 1901.
Sources: Eric Hobsbawm, *Labouring Men: Studies in the History of Labour* (London: Weidenfeld and Nicolson, 1964), 180; Gerald Friedman, "Historical Statistics: New Estimates of Union Membership in the United States, 1880–1914," *Historical Methods: A Journal of Quantitative and Interdisciplinary History* 32, no. 2 (1999): 78; Stephen N. Broadberry and Douglas Irwin, *Labour Productivity in the US and UK During the 19th Century* (discussion paper no. 4596, London: Centre for Economic Policy Research, September 2004), 29, 31.

Britain's industrial revolution had lost momentum by the 1870s; its industries became more or less geographically anchored, and the flow of technological innovations slowed by this time. Hobsbawm writes of Britain's industrial revolution that "if it began with the 'take-off' in the 1780s, it may plausibly be said to be concluded with the building of the railways and the construction of a massive heavy industry in Britain in the 1840s."[215] Kindleberger puts the beginning of Britain's decline as an industrial power "from at least 1870."[216] America's industrial "take off," on the other hand, began accelerating in speed, dimension, output, and technological change in the years following the Civil War, with no secular slowdown during the Gilded Age. The difference can be seen in the figures for relative economic and population growth per decade. According to calculations by Murphy and Zellner, between 1860 and 1869 and 1905 and 1914 the economy of the United Kingdom grew by 25 percent per decade in real terms, or 2.5 percent a year on average, while between 1869 and 1878 and 1904 and 1913 that of the US grew by 56 percent per decade, or an average of 5.6 percent a year. The figures for population growth were 11.1 percent per decade for the UK and 22.3 percent for the US, much of this growth provided by immigration.[217] Thus, by both measures, the US was growing at twice the rate of the UK, indicating less rapid changes and greater stability in the UK. The United States, in other words, was still a society in transition from a mostly rural economy to a predominately industrial one in which the process of class formation was still highly uneven and labor migration a necessity for industrial and urban development.

This difference made the scale of internal migration a major factor in the relative weakness of American trade unions and working-class political organization in the late nineteenth century. In examining the degree of migration in other industrialized countries, it is possible to narrow the comparison to Britain by looking at what major studies of relative internal migration have revealed. Urban geographer David Ward states, "Internal migration in Britain was by far the greatest in Europe,"[218] a fact that allows for a proxy comparison with the whole of western Europe. Adna Weber's comprehensive 1899 comparative study of internal migration in the US and Europe further provides evidence for that proxy. Comparing migration from English counties to migration from much larger US states, which average about three times the population and are usually of much greater size, Weber wrote,

> This brings out the fact of the superior mobility of Americans, which has long been familiar to us in a general way. Indeed, it appears . . . that Americans are more accustomed to migrate from State to State than are Europeans from county to county. The English are apparently the most mobile people of Europe, as regards internal migration at least; and yet the percentage of native Englishmen living outside the county of birth was in 1871 almost exactly equal to the percentage of native Americans living outside the State in which they were born—the percentages being 25.66 and 26.2 respectively.[219]

Ravenstein in his 1889 study of internal migration in Europe and North America noted that among those Germans he labeled the "provincial element"—that is, those who were born in the province of their residence—as of 1885 amounted to 90.23 percent of the population. This may understate the actual amount of migration, as this grew toward the end of the nineteenth century along with emigration particularly after 1900. As one study of Germany's economy in the nineteenth century argued, however, "For most of the century, however, internal migration was largely short-range and seasonal." In any case, the scale was nothing like that in the US, and Ravenstein drew the same conclusions as Weber about the relative degrees of internal migration when he wrote of the Americans, "They are greater wanderers, less tied to home associations, than are the inhabitants of Europe."[220] Thus, it seems the major comparison here should be that of Britain and the US.

Before looking at quantitative measures of internal migration in the US and UK, it is worth mentioning an important difference that arose within broader migrations by the 1870s, if not sooner: namely, the degree of "tramping" by skilled workers aided by the trade-union traveling card. The "tramping artisan" was a fixture of British working-class life during the Industrial Revolution in the years following 1790. Before the railroad became widespread in the UK, the traveling worker often rode the coastal ships or hoofed it on "shank's pony." According to Hobsbawm, however, by the 1860s or '70s "tramping declined rapidly."[221] Hunt states that labor mobility rose between 1830 and 1860 and dropped in the 1880s, while Pelling notes that some unions abandoned tramping in favor of emigration from Britain in this period as an alternative way of dealing with "surplus laborers and mechanics."[222]

It was at this time, in contrast, as industry expanded westward after the Civil War, that skilled workers in America accelerated the practice of tramping and the use of the union traveling card. Chapters 3 and 4 will deal with this in some detail. Here it will be noted that such occupations as the building trades, printers, telegraphers, cigar makers, iron molders, machinists (engineers), railroad workers, and both coal and metal miners, among others, were famous for their "roving dispositions." The important point is that just as British craft workers became more geographically sedentary, their American counterparts took to the roads and rails in growing numbers. The reason for this difference lay in the different phases in the processes and contours of industrialization and urbanization the two countries had reached by 1870. It was the continuous growth and geographic expansion of industry into new areas of the US that made the high levels of internal migration possible.

As Ravenstein pointed out in 1889, "Wherever I was able to make a comparison I found that an increase in the means of locomotion and a development of manufactures and commerce have led to an increase in migration."[223] Thus, rural–urban migration increased during Britain's industrial revolution between the late eighteenth and the mid-nineteenth century, only to slow down in the second half of the century as the speed of development declined.[224] In particular, migration into the northern towns of England, where most manufacturing was located, slowed to well below the level of the 1840s despite a slight uptick in the 1890s. In the 1880s these northern industrial towns actually lost population.[225] In the US, on the other hand, the newer industrial cities of the Midwest and West all grew most rapidly in this period. Furthermore, they grew mostly from migration. So while, according to Searle, the percentage of residents born in England's northern industrial cities was around 70 percent toward the end of the nineteenth century, in the comparable cities of the US it was closer to 40 percent to 50 percent.[226]

To give an even clearer picture of the role of migration in urban growth in newer industrial areas, table 5 shows the proportion of migration in population growth for the two decades from 1880 through 1900 for four cities in the Midwest and one in the mountain West. Two things stand out. The first is the enormous growth of these cities, with Chicago, Detroit, Cleveland, and Milwaukee all more than doubling, and with Denver growing by almost four times in this twenty-year period.

In these two decades, the five US cities in table 5 saw an increase from migration of 1,849,400, while eight northern industrial cities in England grew by only 164,979 as a result of migration. The UK figure for the 1880s was unusually low "due to heavy emigration," according to Cairncross.[227] In the 1890s, emigration "slowed to a trickle" and internal migration grew again.[228] There was, of course, no net emigration from the US in these years. Thus, the average growth of the five US cities from 1880 to 1900 ranged from 138 percent for Cleveland to 276 percent for Denver—an average of 188 percent. To give an even starker example, while Manchester's population doubled between 1851 and 1901, according to Briggs, Chicago's grew by 66 times in that period—most of it by migration.[229]

Table 5. Urban Growth by Migration, 1880–1900 (Thousands)

City	1880	1900	Growth	Natural	Migration	Percent
Chicago	508.2	1,698.8	1,190.6	321.6	869.0	73 percent
Detroit	116.3	285.7	169.4	64.5	104.9	62 percent
Cleveland	160.2	381.8	221.6	84.3	137.3	62 percent
Milwaukee	115.6	285.3	169.7	64.0	105.7	62 percent
Denver	35.6	133.9	98.3	28.5	69.8	71 percent

* Natural growth (births minus deaths) is 20 percent per decade according to Higgs, *The Transformation*, 22; US Census Bureau, *Historical Statistics*, pt. 1, 49, 59, 63.
Source: Bureau of the Census, *Abstract of the Twelfth Census of the United States*, 3rd ed. (Washington, DC: US Government Printing Office, 1904), 100–101, 353, 354; Simon Kuznets and Ernest Rubin, *Immigration and the Foreign Population* (New York: NBER, 1954), 3; US Census Bureau, *Historical Statistics of the United States: Colonial Times to 1970*, pt. 1 (Washington, DC: US Government Printing Office, 1975), 25, 27, 29, 33, 93.

Table 6. State Growth by Migration, 1880–1900 (Thousands)

State	1880	1900	Growth	Net Migration	Percent
Illinois	3,078	4,822	1,744	510.3	29 percent
Michigan	1,637	2,421	784	234.3	30 percent
Ohio	3,198	4,158	960	119.2	12 percent
Wisconsin	1,315	2,069	754	184.8	25 percent
Colorado	140	540	400	198.7	50 percent

Source: US Census Bureau, *Historical Statistics of the United States: Colonial Times to 1970*, pt. 1 (Washington, DC: US Government Printing Office, 1975), 25, 27, 29, 33, 37, 93.

The vast majority of the growth of these five US cities, an average of 66 percent, came from migration and much of that from *within* the same state. The growth from interstate migration of the states that are home to these cities was, as shown in table 6, much slower than that of the cities—an average of 24 percent for the four Midwestern states and 50 percent for Colorado. So the difference in the rate of growth by migration of cities compared to their states ranged from 42 percent for Denver to five times for Cleveland. On average these cities grew by migration at about two and a half times as fast as their states, pointing to a huge amount of intrastate migration.

Michael Conzen's study of internal migration in Iowa reveals the same phenomenon, with 24 percent of native Iowans living in a county other than that where they were born in 1895, while the growth of Iowa's state population by interstate migration was only 11 percent—less than half of intrastate movement.[230] Joseph Ferrie shows that among native-born white males, the rate of intercounty migration was almost twice that of interstate migration for the US as a whole.[231] All these studies indicate that the growth from migration *within* these states was responsible for far more urban growth than migration from out of state by a factor of two or even two and a half times. Indeed, internal migration theory tells us that most migration to cities is by short distances, or "step-by-step" in a sequence of short movements.[232]

Even allowing for a greater proportion of long-distance migration in the case of the US, David Ward observes that, as opportunities in the West diminished after 1870, "the proportion of long-distance movements within the total internal movement declined, and even newly settled areas began to experience the effects of the cityward movement."[233] That is, much of urban growth in the last two or three decades of the nineteenth century came from within the state where the city was located. This observation is further supported by geographer Allan Pred, who shows that many rural or semirural counties in the Midwest lost manufacturing jobs during this period as industries and their workers moved from small towns into large cities like Chicago, Detroit, Cleveland, and Saint Louis.[234]

In order to make a comparison with Cairncross's comprehensive calculations for internal migration in England and Wales, the net intercensal/interstate migration figures for the US need to be adjusted since each state contains many counties and towns. While English counties are significantly larger than American counties, potentially masking some intracounty rural to urban migration,[235] Cairncross uses town and city figures so that any masking of intracounty migration should be minimal. Nevertheless, to err on the side of caution I will conservatively estimate that combined interstate and intrastate migration for the US should be adjusted by 50 percent above the interstate level, rather than the doubling or more that the figures above might justify.

Table 7 compares the figures for the US Northeast, Midwest, and West regions to those for England and Wales. The US South is excluded because of its agrarian economy and significant out-migration, while the rural counties of England and Wales are excluded for the same reason. The results of these calculations indicate that the migration rates for the US were over five times that of England and Wales over this period. The patterns were somewhat different: whereas the US saw a big increase in migration and its rate during the 1880s followed by a drop in the 1890s, England

and Wales experienced a decline in the 1880s and a rise in the 1890s. It is at least plausible that the increased migration of the 1880s contributed to the instability and decline of US union membership in that decade, while in the UK a relative drop in migration and rise in emigration aided the burst of the new unionism at the end of that decade. Indeed, as John Charlton points out in his study of the new unionism, "It was true that 1889 was one of those rare points where the demand for labour in the docks actually outstripped supply."[236] In any case, given the relatively low level of migration in England and Wales compared to the US, it seems unlikely that migration had as significant an impact on unionization in the UK as it did in the US.

Table 7. Net Interstate and Estimated Intrastate Migration, US Northeast, Midwest and West

US NE, MW, and W	1870s	1880s	1890s
Population*	26,201,000	33,672,000	42,960,000
Adjusted migration	2,324,550	5,279,400	3,864,300
Adjusted rate	8.9 percent	15.7 percent	8.9 percent
Net Migration Into Urban and Colliery Districts of England and Wales			
UK England and Wales	**1870s**	**1880s**	**1890s**
Population*	22,712,266	25,974,439	29,002,525
Urban and Colliery District	689,154	228,063	605,980
Rate	3 percent	0.8 percent	2 percent
Average Population, Adjusted Migration, Rate: UK (England and Wales) vs. US (Northeast, Midwest, and West), 1870–1900			
Country	**Population**	**Migration**	**Rate**
US	34,277,666	3,822,750	11.2 percent
UK	25,896,367	507,732	2.0 percent

* Beginning of decade.
Sources: US Census Bureau, Historical Statistics of the United States: Colonial Times to 1970, pt. 1 (Washington, DC: US Government Printing Office, 1975), 22, 25, 27, 29, 33, 93; A. K. Cairncross, Home and Foreign Investment, 1870–1913 (Cambridge: Cambridge University Press, 1953), 70; Bureau of the Census, Abstract of the Twelfth Census of the United States, 3rd ed. (Washington, DC: US Government Printing Office, 1904), 100, 102, 353, 354, 345; Simon Kuznets and Ernest Rubin, Immigration and the Foreign Population (New York: NBER, 1954), 3.

There is another difference in the internal migration patterns in the US and UK that bears mentioning. This is the size of the two countries. Below we will recount the speculation of the American *Iron Molders' Journal* to the effect that if US iron molders had faced a country the size of England, the equivalent of the state of

Pennsylvania, "with no opening for them except by traveling thousands of miles to a new country . . . we believe a Union like that of England would be a forgone conclusion."[237] As testimony by union leaders and activists will show in a subsequent chapter, keeping traveling union members in the union was no easy task given the many places a skilled worker might find employment in America's expanding economy. The "compactness" of England, the journal argued, was a distinct advantage the American Iron Molders' Union did not have.

The size of the US also involved a greater degree of economic and geographic diversity in terms of development. This is captured in Stromquist's analysis of the "moving frontier of labor scarcity" elaborated below.[238] Internal migration theory postulates that people will move toward places with higher wages and more employment opportunities, or as Ravenstein put it, the combination "of locomotion and a development of manufactures" put migrants on the road.[239] Thus, nations with greater diversity of development will have higher rates of migration. It seems clear that the US with far more areas of new and growing development and higher wages would have more migration as long as the differentials remained on the "moving frontier of labor scarcity."

The relative impact of size is even clearer when concentrations of growing industry are included. The lion's share of migration in England and Wales in the late nineteenth century was concentrated in three industrial districts composed of ten to fifteen of their fifty-three counties. These districts were the industrial North, the London area, and South Wales.[240] Thus, British unions had an advantage of "compactness" even beyond the relatively small size of England and Wales envied by the American iron molders. In the US such industrial districts were more numerous. The expanding coalfields of the upper South, Midwest, and far West, for example, provided more areas of attraction to experienced or potential miners than the pits of South Wales could for British workers. American workers in search of improved conditions and income simply had many more places to aim for. The point here is simply that both size and the multiplicity of developing areas created more "pulls" to potential migrants. This, in the context of the different phases of industrial development of the two countries, helps explain the much higher rate of migration in the US.

"Pull" or "Push"?

The two greatest forces of attraction to prospective migrants during the Gilded Age were the growth and movement of industry on the one hand and the interrelated process of rapid urbanization on the other. Ravenstein's "laws" of internal migration, after all, rested on the assumption that, as he put it in his 1885 paper, "It does not admit of doubt that the call for labor of our centers of industry and commerce is the prime cause of those currents of migration which it is the object of this paper to trace."[241] Stanley Lebergott agrees that the pull factor was dominant. Thus, writing about the migration from "farm to city within the United States," he says that a gap in "economic advantage is a first requirement," but that "variation of employment opportunities in the urban areas becomes the decisive complementary factor."[242]

Thus, unemployment itself was not necessarily a cause or incentive to migrate or tramp. Without knowledge of work elsewhere, traveling was not likely to be a good bet during a depression. This was the case despite the large (over)estimates of tramps and hoboes made by contemporary observers in the 1870s and 1890s. For the poorest, unskilled workers caught in the midst of a depression, migration may have been unaffordable, hence the large concentrations of unemployed in the cities during the major depressions. The New York Society for Improving the Condition of the Poor reported that between seventy-five thousand and one hundred thousand workers in the city were unemployed in the winter of 1874–1875, while the number of families on relief rose from five thousand in 1873 to twenty-four thousand the following year. Not surprisingly, the weight of the jobless in the city overstretched available relief and charity, as well as produced mass demonstrations for relief by the unemployed.[243] *John Swinton's Paper* described the situation in New York City in 1884 during the depression of that decade. He wrote of the city's unemployed, "Five, ten, fifteen on almost every corner around the river bank."[244] During the 1893–1897 depression, the New York police estimated some 67,280 resident unemployed and an additional 20,000 homeless. In Chicago, the estimate was 100,000 in the winter of 1893–1894. In both cities, thousands were allowed to sleep in police stations.[245] Clearly, these workers did not have the option of seeking work elsewhere. In all likelihood, for every unemployed worker who tramped during a depression, two or more remained "at home," dependent on inadequate relief, charity, and odd jobs. To the employers of the city whom they asked for jobs, the strangers whom they begged for a handout, or the city officials attempting to keep track of "vagrants," they may have seemed like tramps, but they were most likely just the urban unemployed trapped by the depression. Indeed, the newly formed National Conference of Charities and Correction reported street begging by hordes of tramps in New York City, while Josiah Flynt, a sociologist who had traveled with tramps as part of his research, coined such oxymorons as "the tramp at home" and "the city tramp."[246] These "tramps," who figured in the estimates during the depressions of the time, didn't travel beyond the city limits. In any case, the higher migration rate for the most prosperous decade, the 1880s, underlines the importance of the "pull" factor.

"The Moving Frontier of Labor Scarcity"

What characterized the Gilded Age's volatile economy, then, was a rhythm of employment and migration, expressing the contradictory pulls and pushes of uneven capital accumulation as well as its periods of depression. Stromquist has aptly described the incentives that underlay the rhythm of migration as the "moving frontier of labor scarcity."[247] This refers to the fact of wage differentials that appeared as industry grew or moved westward or both, as urban development increased and new industries arose, so that the demand for labor exceeded that available from the local population—at least until migration created surplus labor or depression destroyed demand. The building of the railroad network across the continent is an obvious example, but it doesn't end there. Nor is this allusive "frontier" limited to the West, since both industry and urban development are in many cases renewed in older areas due to new technology, cycles of investment, continued urban growth in the Midwest, whole new industries, and so on.

Table 8 shows some examples of wage differentials that result from labor scarcity that would attract migrants and tramp workers alike. The most obvious is the huge wage differential between the three regions in all mines and quarries, a difference that was still strong in 1902, above all in the West.

Table 8. Annual Average Mines and Quarries Wage by Region, 1902

Region	1902
Region	1902
North Atlantic	$591.59
North Central	$643.74
Western Division	$925.20

Annual Average Manufacturing Wage by Region, 1880–1900

Region	1880	1890	1900
North Atlantic	$357.89	$381.71	$458.68
North Central	$352.99	$438.05	$447.52
Western Division	$475.71	$581.94	$556.21

Source: Bureau of the Census, *Abstract of the Twelfth Census of the United States, 1900*, 3rd ed. (Washington, DC: US Government Printing Office, 1904), 331, 429.

The differences in manufacturing present a slightly more complex picture but follow the rhythm established above. For the whole period, wages in the West remained well above those in both the East and Midwest, as labor was still relatively scarce on the Great Plains and in the mountain and Pacific states. In 1880, wages in the Midwest were slightly lower than in the East. But as capital moved into the Midwest in the 1880s at a faster rate than in the 1870s, 183 percent compared to 39 percent, the workforce doubled as the wage rate outstripped that in the East.[248]

This is consistent with the general picture of accelerated growth in migration, capital accumulation, manufacturing, and population in the Midwest in the 1880s and the subsequent slowing down of these rates of midwestern growth in the 1890s. In the 1890s, despite the deep depression, capital growth in the East surpassed that in the Midwest, offering slightly higher wages. This is probably due to the rise of steel production in the Pittsburgh area and the development of new industries such as electrical equipment in New York State. All of this is a reminder that the "moving frontier of labor scarcity" was not a fixed place or simply a matter of westward movement.

Table 9. Average Annual Manufacturing Wage by City and State, 1880

City	Wage	State	Wage	Differential
Pittsburgh	$477.85	Pennsylvania	$346.33	27 percent
Chicago	$436.44	Illinois	$396.81	9 percent
St. Louis	$424.35	Missouri	$352.34	17 percent
Detroit	$391.46	Michigan	$326.25	17 percent
Cleveland	$391.41	Ohio	$283.78	17 percent

Source: Bureau of the Census, *Abstract of the Twelfth Census of the United States, 1900*, 3rd ed. (Washington, DC: US Government Printing Office, 1904), 331–333, 352–358.

Wage differentials also play a part in the migration into larger cities, attracting not only out-of-state migrants but also those within the state. Table 9 shows the wage differentials in manufacturing for selected industrial cities and the states in which they are located. This is consistent with the observation by Pred that small towns as well as the countryside lost industry and population to the larger cities of the Midwest.[249] We have already seen that migration within most states was at least twice the rate of migration into the same state in the comparison with England and Wales. As important as are the incentives for migration or tramping, it is necessary to have an overview of just what created the "moving frontier of labor scarcity" and its eventual negation during this period of volatile industrialization. The picture of economic development as a more or less linear progression of growth interrupted only by occasional depressions is far too simple to explain the vast movement of people over oceans and across a continent during the late nineteenth century.

Behind the Missing Factor

The high degree of geographic mobility that characterized Gilded-Age America was the result of the convergence of three phenomena: space, that is the massive size of the United States once the conquest of the continent had been completed; the highly rapid, uneven, and contradictory process of capital accumulation and disac-cumulation; and the tightening formation of social classes associated with capitalist development that rendered upward mobility out of the working class far more dif-ficult than in earlier times. This last factor can be understood, as Richard Schneirov argues, as the transition from the "free labor" era in which self-employment dom-inated to one in which capitalist wage labor was becoming dominant and perma-nent for the vast majority of workers.[250] These forces interacted to "pull" and "push" population and the workforce in a variety of directions over the last thirty years of the nineteenth century. Motion, not stasis, was the norm for most of this period.

The first underlying factor behind the huge internal migration was, of course, the sheer size of the United States. With the defeat of the Confederacy and of the Great Plains Indian nations, the US became larger in space than Europe as a whole, while its individual states were often larger than single European nations. In an explicit recognition of the problem of geography and the extensive nature of the United States, an article in the *Iron Molders' Journal* in 1877 noted that the British Friendly Society of Iron Molders had about twelve thousand members in England, which was "not as large as one of our states—Pennsylvania." Thus, the author ar-gued, "here in the very outset England has the advantage of compactness." If British molders chose "flight" over "fight" as a means to more income, they would have to travel across the Atlantic. The American, in contrast, might just move a short distance to Ohio and from there to Indiana, and so on—and that rapidly by rail. The author continued, "Put 12,000 molders in Pennsylvania and organize them into 100 different (local) unions under one head, with no opening for them except by traveling thousands of miles to a new country, and we believe a Union like that of England would be a foregone conclusion." Geography, in short, was a sizable problem for American unions as well as an opportunity to migrate.

There is a certain irony in seeing the expansion of the United States as a problem for organized labor and the wageworker. Antebellum reformers from New York *Tribune* editor Horace Greeley to labor leader George Henry Evans had seen the westward expansion as the salvation or "safety-valve" for the eastern wageworker who could, should wages in the East be inadequate, turn to a farm or independent artisan's workshop farther to the West for relief. Thus, the American worker would not experience the degradation accompanying the status of perma-nent wageworker of his European counterpart.[251] In fact, it was precisely this west-ward expansion that produced the industrial revolution of the Gilded Age with its vast urbanization and increasingly permanent wage-earning class. Not only the factories and overcrowded cities east of the Mississippi River, but the mines, towns and industry of the West rapidly enclosed a workforce drawn from all points of the compass into the dependency of wage labor even as they migrated across and around the continent.

The driving force behind immigration and internal migration in the Gilded Age was above all the rapid, extensive, and uneven accumulation of capital. Capital accumulation was anything but a seamless process of ascending industrial development. Early in his monumental study, *Capitalism*, Anwar Shaikh shows that both industrial production and real investment rose dramatically during the Gilded Age, a sharply upward trend. But he is quick to qualify this appearance by stating that the "first striking feature is the recurrence of fluctuations: successive episodes of boom and bust, of overshooting and undershooting, in never ending sequence."[252] The trend is upward, but jagged. In other words, this was a period of economic turbulence as well as growth in which outcomes for any given business or industry at any point in the swirl of competition and slump were far from obvious. Many business and economic historians such as Thomas Cochran and William Miller, Alfred Chandler, and Alan Trachtenberg have emphasized the organizational changes in business and industry in the Gilded Age—pools, trusts, and the rise of the modern corporation that characterized US industry by the end of the century.[253] From this vantage point, industrialization appears as a more or less continuous ascent toward a known goal characterized more by corporate "monopoly" (the "visible hand') than competition, a process interrupted only by the business cycle. For the most part this is because such historians tend to focus on the winners of the period, the well-known giant corporations, not on the many losers.

More accurate was the understated remark of Edward Kirkland that "the late nineteenth century was not characterized by a very considerable decline in competition." As he observed, "The trust that succeeded in surviving was balanced by the trust that failed or escaped going under only by the most desperate expedients." Kirkland wrote that "in general, the words businessmen most frequently used to explain the situation they confronted were 'chaos,' 'anarchy,' 'ruin,' 'failure,' 'instability.'"[254] Heilbroner and Singer emphasize competition in their popular economic history of the US: "'Cutthroat' price wars repeatedly broke out as producers desperately struggled to find markets for their product when business was slack"—as it was during the depression that each decade experienced.[255] It was this competition that led to the frenetic "mechanization" in search of reducing costs and the failure of businesses that couldn't keep up, both of which displaced workers in vast numbers even as capital expanded and created different jobs.

The third factor in the convergence that underlay the population turmoil of the era was the formation of a permanent class of wage earners itself, creating a major limitation on working-class choices. Self-employment was largely replaced by wage labor, and social mobility out of the working class had become increasingly difficult and even unlikely—facts that were widely recognized at the time.[256] With upward mobility limited, migration became a more viable option for improving living standards.

Accumulation: Movements of Capital as a "Pull" Factor

The central force of accumulation driven by competition and class conflict gave industrialization and urbanization in this period their dynamism, pulling the movement of people across the country in a number of directions. Between 1870 and 1900, capital invested in manufacturing—the heart of the accumulation process—grew by 365 percent. The proportion of capital invested in manufacturing, however, shifted from its older sites in the Northeast to the Midwest.[257] As David Montgomery pointed out, at the end of the Civil War industry moved rapidly westward along the Ohio River on the one hand and the Great Lakes on the other.[258] Thus, between 1870 and 1900, while the manufacturing workforce in the Northeast less than doubled, that in the Midwest and West combined more than tripled.[259]

A further indication of the movement of industry can be seen in table 10, covering the geographic distribution of capital in manufacturing, and table 11, showing the distribution of manufacturing workers. While this does not include all industrial workers, it nevertheless gives us an overview of the movements of capital and labor in this period. Though the Northeast remained the largest center of manufacturing throughout the Gilded Age, there was a significant shift in the geographic distribution of capital, with the Northeast region declining relatively from almost two-thirds to just over a half of investment, and the North Central, or Midwest, region rising from a quarter of invested capital to 30 percent. In growth rates, the capital invested in the Northeast grew by almost 300 percent, while that in the Midwest grew by 455 percent. By decade, it was the 1880s that saw the most rapid growth, 184 percent for the nation and 183 percent for the Midwest. The West and the South also grew more rapidly than the Northeast but remained less developed as manufacturing regions and more invested in extractive activity—mining in the West and upper South, cotton and timber in the Deep South.

Table 10. Growth and Distribution of Manufacturing by Region, 1870–1900 ($ millions)

Region	1870	1880	1890	1900
Northeast	1,344 (63 %)	1,719 (62 %)	3,548 (54 %)	5,300 (54 %)
North Central	523 (25 %)	716 (26 %)	2,028 (31 %)	2,902 (30 %)
West	61 (3 %)	82 (3 %)	256 (4 %)	430 (4 %)
South	191 (9 %)	273 (10 %)	693 (11 %)	1,200 (12 %)
US Total	2,119 (100 %)	2,790 (100 %)	6,525 (100 %)	9,832 (100 %)

Source: Bureau of the Census, *A Compendium of the Ninth Census, 1870* (Washington, DC: US Government Printing Office, 1872), 796–797; Bureau of the Census, *Abstract of the Twelfth Census of the United States, 1900*, 3rd ed. (Washington, DC: US Government Printing Office, 1904), 331.

Table 11. Growth and Distribution of Manufacturing Wageworkers, 1870–1900 (Thousands)

Region	1870	1880	1890	1900
Northeast	1,274 (63 %)	1,692 (62 %)	2,818 (59 %)	2,772 (52 %)
North Central	498 (24 %)	664 (24 %)	1,250 (26 %)	1,537 (29 %)
West	37 (2 %)	59 (2 %)	133 (3 %)	194 (4 %)
South	215 (11 %)	318 (12 %)	551 (12 %)	811 (15 %)
US Total	2,024 (100 %)	2,733 (100 %)	4,752 (100 %)	5,315 (100 %)

Source: Bureau of the Census, *A Compendium of the Ninth Census, 1870* (Washington, DC: US Government Printing Office, 1872), 796–797; Bureau of the Census, *Abstract of the Twelfth Census of the United States, 1900*, 3rd ed. (Washington, DC: US Government Printing Office, 1904), 331.

From 1870 to 1900, the number of wageworkers grew by 3,292,200, or 162 percent, just under 20 percent of them women. The shifts in capital accumulation noted above necessarily brought wageworkers in their wake so that the Midwest added over a million manufacturing workers to its ranks over this period, while the Northeast actually saw its number of these workers drop slightly between 1890 and 1900. It is important to notice that the gains in the Midwest came most rapidly in the 1880s, when the workforce nearly doubled and migration was at its high point for this period. That is, the shift of workers into the Midwest was not a gradual process, and the timing will be important when we look at the impact on labor organization.

The West was also stamped by industry, often even before the town arrived and even before the Native American population had been defeated and forced onto reservations. As Limerick put it, "Mining placed settlements of white people where none had been before."[260] It was the rapid growth of the heavily metal-based production of industry in the East and Midwest that brought the soaring increase of mining and smelting, as well as other industries in the West, to feed the factories and mills of the East and Midwest. As Gavin Wright argued, "Copper, coal, zinc, iron ore, and other metals were at the core of industrial technology for that era."[261] So, for example, the output of refined lead jumped from a mere 17,830 short tons in 1870 to 367,773 in 1900, while that of zinc rose from 5,400 short tons to 123,886 over those years. Similarly, the growth in the production of copper mined, as telegraph and then telephone wires spread across the continent, increased from 14,112 short tons in 1870 to 303,059 in 1900.[262] The miners who produced these impressive outputs were famously transient, making an accurate count difficult. Nevertheless, the 1900 census put the number of miners in eight states of the West at 103,835.[263] This is a snapshot, so the number of miners who passed through these states over time must have been many times that, rendering union organizing a very difficult task, as we shall see in a subsequent chapter.

Urbanization in this period, again, was largely a function of industrial development. The growth of capital in the Midwest from 1880 to 1900 was concentrated in several newer industrial cities, pulling the migration from country and small town to city. Chicago, the epicenter of industrial growth in the region, saw accumulated capital grow by nearly 700 percent in this twenty-year period, much faster than in the region as a whole, with the lion's share occurring in the 1880s. So great was its attraction that its population growth from out of state in the 1880s accounted for 88 percent of the growth of the whole state of Illinois. Other relatively new mid-western industrial centers, particularly those along the Great Lakes corridor, also saw invested capital grow rapidly: Milwaukee by 488 percent, Cleveland by 405 percent, and Detroit by 360 percent. As with Chicago, the fastest growth came in the 1880s. The manufacturing workforce drawn to these cities by capital also grew in these years, although at a slightly slower rate as mechanization increased productivity. Chicago's manufacturing workers increased by 230 percent, those in Detroit by 184 percent, Cleveland by 171 percent, and Milwaukee by 131 percent, all faster than the national rate of growth of the manufacturing workforce of 94 percent.[264]

Urbanization due to industrial shifts, however, was not just fed from East to Midwest, from farm to factory, or from one city to another. As Allan Pred has shown, there was also a movement of industry and workers within the Midwest from smaller towns to the growing cities of the region. He cites a study that concluded, "The 1880 to 1890 decline of small-town industry in an area stretching from Detroit to Des Moines; and the disappearance of local machine shops, sawmills, flour mills, furniture shops, brick-and-tile-producing establishments, and agricultural implement manufacture was attributed partly to 'the substitution of production on a large scale.'"[265] This production was lost to growing urban industrial centers such as Chicago, Saint Louis, Cleveland, and Detroit, which had enormous transportation advantages over the smaller towns in the region. This tended to concentrate industry in these bigger cities. For example, Chicago went from having 3.5 percent of the agricultural implement output measured in value added in 1860 to 25 percent by 1900.[266] With the movement of production, of course, went many of the wageworkers and their families who had been employed in small-town firms. Thus, the movement of people from the countryside to the city was not limited to farm leavers but also included town-based wageworkers, who might well have then moved from city to city or even region to region in search of work.

While decisions to migrate might be made for many reasons, these "pull" factors underlay most migration and provided the "flight versus fight" option for many workers, which, like the return emigration discussed by Herbert Gutman, served to undermine labor organization. That is, so long as newer areas of development and growth in the West or in growing cities created new jobs, workers could choose to migrate rather than stay and confront their current employer in the first instance or "fight another day" after a defeated strike. At the same time capital accumulation created these new opportunities it destroyed others. It is worth noting again that the industrial areas of potential migration in England and Wales were limited so that the major alternatives for British workers in this period were emigration or resistance, which may in part explain the explosion of the new unionism in 1888–1889.

Machines Eat Men (and Women): Accumulation as a "Push" Factor

One of US industrialization's most dynamic features in the Gilded Age was the continual application of new technology in industry after industry. One way of looking at this is to compare the relative growth of capital and labor as inputs to total national output and its growth. Viewed in the broadest terms for the economy as a whole, the growth of capital as a factor of production grew at twice the rate of labor from 1870 to 1900, while the capital–labor ratio in industry grew by two and a half times from 1880 to 1900.[267] Thus, both agriculture and industry were becoming more capital intensive and requiring relatively less labor, sending redundant workers to where there was still greater demand. But this is only part of the impact of technology.

The rise and fall of industries and firms in connection with technological transformation was a central feature of Gilded-Age industrialization. Noting that the index for manufacturing output had risen from 7.5 in 1863 to 53.0 in 1897, Edward Kirkland commented,

> Within old industries new trends suddenly appeared, grew at an accelerated rate, reached a peak, and then slowed down. On the other hand, retarded growth was also a common phenomenon. In extreme cases growth stopped entirely. Thus, new metallurgical methods erased smelting with anthracite coal and the rolling of iron rails; lubricants from petroleum had very nearly the same effect upon the whaling industry. Changes in these two categories paled in importance before the rapid appearance of new industries. These continually unsettled the economy and gave contemporaries the feeling they were standing always on the edge of a new age of wonders and miracles.[268]

Or disasters, he might have added.

Machines replaced labor. A growing economy might provide a job in another place, but once an aspect of the labor process was mechanized, the labor input was reduced. That, of course, was the whole point from the perspective of capitalists in competition. The displacement of labor, moreover, could be very large. In his first annual report in 1886, the new US commissioner of labor, Carroll D. Wright, showed that while new furnaces used in producing pig iron cut the labor input by 20 percent, automatic hammers in iron and steel replaced employees "in the proportion of 10 to 1."[269] Skilled "puddlers" disappeared from steel mills as new technology took over that work. But the unskilled were also affected. As David Brody observed of mechanization in steel production, "The hordes of common laborers were rapidly supplanted."[270] In a similar vein, the president of the Typographical Union told the Industrial Commission in 1899 that some four thousand typesetting machines had displaced as many as ten thousand to twelve thousand print workers.[271] A mule spinner from Fall River, Massachusetts, told the Senate in 1883 that as a result of the introduction of new machinery in cotton mills, "The tendency has been not only to reduce wages, but also to dismiss help."[272]

The commissioner of labor also calculated that mechanization in the agricultural implements industry in an unnamed western state (most likely Illinois) had displaced 1,545 out of 2,145 workers, a cut of over two-thirds of the workforce. Indeed, the 1886 report included seven pages of examples of machinery replacing labor, where a 50 percent displacement was not uncommon. Not surprisingly, the commissioner saw all this displacement as temporary, soon to be overwhelmed by the creation of still more jobs. But the displaced workers, hundreds of thousands if not more, had to find these new jobs. And as we saw above, the jobs along with the capital that created them were moving, mostly westward, or being transformed in older areas. The evidence above indicates that work and those who sought it moved from region to region, city to city, and town to city in order to fill in the gaps in employment or to seek better wages and conditions.

Disaccumulation: More "Push" Factors

The course of industrial development was anything but a smooth ascent. The unevenness of the process of accumulation meant that within the great movements of industry and workforce were various displacing "push" factors related to what I will call "disaccumulation." These include the destruction of capital, the search for greater efficiency, increasing business failures, industrial relocation, irregular employment, and employer actions that relied on these trends and the migrations they spawned— particularly flooding local labor markets.

The Gilded Age saw a major depression in each decade, roughly between 1873 and 1876, 1883 and 1885, and 1893 and 1897. Whatever their immediate cause (for example, railroad stock collapses), they were endemic in an era of declining profit rates, as Hobsbawm argued. Each such slump brought mass unemployment, though the 1883–1885 depression was the shortest and most shallow with an unemployment rate half that of the 1873–1878 and 1893–1897 slumps.[273] A major cause of dislocation during a depression was the complete failure of a business—the oft-ignored losers of the period. Business failures, however, were not confined to depressions. Their number rose from 64,383 in the 1870s to 88,923 in the 1880s, where growth prevailed for most of the decade. Similarly, the destruction of capital increased from $260 million in the 1870s to $1.3 billion in the 1880s.[274] Regional figures are only available from 1889 on, but what they show is that the Midwest (including the Great Plains states) was not far behind the older industrial Northeast. From 1889 to 1900 the Northeast saw 58,141 failures, while the Midwest experienced 45,244, despite the fact that the invested capital in the Midwest was only about half that in the Northeast.[275]

Ironically, depressions were also opportunities for the better-off industrialists to modernize their plant in order to emerge from the slump in a better competitive position. Not only were new machines brought into factories, but old ones also had to be destroyed as they became less efficient than the newer ones. In 1885 economist David Wells wrote, "Abandonment of large quantities of costly machinery [is] a matter of absolute economical necessity."[276] The necessity was to increase efficiency and lower costs in the face of competition and frequent depressions. Men like Andrew Carnegie saw the depression of the 1890s as the right moment to invest and replace old methods in his fight to defeat the other steelmakers. Between 1893 and 1897, the span of the depression of that decade, Carnegie had the Homestead and Duquesne steelworks rebuilt from the ground up. As a result, the types of workers changed. By 1900 the skilled puddlers had disappeared from US steel mills and more semiskilled "specialist" workers filled the mills.[277] This process, no doubt, forced many to look elsewhere for work.

What is clear is that accumulation and disaccumulation together both expelled workers and attracted them, sending millions to and from regions, states, and cities in search of work. They were simultaneously pulled by economic and geographic expansion and pushed by one type of displacement or another. Although space prevents a detailed look at the differential ways in which these facets of capitalist development made an impact on different sectors of the working class, it is important to bear in mind that race, ethnicity, and gender mattered. The migration opportunities on the frontier of labor scarcity opened to skilled white workers were obviously greater than those available to African Americans, many immigrant groups, and women. Social norms, institutions, and prejudices created barriers for many of these groups. Unskilled "floaters" were unlikely to improve their occupational status even when they achieved higher wages through migration. Women, who migrated in equal numbers to men, might find work in Mr. Carhartt's new "overall" factory in Detroit but were banned from most skilled work even there. Black workers, whether in Detroit or Denver, remained at the bottom of the workforce, with some exceptions like the union bricklayers in Detroit, or carpenters in the South. The new, non-English-speaking immigrants who began to arrive in the mid- to late 1880s mostly found their way into poorly paid employment wherever they went. Whatever their circumstances, however, the path these various groups chose or were forced on to did not actually encompass the entire US. For the most part, this migration did not run from north to south east of the Mississippi or beyond the Mason-Dixon Line, a fact that no doubt led to the eventual crowding of labor markets in northern cities.[278]

Conclusion

The Gilded Age was one of extreme economic and social turbulence. Immigration and internal migration on a massive scale, drawn by rapid and turbulent industrialization, kept the nation's population on the move in a number of directions. Measured by the accelerated accumulation of capital, the introduction of new technology, rapid urbanization, massive immigration, and internal migration all these forces pulled and pushed, the 1880s saw the most intense churning of population and high turnover rates. Workers in the 1880s in particular also experienced the hardening of class lines as wage labor became dominant in the nonfarm workforce. This high point of economic growth, population movement, high turnover, and the hardening of class lines in the 1880s contributed to both the escalating growth and underlying weakness of the Knights of Labor that led to its subsequent decline, which will be analyzed in chapter 4.

The reality of labor migration as a problem for union organization and stability was widely recognized throughout the Gilded Age by observers, academics, and union activists alike. For many middle-class people this was seen as the "tramp" problem that first arose in the depression of the 1870s and continued throughout the period.[279] In fact, more important than the depression tramp or the feared vagrant were those workers who tramped and traveled as a necessary part of their occupation and livelihood, pulled and pushed by the forces we have analyzed in this chapter. In order to better establish the importance of internal migration as a labor problem, we turn now to the experiences and voices of both observers and participants concerning labor migration in the Gilded Age.

Chapter 3

OBSERVATIONS AND AWARENESS
OF LABOR MIGRATION

And when we enquire into the motives which have led these migrants
to leave their homes, they will be found to be various too. In most
instances it will be found that they did so in search of work of a more
remunerative or attractive kind than that afforded by the place of birth.
—E. G. Ravenstein, 1885[1]

Every workingman is a tramp in embryo.
—*Alarm*, October 11, 1884[2]

FACED WITH irregular work, displaced by machines, or simply attracted
by the lure of better pay and conditions, as Ravenstein argued, workers in
Gilded-Age America traveled and tramped across the continent, often "in
search of work of a more remunerative or attractive kind." While Britain had
seen tramp artisans in the late eighteenth and early nineteenth century,[3] the tramp,
or hobo, was a new figure in the post–Civil War United States. As Tim Cresswell put
it, "The technology of the railroad provided the conditions for a new social type—
the tramp—to exist."[4] Cresswell's work provides an important and much-overlooked
examination of the female tramp. At the same time, however, his investigation is limited to the "professional tramp," who "worshipped idleness," rather than the larger
numbers who sought work. The professional tramp was mostly a younger man,
though some studies in the early twentieth century found that perhaps 5 percent of
tramps were women—often dressed as men or boys when riding the rails.[5] Male or
female, these unwanted tramps may have come from abroad or the next town. Often
despised by "respectable" middle-class citizens as beggars or thieves, tramps were described by one 1876 German-language paper as, "This scourge of the land numbering
in the thousands, comes to the northern towns of Iowa and with them robberies,
break-ins [and] thieving."[6] Indeed, between 1876 and 1886, nineteen states passed
laws designed to discourage and punish the tramp who had no work or was between
jobs. Eventually forty out of forty-four states would pass such laws.[7]

While the image of the tramp lingered on into the twentieth century in Charlie Chaplin's 1915 silent film *The Tramp*,[8] the focus on the professional tramp as a beggar and vagrant goes back to the Gilded Age itself. Foremost among those who expressed expertise about the tramp was Allan Pinkerton, the founder and head of the notorious Pinkerton National Detective Agency. In his *Strikers, Communists, Tramps and Detectives*, Pinkerton contributed to the "tramp scare" of the 1870s by reminding his reader that while tramps, like the poor, have always been with us and while some are simply happy-go-lucky fellows, "you oftener get a vagabond" and that "shiftlessness, discontent, restlessness all reach in and take possession of him." Although Pinkerton expresses some sympathy with the plight of the tramp in the context of the depression of that decade, nevertheless, "once a tramp, they are always the tramp in feelings and sympathy." It must also have been alarming to the reader that his discussion of the tramp is followed without a break by a most unsympathetic description of the Paris Commune and the bloody mobs of the railroad strike of 1877.[9]

Among other Gilded-Age observers of the professional tramps were two "visiting anthropologists" who rode the rails with them in the 1890s. One was Josiah Flynt, who reinforced the view of the tramp as "the criminal in the open," indeed as a "parasite" in his book *Tramping with Tramps*.[10] Another was Jack London, who took a more sympathetic, even romantic view of his fellow knights of the road as adventurers but still saw them as beggars rather than workers. Oddly enough, London dedicated his book *The Road* to Flynt.[11] Writing somewhat later in the respectable *Annals of the American Academy of Political and Social Science*, O. F. Lewis, the general secretary of the Prison Association of New York, took the common middle-class view of the tramp as a "problem" about which he advised, "What we in the United States need to do first with the tramp problem is wake up."[12] Even fairly recent literature that has sometimes taken a more kindly attitude toward the tramp or hobo still emphasizes the tramp as a vagrant. Clark Spence, president of the Western History Association from 1969 to 1970, wrote of the tramp in the old tradition as "riding the boxcars from 'no place in particular to nowhere at all,'" speculating on whether it was alcoholism or "the virus of restlessness and wanderlust" that drove these poor creatures. Nevertheless, he does grant that some worked "piecemeal" during harvests, though "most floated aimlessly from job to job."[13] More recent works by historians of migratory labor such as Mark Wyman, Frank Higbie, Donna Gabaccia, and Marc Rodriguez, to mention a few, have dealt in great detail with patterns of migratory labor and will be looked at later in this chapter.[14]

Early in the twentieth century, physician Ben Reitman of Chicago attempted to define the different types of migrants. He wrote, "The hobo works and wanders, the tramp dreams and wanders."[15] For many of these Gilded-Age workers, however, there was no real distinction between these terms. For them the tramp was a product of necessity and a victim of the system to be defended, sometimes pitied, and only occasionally denounced. Though the tramp was reviled in middle-class opinion, as we saw above, these wageworkers in search of work or better pay took on the name, perhaps in defiance of those who looked down on these often involuntary migrants.

The attitude of the skilled granite cutters, who themselves "travel from State to State and city to city," according their union's president,[16] probably expressed the views of many migrant craftsmen. Testifying before the Senate in 1883, Boston granite cutter Charles Harrington said of the oppressive tramp laws passed in his state,

> I am also of the opinion that the tramp laws should be abolished. I can speak intelligently on that subject, having worked on public works, where the custom is, upon completion of, for instance a railroad, for the men immediately to walk to some other place where, perhaps, a railroad is building, or, at any rate, for another job . . . This class forms a large portion of the so-called tramps, and, like all classes of society, have some of the vicious among them; but they are the exception, not the rule, the greatest part of them being peaceful and law-abiding men who take hold of work to which they are adapted as readily as any other class of workmen.[17]

As we will see, other workers also saw the tramp as more than a vagrant or shirker.

The previous chapter established that it was not only the job displacement caused by depressions, "part-year" employment, and mechanization that sent people on the road, but also the pull of what Shelton Stromquist calls the "moving frontier of labor scarcity."[18] This "frontier" had little to do with Frederick Jackson Turner's line of white settlement. This movable "edge" of economic development could leap over that line of settlement with the railroad and mining camps of the far West or arise in growing cities of the long "settled" Midwest or in the new steel mills of Pittsburgh. It would rise and fall with commodity prices on the world market and draw its diverse and competing workforce from all points of the compass—only to disappear as new arrivals overwhelmed the local labor market. The flow of people was, therefore, one of constant migration into and out of areas of opportunity. It was not simply a matter of the whip of unemployment, but often the draw of serial employment or higher wages and better conditions or simply escape from the "foreman's empire." Indeed, as we have seen, depression-level unemployment was more likely to trap the urban poor in their city of residence than to send them on the tramp.

This chapter will examine how participants and observers viewed the migration and tramping of those seeking employment; how they characterized certain occupations as footloose; and how they thought this migration affected their livelihood. What is revealed here is the degree to which people of that era recognized the widespread use of migration for employment as virtually inevitable. The two main attempts to dampen the negative effects of constant migration on labor market conditions, the union traveling card and the "keep away" notice in the labor press, rested on this assumption. The "keep away" notice appeared in both the official union journals and in the independent labor press, which grew to some four hundred to eight hundred local weekly newspapers by the mid-1880s and will be discussed below.[19] The "keep away" notice, in particular, has received little attention from labor and social historians.

Rails and Wires

E. P. Thompson warns us against the simple equation "steam power and the cotton-mill = new working class" in favor of an understanding of the occupational and social diversity of that new class and, indeed, who rebelled first.[20] Similarly, in the United States it was not the factory workers who first rebelled against the rule of capital on a national scale. Nor was it the hand weavers or other archaic forms of artisan labor described by Thompson. In the United States it was precisely those who worked with relatively new technology, in the most organizationally advanced and geographically extended industries in the early years of the Gilded Age—the railroad workers and to a lesser degree the telegraph workers. As Alfred Chandler noted, "The rail and telegraph companies were themselves the first modern business enterprises to appear in the United States."[21] Unlike the "dark satanic mills" of England or even New England in the early nineteenth century, with their tight geographic concentration, the railroad and telegraph spanned the continent well before manufacturing. It was also these two industries that saw the first nationwide strikes. The railroad strike of 1877 was arguably a turning point in the development of class consciousness in America, as it drew in active support from many sections of the new wage-earning class and simultaneously defined capital as a highly visible enemy.

As John R. Commons put it concerning the 1877 railroad strike, "The spirit of labor solidarity was strengthened and made national. This was the first time in the history of the American labor movement that Federal troops were called out in time of peace to suppress strikes." He continued, "The feeling of resentment engendered thereby began to assume a political aspect, and during the next two years the territory covered by the strike became a most promising field for labor parties of all kinds and descriptions."[22] No less important was the reaction of the capitalist class and the respectable middle classes who saw in the violence of this strike the specter of the Paris Commune.[23] Six years later, the telegraphers would wage the second nationwide strike and go down to defeat at the hands of the flamboyant robber (and rail) baron Jay Gould and his Western Union Telegraph Company.[24] It was, of course, the railroad and the telegraph, and the migrating workers that produced and ran them, that contributed disproportionately to knitting the nation and the social classes developing within it together in this period. The railroad, however, was also the chief enabler of the job-seeking tramp, including those who worked on it.

Wherever the migrants came from, by the 1870s they were no longer led across the continent by the frontiersman and pioneering farmer imagined by Frederick Jackson Turner.[25] Looking with alarm on the growth of what he saw as the twin threats of concentrated wealth and immigration in the mid-1880s, the Reverend Josiah Strong noted the changing pattern of settlement across the US as the nation moved beyond the Mississippi and Missouri Rivers. He wrote, "In the middle states the farms were first taken, then the town sprang up to supply their wants, and at length the railway connected it with the world; but in the West the order is reversed—first the railroad, then the town, then the farms."[26]

This spread of settlement via the railroads was not just a matter of laying the transcontinental tracks, but of filling in the transportation network that created markets, towns, and cities. As Stromquist observed, "In many ways the railroads directed the settlement process west of the Mississippi."[27]

Before settlement came those who laid the track and drove, fueled, and maintained the trains. Built across unsettled or sparsely populated expanses, including those where the Plains Indians had not yet been conquered, railroad labor had to come from somewhere else—be that from China, Europe, Canada, or just back East. Whether laying or following the tracks, these workers moved from job to job. The Eight-Hour Commission of the US Congress reported in 1918 that "train hands who drift about the country, working first for one road and then another are called 'boomers.'"[28] These "boomers" were drawn by the higher wages to be found in the West from the Great Plains to the Pacific coast on the edge of the "moving frontier of labor scarcity." As the report on railroad labor prepared for the United States Industrial Commission noted, "There is no standard wage for any class of railroad labor for the whole country."[29] Hence, wages differed significantly from region to region and from small town to large city. For example, the daily wages of engineers in 1880 were over $3.75 in the West compared to less than $3.25 in the East, while those for switchmen were $1.49 in the East compared to $2.02 in the West.[30] Thus, the incentive to move from small town to big city or to move west was significant.

These "boomers" composed three distinct groups: the section men who laid and maintained the tracks; operating or "running" crews of engineers, firemen, and conductors; and the shop men who will be discussed separately below. The section hands had no chance of promotion, so that the only way to improve their livelihood was to move on. The operating crews had a system of promotion that allowed a fireman to become an engineer or a brakeman a conductor. If, however, newly recruited engineers or conductors were young, the firemen and brakemen faced a long period of stagnation and might well migrate in search of a better opportunity so long as the rail network continued to expand.[31]

Like other workers in this period, railroad workers of all kinds seldom had full-time work. Railroad traffic was affected by the seasonal nature of the industries it served. Commissioner of Labor Carroll D. Wright's 1889 study of railroad labor found that on average railroad employees worked about 147 days out of a 313-day employment year. This is all the more significant as 1889 was a year of economic growth, underlining the tendency of many workers to travel in search of better conditions in times of relative prosperity. Table 1 shows the number of days worked by several major railroad occupations on sixty railroad systems covered by the study. It also shows the number of actual employees required to cover the equivalent of the work if it had been done by full-time workers working 313 days in the year. On average for the sixty railroad systems surveyed, this came to two "actual" employees for each "theoretical" full-time worker, revealing the enormous circulation of workers from job to job and even company to company. It is highly unlikely that skilled workers such as brakemen or firemen worked only half a year. Rather they moved from one road to another, some probably outside the sixty systems covered by the study.[32]

Table 1. Average Days Worked by Railroad Employees, 1889*

Occupation	Average Days	Necessary F-T	Actual Workers
Brakeman	153	1	1.56
Conductor	207	1	1.51
Engineer	237	1	1.32
Fireman	155	1	2.02
Laborer	98	1	3.20
Machinist	193	1	1.68
Telegrapher	164	1	1.91
Average All	147	1	2.12

* Full-time = 313 days.
Source: US Commissioner of Labor, *Fifth Annual Report of the Commissioner of Labor, 1889* (Washington, DC: US Government Printing Office, 1890), 146–161.

What also stands out is the relatively short time that unskilled laborers, who composed 40 percent of the workforce and had no hope of promotion, spent in the employment of the railroads. Many of these workers were also part of the seasonal harvest workforce, sometimes creating labor shortages in the railroads during harvest season.[33] No doubt they also drifted to construction sites, timber camps, and other sites of casual unskilled labor. Not surprisingly, these itinerate workers were the least likely to be unionized. The railroad brotherhoods accepted only skilled workers. Some laborers, however, belonged to the Knights of Labor. They were also a large proportion of those who flocked to the American Railway Union during its brief life from 1893 to 1895. But permanent unionization eluded them until the twentieth century. Altogether as of 1890, about sixty-one thousand railroad workers, or 12.72 percent of the total workforce, belonged to unions. This would double by the end of the decade as 85 percent of the rail network was consolidated into seven corporate systems, the Erdman Act of 1898 provided a framework for labor-management negotiations, and the brotherhoods solidified a system of collective bargaining.[34]

Technically, the railroad workers weren't the first to move across the continent, tying East to West. By 1861, the telegraph, the midcentury's other great technological advance, spanned the country, beating the transcontinental railroad by eight years.[35] By 1870 Western Union alone had 112,191 miles of telegraph wire across the continent, 933,000 by 1900. In addition, the railroad lines had their own telegraph systems.[36] As wires extended and thousands of offices and rail depots opened, a brand-new workforce was drawn from place to place. Edwin Gabler, the historian of the American telegrapher, notes, "Like his fellow Americans, the late nineteenth century [telegraph] operator drifted or swam in the period's great streams of migration."[37] Testifying before a Senate committee in 1883, telegrapher John McClelland said that telegraph operators "have been looked upon in the past as quite a migratory class," though he speculated that this was less true "of late years."[38]

The employment histories of some telegraphers, two of whom also testified before this Senate committee in 1883, reveal quite a transient past. John Mitchell came to New York City in September 1882, just ten months before the month-long nationwide "Great Strike" of telegraph workers against Jay Gould's recently merged Western Union Telegraph Company. Soon he was chosen master workman (chief officer) of the New York local assembly of the Brotherhood of Telegraphers, District Assembly 45 of the Knights of Labor. Like many of his colleagues, Mitchell had been in and out of the industry and had traveled far and wide. Several years before coming to New York, he had worked at a Western Union cable station in Cape Bretton, Canada, where he got into a conflict with the manager. Despite being told that if he left his job he would never get another position with Western Union, he reported, "I resigned all the same, and left the business and remained out of it for about six years, and only returned to it in Chicago a little over two years ago." After about a year there, he moved to New York and was elected master workman and in only a few months went on strike.[39] Mitchell's story is, perhaps, only slightly more turbulent than that of other telegraphers. P. J. Tierney began his career in New York as a Western Union messenger in 1870 at the age of fifteen. Two years later he moved to Omaha, where he became a telegraph operator. Four years after that he returned to Western Union in New York.[40]

While this wandering was mostly a male preoccupation, some women, too, took to the road. "Country operator" Minnie Swan Mitchell, one of the most prominent women in the Brotherhood of Telegraphers, remembered that free railroad passes "made it possible for telegraphers, with youth and the great wide world beckoning, to give ear to the siren song of adventure. Wherever one stopped he (or sometimes she) could find employment, or, barring that, friends."[41] Most telegraphers, however, were male, single, and, as one testified, "generally board or have a furnished room in an apartment house or a boarding house, or sometimes in a hotel."[42]

Tramping was encouraged by wage differentials between cities in the Western Union system. This did not follow the East-West divide such as that on the railroad network. So, for example, the monthly rate for New York, the company's headquarters, was $80–$85, while that in Boston and Buffalo was $70–$75. Tierney reported that he was refused a job in Omaha at a promised rate of $100 a week because the New York office complained that Omaha was "outbidding the New York office for the services of the best men." To this was added the fact that employees were kept on the same salary as long as they worked in the same office.[43] Thus, the incentive to travel was strong. As with railroad workers, however, there was a tendency for this flow of people to "crowd" the labor market. In 1881 a Union Pacific telegrapher warned easterners that "the entire Western country is flooded with idle operators, all having flocked West with a mistaken idea." This formed a sort of cycle of migration. Like many other occupations in this era, tramping by telegraphers fell with the deep depression of the 1870s and rose during the recovery of the 1880s, sometimes creating a glut on the market.[44]

The telegraph workers had formed an industrial union, the Brotherhood of Telegraphers, Knights of Labor in 1882. Like many sections of the Knights of Labor, its life as a viable union was a short one. The ill-prepared "Great Strike" of 1883 was lost due in part to the newness of the organization, the lack of a strike fund, the high level of turnover in its membership, and ultimately the wealth and power of Jay Gould and his newly merged giant, Western Union. With the failure of the brotherhood, railroad telegraphers organized the Order of Railroad Telegraphers in 1886, while those at commercial firms would organize the Commercial Telegraphers Union of America at the end of the century.[45] An early experiment in industrial unionism had ended in defeat.

"A Roving Disposition"

The skilled workers in the printing trades were also famously transient, moving first from country to city and then from town to town. As with other unions of the period, tramping was facilitated by the union traveling card, which gained the union member entrance to a local union other than their own, where, hopefully, work could be found.

The percentage of members of the International Typographical Union using travel cards to seek work rose from 22.5 percent in 1880 to 66 percent by 1889. Thus, by the early 1890s, just before the depression of that decade, the equivalent of two-thirds of the recorded membership had gone elsewhere to seek employment. Note here that the proportion of traveling members dropped in 1885 as a result of the brief depression of 1883–1885, with a lag as members became aware of the depressed circumstance.[46] Thus, these skilled workers were more likely to tramp during favorable economic times, presumably when better pay could be found farther afield.

Testifying before the Senate Committee on Education and Labor in 1883 as to the itinerate nature of print workers, Frank K. Foster, an official of both the International Typographical Union (ITU) and the Knights of Labor, said,

> Either from a peculiar nature of the trade, or from some cause I am unable to ascertain, there is a Bohemian disposition among printers—a roving disposition. The nature of the trade permits them to wander from place to place, and a great many availing themselves of this privilege, preferring to live nomadic lives instead of remaining in one locality.[47]

Table 2. ITU Traveling Cards as Percentage of Membership, 1880–1892 Admission by Traveling Card

Year	Traveling Card	Total Membership	Percentage
1880	1,467	6,520	22.5 percent
1881	2,487	7,931	31.4 percent
1882	3,813	10,439	36.5 percent
1883	4,993	12,273	40.7 percent
1884	7,754	16,030	48.4 percent
1885	7,006	16,138	43.3 percent
1886	7,726	18,484	41.8 percent
1887	8,588	19,190	44.8 percent
1888	9,157	17,491	52.4 percent
1889	11,647	21,120	55.2 percent
1890	12,387	22,608	54.8 percent
1891	16,268	25,165	64.7 percent
1892	18,559	28,187	65.8 percent

Source: Ulman, *The Rise of the National Trade Union: The Development and Significance of Its Structure, Governing Institutions, and Economic Policies* (Cambridge, MA: Harvard University Press, 1955), 65.

Foster in fact described the rather poor conditions faced by printers in Massachusetts, one reason for moving on. But there was something in the nature of the industry for most of this period that kept many printers on the road as well.

In a 1912 article on the government of the ITU, George Barnett described one aspect of the industry that put those printers working in the job and book trades on the tramp. He wrote,

> Printing products are not standard goods like the goods produced by the cigar maker or the coal miner. They are made to order and the taste of the customer must be consulted. In the absence of a cheap means of communication, work ordinarily had to be done in the vicinity of the customer. As a consequence, demand in any particular locality varied greatly. During the sessions of the state and national legislatures, for example, it was formerly customary for printers to come to the capital city. Migration was, therefore, common among printers.[48]

This along with the slow growth of the ITU indicates that membership loss through withdrawal was not highest during recessions, but when members tramped.

It was also the case that the growing population and booming cities that spread across the nation called forth more daily newspapers, their number jumping from seven thousand in the 1870s to twelve thousand in the 1880s.[49] But even this work was often seasonal. The *Typographical Journal* reporting on conditions in Buffalo, New York, wrote in 1900, "The usual summer dullness has struck all the newspapers this month."[50] Printers employed by newspapers also shared jobs during good and bad times through a system of substitutes. The regular employee who controlled the "sit," that is his or infrequently her position in the printing firm, often took time off and chose a substitute. As Barnett noted in an earlier work, "The ease with which work as a substitute could be secured was partly responsible for the existence of a class of tramp printers who lived almost entirely by 'subbing.' These were known as "tourists."[51] Thus, like the union printers in the book and job sector, newspaper printers also had incentives to travel.

Printers were also affected by the general trend of much of industry to move from its small-town origins in an earlier period to the large cities, particularly in the Midwest, as industrialization and urbanization accelerated.[52] Samuel Donnelly, president of the International Typographical Union (ITU), testified that "the majority of printers in the large industrial centers come from country towns. They learn their trade in country newspaper offices." But industry had left those towns and moved to the cities where the erstwhile country printers "crowd out other workmen"—that is, other print workers. Thus, the country printer became a threat to the wages of those in the cities.[53] This was, in fact, a problem for many unionized workers. As the *Detroit Unionist* reported in 1882, "The country towns are the source from which come most of the non-union men . . . They leave their homes go to the cities, and when asked to go to work do so, with no intentions of doing wrong."[54] Yet, their presence put pressure on wage levels in the city. Sometimes, union members reversed this process. Printers, of course, also moved as disaster arose and new and better opportunities appeared. One ITU organizer reported to the union's 1890 convention, "In these days, too, competent printers remained in cities like Fargo and Bismarck, earning good wages, but departing when the boom crossed the mountains, leaving famine and wrecked speculation behind it."[55]

The seasonal nature of employment that caused tramping led to many printers working in "unorganized towns" according to one union organizer's report. This led to members withdrawing from the union. To correct this, this organizer proposed that "members working in unorganized towns should be properly registered at headquarters, and granted privileges now denied them . . . thus keeping them at all times in touch with the organization."[56] In other words, under the current rules of the union, members were leaving in significant numbers as they looked for work elsewhere. As we will see in a subsequent chapter, it was only toward the end of the nineteenth century, as the industry became concentrated in a relatively small number of larger cities, that the union secured growth and a more or less stable system of collective bargaining.

Mobile Machinist "Boomers"

If the printing trades were an old pursuit, then machinists, the historian Norman Ware reminds us, "were a product of the industrial revolution." As a builder of machines, Ware wrote, "He had to follow the machines he made and repaired."[57] The machinist, however, was also central to the railroad repair shop, and as David Montgomery writes, "Among the railway repair-shop machinists, transient 'boomers' were legendary." As on the railroads, so in the factories where they also worked, in the 1880s the machinists "defended their own notoriously migratory propensities as necessary for their self-education and for their economic security." It was their experience rather than a formal apprenticeship that made these machinists attractive to employers. As a letter in the industry's *American Machinist* argued, "A machinist who has travelled and worked in a variety of shops, is always a more valuable and desirable man than the one who has not."[58] One machinist who sought work away from home was the young Terence Powderly, later to be grand master workman of the Knights of Labor. In his autobiography, he recalled of the early 1870s,

> It used to be the custom in those days for machinists, not held back by home ties, to lend an attentive ear to the call of the wanderlust when the blue birds ventured north in the spring. In our shop were quite a few who had intimated

to me that they would like to 'go west' or somewhere with the opening of warm weather.[59]

Powderly would experience such a flight himself in 1873. Having lost several jobs as a result of being president of the Scranton, Pennsylvania, local of the Machinists and Blacksmiths International Union, he wrote, "I began a tramp through some of the western states in search of work." He continued, "In the hope of finding employment in Canada, I invaded that country in the winter of 1873–74, and walked the ties (the rails) from Windsor, Ontario, to Buffalo, New York, a distance of two hundred and fifty miles." He describes shoveling snow and driving a herd of pigs, but no work as a machinist across the border. He had "chosen" the depth of the depression for this journey and said he had "sampled in all its reality the desolation and misery of tramp life."[60]

The Molders' "Roving Habits"

Also drawn across the country as industry spread and grew was the iron molder, who made everything from stoves to parts for mechanical farm implements to the cast-iron facades of buildings. As one early history of the Iron Molders' Union put it, "Molders, like printers, have always been noted for their roving habits."[61] As a result, their union publication frequently ran stories about tramps and tramping. In 1880, for example, the *Iron Molders' Journal* reported that New York police were hunting down tramps, while the "capitalistic press" called them "pests of society." The journal attacked the mainstream press for lending "their venal pens to the support of the system that has produced these tramps."[62] A few years earlier, the same publication quoted a Rochester, New York, newspaper when it wrote, "It ought never to be lost sight of that the tramp is the legitimate outgrowth of our social system."[63]

The *Iron Molders' Journal* also carried frequent fictional stories of tramps, such as the redemptive story of Chip, Pat, and Tramp, who finally realize that working as an "*Independent*" (that is, nonunion) molder would make them "a barnacle on a ship's bottom." As a result, they joined in the reorganization of the local molders' union.[64] In a more poignant mood in 1877, the journal ran a poem titled "The Old Tramp." The old tramp had helped to "build up this nation" for "thirty years and more. Seventy-two are the years I've seen, / And twenty of them on the road I've been, / Thousands of miles have known my feet, / But I'm nearing, thank God, the end of the beat."[65] Of those tramps not belonging to the union, however, the *Molders' Journal* complained that same year, "Those drifters are the real bane of the working class."[66]

Part of the problem stemmed from the irregularity of work in the craft. Like about 40 percent of all manufacturing jobs by the 1880s,[67] iron molding in such important lines of production as cast-iron stoves and agricultural implements was seasonal or, as it was called then, "part-year" work. An 1886 article in the *Iron*

Molders' Journal remarked of shops "running steady the year around" that "such shops are exceptional instead of the rule."[68] After the spring production season, many members tramped country areas in search of work. This, even more than the recurrent depressions, was at the root of much tramping in this craft, and one of the Iron Molders' Union's major problems.

This seasonal aspect of the craft also affected bargaining, particularly in the winter down-season. In March 1877, the *Iron Molders' Journal* brought attention to the fact that tramping weakened the unions' position in the face of the predictable assault on wage levels. In an editorial it commented,

> The experience of the past four years has certainly convinced our members that it is not in the spring, summer, or early fall that our wages are attacked, but that it's in winter, when foundries are closing or closed, when the molder cannot well go on tramp, when work of all kinds is stopped, leaving the molder nothing to depend on but the foundry, then is when wages are attacked and too often successfully.[69]

Noting that the employers' attack will surely come in the winter, the journal continued that it "would be natural to suppose that all would prepare for the fight; not when it comes, but prepare *now* for the fight that is sure to come in nine months from now." But the editorial also warned, "The opening of spring will also start many of our members on tramp" and urged them to keep whatever job they had at the moment, as going on the road would only encourage the employers who welcome a "steady stream of molders" asking for work.[70] Once again, while going on the tramp with a traveling card might bring relief to the unemployed individual, it could also put pressure on wages in labor markets in which too many migrants sought work.

The "Traveling Fraternity"

In the late nineteenth century, cigar factories were located all over the country, serving mostly local markets, hence "the cigar maker is a wanderer," wrote one former member of the craft, looking back on his career in the early twentieth century. Another told interviewer Patricia Cooper, "They were great travelers. They'd work so long in a factory, then off they'd be."[71] While "hoboing" on a freight train was a sort of rite of passage for younger cigar makers, unlike the machinists and many others, the union cigar maker usually rode the train in the passenger car, for the Cigar Makers' International Union (CMIU) was one of only two or three unions that provided a traveling loan in addition to the traveling card, according to the Industrial Commission.[72] This loan consisted of the train fare to the next town in the direction the member wished to go, plus fifty cents for food, up to a maximum of eight dollars per trip.[73]

Table 3. Cigar Makers' International Union Traveling Loans, 1880–1903

Year	Membership	Travel Loans
1880	4,440	$2,806.15
1881	14,604	$12,747.09
1882	11,430	$20,386.64
1883	13,214	$37,135.20
1884	11,871	$39,632.08
1885	12,000	$26,683.54
1886	24,672	$31,835.71
1887	20,566	$49,281.04
1888	17,199	$42,894.75
1889	17,555	$43,540.44
1890	24,624	$37,914.72
1891	24,221	$53,535.73
1892	26,678	$47,732.47
1893	26,788	$60,475.11
1894	27,828	$42,154.17
1895	27,760	$41,657.16
1896	27,318	$33,076.22
1897	26,347	$29,067.22
1898	26,460	$25,257.43
1899	28,994	$24,134.33
1900	31,955	$33,238.13
1901	33,974	$44,652.73
1902	37,023	$45,314.05
1903	39,391	$52,521.41

* Does not include members traveling at the time of the count, which was for November from 1880 through 1883 and December of each year from 1884 onward.
Source: *Cigar Makers' Official Journal* (May 1904): 7.

Looking at figures in table 3 for traveling loans from the *Cigar Makers' Official Journal*, we can get a rough idea of the extent and pattern of tramping for the 1890s. Over eighteen years from 1879 to 1897, the CMIU spent $3,718,686, or 17 percent of all benefit payments, on travel loans.[74] The pattern also reveals that during the depressions, "cigar makers stayed home."[75] As table 3 shows, with the short depression of 1883–1885, the value and number of travel loans fell by 1885 and then with the recovery rose again. Even more sharply, with the deeper depression beginning in 1893 and hitting its low point in 1897, the number of loans declined by more than half.

This is the same as the pattern for printers and tells us, as we saw in the last chapter, that in general the rate of migration was in inverse proportion to periods of depression and high unemployment.

To aid traveling members, the *Cigar Makers' Official Journal* carried a monthly column called the "State of the Trade," which listed labor market conditions as "good," "fair," or "dull" in all the cities where it had local unions.[76] The CMIU also dispensed "out-of-work" benefits of three dollars a week up to a total of fifty-four dollars, according to CMIU founder Adolph Strasser.[77] This further helped to regulate the traveling system, and gave the individual a greater choice as to whether to stay at home when the trade was "dull" or to travel where it was said to be "good." To a greater extent than most US unions in this period, the CMIU had a comprehensive set of benefits designed to hold members. As Strasser told the Industrial Commission in 1899, "Prior to the establishment of the benefits I called the organization a pigeon coop—they were flocking in and out all the time; but now a member is going to lose something, and he will think twice before he allows himself to be suspended, for his family is thereby losing something."[78]

Despite this, during the 1880s membership fluctuated significantly, and the Industrial Commission reported, "During the three years ending September 1, 1896 (preceding the last convention) 16,576 members were initiated, and 13,075 were suspended."[79] Suspension was the term most unions used to describe what happened when a member no longer paid dues after a certain period. In other words, the union could lose almost as many members as it recruited despite the elaborate benefit system. Much of this loss must have been due to the holes in the traveling-loan and card system. Like other unions, the CMIU did not count traveling members in its official statistics, indicating it could not fully keep track of them.

"Birds of Passage"

Just as urbanization spread across the country and the railroad network increased in density, so in the years following the Civil War coal mining moved beyond its Pennsylvania origins into the Appalachians of the upper South; the central coalfields of Ohio, Indiana, and Illinois; and the far West to feed the iron and steel mills, fuel the spreading railroads, and heat the homes and workplaces of the nation's growing workforce.[80] From 1880 to 1889, coal production nearly doubled from 71,481,570 short tons to 141,229,513.[81] With the increased density and extension of the railway network by the 1890s, coal production was extended west and south, while regional markets for coal gave way to overlapping and national markets.[82] As a result, John McBride, a leader of one of two coal miner unions at that time, wrote in the mid-1880s, "The coal miner has been of necessity a bird of passage. Different seasons have found him in different localities, as the opportunities for work has offered."[83]

In addition, coal mining in this era was, like so many other industries, not a full-time, year-round job. So, John Mitchell, president of the United Mine Workers of America (UMWA), testified to the Industrial Commission in 1899, a year of economic growth, that due to constant overproduction "it is impossible for miners, even under the most favorable circumstances, to work more than two-thirds of the time."[84] As a result of this part-year work, Daniel Rodgers cites a Pennsylvania miner who had changed jobs five times in 1885, saying, "If I had stopped at one place, I should not have worked half of my time."[85] In the same year that Mitchell addressed the Industrial Commission, a Colorado coal miner testified that "the year before at the mine where I was working it was 11 days per month." He also pointed out that, "The introduction of machinery has displaced, I expect, about one third of the men that were employed in that district." When asked what happened to those men, he replied, "Oh, some go in the hills, some go on the farm, some go East, and some go West."[86]

Table 4. Average Annual Mining Wage by State, 1902

Bituminous Coal Mining

State	Average Annual Wage
Alabama	$606.45
Ohio	$642.85
Pennsylvania	$649.86
Iowa	$662.34
Kansas	$672.59
Illinois	$679.36
Colorado	$755.02
Wyoming	$764.25

Source: Bureau of the Census, *Abstract of the Twelfth Census of the United States, 1900,* 3rd ed. (Washington, DC: US Government Printing Office, 1904), 331–333, 352–350, 430–438.

With or without technological displacement or part-year work, the incentive to move westward to newer areas where mining labor was scarce and wages higher was strong. As table 4 shows, with the exception of Ohio, wages increased as one moved west into the newer coalfields. Furthermore, the table shows that although the United Mine Workers had a relatively stable membership by 1902, it still did not have the power to equalize wages across the different fields.

Beginning in the 1880s, coal miners from the East and from Europe followed the industry into the new, typically rural or unsettled areas where the wage differentials were at least as large as those in 1902. Towns and camps were thrown up by the coal barons, often the same people as the rail barons, with the "truck system" and its "pluck-me" company stores. Writing in his 1891 book, *Labor and Capital*, "the prominent and well known author" of such works as *History of Civilization* and *Bible Companion*, E. A. Allen, told the story of Spring Valley, a story he assured readers was typical in the newer coalfields. Spring Valley was a new mining community in Illinois set up in 1885 by a consortium of railroad investors. As was standard, they advertised for miners, assuring them of "steady work and good wages, where they could procure homes on most excellent terms." And the miners came from "as far away as Pennsylvania and Colorado, and even from Europe."[87]

Unions also followed but ran into several difficulties associated with a transient population that was often new, ethnically diverse, and unfamiliar with one another.

When the rail and coal entrepreneurs of Spring Valley had assembled a population of about five thousand, they determined to break the miners' union. To do this, they first closed three mines in December 1888 and then all the mines in April. Deprived of any income or assistance, Allen wrote of the miners, "Within a month nearly two-thirds of the men had scattered out in search of work elsewhere." In the end, he reported, "capital triumphed."[88] It triumphed not only by the defeat of the union in Spring Valley, but by the large numbers of miners who, as a result of that defeat, would subsequently flood other mining camps.

To a greater extent than that of the occupations discussed above, the migration of coal miners changed in ethnicity over time, complicating things even more. Beginning in the mid-1880s, emigration from eastern Europe and Italy increased rapidly. In 1899, UMWA president John Mitchell testified before the US Industrial Commission that nearly half the miners in the anthracite district could not speak English.[89] C. H. Cramp, a shipyard owner in Pennsylvania, testified at the same hearings concerning the mines near to his shipyard that "the miners at one time and all the laborers of the country here were Irish." But they had left, and now "their places were supplied" with "Poles and Huns," meaning Hungarians.[90] Also testifying before the commission that year was Benjamin James, a member of the executive board of the United Mine Workers, who reported that of the miners in the anthracite fields, "the largest number are Polish, Slavish, Lithuanians, Hungarians,

Italians, and many others."[91] When asked about "non-English-speaking foreigners" in the coalfields, he complained that they "are continually moving."[92] Like their English-speaking predecessors, they no doubt sought the higher wages in the new fields to the west. To the cycle of labor scarcity followed by a surplus was added the dimension of ethnic friction.

The mining camps and towns that spread across America in the Gilded Age bore no resemblance to the more stable English or Welsh "pit village" of the late nineteenth century. For one thing, the "truck system" of company stores and housing that characterized US mining camps and towns of this era had long been abolished by law in England.[93] The American coal-mining towns of the Gilded Age were shabbier and often temporary, their populations barely settled and more diverse, and their turnover higher, and because there was likely to be work in the next mining camp, a journey "on the tramp" facilitated by the same rail network that followed or led the opening of new coalfields seemed sensible.

"Coming and Going" in the Metal Mines of the West

Life in America's metal mining camps and towns in these years was, if anything, even more transient than that of the coal mines. For one thing, metal mines often went dry or became unprofitable if the world price of its output plunged. The fate of silver mining in Lawson, Colorado, for example, was described in the *Pueblo Courier* in 1898: "What a contrast there is between the silence of the mines and depopulation of the place today and the bustling, prosperous and happy community of a few years ago."[94] In any case, metal miners seldom stayed long on a job. One metal miner wrote in his memoirs that he was told by his fellow miners that three months on one job was about right.[95] Another "old-timer" explained that when that they were young, "We'd usually work one job for no more than a month or two, long enough to sample the cooking, wink at the waitresses, and make enough to carry us to the next camp." And lest there was any doubt about how they got around, he added, "No, we never paid to ride the train."[96] No wonder Bill Haywood, who was a vice president of the Western Federation of Miners (WFM) and later a leader of the IWW, said of his efforts to organize miners in Silver City, Colorado, "There was a continual coming and going." Indeed, Haywood himself worked in several mines in the West before and after Silver City.[97]

The roving habits of these miners often started far away from the western mines. The *Miners' Magazine*, official journal of the WFM, told the story of Paul Corcoran, a local leader of the WFM in Burke, Idaho, who by 1899 found himself sentenced to seventeen years in an Idaho prison for a shooting, the magazine said, he didn't do. Corcoran was born in County Sligo, Ireland, in 1865. At the age of twenty he moved to New York and, after a couple of years there, to Leadville,

Colorado, where he became a miner and "received his first lesson in unionism." Next he was off to the goldmines of South Africa, then back to Ireland for a time, where he married. In 1893 he and his wife moved to Granite City, Montana, and finally to Burke, where he became secretary of the local union. Burke, however, was under martial law as part of the effort to break the WFM in the Coeur d'Alene area, and Corcoran got the blame for a shooting that took place during that fight.[98] Fortunately, the WFM successfully campaigned for his pardon, and Big Bill Haywood reported receiving a cable from the union that read simply, "Paul pardoned."[99]

Table 5. Copper Ore Mining

State	Average Annual Wage, 1902
Michigan	$629.72
Arizona	$921.13
Montana	$1,148.99

Source: US Census Bureau, *Abstract of the Twelfth Census of the United States, 1900,* 3rd ed. (Washington, DC: US Government Printing Office, 1904),430–438.

Corcoran's story was probably more extreme than that of many western metal miners, but his origins abroad, his migration within the US, and his roving nature were typical of the trade. The workforce in metal mining was often drawn from areas where these workers had done similar mining, attracted by the higher wages in the West, shown in table 5. Finns came to Butte, Montana, via the copper and iron ore mines of Michigan, as did the "Cousin Jacks" from Cornwall. The "Cornish grapevine" was said to be the best recruiter, bringing "thousands of miners to America from Cornwall's declining tin-mining industry."[100] Less well known were the Irish hard-rock miners who followed a similar path from Ireland to Michigan and then to Montana, as cooper and tin mining declined in Ireland during the 1860s and 1870s.[101] Chinese workers also came to the western mines but were opposed by white miners who frequently attempted to drive them away, often violently. The miners, Wyman notes, were in a state of "continuous movement" from one mine to another.[102]

Boom and Bust in the Building Trades

To this stream of mobile labor must be added the construction workers who followed the growth of towns and cities across the country. Indeed, in these years the basic infrastructure of industrial capitalism and its burgeoning urban centers was built. By 1900, 63 percent of all building trades companies were located in the country's 209 largest cities. The construction industry, however, was cyclical in nature. In real terms, new building permits rose by 282 percent between 1880 and 1892 to an index level of 84 (1913 = 100), then slowed down to an average of 61 during the depression of the 1890s. Nevertheless, as Montgomery argues, "Even during the worst years of the depression, new commercial buildings and urban street car lines continued to be constructed."[103] Those employed in construction rose from 900,000 in 1880 to 1,510,000 in 1890, increasing by 40 percent, while from 1890 to 1900 employment continued to grow, but at a much slower rate, by another 155,000 jobs, or an increase of 10 percent.[104] As a result, for example, the United Brotherhood of Carpenters and Joiners, which had grown from a mere 2,042 members at its founding in 1881 to a high of 56,937 in 1891, then fell to 28,269 in 1897 before rising again to 68,463 in 1899.[105] Even within this fluctuation, the frequent "boom-bust" cycles of construction led not only to migration but also to constant labor surpluses as work came to an end for a time and building workers of all kinds kept flowing in. Writing of carpenters in this period, Jules Tygiel observed that the spread of new towns and the expansion of older ones "launched building booms which increased job opportunities in a given city." He continued,

> Once the boom had run its course, most of these men were no longer needed to meet the normal demands of the local market. But, as employment de-clined in one area, the cycle was repeated in another. In order to find work, it was therefore necessary for building tradesmen to travel from place to place, buffeted by the vicissitudes of a growing urban nation.[106]

This, in turn, however, led to overcrowding of the next local labor market. A Kansas City carpenter wrote to the union's magazine, "The city is flooded with carpenters from other cities."[107] Sometimes this inhibited the organization of a local of the Carpenters. Tygiel writes that a report from Cheyenne, Wyoming, in 1882 lamented that "it is hard to start [a union] up owing to the roving disposition car-penters get after coming West."[108]

The bricklayers offer another example of almost constant movement as cities grew. As Lloyd Ulman pointed out, there were occasionally "abnormally prosper-ous conditions" in some markets, and the union published notices of these places. The locals in those areas didn't appreciate this because they feared a rapid flooding of their market and an end to the favorable economic conditions. Like the carpen-ters, bricklayers were drawn to rapidly growing cities and the higher wages they promised. This created the problem of too many bricklayers migrating to areas of higher wages, thus depressing those wages. The president of the bricklayers told the 1867 convention that these higher wages "cannot long be maintained without a corresponding increase in other cities adjacent to them, because there is an imme-diate rush to obtain the higher wages, and all our efforts are neutralized." Chicago, for example, was described by the union's secretary in 1899 as "the dumping ground for all bricklayers going West, and those traveling East, thereby being subjected to a greater influx of men than other cities."[109] The movement of these organized workers from the East to the Midwest cities in the trail of capital accumulation and urbanization is part of the explanation for the phenomenal growth of these urban-industrial centers in this period noted above, but also of the instability of union membership in the building trades. Thus, although union membership in construction soared in the 1880s, union density actually fell in the 1890s as the number of building workers outstripped union membership.[110]

Harvests of Grain and Ice

Seasonal migratory workers that followed the harvests or other jobs to create serial employment seldom even had the aid of a union traveling card. Their job "security" depended, above all, on the railroad network that unfolded in this era. Frank Higbie argues, "Railroads tightly tracked the location of seasonal jobs, services and homes, and they were the most common mode of travel until inexpensive automobiles came on the market in the mid-1920s."[111] Mark Wyman points out there were numerous crops that required transient labor across the West in the closing decades of the nineteenth century. One of the most prominent was the annual wheat harvest, which drew an estimated one hundred thousand workers. Summarizing its sweep, Wyman writes, "The annual wheat harvest began in the Texas and Oklahoma fields in early summer, edged steadily northward as the grain was ripening at some twenty-five miles a day, and ended in the autumn fields of Saskatchewan."[112] Looking back nostalgically, the North Dakota correspondent of *Country Gentleman* wrote in the 1920s, "Like a flock of swallows that come in the springtime, they harvest the wheat and then vanish into the unknown again."[113]

Probably more typical, however, were those who moved from one area of casual labor to another, often in a pattern they would repeat year after year. Higbie writes,

> During the late nineteenth and early twentieth centuries, millions of people worked in highly seasonal occupations, piecing together a living by whatever means they could find. These were young immigrant and American-born men—often called floaters or hoboes—who worked in logging, crop harvesting, construction, and other seasonal industries.[114]

The list of industries that depended on these transient laborers tells us why they were so indispensable in this period. They were producing the raw materials that fed and housed America's less transient population.[115]

Gunther Peck provides a description of how one immigrant worker fit into this pattern of iterant work:

To newly arrived Greek immigrant Harry Mantos, the North American West was less a particular fixed place than a process of constant movement. Like a well-polished ball in a pin-ball machine, Mantos rapidly bounced from job to job between 1906 and 1909. He began laying railroad track near Salt Lake City, Utah, then took a water-main construction job in Twin Falls, Idaho, and later a position loading mail for the Union Pacific Railroad Company in Green River, Wyoming, before securing a position as a cooper mucker in Bingham, Utah, that summer. The next year brought more movement.[116]

Using testimony from the 1915 *US Commission on Industrial Relations*, Higbie traced the migration routes of three itinerant workers. Although these stories take place in the beginning of the twentieth century, the circuits described would have been well trodden in the last decades of the nineteenth as well. One showed a worker traveling form Galveston, Texas, to the harvests in Nebraska and North Dakota, followed by railroad work in Minnesota, an urban rest in Saint Louis and Kansas City, and then another round of harvest work in Kansas and Oklahoma. Another found construction work in Milwaukee, then went north for the ice harvest, a week's rest in Milwaukee, and then railroad work up north.[117]

Less well known than the agricultural harvests, the Great Lakes ice harvest deserves some attention. Here ice was cut from the lakes to chill meat in Chicago's stockyards and in the trains that carried it eastward, as well as being exported as far as India. As Marco d'Eramo describes it, "To meet the demand, thousands of ice cutters were packed off to the frozen lakes in the middle of winter, with additional thousands of laborers needed to construct infrastructure (roads, depots, accommodation huts for themselves) and still thousands more to maintain them." The invention and application of refrigeration, however, eventually put an end to this "industry."[118]

As Higbie points out, these itinerant workers combined urban and rural work and rest. For these migrants, unemployment was usually voluntary. Marc Rodriguez notes that the routes of these migrants were not from east to west, but were typically circular in nature, allowing for serial employment.[119] Paul Douglas's 1918 study showed the average duration of a job in the lumber camps was fifteen to thirty days, construction ten days, in harvesting seven days, and orchard work seven to ten days.[120] All of this made unionization of migratory workers extremely difficult. J. B. Dale, an organizer of day laborers in California for the American Federation of Labor, told the 1915 Industrial Commission that after four years of organizing, "there is not many agricultural—that is, men that work on the ranches, that belong to these organizations so far." As far as collective bargaining for California fruit workers went, he said, "It had not reached that point."[121] Not until the second decade of the twentieth century did the Industrial Workers of the World succeed in mobilizing, if not quite organizing, migrant farmworkers in the grain harvests of the Great Plains, and then only temporarily.[122]

Industrial Laborers

The unskilled laborer, of course, was not limited to harvests, or railroad construction. Although nineteenth-century statistics do not make a separate count of them, the 1900 census, the first to distinguish between farm and industrial laborers, reports 3,620,000 manual laborers (except farm and mine) and another 5,125,000 farm laborers and foremen.[123] Nevertheless, these figures hardly capture the reality of the size of this labor force. As David Montgomery writes of the common laborers,

> In the researches of quantitative students of social mobility, they simply disappear in droves between one census and the next. They moved continually, and unlike the iron puddler or railroad machinist who might also rove about in search of work, laborers belonged to no particular industry. On the contrary, they were necessary to all forms of manufacturing, transportation, and commerce.[124]

Writing in 1905 much closer to that time, Edith Abbott offered a similar assessment of the unskilled laborer: "Whether a common laborer, coal-wheeler, teamster, or a man policing a machine, he is in high degree an unspecialized worker, who is not really bound within the limits of any industrial, or even occupational, group. He is a kind of free-lance in the labor world, a man who hunts for a 'job' irrespective of its character." His existence is "precarious," while "unskilled has come to be in a measure synonymous with unorganized and underpaid," Abbott wrote.[125] Indeed, as of 1880 the daily wages of the unskilled amounted to 58 percent of those of the average skilled worker.[126] In addition, these workers were part of the army of "floaters" who filled unskilled jobs in areas of new development. Writing of Chicago's growth as an industrial and railroad center, Richard Schneirov said, "Employers could now draw on the nation's floating reserve labor force, consisting of recently arrived immigrants, tramping artisans, and the poor and unemployed generally."[127] These were workers who were sure to be seen as tramps and vagrants by middle-class observers.

Some unskilled workers did organize unions. Chicago's workshop inspector estimated that the city had a workforce of "open-air" laborers of twenty thousand who circulated from one outdoor job to another in warm weather and worked in the meatpacking plants in winter. Among these the salt shovelers, lumber shovers, and brick makers all had unions, although they were small in comparison to the workforce, and it is impossible to say how durable or effective they were.[128] Montgomery notes that those common laborers who worked on the docks often organized by ethnicity or race.[129] Tens of thousands joined the mixed assemblies of the

Knights of Labor in the 1880s, mostly for a brief time. But the vast majority remained outside organized labor both by their exclusion from most craft unions as
well as by their circumstance. John Mitchell, president of the United Mine Workers
at the turn of the century, which did organize the unskilled in the mines, said that
"in this question of the unskilled lies the very essence of the trade-union problem."[130]

The unskilled worker, moreover, lacked the bargaining power associated with
a relatively high level of skill. The less-skilled worker's source of power lay in the
informal work group and the gang structure of most common labor, whether that
was in railroad maintenance, building construction, "ditch digging," or factory
work. It was just such groups that Frederick Winslow Taylor identified in the 1880s
at Midvale Steel and whose behavior he called "soldiering"—the ability of a group
of workers to set the pace of work and hence output. Taylor later explained how
this worked to a committee of the House of Representatives in 1912: "We who were
the workmen of that shop had the quantity output carefully agreed upon for everything we turned out in the shop. We limited the output to about, I should think,
one-third of what we could very well have done."[131]

The fight to restrict output was a form of resistance that could unite those
who did not share a craft culture, one that was rooted in collective self-interest
and the organization of work itself. Also, this form of resistance was important
precisely because less-skilled workers who went on strike were too easily replaced.
The linking together of such work groups was the key to organizing the less skilled.
But building such informal primary groups required trust and at least a core of
more or less permanent workers to give continuity and bind the group together.
Laborers who "moved constantly," as Montgomery put it, were in a poor position
to do this. Here was a case of "fight or flight," and while we have no way to measure
the frequency of either among unskilled workers, it seems clear that while tran-
sience might bring relief to some, it undoubtedly undermined the binding of the
collective in many cases. The high turnover rate for many jobs in this era also points
to this problem.

All of the groups of workers we have looked at not only showed a tendency
to tramp or migrate but also revealed a high turnover of employment that both resulted from and encouraged migration. This constant movement posed a threat to
the wage levels as the "frontier of labor scarcity" inevitably gave way to the "crowding" of the labor market in one place after another. If he or she was lucky enough to
be a union member, the traveling card might help the individual worker get a job in
the next town or city, but it could not blunt the downward pressure on wages and
on union organization that the constant movement of workers created. So, workers
in the Gilded Age created an additional means of trying to gain some measure of
control over this flow of labor in the various publications that characterized the
labor movement of the late nineteenth century.

A Gilded-Age Social Network: The "Keep Away" Notice

The network of labor newspapers discussed in chapter 1 represented an important aspect of the self-activity, or the agency, side of the process of class formation following the Civil War. This communications web not only served as a forum for political debate, a means of education, and a disseminator of news, but also as a method of controlling the constant flow of workers, both union and nonunion, across the country. Its existence forms one of the most concrete pieces of evidence of a contemporary awareness of the universal nature of tramping and migration. At the center of the labor press was what I will call the "keep away" notice.

The "keep away" notice addressed all aspects of migration and traveling in national, regional, and local labor markets. Its purpose was to inform traveling workers or those intending to travel of where labor markets were "crowded," where work was "dull," and where strikes and lockouts were in progress. Individual unions employed the notice to overcome the ignorance of their members about conditions in different regions that led to wasted traveling. In his 1886 book, *The Labor Movement in America*, economist Richard T. Ely, explained that "the trades-unions, and other agencies of the labor movement, such as the labor press, assist the laborer to find the best market for his commodity."[132] Stromquist notes that the railroad brotherhoods, the unions of the running crews, provided "information on conditions of employment and availability of work in various parts of the country" through their journals.[133] More frequently, union papers warned of places to "keep away" from. In 1884, the *Molders' Journal,* for example, advised, "Molders should steer clear of Troy, Albany, Cincinnati and Quincy for the present, and all other places where there is any trouble."[134] In one of the most difficult strike or lockout situations of the late 1890s, the Coeur d'Alene miners' strike in Idaho, the *Miners' Magazine* of the Western Federation of Miners wrote, "We earnestly appeal to all labor unions, particularly the labor unions of the Western Federation of Miners, to do all in their power to keep men away from the Coeur d'Alenes."[135] Official union publications of one union might also carry such warnings from other unions, as when the *Typographical Journal* countered the Coeur d'Alene mine owners' ads in Michigan, Ohio, and elsewhere for scab miners, writing, "Those now working are practically slaves, and it is not believed that eastern miners will give much, if any, heed to the elusive ads of the Coeur d'Alene slave-drivers."[136] Union papers also reported on employment conditions in places where work was scarce. The Knights of Labor's *Journal of United Labor* carried an 1885 report from a district assembly in Kansas that warned, "I would caution all Knights of Labor who are looking towards some other land, whereby they can go and better their condition, not to consider Kansas that promised land."[137] The most consistent source of information for cigar makers was undoubtedly the *Cigar Makers' Official Journal,* with its "State of the Trade" column.

The independent labor papers, with their "keep away" notices, however, reached across the whole movement. Such notices usually appeared simultaneously in several papers around the country. Probably the most common notice had to do with local economic conditions related to periods of depression or fluctuations on the world market that affected a particular area, where conditions were described as "dull." While they tended to be more frequent during the many economic downturns, these notices would appear to one degree another at all times to address the problems of different groups of workers. They also informed workers of where strikes were taking place or where employers were attempting to "crowd" the local labor market.

One such notice, published in the Detroit *Labor Leaf* in 1884, addressed specifically to the situation in the New York printing trades, read, "Job printing business is very dull in New York and printers are advised to keep away from there."[138] A notice directed at both skilled and unskilled workers said, "Laborers and mechanics are requested to keep away from Owoso, Mich. owing to the fact that work is scarce."[139] In early 1884, the *National Labor Tribune*, published in Pittsburgh, concluded, "Trade is generally dull throughout the country."[140] Addressing the potential tramping that sometimes accompanied economic downturns, the *Labor Leaf* advised later in 1884, "Business all over the country in all trades is dull. It is better to stay where you are and save your shoes than it is to tramp through the country and wear them out."[141] Occasionally, under better circumstances, notices might appear such as those announcing, for example, that the shoe business and cabinet making in Detroit were "brightening."[142] More frequent, however, were those like the notices in the Denver *Labor Enquirer* as the depression unfolded in 1883: "Omaha, Nebraska has more molders than can find employment" or "reports from the principal centers indicate a general dullness in the shoe trade."[143] In a longer editorial, the *Enquirer* in July of that year bemoaned that "the workingmen of our country are roaming from place to place seeking to better their condition, but it is lost time and labor in vain."[144] Even in better times, the labor press could report on the irregularity of work common in many industries often far away. The *Patterson Labor Standard* in New Jersey, for example, noted in May 1882 that "the miners in Zanesville, Iowa, have about one day's work in seven."[145]

Also addressing labor market conditions were warnings of employer efforts to "crowd" or flood a local labor market in order to reduce wages by raising supply well above demand. A notice in the *Labor Leaf*, for example, addressed employer ads for "a large number of men to work in lumber districts of Michigan. Good wages; steady work; pay certain." The ads were false, the *Leaf* said: "There are thousands of idle men in the State and you stand a splendid chance to join the vast army of tramps if you get here without money."[146] Similarly, from the *Detroit Unionist*, "All bricklayers are requested to keep away from Omaha, Neb., as the contractors are making an effort to reduce wages."[147]

Efforts to reduce strikebreaking, or even unintentional pressure on local strikers, included those notices advising workers of strikes in various places. In April 1883, the Denver *Labor Enquirer* wrote, "Molders should keep away from Pittsburgh, Pennsylvania, as a strike is in progress at the place."[148] Again, a couple of weeks later, "At Kansas City the molders are still out and both sides seem determined not to yield. Molders should steer clear of there."[149] In a similar vein, the *Detroit Unionist* warned printers, "Let 'tourists' keep away from New Haven, Ct. Both the *Courier* and *Paladium* have been closed by the union."[150] This Gilded-Age social network also provided a way to raise support for strikes. Joseph Buchanan, editor of the *Labor Enquirer*, related how he used the paper to raise funds for the 1884 strike of Union Pacific shop men. Like other local labor papers, the *Enquirer* had a national circulation. Buchanan wrote in his memoir, "'The Enquirer' had subscribers in every state of the Union—in fact, its 'outside' circulation, including Colorado towns, was larger than that at home; and through the paper considerable money was sent to the strike committee."[151]

Although it was probably unusual, one union addressed the problem of tramping by encouraging readers of the *Detroit Unionist* to join the Harness, Saddle, and Collar Makers' Union, stating the advantages of union membership. They wrote,

> It is a grand thing when one of us goes to a distant city in search of work to meet friends who will shake you warmly by the hand, instead of trying to discourage you and get you out of town for fear you will get his job. Union obliterates all of this bitter feeling to strangers when seeking employment at strange places, and besides saves all this unnecessary tramping over the country in search of work, as all unions will be posted as to where there is work, the kind of men required, and the price for the work.[152]

It is not possible to determine just how effective all these appeals and notices were. Although Buchanan's strike appeal appears to have been successful, keeping workers already on the tramp away from some area where a strike was on or trade was "dull" was certainly another matter. The fact that the practice continued throughout the period, however, indicates that many thought it made a difference. Included among those with an optimistic view of the labor market role of the labor press was economist Richard T. Ely, who wrote in 1886, "This idea of labor-market reports is certain to have a further and a beneficial development in the future."[153] What is perhaps equally important, however, is that the effort was made to broadcast across the country, as well as in Canada, and at times over the Atlantic, promoting a general class consciousness and broader understanding of the volatile nature of the capitalist labor market of the day to the thousands who read these papers, as well as those to whom the readers passed on the information.

Conclusion

In this chapter we have seen that those who did the work and those who observed or studied them were well aware of the necessity of migration and tramping. If many middle- and upper-class people thought the tramps a social problem, most of those who migrated for employment knew well they were not vagrants but wage-workers in search of better pay, better conditions, or just employment. Not only skilled workers such as printers, cigar makers, machinists, and iron molders constantly sought employment in new places, but, as we have seen, hordes of mostly unskilled and uncounted itinerant laborers moved across and around the country. Thus, the Gilded-Age tramp was not primarily a vagrant or the hapless Charlie Chaplin character, but was far more likely to be a worker than a shirker and was often even a union member. Ravenstein's observation about the wandering proclivities of "native" Americans, as compared to Europeans, was wrong in only one respect. The tramp or the migrant was as likely to be a transplanted European as a native-born American. It was not, as participants themselves often said, the roving disposition or habits of this or that occupation that created a level of migration many times that of Britain, but the contradictory processes of rapid industrialization and urbanization that drew millions on an industrial trek across a continent and sometimes, as Robert Louis Stevenson saw firsthand, back again.[154]

Chapter 4

THE RISE, FALL, AND REVIVAL OF ORGANIZED LABOR

Looking at the past fate of unions of various kinds, does it not
seem as if the order were growing too fast to be permanent?
—J. F. Bray of Pontiac, Michigan, in the
Labor Leaf, November 11, 1885

T
HE "NOBLE and Holy Order of the Knights of Labor" was America's
first truly mass working-class organization. Unlike the craft unions that
arose more slowly alongside it, the Knights of Labor, or simply "the order," as it was often called, welcomed the skilled and the unskilled of all
trades. Its doors were opened to immigrants and the native-born, to African American and women workers as well. It stumbled only on the "Chinese question."[1] It
challenged the wage system and sought a cooperative commonwealth, a position
that Eleanor Marx and Edward Aveling thought to be "pure and unadulterated socialism."[2] Though never officially socialist and almost more a social movement than
a trade union, the Knights nevertheless contained some of the era's most effective
socialist and trade-union organizers. Founded in 1869, its growth really began in
the wake of the 1877 railroad strike, accelerating during the first half of the 1880s
and then exploding in 1886. Its leap from 111,395 members in 1885 to 729,677 in
1886 astounded labor's friends and enemies alike.

The escalation of strikes mostly initiated by its members from 645 in 1885 to
1,432 the next year, in what became known as the "Great Upheaval," surpassed the
great railroad strike of 1877 and brought forth a powerful reaction from organized
capital. The launch of labor parties by the Knights' local and district assemblies in
1886–1888, often in alliance with local trade unions across the country, stoked the
political hopes of labor and commanded the attention of mainstream politicians.
For a moment, these political efforts undermined the two-party system in several
industrial cities, forcing realignment along class lines. It was the proof that American workers were not adverse to unionization, striking, or class-based politics despite the racial and ethnic divisions and tensions of the era. As Eleanor Marx and

117

Edward Aveling reported on their visit to the US in 1886, "The real significance of all this lies in the fact that in the Knights of Labor we have the first spontaneous expression by the American working people of their consciousness of themselves as a class."[3] Yet almost as soon as it peaked in 1886, it began to decline, and by the early 1890s it ceased to be an important factor in the labor movement.[4]

This chapter will analyze the underlying trends and forces that explain both the Knights' growth and decline as well as the slow growth of the trade unions during the period. In fact, two distinct patterns of labor organization appeared from the late 1870s through the 1890s. The first pattern was set by the Knights of Labor with its rapid growth and subsequent decline. The high point of economic growth, population movement, employment turnover, and the hardening of class lines in the 1880s contributed to both the escalating growth and underlying weakness of the Knights of Labor that led to this decline. In contrast, for many trade unions, a pattern emerged of slow growth and considerable member turnover during the period of greatest economic turbulence from 1873 into the mid- or late 1890s, followed by some stabilization once prosperity returned and capital had settled down and adopted the organizational norms and locations that would characterize the early to mid-twentieth century. As Shelton Stromquist and Richard Schneirov both argue, the high and costly level of intense labor conflict from 1877 onward into the mid-1890s, involving three upsurges in capital–labor conflict (1877, 1886–1887, 1892–1894), may well have been a factor leading some employers to attempt more regular relations with their employees' organizations.[5] This in turn allowed the increased institutionalization of trade unions through established collective bargaining arrangements toward the end of the Gilded Age.

The years 1886 and 1887 saw the most rapid escalation of class conflict of the period as the number of strikes and union members more than doubled between 1885 and 1886. The Great Upheaval was one of those "leaps" in working-class activity that Eric Hobsbawm identifies, comparable to that in Britain in 1889–1890, Scandinavia and Russia in 1905–1907, and the US in 1936–1937. Arguing that the ups and downs of the economy do not explain these, he suggests, "Perhaps the most useful assumption is that, under nineteenth- and early twentieth-century conditions, the normal process of industrial development tends to produce explosive situations, i.e., accumulations of inflammable material which only ignite periodically, as it were under compression."[6]

"Compression," characterized by intensified labor performed over long hours, two years of wage cuts, irregular employment for unpredictable periods, and the realization by most that their status as wageworker was now permanent, well described the moment.

The recovery that commenced by mid-1885 provided the possibility of improvement. The universal "solution" or palliative, already widely embraced, was the shorter workday—the eight-hour day. Thus, a common goal already existed. Successful high-profile strikes by the Knights of Labor on the Union Pacific Railroad in 1884, in the lumber mills of Michigan's Saginaw Valley in 1885, and across Jay Gould's Southwest railroad system also in 1885 provided the spark of encouragement that ignited the explosion, not only of more strikes but also in the acceleration of the boycott and the sympathy strike as widespread forms of solidarity, and the launching of local and state labor parties across the country. The Federation of Organized Trades and Labor Unions, at the behest of P. J. Maguire of the Carpenters, had provided the timing by setting May 1, 1886, as the date when labor as a whole would establish the eight-hour day by direct action.[7] As James Green put it, "Many of the workers who flooded into the new assemblies of the Knights of Labor said they were joining the union so they could prepare for the strike on the great day to come."[8] At the same time, many, like the 1884 Union Pacific strikers and those in the Saginaw Valley in 1885, struck first and joined later in the wake of victory. As Commons et al. summarized this, "They struck first and joined the Knights of Labor afterwards."[9]

Although most unions grew during the Great Upheaval, it was the Knights that saw its membership rolls soar from 111,395 in July, 1885 to 729,677 in July 1886—in terms of "members in good standing" from 104,066 to 702,924.[10] That is, some 600,000 workers had poured into the Knights in one year. Overall, organized labor had grown from 492,793 members to 1,197,739 as the number of strikes rose from 645 in 1885 to 1,432 in 1886. The upheaval would last through 1887 with 1,436 strikes and the proliferation of labor-party efforts across the country. Yet, in the midst of the upheaval, by July 1887, the membership of the Knights fell precipitously, with a loss of 191,573 members in good standing. A year later it had lost another 289,733 of those in good standing.[11] There was no economic depression throwing thousands out of work as in 1873 or 1893, no massive military intervention, while, according to Currie and Ferrie, "Injunctions generally came into effect only after 1886," most of them in the 1890s.[12] What then caused this sudden collapse of the era's most promising labor organization?

Naturally, this has been grist for the mill of historical debate. Among the explanations for the rapid decline of the Knights are the flight of unskilled workers, the loss of strikes, the aftermath of the Haymarket bombing, internal factionalism, the fight with the AFL, and poor leadership. John R. Commons et al. tended to argue that it was the collapse of mixed assemblies of unskilled workers on the one hand and the flight of skilled workers into the superior craft unions of the AFL on the other that led to rapid decline.[13] Norman Ware suggested the events of 1886, such as the loss of the second Southwest railroad strike, the failure of the eight-hour strikes, and the Haymarket bombing, but in his final analysis he seemed to blame the Powderly leadership for having "enlarged the breach between the general officers and the rank and file."[14] Robert Weir raised the question as to whether the intense factionalism within the Knights' leadership might have played an important role—although in the end he rejected this idea.[15] Kim Voss also rejected the idea that internal factionalism destroyed the order, asking whether such conflict was "a cause or a symptom of collapse."[16]

Internal conflict does not provide much of an answer, since it was and is common to many unions, almost none of which experienced this sort of decline. More importantly, the timing is off. As is often the case, it is failure that accelerates factionalism. Although differences were manifest within the Knights between Powderly and the pro-trade-union forces led by Joseph Buchanan and others, Powderly had actually given Buchanan an organizers' commission after the Richmond General Assembly in 1886. Matters escalated when Powderly withdrew the commission in February 1887 and became open in the spring when Burnette Haskell, an associate of Buchanan's in the socialist International Workingmen's Association, presented a "bill of particulars" against Powderly for insufficient support to strikes and the eight-hour movement, failure to support the Chicago Haymarket anarchists' case, expulsion of the cigar makers, and other complaints. The many differences within the Knights of Labor leadership did not take an organized form until after the October 1887 General Assembly when the Provisional Committee of the Knights of Labor was formed by opponents of the Powderly leadership, well after the collapse began.[17] Indeed, according to Richard Oestreicher's calculation based on quarterly per capita tax (dues) payments, the order had already lost over sixty thousand members by October 1886, three months after it reached its peak in July. By January 1887 it had lost over one hundred thousand, so that decline was obvious well before the October 1887 convention where factionalism exploded, in part because of the decline already underway.[18]

The tone in Powderly's opening addresses in 1886 and 1887 could hardly have been more different, the former consisting of four pages of more or less straightforward reports with a few defensive complaints and even a plea not to reelect him if the delegates didn't have faith in him, the latter consisting of sixty-three pages of recorded "documentation" and bombast to justify his leadership and attack his opponents.[19] Joseph Labadie of Detroit, an opponent of Powderly's, in his report to District Assembly 50 on the 1887 General Assembly pointed to the loss of two hundred seventeen thousand members over the past year, which he blamed on the leadership. In describing what he called the "inharmony" of the meeting, he wrote, "The most illogical, cowardly, brutal and violent speeches made came from the general master workman himself"—that is, Powderly.[20] While differences had been festering for some time, it was the visible decline of the organization that accelerated the internal conflict—more a "symptom of the collapse" than a cause, as Voss suggested.

In fact, most internal explanations are too superficial to help and, in any case, can be attributed to many labor organizations throughout the history of organized labor that didn't collapse, the Cigar Makers of the late 1870s and early 1880s being a good example of intense factionalism and union survival.[21] The Haymarket bombing is often seen as the cause of the counterassault and of the rapid decline of the Knights.

Indeed, Samuel Gompers expressed this view. He told the Industrial Commission in 1899, "The effect of that bomb was that it not only killed the policemen, but it killed our 8-hour movement for that year and a few years after."[22] Writing of Chicago, where the reaction to Haymarket would have been most intense, Richard Schneirov argued a different position: "Yet, contrary to the myth, started by labor leaders themselves, the success of the antilabor reaction was highly selective. Generally, those strikes that resorted to crowd actions, like Bisno's garment workers' strike, succumbed to police attack. Many other strikes, however, were well organized and could not be so easily crushed by overt action."[23]

Strikes not only continued but grew in frequency into 1887 and were more often called by the unions.[24] Speaking specifically of the Knights, John R. Commons et al. argued that the upsurge of 1886–1887 actually "resulted in a considerable number of trade agreements with employers' associations and individual employers." Although this was not the norm, "Trade agreements multiplied, especially beginning with 1887."[25] At the same time, the Knights and other working-class organizations turned to the formation of labor parties to counter capital's attacks. To be sure, in the war of words that followed the bombing, employers, authorities, and the mainstream press would use Haymarket against the Knights and unions, but the actual struggles that followed were matters of power more than propaganda.

Another explanation, basically that of Commons et al. mentioned above, was that the decline of the Knights was a result of the rising conflict with the AFL and subsequent exit of skilled workers to the craft unions that would form the AFL in December 1886. For all the intensity of the fight over the Cigar Makers' Union labels in 1886, at the grassroots this fight was largely limited to New York at least until 1887, while Knights of Labor and trade unions continued to work together in local trades assemblies around the country for some time. Furthermore, the decline actually began even before the expulsion of the Cigar Makers from the Knights in October 1886. While the conflict did intensify in 1886 and after, the idea that this drove large numbers of Knights into the AFL trade unions is dubious because the numbers don't hold up. From July 1886 to July 1887, the Knights lost nearly 200,000 members, but the AFL unions gained only 22,000 from 1886 to 1887. By 1888 the Knights lost another 181,438 members, but again the AFL saw a rise of only 15,000 that year. Even if we extend this to 1889, the total gain of AFL members from 1886 was only 72,000, while the loss to the Knights was over half a million, so that only a small proportion of this could be explained by craft union or AFL growth, particularly since at least some of their growth was rooted in their own organizing efforts.

Of course, some Knights did move into AFL unions after the rapid decline began after July 1886, while many who had been joint members of both the Knights and their own craft union, such as Gompers himself, left the Knights of Labor during these years. This contributed somewhat to the Knights' losses, but the scale of this shift in 1886–1887 was not large enough to explain the Knights' precipitous decline or change the level of membership in the craft unions much. Nor did most of the fleeing Knights go into unaffiliated trade unions, where membership dropped from 354,193 in 1886 to 181,025 in 1889. Altogether, organized labor lost nearly half a million members from 1886 through 1888, mostly from the Knights, and only in 1889 did membership in the trade unions begin to grow gradually.[26]

The other problem with the escalating fight between the Knights and the AFL as a cause of the Knights of Labor's initial decline is, once again, the timing. Looking at Detroit, for example, Oestreicher notes that the relations between the largely AFL Trades Council and the Knights of Labor District Assembly 50 "were quite amicable" and that they worked together on many projects through 1886. Hence, "until the end of 1886, a semblance of unity was maintained." Only in the spring 1887, as factionalism escalated nationally, did it become "literally impossible to hold any labor gathering in Detroit without engaging in factional debate."[27] The rapid decline of Knights membership, however, began by mid-1886, well before hostilities broke out. In Chicago, representatives of Knights of Labor Local Assemblies continued to attend and work with the Chicago Trades and Labor Assembly (CT&LA) into 1888, until in the spring of that year Knights of Labor Local Assemblies finally withdrew from the CT&LA when that body sided with the AFL Cigar Makers' International Union on the label question.[28] The loss of members in Chicago, however, began well before the split.

The one factor underlying this rapid decline that most historians seem to agree on, even if they give it different rankings, is the counteroffensive of capital that began in 1886 and accelerated into the mid-1890s. Commons et al. stated,

> While a share of this retrogression may have been due to the natural reaction of large masses of people who had been suddenly set in motion without experience, a more immediate cause came from the employers. Profiting from the lessons of May, they organized strong associations and began a policy of discriminations and lockouts, directly mainly against the Knights.[29]

Schneirov places the wave of employer opposition prior to May 1886. He writes,

> The employers' attempt to turn back the gains of the labor movement actually began with the failed strike by the Knights against Jay Gould's southwest

railroad system in March through May, 1886. This strike triggered the sudden growth of law and order leagues in small Midwestern railroad towns. During and after the eight hour strikes the employers' movement broadened into, in the words of historian Clarence Bonnett, "a tidal wave of formation of employers' associations."[30]

Weir sums it up when he argues, "For all the many shortcomings in the Knights of Labor's structure, its decision-making processes, and its leaders, I believe the Knights of Labor was done in by opposition, not primarily by structural or ideological ineptitude." The opposition he refers to came primarily from "the fury of capital's counterassault" as well as the state and the press that backed capital's offensive.[31] Voss draws a similar conclusion, particularly in relation to skilled workers, writing, "Instead, the mobilization of employer opposition, especially against skilled craft workers who maintained their allegiance to the Knights in the hostile years following the Haymarket bombing, was the most important reason for the decline of the Knights."[32]

The impact of the employers' offensive of these years, however, simply raises another question. After all, many strikes succeeded. If nearly half were lost, just over half were wholly or partially won. Furthermore, nationally the trade unions of the new AFL did not lose members.[33] Why, in the case of the Knights, was the employers' counterassault so utterly effective, so fast? For an answer to this question it is necessary to turn first in greater detail to the *context* of the 1880s in which the Knights grew and then so rapidly declined.

The Perfect Storm, 1886–1887

The 1880s provided a climate in which labor organizations could grow, but also be undermined by the sheer volatility that underlay the economic growth of that decade. Measured decade from decade, the gross national product of the years 1879–1888 averaged 84 percent above the previous ten-year average in real terms, while the nominal amount of capital invested in manufacturing grew by 134 percent over the decade for the country as a whole, about four times the rate of the 1870s. In the Midwest, manufacturing capital grew by 183 percent in the 1880s, compared to 37 percent in the 1870s. As Commons et al. argued, "the factory system of production, for the first time, became general during the eighties," along with the "introduction of machinery upon an unprecedented scale."[34] Furthermore, growth often meant geographic shifts. The number of gainfully employed workers rose by 31 percent across the country in the 1880s, while wageworkers in manufacturing increased by 74 percent nationally and 88 percent in the Midwest.[35] Under twentieth-century conditions this might simply indicate a healthy climate in which unions could be expected to experience sustainable growth. But as we have seen, capital

accumulation in the late nineteenth century was far more contradictory and employment more irregular even in the best of times. In this context, this expansion
of industry provided the major "pull" factor in what became a "perfect storm" that
undermined the Knights of Labor and limited unionization as a whole for a time.
Table 1 shows the relative rates of change rendered as indexes to emphasize the
speed of change for seven important measures of the perfect storm for the three
decades of the Gilded Age, with the 1880s clearly standing out by all measures.

As table 1 shows, the rates of growth of accumulated capital both nominal and
adjusted for inflation, the manufacturing workforce, the number of construction
workers, and both measures of migration were far higher in the 1880s than either
before or after. Only the rate of growth in the number of urban dwelling unit starts
increased slightly in the 1890s despite the depression as people filled the growing
cities of the Midwest and West, outstripping the growth of the workforce. The lag
in the construction workforce is likely the result of the increase in prefabricated elements of new buildings and economies of scale from the growth in building size in
the 1890s.[36] Doucet and Weaver point out, for example, that machine-made bricks
raised the productivity of bricklayers dramatically, while factory-made building
parts, such as window and door frames, meant that "machined products moved
jobs away from the construction site and concentrated them in wood-finishing
mills."[37] In any case, the rapid growth of urban housing units and the construction
workforce in the 1880s reflects a workforce on the move in the wake of spreading
urban growth in that decade. Indeed, the level of interstate migration during the
Gilded Age reached its highest point during the 1880s, with a total of 3.5 million
people crossing state lines between the 1880 and 1890 censuses, two-thirds of them
moving to the Midwest or West. This was over twice the number who did so during
the 1870s. As we saw in chapter 3, migration between counties within the states
generally ran about twice that of interstate migration, while a great many migrations within the decade are not captured by these figures.[38] Thus, the adjusted rates
of migration per population also show a much higher level in the 1880s.

The measurement of migration by decade, however, does not fully capture the
intense impact of migration in the mid-1880s at the time of the Great Upheaval.

Following the pattern that migration increases with economic growth, the
rising curve of migration in this decade would have started its ascent after the end
of the relatively mild depression that lasted from March 1882 to May 1885.[39] This
suggests that migration accelerated just as the Knights of Labor began its ascent,
followed a year later by its rapid decline. The correlation between rising migration
and falling Knights membership strongly suggests a causal link.

Along with the "pull" of economic growth that characterized this period, at
least three important "push" factors were simultaneously at work producing this
intensification of internal migration. The first was the high level of technological

displacement described by the US commissioner of labor in his 1886 report, cited in chapter 2, in which displacement rates of 50 percent were not uncommon.[40] In other words, even though there was net job creation in this decade, the high level of capital investment simultaneously transformed and destroyed jobs, providing both push and pull forces behind the high levels of migration. One machinist who told the Senate in 1883 "I work in different shops" expressed the contradiction between capital's simultaneous creation and destruction of jobs when he related that in his trade, "The invention of machinery produces a little more work; but at the same time there are inventions in our own trade which take it away again."[41] Another push factor related to the volatile nature of accumulation was the increase in business failures in the 1880s, which ran about 40 percent above the 1870s at 88,923. This is all the more remarkable because the 1882–1885 depression was much shallower and shorter than that of the 1870s, a sign that growth was never a simple, linear phenomenon in the Gilded Age and that the ruthless competition of the era could destroy more firms in good times than bad.[42]

Table 1. Relative Indexes of Rates of Change
per Decade, 1870–1900 (1870–1880 = 100)

Item	1870–1880	1880–1890	1890–1900
Nominal Manufacturing Capital Growth Rate	100	419	159
Real Manufacturing Capital Growth Rate	100	249	91
Increase in Manufacturing Wage Earners	100	211	34
Interstate Migration (NE, MW, W)	100	227	166
Adjusted Migration Rate per Population	100	176	100
New Urban Dwelling Units Started	100	257	284
Increase in Construction Workforce	100	262	67

Sources: See chapter 2 tables 1, 8, 11, and 12; US Census Bureau, *Historical Statistics of the United States: Colonial Times to 1970*, pt. 1 (Washington, DC: US Government Printing Office, 1975), 139; US Census Bureau, *Historical Statistics of the United States: Colonial Times to 1970*, pt. 2 (Washington, DC: US Government Printing Office, 1975), 627.

Class conflict itself provided another push factor as lost strikes or lockouts sent workers elsewhere in the context of growing employment possibilities. For the decade of the 1880s as a whole, some 208,531 workers, or about 11 percent of all strikers, were replaced by "new hires" in the wake of lost or prolonged strikes.[43] The years 1886 and 1887 saw a leap in the number of strikes, largely due to the rising eight-hour movement. In both of these years almost half of these strikes were lost, according to the commissioner of labor. Some 680,000 workers went on strike in these two years compared to only 239,000 in the previous two years.[44] In 1886–1887, 79,403 new hires replaced 12 percent of all strikers, but as Currie and Ferrie conclude, "When strike replacements were used, typically about a quarter of the prestrike workers were replaced."[45] In any case, the loss of nearly 80,000 jobs by strikers in these two years would itself account for much of the loss of nearly 200,000 members for the Knights of Labor from July 1886 to July 1887.

Equally important for this analysis is the high geographic concentration of strikes, as it was in the most industrialized states where much of the initial collapse of the Knights occurred. In his 1887 *Annual Report*, the commissioner of labor noted that 75 percent of all strikes from 1881 through 1886 occurred in business establishments in just five states.[46] Table 2 shows the number of replacements used during these years in these five states and the percentage of those that occurred in 1886 at the height of the Knights' growth and the beginning of its rapid decline. Of the total of 64,529 replacement workers used in these five states over this period, 21,357 (or a third) were "brought from other places"—namely, out of state.[47] Nationally, in 1886, 39,854 replacement workers displaced as many strikers, while 1887 saw virtually the same level of replacements at 39,549.[48] It seems evident from this that the use of replacement workers throughout these years and their acceleration in 1886 and 1887 was another force in the "perfect storm" pushing workers from place to place and undermining both the Knights and unions, for as we will see, the collapse of the Knights was centered in about ten urban industrial cities.

In Chicago, the center of the May 1 strikes in 1886, replacement workers, often brought from "other places," were used in over a third of all strikes. Of the 6,040 new hires in Chicago in 1886, 1,874 (or 31 percent) came from out of town. In some cases, the proportion of replacements was even greater. For example, of the 3,722 who struck the McCormick Reaper Works twice in Chicago in 1886, 1,445 (39 percent) were replaced, 600 of those replacement workers (42 percent) were brought from out of town.[49] In addition, of course, as a result of the employers' offensive of 1886, many Knights were simply fired for trying to organize. As Commons put it in his study of meatpacking in Chicago, "For fifteen years after the Knights of Labor [stockyards] strike in 1886 every man or women who ventured to start an organization was discharged; and after 1890 when the 'combine' of packers became effective, many of them were blacklisted."[50] Thus, the number of workers replaced or fired was substantial and the question remains as to where they would be able to find work.

While we can't know how many of these replaced strikers or fired organizers left town to find other work, we do know that hunting for work in the wake of a lost or even a prolonged strike often meant looking elsewhere. Kim Voss, for example, reports of an 1885 leatherworkers lockout in Newark, New Jersey: "By mid-September, however, it was clear that the leatherworkers had suffered an absolute defeat. Some reapplied for their old jobs, but at least one-half were turned away, and all the shop stewards were blacklisted. Other leathermakers left Newark to find work elsewhere."[51]

Table 2. Number of Replacement Workers: Illinois, Massachusetts, New York, Ohio, and Pennsylvania, 1881–1886

State	Total 1881–1886	1886	Percent in 1886
Illinois	16,590	8,378	51 percent
Massachusetts	6,185	3,180	51 percent
New York	24,889	9,023	36 percent
Ohio	5,172	1,163	23 percent
Pennsylvania	11,693	3,657	31 percent
Five State Totals	64,529	25,401	39 percent
US Total	104,518	39,854	38 percent

Source: US Commissioner of Labor, *Third Annual Report of the Commissioner of Labor, 1887* (Washington, DC: US Government Printing Office, 1888), 690–705; US Commissioner of Labor, *Sixteenth Annual Report of the Commissioner of Labor, 1901* (Washington, DC: US Government Printing Office, 1901), 343.

Knights of Labor leader Joseph Buchanan described the confused outcome of a yearlong strike by coal miners in the mid-1880s in which some companies settled and others didn't. He wrote of its end, "It finally wore itself out; many of the miners leaving for other parts, some returning to work as union men, under union conditions, and some 'black-legging.'"[52] After a long lockout of coal miners in Spring Valley, Illinois, that began in December 1888 and lasted several months, "two-thirds of the men had scattered out in search of work elsewhere," reported E. A. Allen in 1891.[53] Daniel Walkowitz describes the result of a similarly prolonged strike of cotton mill workers in Cohoes, New York, in 1882, writing, "By the time the conflict had ended, from a third to half of the Harmony Mills workforce had either left Cohoes or found other work in the city."[54] In other words, flight or migration during or after prolonged or defeated strikes was common throughout this period. This was a pattern of migration that involved both the outgoing strikers and their incoming replacements, thereby undermining labor organization in two directions.

Simultaneous growth of employment and displacement by mechanization, business failures, and lost or prolonged strikes accompanied by blacklisting and replacement workers created a perfect storm of labor migration that accelerated in the years 1886 and 1887. Further, all of these trends were most intense in those industrial states and cities where most of the initial decline of the Knights of Labor from July 1886 to July 1887 occurred, as we will see below. It stands to reason that the apparent correlation between all of these figures and their simultaneous collision in this two-year period must explain a good deal of the sudden decline of the Knights. This, then, was the unfolding context in which the Knights of Labor faced the accelerated employers' offensive of these years. To understand how this context affected the Knights' decline we need to look at how the Knights grew prior to its rapid takeoff from mid-1885 as this perfect storm gathered strength.

Knights of Labor's Unstable Growth and Turnover, 1879–1884

The violent nationwide railroad strike of 1877 was the prelude to an escalation of class conflict characterized by a new wave of Workingmen's Parties and Greenback Labor Parties and the return of union growth, with the Knights of Labor emerging as the vanguard of organized labor. While as yet still smaller than the Federation of Organized Trades and Labor Unions, in the years 1881 through 1884 the Knights were growing at two to three times as fast as the federation, at least after the temporary slump of 1882, having added some fifty-two thousand members by 1884. Furthermore, between 1881 and 1884, the Knights of Labor had organized or chartered almost eighteen hundred Local Assemblies (LAs), its basic local organization.[55] Such net increases might give the impression of solid growth. Yet there was something in the way the Knights grew as the 1880s unfolded that revealed an underlying weakness. At its 1879 annual General Assembly, Grand Secretary Charles Litchman pointed to a problem that would only increase:

> I regret to announce the demise of L.A. 1035, of Tiffin, Ohio. It started under very favorable auspices, and knowing personally many of its members, I had great hopes it would prove one of the best locals in the Order. The failure of the employers for whom most of the members worked, compelled them to seek "fresh fields and pastures new."[56]

As will be discussed in the concluding chapter, the Knights had a number of organizational problems that made them more susceptible to both employer opposition and the winds of economic change and mass migration. From 1880 through 1886 the average size of a Knights of Labor Local Assembly was under 100 members, generally smaller than the citywide local unions of the trade unions.[57] In fact, almost 500, or over a quarter of the 1,792 Local Assemblies, organized between 1880 and 1884 "lapsed."[58] To be sure, some were reorganized. In 1882, for example, the grand secretary reported that while only nine LAs had become defunct, eighty-six had been reorganized.[59] But often it was not enough. From September 1882 to September 1883, the 1883 General Assembly was told that thirty-four LAs had been reorganized, while 221 had become defunct.[60] Even the process of collapse and reorganization showed an instability and discontinuity of organization and personnel that would undermine the solidity of any organization. In contrast to the continuity of the order's top leadership, its base was characterized by almost continuous turnover. The turnover of members, in fact, was even more severe than that of LAs'. As table 3 shows, between the 1879 General Assembly and that of 1884, the Knights initiated 161,234 members but lost 120,708, or the equivalent of 75 percent of its new members.[61] Despite net growth, the Knights were unintentionally building an edifice with a very shaky foundation even as the perfect storm was about to gather momentum.

Table 3. Knights of Labor Members Initiated & Lapsed, 1879–1884

Year	Initiated	Lapsed
1879	4,870	4,089
1880	20,206	12,843
1881	10,459	12,357
1882	26,139	11,118
1883	44,319	33,901
1884	55,241	46,400
Totals	161,234	120,708

Source: Record of the Proceedings of the General Assembly, 1879–1884.

All of the push factors mentioned above were at work during these years of early growth. Indeed, due to industrial conflict alone, between 1881 and 1884, 45,592 strikers lost their jobs to new hires—over three-quarters in the five key states listed in table 2.[62] Assuming most sought work elsewhere, that alone would account for over a quarter of all the Knights' lapsed members. We saw this in 1879, a year of relative prosperity, in the case of LA 1035, whose members had to seek "fresh fields and pastures new," and after as the order lost three-quarters of the members it had initiated. A hint of the problems caused by traveling also came up at the 1880 General Assembly when a delegate from Pennsylvania moved, "*Whereas,* Much inconvenience and loss falls to the lot of our members when traveling to cities where their trade is controlled by some other organizations which do not recognize our cards." It is worth noting that he didn't say "if" members were traveling, but "when"—it was assumed that traveling was a routine matter for many occupations.[63]

As we will see below, the rapid decline that commenced in mid-1886 was centered in urban industrial areas where the impact of the perfect storm was most severe.[64] So, the basis on which Knights of Labor LAs and District Assemblies (DAs), the county or citywide coordinating bodies, were built is particularly important. In table 4 we look at a sample of four industrial cities: Philadelphia, the home of the Knights; Detroit, a midsize industrial center; Chicago, the new dynamo of this era; and San Francisco, the industrial giant of the far West. The figures are for those Local Assemblies for which membership figures are available. The higher turnover rate for the Midwest cities most likely reflects their faster rates of urban entrance and exit. While the proportion of lost members to those gained varied from city to city, in all it was dangerously high.

Table 4. Knights of Labor Members Initiated and Lapsed in Philadelphia, Detroit Chicago, and San Francisco, 1881–1884

City	LA Sample	Initiated	Lapsed	Percent Lapsed
Philadelphia, DA 1	37 of 112 LAs	10,317	6,792	66 percent
Detroit , DA 50	15 of 21 LAs	1,202	1,348	112 percent
Chicago DAs 24, 57	36 of 62 LAs	4,101	4,338	106 percent
San Francisco, DA 53	15 of 18 LAs	1,634	991	61 percent
Total Four Cities		17,254	13,469	80 percent

Source: Jonathan Garlock, *Guide to the Assemblies of the Knights of Labor* (Westport, CT: Greenwood, 1982), 25–26, 65–73, 225–228, 450–460, 588–660.

Although there are no available statistics on residential persistence for all four of these cities, population turnover was large in all urban areas, as we saw in chapter 2. From this, Stephan Thernstrom concluded,

> The extreme transiency of the urban masses must have severely limited the possibilities of mobilizing them politically and socially, and have facilitated control by the more stable and prosperous elements of the population. Effective organization demands some continuity of membership, and this was glaringly absent among the poorest city dwellers of nineteenth- and early-twentieth- century America.[65]

Clearly this lack of continuity applied to the Knights of Labor, whose strength in the first half of the 1880s was in urban centers where turnover was high and the perfect storm most intense. All of this meant that even as it grew up to 1886, the Knights were virtually undermining their own organizational stability, losing a huge proportion of those who joined and rendering the development of a stable resident leadership difficult. This in turn almost certainly meant that it was not simply the inexperience of those who joined during the acceleration of growth from mid-1885 through mid-1886, as the top leaders tended to argue. Rather, the base of those who had joined before was necessarily too weak, too riddled with turnover, too lacking in ongoing grassroots leadership to provide a solid organizational foundation that could accommodate the rapid influx of those joining in the midst of the growing strike wave of 1885–1886.

The Decline of the Knights of Labor

J. F. Bray, who is cited at the beginning of this chapter referring to the collapse of unions in the past, was no doubt referring to the 1870s when, as Lloyd Ulman calculates, as many unions "disappeared" as were formed.[66] The 1870s, however, saw the Gilded Age's longest depression, while the years 1886–1887 when the Knights grew and declined were years of growth, so that a different explanation for their rapid decline is required. The decline of the Knights occurred in the face of the intensified employer offensive of mid-1886 and was facilitated by the unstable manner in which that organization grew in the preceding period. Battered by the perfect storm of growth and migration, the order saw enormous turnover of Local Assemblies and members.

In early 1885 the number of new Local Assemblies jumped from 42 in March to 80 in April. With a slight slump in growth during the summer, the numbers just kept going up, to 260 formed in December 1885. As growth accelerated in the early months of 1886, reaching over 800 new LAs in May, General Master Workman Powderly issued an order suspending organizing activity for forty days and rejecting three hundred applications for the position of organizer. He called a special General Assembly for May 25 to June 3, 1886, where the leadership ratified Powderly's order and required all future organizers to attend a training program in Knights of Labor principles.[67] Not surprisingly, growth slowed down to less than half that, with only 397 LAs formed in June. While there was still growth as measured by new assemblies, the rate slowed down to 133 by November.

After that, the *Journal of United Labor* stopped reporting these figures.[68] Yet despite the leadership's desire, recruitment did not stop. In his report to the 1887 General Assembly, General Secretary Frederick Turner stated what he thought the reason for the rapid decline was: "People came into the Order by the hundreds of thousands, so that a suspension of initiation for forty days was ordered. After this forty days had expired the rush again commenced, and the result was to bring to the organization a mass of material that proved itself to be a weakness rather than a strength."[69]

The idea, expressed by Turner and other leaders of the Knights, that the sudden decline was the result of the rapid influx of a weak "mass of material" or an inexperienced and undisciplined rabble leading up to mid-1886 needs critical examination if we are to get at the real roots of the decline. While most of the half million or more who flooded into the Knights from mid-1885 through mid-1886 would not have been union members prior to joining, most would certainly have had some organizational experience and significant exposure to industrial conflict. Given the high turnover of Knights members prior to the upsurge, it is likely that some were returning Knights. As Ware argues, "Thousands who had once belonged to the Knights and had dropped out because nothing much was happening, flocked back after the strike, boycott, and other successes of 1885."[70] Also, many would have been among the more than one million Union Army veterans of the Civil War "identified as mechanics and laborers"[71] experiencing the discipline of the military *and* for many acquiring or reinforcing an egalitarian vision of society that eventually justified that war and was often expressed by Knights and trade unionists in this period. Additionally, many would have had some organizational experience in the dense web of fraternal orders, mutual-aid and beneficial societies, and ethnic organizations that characterized the Gilded-Age working class of all races and ethnicities, a fact often noted by several labor and social historians.[72] Furthermore, in the five years prior to 1886, there had been 2,471 strikes involving 630,000 workers, while total union membership rose from 189,062 in 1881 to 403,061 in 1885,[73] so that even many nonunion workers would have experienced labor activity as supporters, relatives, or simply observers, particularly in the industrial cities where most of this highly visible growth of class conflict occurred and where the Knights saw both their rapid growth and decline. All of this tells us that the huge acceleration of 1885–1886 was not the rush of the mob, but an upsurge of those already affected by the "compression" of the previous years, many of whom possessed enough organizational experience to see the benefits of collective action.

Thus, the decline turned out not to be a momentary aberration caused by inferior recruits, as Turner seemed to think, but a continuous slide that lasted for the next few years as lost members far outstripped new recruits. There was more at work than the caution of the leaders or the inadequacies of the new members. In terms of membership, we know that by mid-1886 the Knights had hit their highpoint. It was only after this that there was a rapid growth in "mixed" assemblies. As Ware argues, "The change in distribution between mixed and trade assemblies is explained not by changes in the older sections of the Order, not by the inrush of the unskilled, but by the expansion into the agricultural West and South."[74] It was not among these that the first phase of rapid decline from July 1886 to July 1887 came, but precisely from the older urban-based District Assemblies where turnover was large and trade assemblies dominated. And it was, of course, in the nation's urban industrial concentrations that the eye of the perfect storm hit hardest.

As Commons pointed out, between July 1886 and July 1887, "The falling off of the largest district assemblies in 10 large cities practically equaled the total loss to the Order which amounted to approximately 191,000."[75] As table 5 shows, the losses in these ten cities amounted to 85 percent of the total drop in membership from July 1886 to July 1887. Furthermore, several of these cities were also the sites of a large proportion of the strikes in this period, including those where large numbers of replacement workers were used. Bennett and Earle conclude that "strikes were unusually concentrated in large urban counties." New York led the way, with Chicago (Cook County) second.[76] Since almost half of strikes were lost and strikers replaced by nonunion workers in many cases, as we saw above, this, too, points to a significant cause of migration and decline. These facts strongly indicate that whatever initial dampening effect Powderly and the decisions he made at the 1886 special session he called to deal with the Knights' rapid increase in members may have had on growth, they cannot explain the scale of the sudden decline that commenced by late 1886.

Table 5. Knights of Labor Membership* Losses, mid-1886 to July 1887

City	July 1886	July 1887	Loss
New York, DA 49	60,809	32,826	27,983
Philadelphia, DA 1	51,557	11,294	40,263
Boston, DA 30	81,197	31,644	49,553
Baltimore, DA 41	18,297	7,549	10,748
Providence, DA 99	11,512	1,735	9,777
Hartford, DA 95	14,148	5,622	5,890
Newark, DA 51	10,958	4,766	6,192
Chicago, DA 24	12,868	10,488	2,380
Chicago, DA 57	7,389	4,656	2,733
Milwaukee, DA 108	7,724	3,178	4,546
Detroit, DA 50	4,615	2,213	2,402
Total Loss of Ten Cities			162,567 (85 percent)
All Members*	702,934	511,351	191,583

* In good standing.
Source: *Record of the Proceedings of the Tenth Regular Session of the General Assembly,* Richmond, VA, October 4–20, 1886, 326–328; *Record of the Proceedings of the Eleventh Regular Session of the General Assembly,* Minneapolis, October 4–19, 1887, 1847–1850.

Nor can it be blamed on the unskilled, since, as Ware points out, most of the large city District Assemblies were composed in their majority of trade assemblies of skilled workers, not "mixed" assemblies of the less skilled.[77] Chicago, for example, had only ten mixed assemblies out of seventy-four Local Assemblies formed before 1886, and only twenty-six out of 116 formed during or after 1886 as the number of assemblies increased. The Illinois Bureau of Labor Statistics shows that only 13 percent of the Knights in Chicago (Cook County) were listed as "laborers" (including helpers and hod carriers). For Detroit, the figures are four out of eighteen for those assemblies formed before 1886 and twelve out of thirty-nine for those after 1886.[78] Thus, a good deal of the initial decline of almost two hundred thousand had to have come from urban-based trade assemblies, the very workers who were most likely to travel for other work in the wake of lost strikes, technological displacement, industrial shifts, and the like, as long as work was available elsewhere—as it was in 1886–1887.

The fledgling labor organizations of the 1880s were tossed and turned in this sea of human motion. In the end, the Knights saw both continued decline and a shift from urban centers to more rural areas just as population and older industries were leaving those areas. By the 1890s the task of organizing industrial workers fell to the surviving craft unions and to new efforts to organize on an industrial basis in the mines, in the garment shops, and on the railroads. Most of these trade unionists, whether in craft or industrial unions, whether led by pure and simple or socialist officials, were faced with the same forces. But the story was somewhat different—a story more of limitations on growth that allowed for survival into the end of the Gilded Age as industry settled into its twentieth-century patterns. We turn now to that story.

Trade Unions in the Storm

As with the Knights of Labor, those workers organized in local or national trade unions were, of course, subject to the forces of the perfect storm that undermined growth. So, unaffiliated local unions grew from 153,655 members in 1885 to 354,193 in 1886 during the strike wave and then shrank in 1887 to 236,910 members—spectacular growth followed by serious and rapid decline in a time of economic growth. Again, the decline in the number of local unions cannot be fully explained by those that entered national unions affiliated with the Federation of Trade and Labor Organizations, and subsequently the AFL, as the federation's growth was not big enough to account for such a shift. During the strike wave of 1886, the national unions affiliated with the AFL gained a mere thirteen thousand members, while in 1887 they defied the trend toward decline by gaining an additional twenty-two thousand members.[79] As Norman Ware put it, "In 1885–86, when the Knights of Labor were making their phenomenal gains, the national trade unions were adding to their numbers more slowly but more surely."[80] If more careful growth and more coherent organization helps to explain why these national trade unions didn't follow the Knights or the isolated local unions into decline, the question remains of why these unions and their new federation, the AFL, failed to experience rapid growth until the final years of the Gilded Age.

Slow growth, after all, was not usually a preference when even the strongest of the AFL unions embraced only a minority of the workforce in their trade or industry for most of this period. The majority of these unions depended on a near "monopoly" of their labor market, whether local or national, in order to increase wages or shorten hours, but very few had anything like a majority outside of a few cities. G. W. Perkins, president of the Cigar Makers' International Union (CMIU), testified before the Industrial Commission in 1899 that "the actual number of cigar makers proper is about 75,000 or 80,000, and we have 27,000." In New York, he admitted, "There are 20,000 cigar makers . . . and we only have about 6,000 of them."[81] In other words, the CMIU had only about 30 percent of all cigar makers nationally and in New York City by 1899. In printing, another site of relative union strength in the International Typographical Union (ITU), union density grew from 11 percent in 1880 to 28 percent in 1899, still a small percentage of the workforce. For all of mining, union members composed only 12 percent in 1880, rising to 25 percent in 1890 then falling to 15 percent in 1899. In construction, where the building trades unions would eventually form a large part of the AFL membership, the comparable figures were 2 percent in 1880, 13 percent in 1890, and 13 percent in 1899. Shortly after the turn of the century, these proportions would grow significantly in most industries for reasons we will examine later.[82] But what stands out for the Gilded Age is how slow trade-union growth was in good times and bad. What then were the forces behind this slow growth?

First, of course, is the fact that these unions were tossed and turned by all the contradictory forces of capital accumulation and urbanization analyzed in chapter 2, as well as by the perfect storm of the mid-1880s. As we have seen in chapter 3, traveling was second nature to the members of many of the most important trade unions and occupations of the period. The pulls and pushes of the era, and especially the 1880s, lay behind much of this labor migration. The displacing impact of technology, for example, hit a great many of the industries in which the AFL unions were rooted.

Former president of the Amalgamated Association of Iron and Steel Workers, Mahlon Garland, told the Industrial Commission in 1899 that the effect of new machinery "has been more startling in the steel mills. One can hardly explain the great changes in that direction, because they are so constantly occurring. Machinery is doing the work that everybody thought utterly impossible eight or ten years ago."[83] The idea that it was the depression of 1893–1897 that undermined the Amalgamated Association (AA) does not stand up as production actually grew, with some ups and downs, from 3.9 million tons in 1891 to 8.9 million tons in 1898. Yet, between 1892 and 1896, the AA lost over ninety lodges (local unions) and nearly nine thousand members.[84] Indeed, David Brody concluded that "mechanization undermined the power base of the union." The same conclusion was drawn by Jesse Robinson in his 1920 study of the AA.[85]

Many other craft workers saw the mechanization brought by rising capital accumulation push them out of work and on the road. According to Frank Stockton, an early historian of the International Molders' Union of North America, "The first important efforts to introduce the use of molding machines in America took place in the eighties."[86] As we saw in chapter 2, Samuel Donnelly of the ITU told the Industrial Commission, "I would estimate that there are being used about 4,000" and affirmed that this meant the displacement of ten thousand to twelve thousand men. He added that in addition to the typesetting machines, "There are machines in all branches of the printing trade—that is new, improved labor-saving machinery is being introduced at all times in press rooms and binderies and in electrotyping and stereotyping establishments."[87] Machinist John Morrison told the Senate committee in 1883, "Also, there is more machinery used in the business, which again makes machinery." He continued, "In fact, through this system of work, 100 men are able to do now what it took 300 or 400 men to do fifteen years ago."[88] Horace Eaton of the Boot and Shoe Workers' Union linked the new machinery in his industry with the rise of part-year work. He told the Industrial Commission that eleven years ago (1888),

> Where a man at that time would likely get 8 or 9 months' good work in a year, at the present time the season is shorter. Machinery is more largely used and of a more improved type. The manufacturers equip themselves to turn out their product in a shorter time, and the seasons of employment are shorter and more uncertain.[89]

Thus, in various ways, mechanization forced these craftsmen to seek employment elsewhere, and as often as not, this meant joining the streams of labor migration that reached new highs in the 1880s. The high proportion of members using the traveling-card systems testifies to this, as we will see below.

The movement of capital into the Midwest accelerated during the 1880s, causing major relocations in a number of industries. The ironworkers, the strongest section of the AA, faced just such a geographic shift of the industry. As early as 1876, the *Iron Molders' Journal* reported the shift of iron production to the West when it wrote, "The growth of iron manufacturing in the West is well illustrated in the case of Chicago," where "200 establishments employ 10,000 workmen."[90] In 1883, testifying before the Senate hearings, John Jarrett, then president of the AA, agreed that the new processes in steel mills were displacing men but that new mills were opening "and the men have got work in those." He specifically mentioned new mills in Chicago in 1882, which he supposed provided some two thousand jobs.[91] Concerning the eastern iron mills, former president Garland stated in 1899, well after the economic recovery was underway, "The fact is they are going out of the business."[92] By 1900 production in the East was down to 65 percent, while that in the Midwest had risen from 16 percent to 27 percent of the total.[93] The production of pig iron in Illinois rose from 7 percent of the national output in 1882 to 10.4 percent in 1892,[94] enough to cause problems for a union with roots in Pennsylvania. In addition, Allan Pred showed that within the Midwest, iron production had moved from smaller towns to big cities, notably Chicago, Cleveland, and Detroit and along with this movement went much of the labor force.[95]

By 1891, before its crippling defeat at Homestead, about half of the local lodges of the AA were in Pittsburgh and Philadelphia. By 1902 they composed only 22 percent of all lodges. A good deal of the drop in Pittsburgh is explained by the disastrous defeat of the AA at Homestead in 1892, where 1,600 new hires replaced many of the Homestead strikers and the 1,250 who had struck in sympathy.[96] The equally large decline in Philadelphia, however, appears to be more the result of the geographic shift of the industry. Yet this drift of members away from Pennsylvania was not a reflection of any growth of the AA, the membership of which remained well below the level of 1892, but a shift westward.[97]

The iron molders also saw their industry shift toward the Midwest. In 1884, the *Iron Molders' Journal* reprinted an article from a management magazine saying that Chicago was now the largest stove market in the world and that "the stove foundries are annually enlarging their capacity and volume of goods turned out." By the mid-1880s some stove companies moved from Troy, New York, a union stronghold, to Cincinnati and elsewhere to the West, while the number of stove foundries in New York City had fallen from sixty or more to nineteen by the mid-1890s.[98] Molders also faced that other feature of the era, part-year work, as we saw in chapter 3. In 1886, a year of economic growth, the *Iron Molders' Journal* complained that shops "running steady the year around" were "exceptional instead of the rule."[99] As a result of these trends, the union lost locals. In 1876, the convention was told that while seven new local unions had been organized, sixteen had lapsed. In 1882, things looked better as eighty-eight new locals were formed or reorganized, but still eleven were suspended, "some on account of shops changing locations, others on account of strikes and members leaving."[100]

These trends also meant that the Iron Molders lost members even as they grew. The union secretary reported to the union's convention in 1888 that while the union had initiated 5,336 members in the last two years and reinstated 2,199, it had lost 3,924, not including deaths, or about half those they had gained.[101] Even the large number of reinstated members speaks of instability and, as we will see below, the leaky nature of the traveling system of these unions. Again, the forces of the perfect storm along with industrial relocation had united to cost the Iron Molders members and restrain the growth of a union widely considered to be one of the strongest in the country.

Gilded-Age machinists had seen their old union, the International Union of

Machinists and Blacksmiths, virtually destroyed during the long depression of the 1870s. When growth returned at the end of that decade and in the 1880s, machinists joined the Knights of Labor in growing numbers. Indeed, by the 1886 General Assembly of the Knights, they composed eighty-six of the six hundred delegates. Their efforts to form a national trade assembly were thwarted, and as the Knights declined, machinists held on to organization only in railroad maintenance shops, notably those of the Union Pacific Railroad. In 1888, former Knights in southern railway shops organized the National Association of Machinists, but as David Montgomery pointed out, this union, even under its new name as the International Association of Machinists (IAM), remained weak well into the 1890s.[102] As we saw in chapter 3, machinists possessed "notoriously migratory propensities" as they followed the railroads and the growing industries of the Midwest, such as farm-implement production. These migratory propensities inevitably had an impact on efforts to organize. Thus, on the eve of the depression that began in late 1893, five years after its formation, the IAM could claim only twelve thousand members.[103]

In his detailed comparison of the relative workplace power of British "engineers" and US "machinists," Jeffrey Haydu notes that one reason why the British union was stronger was that "American workers were also more nomadic than British ones. Frequent job changes—in search of high wages, in response to grievances, or to evade blacklists—undercut work group cohesion and stable shop organization." As he pointed out, "The IAM enrolled only 11 percent of American machinists by 1900, compared to perhaps 50 percent of engineers enrolled in the ASE [Amalgamated Society of Engineers] and other craft unions."[104]

Coal miners faced a similar dilemma as their industry moved westward with the opening of new fields in the Midwest and far West in the 1880s and 1890s. In his study of Alabama coal miners, Daniel Letwin wrote, "Whatever the causes, it was not unusual for a miner's career to take him far and wide: from the central competitive fields of Illinois, Indiana, and Ohio through the upper and central Appalachian coal districts of Pennsylvania, Kentucky, West Virginia, and Tennessee."[105] Writing in the mid-1880s, John McBride, then secretary of the National Federation of Miners and Mine Laborers and later president of the United Mine Workers of America, described some of the migration-related "difficulties which have stood in the way of organization and united action" of these "birds of passage," including the fact that "different seasons have found him in different localities, as the opportunities work has offered." Many of these different localities were, "Scattered in remote districts— frequently miles away from the towns—and shut off almost entirely from all social intercourse, the opportunities for the interchange of ideas and the upbuilding of compact, serviceable organizations have necessarily been slight."[106]

In addition, coal that had to be transported by rivers or on the Great Lakes was necessarily seasonal in nature. McBride stated that "these conditions have been serious obstacles to miners in the labor movement," above all "because they have had a tendency to disrupt local organizations and injure their efficiency." He also complained of the "employment of farm-hands in the mines during the winter season, since they have nothing to gain by such organization as the skilled miners were striving to build up."[107] Thus, unionization was negatively affected by both the movement of miners out of a camp or town on the one hand and the influx of lower-paid, seasonal farmhands on the other. Furthermore, the company town system that prevailed in many coalfields often meant miners could be fined for "unruly" behavior or other trivial offenses against company rules. If the fine was not paid, the miner could be evicted from company-owned housing and "sent down the road." Lost strikes or lockouts could also mean migration, as the example of Spring Valley showed.[108] Similarly, after miners were defeated by a 1873–1874 lockout in the Tioga area of Pennsylvania, "some of the men and their families left the Tioga region for other mining areas. A few actually returned to Scotland."[109]

Both economic forces and lost strikes as well as the search for better jobs contributed to the turnover of local affiliates of the national and international unions. In 1885 the president of the ITU, whose members were famous for their "roving disposition," stated, "It appears that since the permanent organization of this body the number of new unions having lapsed is about equal to the number now in existence." Concerning the number of membership cards issued to defunct locals, he added that the number of cards issued to "persons who are not justly entitled to them it is impossible to estimate."[110] Although a single year's figures may not be representative, from June 1886 to June 1887, in the midst of the Great Upheaval and economic growth, the ITU gained 1,463 new members but lost 1,339. While other unions were growing, the ITU grew by a slim 706 members in that year. Significantly, the number of traveling members grew from 7,006 in 1885 to 8,588 in 1887. By this time, the ITU membership had become highly concentrated in eight large cities, giving it more organizational stability than many other unions. Thus, during that period the ITU gained 111 local unions and lost only 7. During those years, however, an average of 43 percent of its members were on the tramp, so it was losing members via the traveling-card system rather than through lapsed locals.[111] As will be argued below, the traveling-card system in general was a significant drain on the membership of most unions whose members engaged in regular tramping.

The Cigar Makers are one of the few unions for which figures for the turnover of local unions are available for the 1880s. In this case, unlike the ITU, the union did experience a fairly high turnover of local unions. This difference can be explained by the fact that while printing was highly concentrated in a few big cities by the mid-1880s, cigar making was scattered all over the country and most of the union's locals were small. As table 6 shows, while not as extreme as that of the Knights, the turnover of Cigar Makers' locals was significant. The reasons for a local union dissolving were explained in the president's report to the 1883 convention of the Cigar Makers, where he stated, "With few exceptions, the unions dissolved because trade left, and cigar makers had to seek employment elsewhere. In some instances the members left in consequence of losing a strike, and surrendering their charter."[112]

Table 6. CMIU Local Union Turnover: Charters Issued–Unions Dissolved, 1881–1889

Years*	Issued	Dissolved	Percent Dissolved
1887–1889	38	21	55 percent
1885–1887	109	40	37 percent
1883–1885	63	50	79 percent
1881–1883	95	36	38 percent

* September to October.
Source: Supplement to the Cigar Makers' Official Journal, September–October 1883, 1–2; Proceedings of the Sixteenth Session of the Cigar Makers' International Union, Cincinnati, October 1885, 3; Proceedings of the Seventeenth Session of the Cigar Makers' International Union, Buffalo, NY, October 1887, 3–4; Proceedings of the Eighteenth Session of the Cigar Makers' International Union, Buffalo, NY, October 1889, 3.

The dissolving of a local could mean the remaining members would either transfer to another local or enter the traveling-card system, which often meant disappearing from the union's rolls.

The Western Federation of Miners (WFM), an industrial union, also provides evidence that lost strikes as well as larger economic forces were a major cause of migration and, hence, of the turnover of local unions. Jim Foster, in his study of the WFM, shows that high levels of (failed) strike activity and tramping were tightly correlated. Defining "tramp locals" as those with 70 percent or more membership turnover, he writes, "The tramp locals existed for a shorter period on the average, were involved in more strikes, and were less likely to win those strikes than more stable WFM locals."[113] The WFM executive board's ledger shows that the turnover of locals was high. From 1894 through 1905, 145 locals of the WFM were organized, while 45 dissolved. As we will see below, the roving nature of these miners also produced an average turnover of nearly half for each local union each year.[114]

For both the craft and industrial unions of the Gilded Age, the most important tool in managing this continuous drift of workers was the union traveling card. Lloyd Ulman theorized that it was this mobility and the traveling card in both local and national labor markets that made national unions necessary in the years following the Civil War.[115] At the same time, however, the slowness of their growth compared to unions in Britain, where tramping had largely disappeared, suggests that tramping and migration were a significant cause of slow growth through most of the Gilded Age.

The traveling-card system whose intention was to control member migration in fact played a role in the loss of members and, as a result, in the limitation of union growth.

The Traveling-Card System: A Leaky Ship of State

As the Industrial Commission pointed out in its summary of its hearing in 1899–1900, "Every national union issues some form of certificate of membership, by which its members, going on to new places, are able to obtain admission to local branches."[116] From the point of view of the union leadership, the traveling card was meant to provide some level of control over the flow of members in and out of various labor markets.[117] The contention here is that, in the context of America's volatile economy, it was a very blunt instrument for controlling the movement or retention of union members. The formation of national union governance of which Ulman spoke had created a leaky ship of state riddled with problems and limited as a system of controlling labor migration. It was, nevertheless, a widely used system among those belonging to trade unions.

Unfortunately, there are only very limited data on the quantity of traveling cards issued by most unions. Looking at figures for two unions for which statistics on traveling members are available, however, can give us an idea of the extent of the use of the traveling card. During the 1880s, for example, the Typographical Union saw the proportion of members admitted to local unions by traveling card to stationary members rise from 22.5 percent to 55 percent by the end of the decade. For the second half of the 1880s the average proportion of traveling members was 49 percent, a total of 37,118 between 1886 and 1889, or an average of over 9,000 a year.[118] In the case of the Cigar Makers, in the second half of the 1880s, when data on the number of members traveling was published, there were 35,338 traveling members of the Cigar Makers recorded, equaling 44 percent of the average number of stationary members between 1886 and 1889.

On average, just under nine thousand CMIU members traveled each year.[119] The amount of traveling loans rose from $26,684 in 1885 during the recession to $43,540 in 1889, indicating a considerable increase in traveling over this period.[120] Thus, the number and proportion of traveling members for both unions was high.

Altogether, from 1886 through 1889 these two unions alone saw over 70,000 members on the road, or an average of about 18,000 each year. In these years members of other trade unions would also have taken to the road for many of the reasons discussed earlier. This would have included those trades known for their traveling proclivities, such as the typographers and cigar makers discussed above, telegraphers seeking higher wages, iron molders and steelworkers following the geographic shift of their work, coal miners in regional unions moving from one coalfield to another, and bricklayers and carpenters building the cities of the Midwest and West, as well as granite and stonecutters supplying the materials, among others. These unions were comparable or larger in size than the Typographers and Cigar Makers and would certainly have had an additional 30,000–40,000 traveling members. Also contributing to the geographic flow of workers were the railroad workers, who, as the commissioner of labor's 1889 report showed, had enormous turnover and a "tendency of labor to migration" that he had never seen before in such clear statistical terms.[121] With half again as many members as the Typographers and Cigar Makers combined, the three major railroad brotherhoods would have seen at least 20,000 members on the road in any year in the second half of the 1880s. Including only these occupations, which we know to be characterized by extensive migration and tramping, it is reasonable to assume that there were at least 70,000–80,000 trade-union members traveling each year between 1886 and 1889. In those years, AFL-affiliated unions averaged a little over 180,000, while non-Knights, non-AFL national unions (such as the railroad brotherhoods) averaged about 160,000, bringing annual average total non-Knights trade-union membership for these years to roughly 340,000.[122] Thus, traveling union members would have amounted to about 20 percent or more of all members of national trade unions each year between 1886 and 1889. Obviously, that is a significant proportion of trade-union membership. The question is how many of these traveling union members exited the traveling system due to the pulls and pushes of the period, above all in the 1880s, thus slowing down the overall growth of the unions. A closer look at the effectiveness of the traveling-card system will help provide an indication.

The Iron Molders also had a system of loans for travelers, but unlike the Cigar Makers, the responsibility for the loans fell on the local unions. Frank Stockton, in his history of the union, noted that this system became unpopular because it was hard to collect on the loans. "In many instances," he wrote, "all trace of the borrowers was lost."[123] The president of the Iron Molders' Union concurred in 1874 when he told the union's convention, "On average, there are at all times from twelve to fifteen hundred members scattered over the country with their cards in their pockets"—that is, working nonunion rather than using their traveling cards. That amounts to 16–20 percent of the total membership of 7,500 in 1874.[124] Presumably, the total number of traveling members was much larger, as most would have deposited their cards. Two years later he reported to that convention that "a considerable number of members are working country shops, and we lose all track for them for months and even years at a time."[125] In other words, the union was losing significant numbers of traveling members, which it could not even keep track of.

In a similar vein, Secretary O'Dea of the Bricklayers told the 1886 convention of that union, "The country is full of members of different subordinate [that is, local] Unions who hold traveling cards in their possession, who do us more injury than good, and when they do deposit their cards in a Union, do so after having had them in their possession for sometimes two years."[126] At the Bricklayers' 1901 convention, the secretary reported on the previous year: "I find that 6,065 traveling cards were issued, while I can find deposited for the same term 5,176, a loss of almost 1,000 members in traveling cards alone."[127] Thus, about 17 percent of its traveling workers simply disappeared from the Bricklayers' membership rolls. The union could not actually keep track of the members on the tramp, who while working nonunion were undermining the wages of the paid-up members. In this situation, the traveling card turned out to be a poor defense.

The Machinists also faced problems with a decentralized traveling-card system that left the loans to local lodges. At the 1895 convention of the IAM, Grand Master Machinist James O'Connell told the union's convention, "I estimate that in the past two years there has changed hands between our local lodges, on account of loans given to our traveling brothers, $5,000. Notwithstanding all the assistance given to our traveling brothers, our traveling card has been most unmercifully abused." The difficulties of the traveling-card system adopted by the IAM led to problems of the repayment of loans.

O'Connell said this had led to "an unlimited number of disputes between our local lodges as to the returning of borrowed money, and the transfer of brothers from one lodge to another." He called for a new uniform card on which each member would have a number.[128]

Because of the many difficulties in keeping track of migratory members, the leadership of other unions also sought changes in the rules governing the use of the traveling card. As Tygiel wrote of the Carpenters, "During the first seven years of the Brotherhood's existence, the national union experimented with several ways of enforcing the travel card system." This included secret passwords and hand grips, and the signing of cards. "The system was confusing and not very effective," writes Tygiel, and was changed in 1886 for a two-card system, which "proved highly unsatisfactory." This was abandoned in 1888 for a single "clearance card," but this too "did not eliminate all of the problems inherent in the travel system."[129] Some unions, such as the Carpenters, Printers, and Iron Molders imposed time limits on the card. If a member failed to deposit the travel card with a local union within the time limit, he or she generally lost privileges or was suspended.[130] While this was meant to be an incentive to deposit the card in a timely fashion, it also meant that those who didn't were out of the union, at least until reinstated. The Western Federation of Miners also found that the "traveling card had not proven to be a satisfactory method of controlling tramp miners" and experimented unsuccessfully with various changes.[131]

As we saw above in the case of the Iron Molders and the Machinists, one indication of how leaky these systems were can be seen in the number of travel loans not repaid. The Cigar Makers were one of the few unions with a central travel-loan system, which was established in 1879. The loans had to be repaid or the member would eventually face suspension and be out of the union. As the system got up and running in 1881, the *Cigar Makers' Official Journal* complained, "So far we have paid out a lot of money, and collected very little, considering that the trade is more prosperous than it has been for years."[132] And indeed, the monthly reports on loans made and loans collected in the *Official Journal* in 1881 show that the number of loans exceeded the number of collections fairly consistently.[133] By 1898, the union's financial report showed that "loans outstanding" had accumulated to $83,080.53.[134] In 1905, President Perkins stated that there were still $88,000 in unpaid loans. He estimated that the union granted "from $2,000 to $3,000 more loans each year than we collect."[135] When the travel-loan program was finally dropped in 1928, the union had "a quarter of a million dollars coming for travel loans," but simply wiped the debt off the books as uncollectable.[136] Clearly, from the start, a significant number of members had dropped out of the union before they paid off their loans or had been suspended for failure to pay.

While the turnover of local unions shown above can be attributed mainly to the various contradictory forces of accumulation and urbanization, the turnover and loss of traveling union members must in large part be the result of the leaky travel-card system. Here we look more closely at two unions for which sufficient data are available: the Western Federation of Miners, a new industrial union with a highly volatile membership, and the Cigar Makers' International Union, an old-established craft union with a tradition of traveling.

The Western Federation of Miners (WFM) was organized as an industrial union in 1893 by pulling together local unions and former Knights of Labor assemblies of metal and hard-rock miners from around the West. Despite the long depression of 1893–1897, western mining thrived and grew rapidly during the 1890s as over three thousand new mining firms each with a capitalization of over $1 million were formed, while copper production rose more or less steadily from 129,882 short tons in 1890 to 303,059 in 1900, lead from 157,844 to 367,773, and zinc from 63,683 to 123,886 tons over that decade.[137] The stormy history of the WFM shows that industrial as opposed to craft organization did not reduce the problems of a migratory membership or improve the effectiveness of the traveling-card system. In the early years of the twentieth century, about a third of all WFM members were registered as "tramps" at any one time. This may be an underestimate, as the members seldom kept track of their traveling cards. As one delegate told the 1907 convention of the WFM, "The great majority of the members of the Western Federation of Miners are itinerant. They are traveling around from place to place and pay little attention to what kind of card they have. You can make it of gold and I will guarantee that the so-called tramp miner or ten day miner will not keep it."[138]

Membership turnover in the WFM's local unions averaged about 49 percent a year, according to Foster, so that the union grew slowly from about 20,000 at its founding to 27,154 in 1903. To achieve even this growth would have taken at least 14,000 new recruits or reinstated members, given the high membership turnover. Another indication of the enormous turnover of membership can be seen in the roster of convention delegates from its founding to 1900. At the founding convention in 1893 there were forty-three delegates. Of those only four appeared at the third convention in 1895, which had twenty-six delegates. No delegates from the 1893 convention were present at the 1900 convention, which was attended by eighty delegates, and only two people from 1895 were present in 1900—and they were the president and secretary-treasurer of the union.[139] This discontinuity of convention delegates simply reflected what would have been a nearly 100 percent turnover of members over the two years between conventions in the locals that sent delegates to the biennial conventions.[140] According to Foster's estimates for 1903 and 1905, when figures were available, an average of 32 percent of WFM members were tramping during those years, while total membership fell by over one thousand members.[141] Clearly, the WFM was leaking tramp members at a high rate.

In contrast to the WFM, the Cigar Makers' International Union (CMIU) was a well-established craft union with a highly developed benefit system, including its travel loans, in which President Strasser had expressed such confidence in its hold on his members to the Industrial Commission.[142] In addition, the CMIU had a number of stringent rules to prevent abuses of the traveling-loan system. One of them was that a member failing to deposit his card in a local union was fined ten cents a day for thirty days and then suspended.[143] For those unable or unwilling to deposit, this rule would tend to encourage exit from or expulsion by the union.

Table 7. CMIU Members, Suspended, Those on Travel Cards and Loans

Years*	Members	Suspended	On Travel Card	Loans
1886–87	22,619	14,042	18,798	$86,453
1888–89	17,377	11,737	16,540	$81,112

* September of the previous year to October of the current year.
Source: Proceedings of the Seventeenth Session of the Cigar Makers' International Union, Buffalo, NY, October, 1887, 3-4; *Proceedings of the Eighteenth Session of the Cigar Makers' International Union*, Buffalo, NY, October, 1889, 3.

Table 7 shows the number of CMIU members, those suspended, and those on travel cards. Those traveling were the equivalent of 83 percent of the average recorded stationary membership of 1886–1887 and 95 percent of those in 1888–1889, both very high ratios. In other words, in the second half of the 1880s almost half the total union membership was on the road at one point or another each year.

These years were not depression years, so the drop in membership cannot be explained simply by cyclical economic conditions. Furthermore, we know that cigar makers, like most traveling union members, did more traveling in good times when work was available in multiple places.[144] Thus, the figures for suspensions and travelers suggest at least part of the explanation for the decline. The high levels of suspensions and travelers in 1886–1887 contributed to a drop in membership in the following years as members passed out through the traveling system between union counts, while the number of newly initiated members also fell, failing to make up the difference of those lost. The actual number of suspensions and travelers moved in the same direction as member losses, falling in 1888–1889. This correlation strongly suggests a causal link between the level of traveling, the number of suspensions, and the decline in membership.

Furthermore, if the Cigar Makers lost a percentage of their traveling members similar to the Bricklayers (17 percent) or Iron Molders (16–20 percent), that would have meant a loss of between six thousand and seven thousand members in the period 1886–1889. This would account for almost a quarter of the suspended Cigar Makers members in those years. If we apply the 17 percent to the average of seventy thousand to eighty thousand union members traveling each year in this period, the total loss through the traveling-card system alone would have amounted to just over one hundred thousand for these four years. The 17 percent figure for the Bricklayers, however, is for 1901, when traveling would have been less frequent than in its high point in the period of 1886–1889, so that the loss of members via the traveling card would most likely have been higher. Thus, the loss of members through the traveling-card system alone certainly goes a long way toward explaining the slow growth of the trade unions in this period. Had these members not been lost to traveling, organized labor could have gained at least an additional hundred thousand members in these years alone.

Clearly, the workings of the contradictory process of capital accumulation and the perfect storm of the 1880s that encouraged tramping limited the growth of the trade unions throughout the period in the years between the great railroad strike of 1877 through the mid-1890s. For the Knights of Labor, built on shaky ground during its period of initial growth, this ultimately meant a collapse of membership it could not stem. Together, the continuing decline of the Knights and the slow growth of the trade unions meant that organized labor fell behind the rapid growth of the process of accumulation, the burgeoning businesses it was creating, and the expanding workforce it spawned. In his assessment of union membership trends, Gerald Friedman argues that "business-cycle conditions have little consistent relationship with union growth rates in this period," whereas "industrial output grew faster in years of slow union growth."[145] This is because the impact of the uneven processes of capital accumulation and urbanization, their convergence in the 1880s, the lost strikes resulting from capital's counteroffensive, and the streams of migration these forces unleashed made workers' organization an uphill struggle from the 1870s through the mid-1890s. In the final years of the Gilded Age, however, new trends in the development of business organization, along with a period of prolonged growth, provided a breathing space in which organized labor made significant gains.

A Breathing Space: Relative Stability and the End of the Gilded Age

The long depression that began in 1893 bottomed out in June 1897, after which the economy experienced growth for nearly a decade. The gross national product more than doubled in nominal terms between 1897 and 1907, with only a slight pause in 1904, while in real terms it rose 63 percent over those years, or more than 6 percent a year on average. Over this period the average annual business failure rate ran at about 14 percent below that of the depression years, while the index of manufacturing output almost doubled. In real terms, the value of output of fixed capital rose from $2.7 billion in 1889 to $3.4 billion in 1899. It was also in the late 1890s that total US exports and those of finished manufactured goods surpassed imports. What is more, the proportion of income accruing to capital grew from 47.5 percent of the total in the 1880s to 50 percent in the 1890s and 53 percent in the first decade of the twentieth century.[146] Clearly, in economic terms all was going well for American capital at the turn of the new century.

At the same time, partly due to the "compression" experienced throughout most of the 1890s and to the improved conditions after 1897, the turn of the century saw one of those leaps of working-class activity and organization cited by Eric Hobsbawm.[147] The number of strikes soared from 1,056 involving 184,000 workers in 1896 to 3,493 strikes and 532,000 strikers in 1903, well above the level of those in 1886–1887.[148] By 1900 two out of three strikes were successful or partially so, no doubt reducing one incentive for migration.[149] Thus, in the wake of this strike wave, over a million and a half workers rushed into trade unions between 1899 and 1904—far more than during the Great Upheaval of 1886–1887.[150] Furthermore, more of them came to stay this time despite some future setbacks. Much of the reason for this lay in the new situation of capital and the employers themselves.

It was in these years that many industries achieved the organizational and geographic stability that would characterize big business for much of the new century. The huge consolidation movement in the final year of the nineteenth century, when the number of mergers soared to 1,208, four times the previous year, created many of the corporate giants of the early twentieth century.[151] This in turn fed the rise of the corporate bureaucratic norms of operation analyzed by Chandler, Jacoby, and others that replaced the volatile era of the robber barons.[152] While competition would remain a constant feature of capitalism, Matthew Josephson concluded,

"After so many storms, upheavals and trials which led to the Great Truce of 1901 between the House of Morgan and the House of Rockefeller, a period of comparative harmony ruled in these high quarters."[153]

Table 8. Geographic Concentration of Major Industries by Percent of Total Dollar Value of Product, 1900

Industry	State	Percent of Dollar Value of Product
Clocks	Connecticut	63.5 percent
Coke	Pennsylvania	62.2 percent
Safes and vaults	Ohio	61.8 percent
Brassware	Connecticut	54.1 percent
Iron and steel	Pennsylvania	54.0 percent
Carpets and rugs	Pennsylvania	48.0 percent
Boots and Shoes	Massachusetts	44.9 percent
Agricultural Implements	Illinois	41.5 percent
Meat packing	Illinois	40.1 percent

Source: US Bureau of the Census, *Abstract of the Twelfth Census of the United States, 1900* (Washington, DC: US Government Printing Office, 1904), 340.

At the same time, as table 8 shows, many major industries achieved a high degree of geographic concentration in specific states—mostly in one or two cities within that state. In combination, these trends also meant large geographic concentrations of the workers in these industries. Equally important from the standpoint of most business leaders was the stabilization of national politics that accompanied the defeat of Populism and the dominance of the Republican Party as a result of the "critical" election of 1896. The McKinley victory of 1896 was in part accomplished by the unprecedented fundraising of industrialist Mark Hanna, who raised over three and a half million dollars, twice what had been raised in the previous election—and a clear indication of the role of business in politics.[154] At the same time, the Democratic Party achieved a new measure of stability with the emergence of the "solid South" following the defeat of Populism and the increasing disenfranchisement of African Americans throughout the South.[155] Along with the turn to extracontinental imperialism with the Spanish-American War, these trends helped create a greater sense of confidence and collective power as a class within the business community.

As Stromquist suggests in the case of the railroads, the high level of intense labor conflict from 1877 onward into the mid-1890s may well have been a factor leading some employers to attempt more regular relations with their employees' organizations.[156] Schneirov describes a similar process in Chicago in the wake of the 1894 Pullman strike as elite elements in the Chicago Civic Federation began to advocate "arbitration"—that is, voluntary collective bargaining—and union recognition. Thus by 1896, William Baker, head of the Board of Trade and president of the Chicago Civic Federation, could declare that "all through the building trades, the printing trades, iron trades in almost every line of skilled labor, trades unions were recognized without any demoralization of business." This approach would be taken up by the National Civic Federation when it was formed in 1900.[157] While much of capital remained hostile to unionism and further mass confrontations lay ahead, these developments allowed the increased institutionalization of trade unions through established collective-bargaining arrangements.

Between 1890 and 1900, national or regional collective bargaining agreements had been established for the Iron Molders (1891, 1899); the United Mine Workers (1898, 1900); and the Machinists (1899).[158] Beginning in the late 1880s, the Typographers won citywide agreements in the cities where printing was by then concentrated, with 44 percent of their members in the six largest printing centers.[159] Building trades unions also achieved local collective bargaining in most large cities. Indeed, by 1900 John R. Commons could comment, "This higher form of industrial peace—negotiations—has now reached a formal stage in a half dozen large industries in the United States." These included not only those workers discussed above, but also the Great Lakes longshoremen and the boot and shoe workers.[160] More broadly, Commons observed of the 1890s, "The coming in of the trade agreement, whether national, sectional, or local, was also the chief factor in stabilizing the [labor] movement against depression."[161]

Yet the geographic settling of industry and the subsequent institutionalization of the trade unions through collective bargaining agreements, along with new growth, also meant that union leaders began to frown on constant traveling. Tygiel documents this for the Carpenters, noting that "as the union became more firmly entrenched, however, there emerged among its leadership a growing disenchantment with the fabled 'tramp carpenter' and by the turn of the century the itinerant had fallen into disfavor with the new class of professional labor bureaucrats." Although tramping could not be entirely eliminated, the union took steps to limit the practice.[162] In a similar effort to limit tramping, the Bricklayers allowed local unions to impose high initiation fees on traveling members to reduce what Secretary O'Dea called the "underground railroad business," particularly where there was more than one local in overlapping labor markets—for example, New York City and northern New Jersey.[163] So unsatisfactory was the traveling-loan system of the Iron Molders that in the early 1890s locals began refusing to grant loans, and the system was finally replaced with an "out-of-work" benefit in 1897 that, it was hoped, would keep more members at home.[164]

The concentration of an industry, increased mechanization, and collective bargaining agreements also tended to reduce tramping somewhat. When asked by the Industrial Commission in 1899 whether "this transient element, then, has largely disappeared from the printing business?," Samuel Donnelly of the ITU replied, "To a great extent." In that same year, he was able to report to the union's convention, "The list of delinquent unions published, as required by [union] law, during the past year, has been exceedingly small."[165] Even in unions where tramping did not diminish, the new institutional framework of collective bargaining and the growth of union administration and bureaucracy it brought meant that traveling members had a less disruptive effect since wages and conditions were fixed for a time and the mechanism for their renewal was in place. In fact, this institutional framework allowed for significant growth.

Table 9. Trade-Union Growth, 1898/1899–1902/1904

Union	1898/1899	1902/1904
Carpenters	31,508	161,205
Bricklayers	33,351	56,279
Cigar Makers	26,460	39,391
Mine Workers (coal)	32,902	300,000*
Iron Molders	28,941	54,251
Typographers	28,614	38,364
Machinists	22,500	32,500**
Total All Unions	831,379	2,383,378

* 1905.
** 1900 and 1901.
Sources: Proceedings of the Sixteenth Biennial Convention of the United Brotherhood of Carpenters and Joiners of America, Des Moines, IA, September 19, 1910, 109, 282; Proceedings of the Thirty-Fifth Annual Convention of the Bricklayers and Masons' International Union, Milwaukee, January 14–26, 1901, 22; Forty-Fourth Annual Report of the President and Secretary of the Bricklayers and Masons' International Union of America, Indianapolis, December 1, 1909, 282; Cigar Makers' Official Journal, May 1904, 7; Frank Julian Warne, Coal-Mine Workers: A Study in Labor Organization (New York: Longmans, Green, 1905), 219–222; Frank T. Stockton, The International Molders' Union of North America (Baltimore: Johns Hopkins Press, 1921), 23; Report of the Officers and Proceedings of the Forty-Eighth Session of the International Typographical Union, Cincinnati, August 11–16, 1902, 27.

In the breathing space created by these changes in business organization, concentration, and collective agreements, unions grew once again, often drawing in new members through strike action. Table 9 shows the growth of some of the unions with large traveling memberships. Overall, total union membership rose from 619,579 in 1896 to 1,170,160 in 1900, reaching 2,383,378 in 1904. Among the biggest winners were the unions in construction, which soared from 151,418 in 1899 to 465,269 in 1904, as well as those on the railroads, which grew from 59,030 to 252,892 during the same period. Both of these groups of unions, it should be noted, were stalwarts in the movement toward "pure and simple" unionism. Union density also rose overall from 5 percent to 11 percent in 1904, while that in noncommercial industry rose from 9 percent to 21 percent in those years.[166]

After 1904, increased immigration and migration, along with a new depression and a revived employers' offensive, would send these figures down somewhat. As Leon Fink points out, by 1904 the aggressively anti-union National Association of Manufacturers eclipsed the more cooperatively minded National Civic Federation and "led the charge against any contractual conciliation with the trade unions."[167] Nevertheless, organized labor had achieved a degree of stability absent in the Gilded Age. This stability, however, came too late to salvage the various efforts at independent political action that had characterized the Gilded Age. The volatility of the fading era and the limits it imposed on union growth that preceded the end of the Gilded Age had undermined the labor-party efforts that arose in the 1880s and 1890s. It is, of course, the failure of these political efforts that often lies at the base of most American "exceptionalist" arguments as we saw in the introduction. The following chapter will examine these political efforts in greater detail.

Chapter 5

WHY INDEPENDENT WORKING-CLASS POLITICS FAILED IN THE GILDED AGE

From a late twentieth-century American perspective, what is perhaps
most striking about the political tumult of the 1880s is the centrality of
worker organization to both the structure and outcomes of the contests.
—**Leon Fink, 1983**[1]

FROM THE late 1870s through the mid-1890s, organized labor activists
in the United States attempted three times to form independent working-
class-based parties: 1877–1878, 1886–1888, and 1893–1894. In each case,
organized labor proved too weak to sustain political action independent
of the two mainstream parties. Looking at the relationship between union organization and labor-party efforts, John Laslett argues that the major reason for the
lack of a labor party in the US by the early twentieth century is that "the labor
movement was relatively small at this time and dominated by conservative craft
unions." In contrast, he writes,

> It is illuminating to compare this situation with that in Great Britain or in
> Germany where mass industrial unionism had already begun to develop in
> the last decades of the nineteenth century, providing the widespread numeri-
> cal base which alone could sustain an independent labor party.[2]

Making the same point to explain the success of the British Labour Party,
G. D. H. Cole also noted that both old and new unions of skilled and unskilled
workers in the UK more than doubled their membership by 1895. Arguing for the
connection between the growth of the unions and "the political Labor movement,"
he wrote, "It was one and the same impulse that, between 1885 and 1895, doubled
the strength of the Trade Unions affiliated to the Trades Union Congress and
brought into being a powerful movement for the creation of an independent party
based on the organized strength of the working class."[3]

In other words, without a sufficient organized mass base in the emerging working class, the possibility of a permanent labor party or even a farmer-labor or populist party in the US was problematic, despite several efforts in that direction during the Gilded Age. All three national efforts show considerable support in the ranks for a more radical political course but at the same time the lack of organizational strength and resources to turn sentiment into sustained political motion.

It was during the Great Upheaval of the mid-1880s that strike levels reached a new high, union membership grew most rapidly, and a mass movement "from below" for independent political action swept the country. Of these years Selig Perlman wrote, "Labor organizations assumed the nature of a real class movement."[4] It was also, however, in the mid-1880s that internal migration reached its highest point of the era and, in the wake of the Great Upheaval, both union membership and the labor-party movement of that decade collapsed despite some promising electoral successes. The problem, then, was not one of consciousness, but of organization that was repeatedly undermined by the massive movement of people in the turbulence of rapid and uneven industrialization described throughout this book.

Reviewing Gilded-Age Politics

Before proceeding to the analysis of the three attempts to build labor-based parties, some of the best-known generalizations about nineteenth-century American politics need some qualification if we are to understand more accurately the barriers facing the labor activists and leaders who attempted to go beyond the limits of the two major parties that emerged from the Civil War, the Democrats and Republicans. The first such generalization is the widely cited high voter turnout in US elections for most of the nineteenth century. The most frequently cited figure by well-respected political scientists and historians alike is that voter participation rates in presidential elections reached nearly 80 percent from the Jackson era to 1896.[5] There are three problems with this view of voter turnout. The first involves the difference between the actual and potential voter turnout resulting from residency and registration requirements, the second the focus on presidential elections rather than state and local elections. A third problem concerns the equally repeated notion that loyalty to the two major parties was particularly intense in this period.

The disenfranchisement of African Americans in the late nineteenth century and the permanent disenfranchisement of women in this era have justifiably been the focus of considerable scholarship in understanding the shape of the political culture of much of the twentieth century. Far less attention has been given to the de facto disenfranchisement of much of the Gilded Age's diverse and growing working class that flowed from its high degree of geographic mobility. As David Montgomery summarized the limitations of the suffrage, even after the passage of the Fifteenth Amendment eliminating racial disqualification, "Foreign citizenship, failure to meet residency and poll tax requirements, and above all gender, sharply curtailed the working class vote."[6] These obstacles were bound to affect the ability of many working-class males to vote as well.

Looking at the question of voter participation rates, at the time of the presidential election of 1884 there were almost fifteen million males over twenty-one years of age, the most basic qualification for voting. However, in that election only a little over ten million people voted. Thus, in 1884 almost five million adult males did not vote for one reason or another. While the official turnout rate of eligible voters was 77.5 percent for that year, the actual turnout rate of those potentially eligible was 69 percent.[7] One reason was that many states had fairly long residency and in some cases personal registration requirements, both of which would have worked against America's migratory working class and its growing immigrant contingent. In some industrial areas this had an extreme effect. Montgomery notes than in industrial Lawrence, Massachusetts, only 15 percent of the population were registered to vote in 1880.[8] With inter- and intrastate migration running in the millions, it is obvious that many adult males, whether citizens or not, would have failed to make the residency requirement, which in many states was quite long in those years. It was not until the 1970 amendment to the Voting Rights Act that residency requirements were limited to thirty days.[9]

Several states allowed foreign-born males to vote if they signed a statement of intent to become citizens, but important industrial states such as Ohio and Illinois had abolished this right before 1870.[10] For immigrants new to their chosen community, residency posed a barrier to voting. For those who couldn't speak or write English, the registration requirement was equally daunting. While few figures are available for voter turnout by ethnicity, in San Francisco as late as 1900, among registered voters 56.5 percent were Germans, 37.9 percent were Scandinavians, and 19.7 percent were Italians. In the state of Michigan in 1884, only 38 percent of Polish male workers of voting age voted.[11] It is worth bearing in mind that in Michigan alone in the 1880s, while 19,700 native-born whites left the state, 193,200 foreign-born people entered it. Obviously, such high turnover would have presented a residency problem for many of the immigrants who entered the state in that decade. In the East North Central region as a whole this turnover saw 483,100 native-born whites leave their state and 865,400 foreign-born people enter the region. Such a spatial churning of population and ethnicity would have had a significant negative effect on many people's ability to vote even where immigrants had the right to do so. Since the labor-party movement of 1886–1887 was heavily dependent on immigrant workers who composed large percentages of the industrial workforce in most cities, low participation rates among the foreign-born, for whatever reasons, put them at an electoral disadvantage. The frequently repeated idea of high voter turnout must be significantly modified for the potential male working-class electorate of the Gilded Age.

The second qualification to the notion of high turnout rates follows from the centrality of state and local politics for labor in this period. It was at these levels of the American political structure that most social and regulatory legislation was passed by labor and most union-friendly officials elected. In these elections for state legislative and local offices, official counts of voter turnout ran between 60–80 percent.[12] If we assume a similar gap in the potential electorate as in national elections, and especially its working-class component, this tells us two things. First, working-class electoral insurgency was at a disadvantage from the start as turnout was even lower than in national elections.

Second and more important, however, was the fact that under these difficult circumstances, working-class voter turnout would have depended on the state of organization of workers in the localities where they challenged the two old parties. Unions could help register voters and increase turnout. Thus, in this context of high levels of immigration and internal migration the relative strength or weakness of labor organization was a key factor in both the successes and the failures of Gilded-Age labor-party movements, particularly those in the mid-1880s.

The third qualification is the oft-repeated proposition that, as one historian put it, "the decades that followed the Civil War became in the eyes of historians and political scientists 'the party period,' the time of greatest attachment to political parties in the country's history"—meaning, of course, attachment to the two major parties. As political scientist Walter Dean Burnham put it, "In this period there was no popular cultural support for the 'independent' voter." The symbol of this party loyalty, as well as of high turnout, was the torchlight parade, or "military style" and "drill" that mobilized voters until the late 1890s.[13] As cited in the introduction, this view has been challenged both before and since, first by John D. Hicks in 1933 and more recently by Mark Voss-Hubbard, both of whom noted that alternative parties were in fact a regular and influencing feature of nineteenth-century politics.[14] No doubt most voters cast their ballot for one of the two major parties in most elections, particularly in congressional and presidential contests. Even there, however, party loyalties often took a back seat in moments of perceived crisis or matters of primary importance to certain voters.

Eric Foner writes of the importance of the Free Soil Party in 1848 despite its poor showing in the election,

> The Free Soil party thus played an important role in the spread of anti-slavery sentiments. In addition, the spectacle of a founder of the Democratic party and an ex-president repudiating the regular nominee of his party and running on an independent ticket "totally dispelled the prestige, sanctity, and domination of 'regular' nominations" in the words of one Hunker.[15]

In 1872, "mugwump" reformers appalled by the corruption surrounding the Grant

Administration deserted the Republican Party and ran reformer and New York *Tribune* editor Horace Greeley as a Liberal Republican with the endorsement of the Democratic Party.[16] In the following presidential election of 1876, southern Democrats threw their Electoral College support to Republican Rutherford B. Hayes in return for the final withdrawal of federal troops from the South and recognition of white-supremacist Redeemer state governments in the notorious Compromise of 1877.[17] In 1878, a million or so voters cast ballots for local, state, and congressional candidates of Greenback Labor or Workingmen's Parties.[18] In 1892, a million voters deserted the major parties for the Populist Party candidate. Lawrence Goodwyn noted of the Democratic Party's 1892 and 1894 losses to Populism, "The old party had taken massive losses in 1892 in the West, and the defections in the South reached such tidal proportions in 1894 as to imperil the party in its 'Solid South' heartland."[19]

In the "critical" election of 1896, Democrats, repelled by William Jennings Bryan's alleged Populism and evangelical style, deserted their party in large numbers to vote for Republican William McKinley. In New York in that year, Tammany, the ultimate urban Democratic organization of that era, chose to ignore their presidential candidate and mobilize only for congressional, state, and local offices.[20] In some states the drop in the percentage of the Democratic vote between 1892 and 1896 was large: in Wisconsin it dropped from 47.9 percent to 37.8 percent; in Massachusetts from 47.3 percent to 25.5 percent; in Rhode Island from 48 percent to 37.6 percent; and in Maryland 51 percent to 44 percent. Even more striking was the drop in the Democratic vote in some major cities between 1892 and 1896: New York from 59 percent to 42 percent; Philadelphia 42 percent to 26 percent; Detroit 50 percent to 41 percent; and Chicago 55 percent to 40 percent.[21] This brought to an end the close election results that had previously characterized national elections. Thus, even in national elections where the fear of wasted votes was highest, there were notable exceptions to the rule of major party loyalty.

Limits of the Urban Party "Machine"

Another frequently mentioned barrier to independent working-class politics in the late nineteenth century concerns the role of the urban and mostly ethnically based political party "machine." Sombart's discussion of "the Political Machine" emphasized the large number of elections and the vast number of professionals and money needed to perpetuate such an organization in New York City (actually Manhattan or New York County). Oddly enough, for a demonstration of the power of urban political machines, the figures he produced for the 1896 election show that the antimachine opposition "fusionists" were able to deploy far more operatives and hold more events than Tammany: 2,500 speakers to Tammany's 1,500 and 4,000 meetings to 3,700 for the machine. No doubt this helps explain the huge drop in the Democratic vote in New York City in 1896 mentioned above. Between 1886 and 1897 Tammany averaged only a plurality of 49.5 percent of the vote in its bailiwick.[22]

Martin Shefter and Ira Katznelson present slightly different views of the importance of the urban machine in the Gilded Age. Shefter emphasizes the dichotomy between the trade union on the one hand and the machine on the other. For Katznelson it is the separation between the workplace, where some form of class consciousness exists, and the ward-level machine where ethnic identity dominates.[23] Both, however, see the machine as the key barrier to working-class independent political action, much as Sombart did.

If by "political machine" we mean that combination of hierarchical and centralized party organization that penetrated working-class neighborhoods, usually with some version of the clubhouse system or "more or less elaborate grassroots organization," and the dispensation of patronage in the form of jobs and contracts by a powerful party boss, it is by no means the case that such machines were widespread before the end of the century despite the use of the term.[24] Sufficient patronage requires high city expenditures and long-term tenure of city offices in order to control patronage, as well as a central authority to dispense them and select loyal candidates. In most cities these conditions did not prevail in the Gilded Age. In the case of patronage jobs, Judd and Swanstrom point out, "Though city governments grew rapidly in the late nineteenth century, the number of public jobs was pitifully small compared to the jobs available in the private economy."[25] Richard Schneirov, in his political history of late nineteenth-century Chicago, *Labor and Urban Politics*, notes the "fiscal restraints on government" and the fact that the principle source of patronage in Chicago, public works, "was under the control of business leaders." He also questions the presence of an omnipotent machine in what had become by 1890 the nation's second city.

For one thing, no single party ran the city throughout this period. For another, there were severe restraints on public spending and, hence, patronage. In this period in the cities under Irish Democratic Party control saw per capita city spending fall by about 40 percent. But most telling is what Schneirov says about Mike McDonald, "who came as close to being a Democratic Party boss as anyone in this era." Schneirov writes, "But McDonald could not be a boss in the manner of Richard Crocker of New York's Tammany Hall, because Chicago, like most cities in the 1880s, lacked a centralized machine for controlling nominations and dictating policy."[26] Without centralized control of city jobs and contracts, such ward-level organization as existed would have had little to distribute to its constituents and, hence, little to sustain loyalty in the nonideological manner attributed to urban political "bosses."

Additionally, Schneirov writes about the ability of the major party organizations in the newer cities of the West, including Chicago, to incorporate the working class: "In the West, however, where party patronage and organization were far weaker, large movements of agrarian and labor reform grew up in this period and proved immune to party co-optation."[27] Regarding Chicago, Bruce C. Nelson points out that "municipal politics remained competitive throughout the period." While Democratic mayor Carter Harrison was reelected four times, "neither major party was entrenched: in ten elections between 1876 and 1893 the Democrats won the mayoralty six times, the Republican's four." Furthermore, the possibility of a genuine "machine" based on ethnic groups was rendered problematic by the political split of the major ethnic groups that dominated most cities by the 1880s: the Irish were Democrats, while the Germans, Norwegians, and Swedes were mostly Republicans.[28]

Machine politics and patronage in this era were mostly dominated by the Irish. As Judd and Swanstrom, as well as Erie, point out, "Scandinavians, Germans, and Jews, for example, participated relatively little in machine politics."[29] The Germans, furthermore, were often divided along religious and party lines, as were native-born whites, while African Americans were Republicans. Olivier Zunz describes a similar lack of political party unity across or even within ethnic lines in Detroit, as well as alternating party government in these years despite ethnic concentrations.[30] The sort of centralized machine that could have held together different ward-based ethnic groups was largely absent. Brown and Halaby's comprehensive study of thirty major cities found only six with citywide machines by the late 1880s and early 1890s, and at least half of these disappeared after 1895. Steven Erie limits the number of Irish-dominated Democratic machines to four.[31] Thus, the likelihood of a single-party citywide machine based in ethnic neighborhoods beyond the Irish was not a possibility in most cities in this period, and without a centralized organization the distribution of even the relatively small amount of patronage would have been problematic.

Even Manhattan's Tammany Hall, by far the most developed of the urban Democratic organizations, did not meet the strictest definition of a machine for the entire period. As Shefter points out, it was only after Henry George's United Labor Party campaign for mayor in 1886 won large votes in Tammany's working-class districts that Democratic Manhattan bosses John Kelly and Richard Crocker "extended throughout the city a mode of organization—the district club—that was found to be a more successful means of ensuring voter loyalty to the machine than working through autonomous neighborhood institutions."[32] It is even likely that prior to this Tammany actually lost some organizational strength not only with William M. "Boss" Tweed's downfall in 1871, but also by new state laws that, among other things, replaced the city's notorious volunteer fire companies with a professional fire department. As Eric Foner put it, these fire companies "formed important cogs in the Tammany machine."[33] Furthermore, during the 1870s and the 1880s, the New York City Democratic Party was split between Tammany and the reform wing loyal to national party elder Samuel J. Tilden.[34] Indeed, as David Montgomery points out, following the demise of Boss Tweed in 1871, New York's "Democrats dissolved into half a dozen competing clubs for the rest of the century."[35] Matters became even worse with the depression of the 1890s, as what patronage there was dried up. Tammany saw setbacks, and virtually all the Democratic machines were "forced to choose the low-cost alternative . . . demands: racetracks, gambling, and drinking."[36] All of this hardly conforms to the twentieth-century view of the centralized urban political machine. A word needs to be said about the huge numbers of political "professionals" and party operatives first put forward by Moisei Ostrogorski in his two-volume 1902 work, *Democracy and the Organization of Political Parties.* Looking at the various levels of party organization toward the end of the Gilded Age, he estimates that the total troops available within the party organizations numbered "of course quite approximately, at from 800,000 to 900,000 men," with another 50,000 or so in the higher party committees.[37] This appears an astounding number and has been cited by historians since as evidence of the strength of professional—that is, "machine"—organization in American politics. As Ostrogorski himself makes clear, however, this legion of party operatives is spread out across the nation into 2,200 counties. If the party operatives were spread out evenly, each county would average about 400 and each party more or less half of that. Of course, they were not spread evenly, and the exceptionally strong Tammany organization could deploy far more than that, though in the most populous county in the nation.

Nonetheless, even the urban party organizations appear less impressive before the turn of the century, when patronage would accelerate.[38]

Furthermore, within these counties are many assembly district organizations and countless thousands of wards or electoral districts. And of course, this vast number is divided not only between the two major parties but also within these parties in many places between competing factions. Tammany, for example, had to compete with Irving Hall and county Democrats within the New York County (Manhattan) party organization.

Ostrogorski takes note of this problem when he writes of the political "clubs" forming at that time and that "they are likely rather to afford the opportunities for the jealousies of the small politicians wrangling over the spoils, and to keep alive the spirit of factionalism."[39]

He notes, however, the growth of these clubs nationally since the late 1880s, as the example above of Tammany after the 1886 elections shows. Thus, the modern machine was still in formation in the 1890s. As Ostrogorski himself points out, one of the most invaluable institutions hosting these clubs were "drinking-saloons."

He writes, "The party organizations and the candidates therefore find that their most valuable helpers for manipulating the electorate are the saloon-keepers, and the latter must be rightly ranked among their regular auxiliaries." Saloon-keepers, however, had been the center of party organizations for decades well before the rise of the clubhouse system he takes note of. British observer James Bryce had noted the importance of the saloon as the grassroots site of electoral activity in New York in 1884 when he wrote,

> The lower sort of city politicians congregate in clubs and barrooms; and as much of the cohesive strength of the smaller party organizations arises from their being also social bodies, so also much of the power which liquor dealers exercise is due to the fact that "heelers" and "workers" spend their evenings in drinking places, and that meetings for political purposes are held there. Of the 1,007 primaries and conventions of all parties held in New York City preparatory to the elections of 1884, 633 took place in liquor saloons.[40]

Bryce describes the developed assembly district-based clubhouse system only after the turn of the century, probably 1914 in the edition cited here. Each district had its own headquarters and "clubhouse." Altogether there were about eleven hundred precincts each with its own captain.[41] It was most certainly the new clubhouse system that brought in the legions Ostrogorski described. Even then, while urban counties like New York County or Cook County (Chicago) would have a much greater concentration of activists than rural counties, Ostrogorski nonetheless suggests just how spread out these party operatives were: "In every village or 'school district' of any importance there is a local committee of three to five militants."[42] The more we look at the nine hundred thousand, the thinner their distribution gets and the less overwhelming is the "professional" core of the party organizations and "machines" outside a handful of eastern cities and even there only toward the end of our period.

A ward- or district-level party organization or "ring," or even a citywide party organization, in other words, was not the same thing as a machine based on widespread patronage in most cities for most of this period, and the type of single-party rule that came to characterize many US cities in the twentieth century was by no means universal in the nineteenth. The dramatic decline of the Democratic votes between 1892 and 1896 in New York, Boston, Baltimore, and elsewhere at the same time as the nine hundred thousand "militants" certainly brings into question just how well organized and influential the urban Democratic machines of the era really were, even in the older cities of the East.[43] What is more, the emphasis of both Shefter and Katznelson on the supposed separation of class consciousness and ethnic identity between work and home seems dubious in the light of widespread participation of both native- and foreign-born men and women in the eight-hour movement, the labor day parades, frequent mass community support for strikes, extensive use of the citywide boycott, and the broad circulation of city-based labor weeklies, as well as in the various labor-party efforts, all of which show a great deal of overlap during the Gilded Age.

Patterns of Gilded-Age Working-Class Political Rebellion

If E. P. Thompson is right in arguing that class consciousness grows in large part from the common experience of workers in capitalist social relations, then the formation of class consciousness in the US in the Gilded Age can in part be attributed to the increasingly shared experience of the turbulent and contradictory processes of industrialization, urbanization, and class conflict that characterized the era. As Steven J. Ross wrote concerning the upsurge of the mid-1880s in Cincinnati, Ohio, "This explosion of class conflict was not an isolated series of episodes, but part of a long-standing tradition of working-class resistance to the detrimental changes wrought by the expansion of industrial capitalism." If the political upsurge of the mid-1880s was greater than earlier alternative-party efforts it was in part due to the fact that "by the early 1880s, as the overall setting and conditions of production grew more homogeneous, the common experiences and needs of Cincinnati workers began to loom larger than their differences." Above all, it was the flow of semiskilled and unskilled workers into the workforce that made the United Labor Party possible.[44] The same was true in Chicago.

As Schneirov writes, "The resounding impact of the boycott, the eight-hour movement and the extension of labor organization among unskilled working people in the first half of 1886 laid the foundation for another independent foray of Chicago's workers into electoral politics."[45]

In other words, working-class political rebellion in this period was closely related to the level and intensity of industrial conflict *and* to the actions of capital and its allies. While some authors have seen these political movements as an alternative to lost strikes or economic conditions, Leon Fink has argued, "In this era at least union organization and labor politics were not juxtaposed to an alternating economic current; rather the industrial struggle was the generator of political action." Further, Fink links the success or failure of these political movements directly to the state of worker organization when he writes, "From a late twentieth-century American perspective, what is perhaps most striking about the political tumult of the 1880s is the centrality of worker organization to both the structure and outcomes of the contests."[46] This fact, combined with the limitations faced by working-class immigrants in terms of voter turnout discussed above and the need to break old party loyalties where they existed meant that preexisting and relatively stable worker organization was essential to the labor-party movements.

Finally, there is the fact that both the political rebellions of 1877–1878 and

1886–1887 were initiated locally "from below," but then rapidly took on a nation-wide character despite the lack of any central coordination. So far as I know, no one has attempted to explain or theorize this unique fact. While it is more or less easy to understand why the 1877 railroad strike spread across the country, spawn-ing the "workingmen's parties" of 1878, due to the nature of the industry with its network quality and mobile workforce, the spread of a labor-based political move-ment across the continent simultaneously in the 1880s requires some explanation. I believe that explanation lies in the changing condition mentioned above, the pre-history of these movements and the rise of the labor press.

First, the idea of independent working-class political action was hardly new in this era. At the end of the Civil War in April 1866, Andrew C. Cameron wrote in the widely read *Workingmen's Advocate*, "So far as we are concerned, from this day henceforth, the policy of the *Advocate* will be to aid in the formation of a Working-men's Party, independent altogether of either political faction."[47] Some continuity between the 1878 Greenback and Workingmen's tickets can also be discerned in local alternative-party campaigns in the early 1880s. As noted earlier, Detroit had its Independent Labor Party as early as 1882, while Knights and unionists in Den-ver fielded a labor ticket in 1883.[48] In other words, the idea of independent political action by organized labor was in the air and part of the culture of resistance, at least among the activists. This, however, only partially explains the national sweep of such efforts in both 1878 and 1886–1887.

Another piece of the explanation lies in the rise of the labor press in both decades. As John R. Commons and John B. Andrews wrote, "The rise and fall of a labor movement is marked by the rise and fall of the labor press."[49] Similarly, the rise and fall of the political movements in this era was related to the ups and downs of both labor organization and the labor press, which in turn depended largely on the level of worker organization for its success. As we saw in chapter 1, the labor press of the 1870s grew to 120 local weeklies. By the mid-1880s it had risen to 400, perhaps even 800, weekly papers, most carrying news of political actions by labor and many supporting it. Just as the labor press provided important labor market in-formation for workers on the tramp or those considering migration, so on a weekly basis they spread the news of both labor's political reactions to the upsurge of eight-hour strikes and the employers' attempt to roll back the gains, as well as the orga-nizational strides that resulted from these strikes. By the mid-1880s, the labor press bound together activists and leaders across the country on a weekly basis and as a result played a role in spreading labor-party efforts despite the lack of any central coordination. Like the Knights and the labor-party movements, however, the labor press also followed their subsequent decline. We turn now to an examination of the three major labor-party efforts of the Gilded Age.

The First Rebellion, 1877–1878

The first rise in labor-based independent political action in the Gilded Age came in the wake of the volcanic eruption of the 1877 railroad strike that spread across America, drawing in workers of all kinds and in some cases taking on near insurrectionary proportions that shook cities and towns the length of the country. Shelton Stromquist summarized the impact of the strikes:

> The railroad strikes that swept across the country in July 1877 were the clarion call of a new class. On the one hand, they foreshadowed nearly two decades of deepening labor conflict on the railroad, and on the other hand, they were the baptismal rite of a broader, urban working class not bound by differences of trade or skill.[50]

The violence of the strike and the fact that it drew in workers from unrelated industries in cities like Saint Louis, Baltimore, Milwaukee, and Chicago raised the specter of the Paris Commune of 1871 in the minds of both employers and local authorities. The use of state and federal troops to put down the strike in turn convinced many workers that the state was in the hands of capital. The result was a turn to independent political action by union activists across the country in an effort to neutralize state repression.

While the elections of 1877–1878 are usually seen as launched by the Greenback Labor Party, with its cohort of middle-class reformers, farmers, and small businessmen, it also saw independent workers' slates. As Commons et al. put it, "Immediately after the strikes workingmen's parties began to spring up like mushrooms."[51] In Louisville, Kentucky, the Workingmen's Party swept the local elections. As historian Michael Bellesiles described the consequence, "Inspired by the Louisville victory, other labor parties formed and won local elections through the fall of 1877 and in 1878, often electing men who had been leaders of the strike. Many of these labor parties formed coalitions not just with the Greenback Party and middle class reformers, but also with black workers."[52]

Workingmen's and Greenback Labor Party candidates won office not only in Louisville but also in Chicago; Milwaukee; San Francisco; Saint Louis; Toledo, Ohio; Elmira, New York; and Scranton, Pennsylvania, where future Knights of Labor leader Terence V. Powderly won the first of three terms as mayor on the Greenback Labor ticket.

Overall, they won about a million votes and elected fourteen congressmen in 1878. However, much of this vote came from farmers, and the attempt to solidify a national party fell into the hands of middle-class Greenback reformers. When the amount of currency increased rapidly in 1879, the reformers lost their issue and the party atrophied.[53]

The relative weakness of workers in the greenback movement was due to the near collapse of trade unions during the depression of 1873–1879. During these years, sixteen unions expired, while many others lost most of their members, according to Lloyd Ulman.[54] The Knights, who played an important role in the 1878 elections, particularly in Pennsylvania, reported only 9,287 members nationally in 1879.

Commons et al. put the number of union members in 1870–1872 at "about 300,000," but by 1880 there were only 167,681 union and Knights of Labor members in the entire country.[55] Thus, the state of the unions by 1878 was not sufficient to support a stable alternative party or preclude the domination of the Greenback Labor Party by middle-class reformers. The crushing of the 1877 strikes almost certainly meant that many strikers were forced to look for work elsewhere, and indeed, the recovery that began in early 1879 would soon have provided the incentive to tramp, limiting union growth for a while. The organizational weakness of the unions and their activists had allowed the party to fall into the hands of the middle-class and agrarian reformers, which in turn left the party a shell.

The Great Upheaval: Labor's Greatest Attempt at Class Political Action

The Great Upheaval of the mid-1880s that began in 1885 and accelerated in 1886 and 1887 not only ratcheted up class conflict but also promoted acute class consciousness among all sectors of the population as 680,000 workers sent the level of strikes to more than 1,400 in each of those years. As economic recovery began in May 1885 and a series of high-profile strike victories against Jay Gould's Southwest rail system and the timber barons of Michigan caught the imagination of many workers, membership in trade unions and, above all, the Knights of Labor grew and with it the self-confidence of thousands of workers. The planned eight-hour strike set for May 1, 1886, drew in still more workers, and the membership of the Knights soared to 729,000, while that of unaffiliated unions more than doubled in one year to 354,193 in 1886. The craft unions of the new American Federation of Labor also saw some growth, so that total membership of all labor organizations surpassed a million for the first time.[56] The basis for a renewed effort at independent political action had been laid.

Leon Fink has given us the most in-depth analyzes of the political upheaval of the mid-1880s. Summarizing the sweep of the movement, Fink writes:

> Indeed, in some 200 towns and cities from 1885 to 1888 the labor movement actively fielded its own political slates. Adopting "Workingmen's," "United Labor," "Union Labor," "People's Party" and "Independent" labels for their tickets, or alternatively taking over one of the standing two-party organizations in town, those local political efforts revealed deep divisions within the contemporary political culture and evoked sharp reactions from traditional centers of power.[57]

This new political movement saw considerable early success. Norman Ware wrote, "The political campaign of 1886 was the most successful ever conducted by labor in the United States."[58] Commons et al. said of the first round of elections in which the various labor parties participated in 1886, "The showing made at the election surpassed even all expectations." Furthermore, the momentum lasted into the municipal elections in the spring of 1887.[59]

The power behind this movement and its early successes was the bourgeoning Knights of Labor. In November 1886 *John Swinton's Paper* declared of labor's electoral victories of that autumn, "The Knights of Labor led the way." Despite the order's official ambivalence toward partisan politics, the membership and most local organizations threw themselves into this movement. By October of 1886, Powderly and the *Journal of United Labor*, following the ranks, had endorsed Henry George's United Labor Party campaign in New York, and the journal proclaimed labor's political goals could not be accomplished "until the workmen send men of their own grade to make the laws."[60]

The electoral victories and near victories in the fall of 1886 rallied Knights across the country to the banner of independent political action. Thomas Neasham, district master workman of District Assembly 82, composed of thousands of Union Pacific workers and headquartered in Denver, told his members in January 1887,

> We must not forget that we live in an age of great and mighty changes, when everything seems to be in a state of transition, and if the interest manifested in the late elections, by the working men, has any signification at all, it certainly tells us very distinctly and in an unmistakable manner, that we ourselves are on the move, and are passing from an old and effete state of things to a new and nobler state of manhood.

He went on to remind his members that unless "we keep the political, intellectual, and moral elements in line with that of the industrial, our labor will be in vain."[61]

Independent political action by labor also attracted support and sometimes grudging sympathy from trade unions as well. Even the newly formed American Federation of Labor, at its founding convention in December 1886, stated,

> The revolution recently witnessed in the election contests of several States, notably the remarkable and extraordinary demonstration made by the workingmen of New York, Milwaukee, Chicago and other cities, shows us that the time has now arrived when the working people should decide upon the necessity of united action as citizens at the ballot-box, independent of the existing political parties.

In consequence, the convention "*Resolved,* That this Convention urge a most generous support to the independent political movement of workingmen."[62]

The force of this new movement brought about "the very dissolution of normal party structures in dozens of Gilded Age communities" that, Fink writes, "signaled an unusual, crisis-ridden moment for the American political culture."[63] In city after city, the old two-party system disappeared as Republican and Democratic elites rushed into fusion "citizens' slates," or united behind a single candidate to oppose the new labor parties in Chicago; Milwaukee; Denver; Cincinnati; Rochester, New Hampshire; and Rutland, Vermont, among others.[64] This led *John Swinton's Paper* to predict in November 1886 that "there will soon be but two parties in the field, one composed of honest workingmen, lovers of justice and equality; the other . . . composed of kid-gloved, silk-stockinged, aristocratic capitalists and their contemptible toadies."[65] Even the *Iron Molders' Journal* noted the irony of this when it reported the reaction of capital to the Union Labor Party campaigns around the country:

> And wonderful to relate, both of the old parties object, and claim the right, and assert that they can do all that is necessary to be done for labor, and it is useless for them to take political action, and the two old parties have joined hands—a veritable fulfilment of the lion and lamb story—to keep the Union Labor Party from coming to power.[66]

For a moment in much of urban America a new class alignment had taken shape and the two parties that faced one another were those of labor and capital. The idea of such a class realignment did not go unnoticed. Observing the early successes of the labor parties on the one hand "and the readiness with which Republicans and Democrats have united in some of the recent municipal elections" on the other, Henry George speculated, much like John Swinton, that "old habits of thought and touch, are so broken down that new issues can readily come to the front and new alignments of political forces take place."[67] It was not to be.

While most of the local and state labor parties held up through the spring of 1887, the elections in the autumn of that year were a crushing disappointment for labor parties in major industrial states such as New York, Massachusetts, Pennsylvania, and Ohio. When Henry George ran for secretary of state in New York State in the autumn of 1887, his campaign made "a disappointing showing." As Commons et al. put it, "The elections of autumn made it clear that the wave of independent political activity by the wage-earners had about spent its force."[68] By October 1887, the *Journal of United Labor* had changed its mind and advised Knights to "abstain from miscellaneous political agitation."[69] The collapse of the Knights that began in late 1886, costing nearly two hundred thousand members by July 1887, and in its trail the labor-party movement, also brought on the decline of the labor press that had played an important role in advancing the idea of independent political action. *John Swinton's Paper* went under in 1887, while Joseph Buchanan's *Labor Enquirer* "ceased to exist" in 1888, and Detroit's *Labor Leaf* succumbed in 1889. According to the French study cited in chapter 1, the number of such papers fell to 150 by the end of 1888.[70] Without the mass base that had grown from the early 1880s through 1886, they could not be sustained, bringing another blow to labor's political efforts. What then was behind the sudden collapse of such an apparently forceful movement?

Many works emphasize the factionalism within the movement that grew in 1887. Philip Foner, for example, emphasizes the disruptive role of Henry George in attempting to impose the single-tax policy as the central program of the United Labor Party, as well as his organization of the largely middle-class Land and Labor Clubs.[71] No doubt Henry George, whose influence played a positive role in the early phases of the movement, became a disruptive force after the November 1886 New York City mayoral election in which he came in second. There were, of course, many political and ethnic differences within this movement, including socialists, greenbackers, former and not-so-former Democrats and Republicans, and those on the way to becoming pure and simple unionists. Naturally, they frequently clashed. But so long as Knights and union membership were growing and the new parties were gaining votes, these differences could be compromised as they were in Chicago, for example.[72] Once the decline of the Knights accelerated in 1887 and the labor parties started to lose activists and voters, the earlier alliances often fractured. The split George fostered between the United Labor Party and the Union Labor Party came in mid-1887 after the movement had, like the Knights, peaked.[73] As with the decline of the Knights, the political factionalism that grew in 1887 appears as much a result of disappointment and failure as a cause. In any case, the common trajectory of the Knights, the labor parties, and the labor press strongly suggests that something deeper than factionalism was at work.

The problem was that, even where it had the support of the trade unions, the nationwide movement for independent labor politics was in most areas dependent on the Knights of Labor and the huge influx of members that more than doubled total union membership in early 1886. With few exceptions, as the Knights collapsed so did the local or state labor parties. Leon Fink's more detailed analysis of the rise and fall of the movement in four cities supports this analysis. In each of the three cities he examines in detail, where the Knights of Labor backed independent labor tickets, he gives a great deal of weight to the united reaction of the city's business elite and the fusion tickets they organized on the one hand and the decline or weakness of the Knights on the other. In the case of Rochester, New Hampshire, he writes, "The labor tickets in Rochester grew up as an extension of the strength of the Knights of Labor. So, too, the decline of independent labor politics was undoubtedly a corollary of the collapse of its constituent organization."[74]

In this case the collapse was triggered by the defeat of shoe workers' strikes in 1886 and 1887. It is interesting to note that in 1886, of the 1,114 strikers in New Hampshire, 389 of them (or over a third) were replaced by new hires, suggesting that some of the loss of Knights was due to out-migration after being replaced by nonunion workers.[75] In Rutland, where the Knights-backed United Labor Party had swept elections in 1886, Fink writes of labor's defeat by the Citizens' Party in the 1888 town elections, "The returns suggest that an erosion of labor's organized strength rather than any massive shift in popular sympathies contributed to the electoral turnaround."[76] Concerning the ultimate defeat of Milwaukee's labor party, called the People's Party, and others, he says, "Parties like Milwaukee's early People's Party and the ULP were only as strong as the organizational influence of the Knights of Labor within the community. As the Knights' membership fell off, the new party's political hold on the working class everywhere fell off too."[77]

Steven J. Ross noted the same phenomenon in Cincinnati when he wrote, "The steady decline of the Union Labor Party after the elections of November 1887 was paralleled and hastened by the gradual disintegration of the party's central force—the Knights of Labor."[78] As Fink generalized, "For without organization of the working class it proved impossible to create and sustain a working-class party."[79] The great workers' political rebellion of 1886–1888 foundered on the collapse of the Knights of Labor.

The decline of the Knights in the major industrial cities listed in table 5 in chapter 4 correlates strongly with the trajectory of the labor vote in several of these cities. Following the national pattern, they generally saw significant success in the autumn of 1886 through the spring of 1887 and then declined. In New York, where Henry George had done so well in the autumn 1886 mayoral election, by mid-1887 the Knights had lost well over half their members, while in Boston they lost almost 40 percent, in Philadelphia 28 percent, and in Chicago a quarter of its membership. In Chicago, for example, of the 116 new Local Assemblies of the Knights formed in 1886, over half were defunct by 1887 and eight out of ten by 1888.[80] In each case, the labor-party vote declined after the spring elections of 1887 as membership in the Knights fell. This decline can be seen as well in the important state-wide elections in Massachusetts, Pennsylvania, New York, and Ohio. While the labor tickets had generally done well in 1886, labor candidates for state office in the autumn of 1887 all did poorly. The results were more uneven in some cities, but the movement had risen with the Knights, peaked when the Knights peaked, and started its decline in the trail of the Knights' collapse. That collapse would continue, and with it splits and factionalism increased and the hopes for independent political action by labor faded for the time being.

The Third Attempt: the "Political Program," 1893–1894

While the labor-party movement of the mid-1880s had taken off in a period of economic growth, the third attempt to push organized labor toward independent political action came during the deep depression that began in 1893, and in the wake of major union defeats in which migration and immigration played less of a role. On the other hand, it also occurred just as the Populist or People's Party seemed to be gaining momentum. This suggested to some leaders and activists the possibility of a labor-Populist alliance as the basis for a serious break with the two major parties. Unlike the two earlier movements, which arose from the ranks, the movement that initiated in 1893 came from within the activist and even upper layers of the unions and particularly from their socialist wing, although it gathered major grassroots support.

The leader in this effort was Chicago socialist Thomas Morgan, who was at the time head of the small Machinists' International Union that the AFL had chartered to compete with the International Association of Machinists, which was denied affiliation because of its "whites-only" clause. Thus, Morgan had a voice in high AFL councils.

Furthermore, he came to the 1893 AFL convention as part of a growing labor-Populist alliance in Illinois that promised to have an impact on Chicago politics. It drew the support not only of some of the leading intellectual lights of the day, such as Henry Demarest Lloyd, Clarence Darrow, and Richard T. Ely, but also Eugene Debs of the newly formed and rapidly growing American Railway Union and other union leaders and activists. In October 1893, just before the AFL convention, the Illinois State Federation of Labor declared the "necessity for independent political action on the part of the producers." Thus, Morgan went to the 1893 AFL convention representing a good deal more than himself.[81]

Not only that, but the movement toward a labor-Populist alliance involved more than the movement in Illinois or the debate within the AFL, having significant support in Wisconsin and Ohio as well as in the mountain West, where it was "a working class movement," according to Dubofsky.[82] W. MacArthur of the San Francisco Central Labor Council reported to the 1894 AFL convention that "the State unions of California are affiliated with the Farmers' Alliance for Political purposes."[83] Similarly, in Texas in 1894 the State Federation of Labor, which included both trade unions and the still significant Knights of Labor in that state, supported the Populists.[84] Just prior to the debate at the December 1894 convention of the AFL, the November issue of the *American Federationist* ran a "partial list of the names of Union members who have been nominated in their respective States, cities, counties, and districts for the offices named."[85] The list included some three hundred union members running for office. The biggest concentrations were in northern industrial states with a major focus on state legislatures. According to David Saposs, "A majority of them ran upon the People's Party, or 'Populist' ticket." Thus, these labor candidates provided a potential urban and northern ally to Populists who were winning in the South and West. Most, however, lost their elections in 1894.[86] No doubt the defeat of so many labor candidates was due in part to the weakness of the AFL and its major affiliates at that time. In addition, many listed in the *Federationist* were from the American Railway Union, which went down to a disastrous defeat before the election in 1894.

What Morgan proposed the federation adopt in 1893 was nothing less than the "Political Programme" of Britain's reform socialist Independent Labor Party. Its preamble "adopted the principle of independent labor politics as an auxiliary to their economic action," while its eleven-point program included the controversial "plank 10" calling for "the collective ownership by all the people of all means of production and distribution." Most of the other planks "were traditional demands of labor," according to J. F. Finn. The program was to be sent to each AFL affiliate for a referendum vote by the members. Remarkably, the motion made at the 1893 AFL convention to strike the word "favorable" from the resolution before forwarding the program to the affiliates was defeated, and the proposal was sent with a "favorable" recommendation. Based on the outcome of the referendum, the program was to be voted up or down at the 1894 convention, and even Samuel Gompers said he was sure it would pass.[87]

The program had the support of the unaffiliated radical Western Federation of Miners and the recently formed 150,000-member American Railway Union, but the debate took place within the AFL. The issue was debated in the pages of the AFL's new publication, the *American Federationist*, among other places. In the very first issue of the *Federationist* in March 1894, Frank K. Foster, a well-known former leader of the Knights and editor of the Boston-based *Labor Leader*, argued for caution in the matter of "party" action as opposed to "political" action. He also opposed plank 10, which he warned would make the trade unions "simply annexes of the Socialistic Labor party." Not surprisingly, Foster was answered by the program's main proponent, Thomas Morgan, who defended plank 10 with the uncharacteristically syndicalist statement that it meant that the ownership of the nation's iron and steel mills would be transferred "to the Amalgamated Association of Iron and Steel Workers and their related labor organizations." In any case, he argued, "The extent to which this radical sentiment has permeated the Union labor movement of the United States, will be shown by the instructions of the Unions to their delegates to the next annual convention of the A.F. of L."[88] And so it was.

The results of the referendum taken by the affiliates as well as by state federations and local central labor councils were astounding, with a large majority of the members voting in favor. The political program was passed in full by the memberships of the Cigar Makers, United Mine Workers, the Amalgamated Association of Iron and Steel Workers, Lasters, Flint Glass Makers, Tailors, Brewery Workers, Painters, Electrical Workers, Furniture Workers, Street Railway Employees, and many others. Even in the birthplace of pure and simple unionism, the Cigar Makers, where the vote was taken plank by plank, the membership voted 86.8–90.9 percent for most planks and 68.4 percent for plank 10 on the collective ownership of the means of production and distribution. The Typographers struck plank 10 out, while the Carpenters amended it. Only the Bakers' Union rejected the program completely. The program was also approved by the state federations of Maine, Rhode Island, New York, Ohio, Michigan, Wisconsin, Illinois, Missouri, Kansas, Nebraska, and Montana, as well as the city central bodies of Baltimore, New Haven, Cleveland, Toledo, Lansing, Saginaw, Grand Rapids, and Milwaukee, according to Commons. In the most thorough account of this debate, J. F. Finn stated, "The rank and file were vociferously radical and had given support to it."[89] No doubt the massive struggles at Homestead and Pullman had stoked up class consciousness.

According to the procedures agreed to in 1893, the delegates from unions that voted in favor of the program were to be instructed to vote for it at the 1894 AFL convention.[90] Had the delegates to the 1894 AFL convention adhered to their unions' instructions, the program would have passed in full. Morgan assumed, therefore, that the convention of 1894 would simply count the results of the referendum. Instead, P. J. McGuire of the Carpenters, Samuel Gompers of the Cigar Makers, and Adolph Strasser, who was a delegate with dubious credentials from the New Jersey State Federation rather than his own Cigar Makers, succeeded in having the program voted plank by plank. They then convinced key delegates from the Carpenters, Miners, and other unions whose members had ratified the program to ignore their instructions and vote against it. The reason this was so easy was partly due to the fact that the delegates of the big unions were leaders who regularly attended AFL conventions. They were regular "insiders" whose interests and political ideas were not always in line with those of the more militant and radical proclivities of the majority of members in these years of intense conflict.[91] As MacArthur of San Francisco complained, those leaders "used every influence in their power to try and prevent the delegates having an opportunity to express the wish of their constituents on the original matters of [the program's] provisions."[92]

The preamble, which advocated independent political action, was voted down 1,345 to 861 on a motion from Strasser. A substitute for plank 10 calling only for the abolition of land monopolies passed 1,217 to 913. Finally, a motion to pass the program as amended was defeated 1,173 to 735, with many supporters of the original program voting against. Ironically, each of the planks, as amended, had been voted up so that technically the program had been approved. Although the program as passed was dutifully run in the *American Federationist* as the program of the AFL,[93] in reality it was a dead letter. There was enough discontent among the delegates in 1894, however, to reject Samuel Gompers for president of the AFL and elect instead John McBride of the Miners, who was not even present, by a vote of 1,170 to 976 by carrying the Miners, Boot and Shoe Workers, and many smaller unions, and splitting the Carpenters' vote.[94]

In his analysis of the defeat of the program, Robin Archer emphasizes the rigid "either-or" (either trade unionism or political action) mentality and sectarian style of debate that many on both sides had learned in the socialist movement. Certainly this applied to Morgan, Gompers, and Strasser, and indeed, the debate was at times vicious and even personal, as the verbatim transcript shows. This led some to feel that the program was simply too divisive and might actually increase the already substantial factionalism in the labor movement. It was in part on this basis that Gompers and Strasser convinced several delegates to oppose the program.[95] There is a good deal of truth in this observation, but there was also another more political and ironic set of differences that led some to oppose the program in whole or part.

It was not a simple pro or con difference over independent political action per se but was, for some, a difference over how the program would affect a labor-Populist alliance. Morgan's reason for putting forth the political program and plank 10 in particular had been to insulate the People's Party from being absorbed by the Democrats. Yet, some of the leading figures in the opposition to the program were precisely those who were supporting a political alliance with Populism, including AFL treasurer John B. Lennon and Frank K. Foster, a member of the Typographical Union, former Knight, and editor of the Boston *Labor Leader*. In that weekly paper in the year or so running up to the vote at the AFL convention, Foster ran many articles praising the Populists in various parts of the country, even predicting in early November 1894 that "the Populists will hold the balance of power in the coming United States Senate."[96] Foster and Lennon thought plank 10 would alienate the farmers who composed the backbone of Populism. Lennon also opposed plank 3, the eight-hour day, for the same reason. At the same time, he left open the door to some form of political action with other groups, presumably farmers, so long as it was "entirely a movement as citizens of the United States and not as trade unions."[97] In the end, the political program was defeated, as Finn argues, not by a majority of pure and simple unionists but by a coalition of pro-Populists who saw it as socialist and inimical to a labor-Populist alliance; philosophical anarchists who saw it as statist; socialists who saw it as divisive or opposed an alliance with farmers; those already connected to one of the two major parties; and, finally, those who saw themselves as pure and simple unionists. In political terms, the pure and simple unionists were probably not yet a majority at the 1894 convention. Interestingly, in the midst of the debate, P. M. McBryde of the Miners (not John McBride) said of some of those who opposed the program, "I noticed the very delegates that assailed socialism and claim to be pure and simple trades unionists, everyone are confessed socialists." The socialists were divided on the question of a labor-Populist alliance. W. MacArthur of the San Francisco Central Labor Council reported that in California the socialists had voted against "an alliance with the farmers." The lack of a clear majority of pure and simple unionists was at least in part because a number of the building trades unions who would form the backbone of pure and simple domination of the AFL after the turn of the century were not yet affiliated orhad not sent delegates to Denver in 1894.[98]

What is most interesting about the 1893–1894 effort to move the AFL toward independent political action in the form of a labor-Populist alliance was the positive attitude of so much of the trade-union membership toward both political independence and a collectivist program. They had, in effect, endorsed the program of the very backbone of British reform socialism, the Independent Labor Party, indicating that at least in the 1890s the consciousness of many American trade unionists was not so different from their British colleagues as Sombart, Perlman, and others had assumed. No doubt this outlook was increased by the disastrous state of the economy and the unemployment and wage cuts that accompanied it, as well as the overt role of the state in defeating high-profile strikes at Homestead, Coeur d'Alene, and Pullman, the latter under a Democratic administration. Even among the leaders, the idea of a labor-Populist electoral alliance had significant support. Furthermore, had the delegates not ignored their instructions to vote in favor of the entire program, it would have passed by a large majority. Could the passing of the program and this discontent at all levels have led to the labor-Populist alliance some sought?

The most likely answer is no. For one thing, in the election of 1894, while Chicago Populists drew tens of thousands of union members to their rallies, in the end, the Illinois Populists received only thirty-five thousand to forty thousand votes in Cook County (Chicago and some suburbs), a return described as "credible," but which Clarence Darrow saw as "wholly disappointing." This was an indication of the relative weakness of support for the Populists among urban workers. For another, Populism was about to succumb to fusion with the Democrats. Perhaps the injection of trade-union support would have prevented that, but that is to be doubted on two grounds. First, even if the "political program" had passed in full, it is doubtful if the leaders of the AFL or most of its larger craft affiliates would have carried out its intention. Gompers, after all, was reelected president at the next convention, which passed a resolution calling on workers to vote in their "class interests . . . outside of party lines."[99] In addition, the program itself was rejected at the 1895 convention by a vote of 1,531 to 359 that declared "the failure to adopt the planks as a whole was equivalent to rejection and therefore we declare that the American Federation of Labor has no political platform."[100]

But even if some union leaders did actively seek the new electoral alliance, as the remnant of the Knights had, the fact was that the AFL was weak. As Neville Kirk has argued concerning the difference in US and British approaches to politics in this period, "And the 'peculiarity' of the US trade-union movement lay in the fact that it had not gained the strength, success and influence of its British counterpart, rather than in the adoption of novel or different political tactics and strategies from those employed by the pre-1899 TUC."[101] Union membership in the US had grown to 872,900 in 1894, but only 275,000 of those members were in AFL-affiliated unions. The Knights, who supported the Populists, still claimed about 85,000, but many of these were now farmers or rural wageworkers. Another 168,979 union members were scattered around the country in unaffiliated local unions. The rest were in unaffiliated national unions, such as the railroad brotherhoods who were then battling the American Railway Union. In other words, organized labor did not form a unified force. Furthermore, all three of these groupings were about to lose members as the depression deepened and the American Railway Union was destroyed by the intervention of the federal government under Grover Cleveland.[102] Perhaps, in light of this reality, Gompers was not altogether wrong, whatever his motives, when he told the 1894 AFL convention, "Before we can hope as a general organization to take the field by nominating candidates for office, the workers must be more thoroughly organized and better results achieved by experiments locally. A political labor movement cannot and will not succeed upon the ruins of the trade unions."[103]

The third and final effort of the Gilded Age to create a labor or farmer-labor party had failed. Independent political action at the opening of the new century would take the form of the Socialist Party of America, supported by only a minority of unions and union members and hence unable to force the sort of class-based realignment that John Swinton and Henry George thought they foresaw in 1887 or Thomas Morgan, John Lennon, and Frank Foster thought they foresaw in 1893–1894. All three attempts at independent political action followed a similar pattern in that each arose in the wake of intense industrial conflict between workers on the one hand and capital and their state allies on the other. As both Fink and Thompson argue above, the "economic" and "political" aspects of these efforts were intricately related, rather than separate swings or alternating currents. The initial success of each indicates, as has been argued throughout, that it was not a lack of class consciousness that underlay this failure. Indeed, the very effort by significant sections of the organized working class to gain political independence reveals a level of consciousness comparable to or even more advanced than that in most of the other English-speaking countries at least until the late 1890s—a phenomenon noted at the time by such foreign observers as Eleanor Marx and Frederick Engels.[104] In each case, it was the relative numerical and organizational weakness of the labor movement that undermined these efforts, much of that due to the unusually high level of geographic mobility of the US working class as well as to a rising arc of state intervention and racial exclusion.

CONCLUSION

The twenty-five thousand strikers had the stock yards completely
tied up, and it was known that the bosses were on the point of
yielding, when a telegram from the General Master Workman
dumped the fat into the fire. This telegram ordered the men to
abandon their demands for an eight-hour day and return to work.
—Joseph R. Buchanan, district master workman,
Knights of Labor District 89, Denver, Colorado.[1]

G IVEN THAT internal migration and the continuous march from one
job to another were a fact of life for many working-class people during
the Gilded Age, was any other outcome possible? Most crucially,
could the rapid initial collapse of the Knights of Labor been avoided
in 1886–1887, since this was the proximate cause of the decline of the labor press
and the failure of the labor-party movement of that decade? It will be argued here
that, in fact, there were at least three things the Knights of Labor could have done
to minimize the damage imposed by the "perfect storm" that sent many workers on
the road. These are: the development of a clear policy on strikes and a strike fund
to back up such actions; the formation in the 1880s of national trade districts, in effect national or international unions, such as the window-glass workers had formed
in 1880; and a turn toward more aggressive and concentrated organizing as the
Knights grew in 1886, instead of the formal retreat sounded by Powderly that year.
While this speculation involves a "counterfactual," at least the first two of these
changes were proposed at the time. There is no way, in retrospect, to determine if
a better strategy adopted by the labor movement would have offset the negative
effects of geographic working-class mobility, but certainly these measures would
have offered a better prospect of counteracting that disruption.

The quote above from highly respected Knights leader Joseph Buchanan,
an opponent of Powderly, gives us some indication of the dissatisfaction of many
members and leaders with the lack of coherence in the Knights' official stance
toward strikes. He was not alone; Joseph Labadie of Detroit, another respected
leader and Powderly opponent, reported that the defeat of the Chicago stockyard
workers created bitterness among the strikers that "will cost the order many members in Chicago alone."[2] The ambivalent, even hostile attitude toward strikes of

General Master Workman Terrence Powderly and his supporters in the leadership prevented the Knights from developing a clear policy or a strike fund to back up the frequent withdrawal of labor that characterized the order in the mid-1880s. This led not only to the failure of the 1886 Chicago stockyards strike but also to defeats at the Southwest Railway, the Reading Railroad and its mines, and the New England textile and shoes mills from 1885 through 1887.[3] This cost the Knights thousands of members. In 1886, in Illinois alone, strikers replaced as a result of failed strikes amounted to over eight thousand workers, many of them Knights.[4] Nationally in that year, almost forty thousand strikers were replaced by new hires during or after failed strikes. The following year another forty thousand were lost to replacement workers in the wake of failed strikes.[5] Together these losses amount to the equivalent of over 40 percent of the Knights' initial losses from July 1886 to July 1887, though of course, not all those who lost their jobs were Knights. Clearly Buchanan and Labadie did not see these massive losses as inevitable.

Caution or even opposition to strikes was common among trade-union leaders as well. The difference was, as Ware pointed out, that trade-union leaders typically sought to bring strikes under some sort of central control through a consistent policy or procedure while at the same time "building up a financial system that would give support to official strikes with some chance of success."[6] Although various funds were set up by the Knights in the 1880s, none actually served as a strike fund. If any benefits were paid, it was by assessments of the members or simply appeals for funds—both ineffective and irregularly used. The failure of this approach became forcefully clear with the defeat of the 1883 Knights' Brotherhood of Telegraphers strike. The leaders of the Brotherhood of Telegraphers had assumed, perhaps naively, that their national organization would back them up financially and morally. In fact, neither was forthcoming despite the popularity of the strike against the much-hated Jay Gould and his Western Union Telegraph Company.[7]

Thus, in late 1883 the general executive board of the Knights declared, "It became apparent in the early history of the year just closing that the laws governing strikes and lockouts were totally insufficient as a means of rendering financial support to members out of employment through any cause." The inefficiency of assessments and appeals "render these provisions useless as a weapon against the present power of concentrated capital in many industries."[8] Certainly this was a realistic assessment of the old policy. An assistance fund was established. Unfortunately, as Ware noted, it "never amounted to much more than $7,000."[9] Tragically and unnecessarily, the Knights of Labor continued to muddle through the question of strike policy and support with disastrous consequences in the mid-1880s.

As with strikes, the policy of the Knights toward the formation of national trade districts (NTDs) was vacillating, while their organization received little encouragement from the top leadership. National trade districts were, in effect, national unions of workers in a specific industry or occupation. The first of these, the Window Glass Workers' "Local" Assembly 300, was organized in 1880 even though the order's laws forbade it. The second was in 1882, with the formation of the Brotherhood of Telegraphers discussed above. In 1884, the order admitted the International Trunk Makers Union as a national trade district. Also in 1884, Joseph Buchanan helped the shop workers in the entire Union Pacific system organize an all-grades union, win its first strike, and affiliate to the Knights of Labor. Indeed, according to Ware it was in 1884 that interest in NTDs first peaked. At the same time, executive board members William Bailey and Thomas Barry—who were, like Buchanan, critics of Powderly—pushed to expand the role of NTDs. Yet, the effort to form a miners' NTD in 1884 was put off until 1886. At the 1885 General Assembly, although the laws allowed it, Powderly stated, "I do not favor the establishment of any more National Trade Districts, they are a step backward." In fact, it was not until 1887, after the AFL had been formed and the Knights' decline had begun, that the movement to form NTDs took off.[10] By then it was too late—the order was in decline, the conflict with the AFL was gathering steam, and the newly forming NTDs were mostly too weak to compete with AFL affiliates or to force mergers with them.

The formation of national unions offered the possibility of regulating wages beyond the local level across state or regional boundaries in an occupation or industry, as the Window Glass Workers did, or conducting nationwide strikes such as that of the Brotherhood of Telegraphers. These were advantages trade unions possessed. Had the Knights encouraged NTDs earlier, they might have had a more solid base and a stronger position in relation to the AFL unions. This in turn might have produced growth through a competition scenario such as the CIO-AFL rivalry of the 1930s if the NTDs had been strong enough by 1886 on the one hand or had there been a greater incentive for mergers of some NTDs and AFL trade unions on the other. Some NTDs that formed before 1887, notably the Union Pacific workers and both coal and metal mining NTDs, survived into the 1890s to contribute to the formation of the American Railway Union, the United Mine Workers, and the Western Federation of Miners. Most NTDs that formed during or after 1887, however, were dragged down along with the general collapse of the Knights or were simply absorbed by AFL affiliates.

The third alternative approach that might have limited the Knights' decline or even turned its initial increases into sustainable growth involved the commission of organizers and the limited tasks assigned them. Knights of Labor organizers were not full-time employees of the order but rather received a daily stipend while initiating members and were often allowed to keep a portion of the initiation fee. Their remit was largely to initiate new members, educate them in the principles of the organization, and help charter new Local Assemblies (LAs). As we saw in May–June of 1886, as tens of thousands of workers entered the order each month,

General Master Workman Powderly ordered a cessation of initiations and the rejection of some three hundred requests for commissions to become an organizer. While these acts were not the major reason for the decline, they bypassed the real weakness of the order. If rather than attempting to halt the influx of new members the Knights had instead increased the corps of organizers and brought the new recruits into existing mixed or trade LAs with more experienced leaders wherever possible, they might have retained more members. Instead, they allowed the proliferation of more than seven thousand new and typically small LAs between 1885 and 1887, contributing to the instability of the organization.[11] If the alternative approach had been combined with consistent support for the rising strike wave of the time and the prior formation of national trade districts in important industries or occupations, the future of the Knights might have been very different. Given that the collapse of the Knights was a major turning point in the history of organized labor in the Gilded Age, had they taken a different course it might have mitigated the enormous forces arrayed against labor caught in the midst of the "perfect storm."

Indeed, if a new strike policy and fund had been implemented in 1883, when proposed, some of the defeats of 1886–1887 might have been prevented. If national trade districts had been organized in 1884 when requests for their formation grew, the subsequent escalation of growth in 1885 might have been more organizationally stable.

Similarly, had the leadership and organizers encouraged new members to enter an appropriate existing LA in 1886 instead of applying the brakes, the subsequent massive loss of these fragile local organizations and their new members might have been reduced and the underlying weakness and instability of the Knights minimized. Had the order, as a result, retained many of those who joined during the Great Upheaval, the state and local United Labor Parties created in 1886–1887 might have survived long enough (three or four years) to flow into an alliance with Populism in the early 1890s just as the smaller alternative parties had merged into the Republican Party in the 1850s. Given the blows to the Democrats in the West and South in the early 1890s, the northern urban base of the various Labor Parties could have contributed to a major realignment along class lines in the 1890s. This, of course, is a lot of "ifs," "hads," and "mights."

Nevertheless, historians need not be blinded by what Eric Foner calls "the mirage of inevitability" that comes with hindsight.[12] For better or worse, alternative paths are, in fact, sometimes taken. Geographic mobility need not have been absolute destiny.

The traditional "exceptionalist" questions of "why is there no socialism?" or "why is there no labor party?" in effect deflected the search for the underlying causes of organized labor's relative weakness in the US for a long time. Most frequently based on the assertion of the lack of class consciousness by workers in the United States, the explanations for this missing consciousness have been sought in the prosperity of the working class, its alleged access to free or cheap land, and the social mobility open to significant numbers of workers. While most of these explanations have been found inadequate in themselves, the assumption of a lack of class consciousness that underlies the exceptionalist questions has tended to linger on despite the mass of evidence that such a consciousness was widespread during the Gilded Age. The more recent efforts to place the power of ascendant capital and the racial and ethnic divisions within the working class as central causes of labor's weakness, on the other hand, have helped to deepen our understanding of the era and contributed to the enrichment of labor and social history. Nevertheless, the obvious and often acknowledged fact of the high degree of internal migration among working-class people in the US during the late nineteenth century and its impact on labor organization has remained outside the analytical framework of most historians. This stands in contrast to the important role of internal migration employed by historians of the African American experience, where both the movement of former slaves from plantation to city in the years immediately following the Civil War and the Great Migration to the North in the second decade of the twentieth century are central to the story of black America.[13] Yet, the centrality of geographic mobility to the epic of working-class formation in all its diversity, involving as it did the movement of millions across and around the United States, at best receives a brief mention in most treatments of Gilded-Age labor history. The connection of this movement to the weakness of American labor organizations in this period is even rarer. There is, thus, much to be gained in the field of labor history by the integration of this side of the demographic history of periods of extreme social flux such as the late nineteenth century with our expanded understanding of the economic, racial, ethnic, and gender demographics in the uneven process of class formation.

Organized labor in the late nineteenth century faced not only mass social barriers in the increasing power of the new industrial capitalist class and its own intraclass divisions of ethnicity, race, and gender, but also the powerful forces of expanding industrialization and urbanization that brought this class into being and drew millions from job to job and place to place across and around the vast spaces of the United States. In the years from 1870 through 1900 over seven and a half million people crossed state lines outside the South, almost half of them in the 1880s, while at least twice this number moved from county to county, countryside to city, and city to city. The majority of the evidence shows this was above all a movement of working-class people. The making of the American industrial working class was accomplished on the run. So, though working-class people struggled to resist the aggression of capital as they saw it and at times attempted to go beyond the system of permanent wage labor through unions, eight-hour leagues, boycotts, cooperatives, mass demonstrations, independent parties, socialist groups, and an independent labor press, the fight was an uphill one until a breathing space opened at the very end of the period—and then only temporarily. Constant labor turnover and spatial movement created a slippery slope that made the struggle seem a Sisyphean labor at times. This in turn created chains of causation in which union weakness or decline undermined each effort at independent working-class political action. This missing factor of internal migration and geographic mobility, therefore, helps to explain what appears to some as "exceptional" about American class relations. It was not the absence of class consciousness and unique working-class values and perceptions that seemed to make the US different from much of Europe in the late nineteenth century, but rather the failure to sustain the many organizations and institutions that reflected and shaped this consciousness. Among the major reasons for that failure, geographic mobility has been the missing factor.

The mere mention of millions of people on the move along with new sites of industrialization and urbanization naturally brings to mind today's world. At any time today across the world, there are approximately 230 million migrants leaving their homes to seek work elsewhere.[14] New technologies in transportation and communications have increased migration, as they did in the late nineteenth century. In the United State alone, there are nearly forty million immigrants, the vast majority of whom are working class.[15] As in the past, these new immigrants have become migrants within the US and today are found in every part of the nation, this time including the South. Many have attempted to join or build trade unions in agriculture, meatpacking, transportation, and elsewhere, as well as other forms of worker organization.[16] Many, however, are in precarious jobs. Indeed, the trend toward "lean production" that originated in Japan in the 1950s and arrived in North America and Europe in the 1980s, with its growth of workforce "flexibility," has reintroduced the sort of precarious work common to the nineteenth century.[17] Once again, both native-born and foreign-born workers face problems similar to those that confronted Gilded-Age workers. While no work of history can provide simple answers to the problems of another era, an understanding of how the forces of immigration and internal migration affected the efforts to build labor organizations in a prior age of new technology and geographic mobility has central relevance to today's world of work and conflict.

APPENDIX

THE NOTION that the workforce, like the population, of the Gilded Age experienced high rates of mobility and turnover inevitably came under attack from some economists. In what might be impolitely considered part of the ongoing dispute between historians and some neoclassical economists, Susan Carter and Elizabeth Savoca in what is probably the most important criticism of high turnover, have questioned much of the evidence used by historians to argue for high rates of geographic and workplace migration.[18] The authors critically cite a number of studies drawing on historical evidence of low urban persistence and high job turnover rates during the nineteenth and early twentieth century from historians such as Stephan Thernstrom and Sanford Jacoby.[19] To question the arguments for high turnover and quit rates recorded in various industries and worksites, in particular, using the mathematical tools popular with neoclassical economists, the authors turn to calculations of job length—that is, the length of jobs held with the same employer. Their findings are based on an 1892 survey by the California Bureau of Labor Statistics that does indeed contain a great deal of useful data.[20] Using the survey's data on "Years Engaged . . . Present Employer," Carter and Savoca have calculated "an average job length of 13 years" for the early 1890s.[21] Considering that the median years for job tenure in the US workforce in 2010 was only 4.4 years, even allowing for the difference between the mean and median length, this would certainly turn our perception of Gilded-Age employment on its head.[22] There are, however, a number of serious problems with Carter and Savoca's calculations and conclusions.

Noting that Carter and Savoca use "modern duration modelling techniques," which make their study important and "likely to influence future research," Sanford Jacoby and Sunil Sharma criticize some of their methods and conclude that "there is a sampling problem that leads to undercounting short employment durations."[23] In addition to their criticism of the type of duration measure Carter and Savoca use and the data's inclusion of white-collar workers and exclusion of Chinese workers mentioned by Jacoby and Sharma, I believe other problems arise from their selection of data. Only nonunion male workers are chosen for their data set on the rather odd grounds that the tenure patterns of union members and women "differed substantially from those of non-union males." If one is researching the

overall patterns of employment, it would seem essential to include a sample of all
those in the relevant labor market. Their choice of a limited group thus distorts
the outcome of the study despite its elaborate mathematical construction. A look
at several occupations in the 1892 survey in which most workers answer "yes" to
membership in a labor organization including printers, bricklayers, carpenters,
cigar makers, tailors, brewery workers, and coastal sailors produced some 883
workers, many of them known for their mobility and others for seasonal work. In
general, the job duration figures for these workers reveal lengths with the same employer shorter than the averages calculated by Carter and Savoca, indeed in many
cases measured in months rather than years. The sample used by Carter and Savoca
includes only 1,158 workers so that the addition of some 880 (and possibly many
more) union members, as well as women and Chinese workers, would certainly
have produced a shorter average duration. Furthermore, the survey itself excludes
some occupations, such as railroad workers known for high turnover and short job
durations as we saw in chapter 4 and who would have been present in significant
numbers in California. Thus, the sample used by Carter and Savoca is not representative of the actual Gilded-Age workforce of California or the nation.[24]

As the job duration figures in the California survey were taken while these
workers still held their current job, the authors speculate that they would continue on these jobs for some time. Rather generously they increase the duration
by a factor of nearly two. The grounds for this lay in the neoclassical fiction of a
"steady state" in the economy—that is, a condition of zero growth or a period of
equilibrium. Jacoby and Sharma question this assumption.[25] The problem here, of
course, is that at no time was the Gilded-Age economy of the US in anything like
a steady state. The idea that job duration figures collected in July 1892 would have
nearly equaled their past length in the following period is negated by, among other
things, the fact that the great depression of the 1890s commenced five months later
in January 1893, according to the National Bureau of Economic Research.[26] Indeed,
Jacoby and Sharma point out that San Francisco was already in a state of depression in 1892.[27] Certainly many of those employed in July would have lost their jobs
within the following year or so, bringing average job tenure down still further.

Carter and Savoca do focus on other data in the survey, showing, for example,
the rather well-known facts that marriage, number of dependents, and home ownership "have a large impact on the job-exit rate."[28] What is overlooked, however, is
the considerable amount of data in the California survey that might have given a
very different and more rounded picture of job turnover and geographic mobility. For example, in the column preceding the time with "present employer" is the
number of years in the "present employment"—that is, time in their occupation as
listed in the survey. In the vast majority of cases, time in occupation is many times
longer than time with the "present employer," indicating a good deal of movement

from one employer to another over time. Similarly, the two columns that compare the workers' time in the US to that in California show that, for most, the time in California is significantly or even greatly less than that in the US, pointing to previous migration. Moreover, a majority of those questioned in the survey were foreign-born so that migration rather than persistence would have been an important feature of their lives. Finally, data in another column also not used by the authors indicates the number of days lost as a result of "no work," which for many occupations was substantial, once again pointing to the relative impermanence of employment.[29] The narrow focus on current job duration with a single employer of a limited group, and its arbitrary steady state multiplication, has meant that the authors' mathematical edifice has been built on a thin and shaky foundation. It may be that the estimates of Thernstrom, Chudacoff, Zunz, and others whose works are citied above were off in some respects due to problems with city registers and census data, but the overall picture from these different authors using somewhat different methods nevertheless supports the broader picture of considerable geographic mobility, residential movement, and, by implication, employment turnover found in other contemporary and more recent sources cited in this book.

BIBLIOGRAPHY

Books and Articles

Abbott, Edith. "The Wages of Unskilled Labor in the United States, 1850–1900." *Journal of Political Economy* 13, no. 3 (June 1905): 321–367.

Allen, E. A. *Labor and Capital.* Cincinnati: Central Publishing House, 1891.

Anderson, Benedict. *Imagined Communities: Reflections on the Origins and Spread of Nationalism.* London: Verso, 2006.

Archer, Robin. *Why Is There No Labor Party in the United States?* Princeton, NJ: Princeton University Press, 2007.

Arnesen, Eric, Julie Green, and Bruce Laurie, eds. *Labor Histories: Class, Politics and the Working-Class Experience.* Urbana: University of Illinois Press, 1998.

Atack, Jeremy, Fred Bateman, and Robert Margo. "Part-Year Operation in Nineteenth Century American Manufacturing: Evidence from the 1870 and 1880 Census." *Journal of Economic History* 62, no. 3 (September 2002): 792–809.

Barnett, George E. *The Printers: A Study in American Trade Unionism.* Cambridge, MA: American Economic Association, 1909.

―――― "Collective Bargaining in the Typographical Union." In *Studies in American Trade Unionism*, edited by Jacob H. Hollander and George E. Barnett, 158–182. New York: Henry Holt, 1912.

――――. "The Government of the Typographical Union." In *Studies in American Trade Unionism*, edited by Jacob H. Hollander and George E. Barnett, 13–42. New York: Henry Holt, 1912.

Bellesiles, Michael. *1877: America's Year of Living Violently.* New York: New Press, 2010.

Bennett, Sari and Carville Earle. "The Geography of Strikes in the United States, 1881–1894." *Journal of Interdisciplinary History* 13, no. 1 (Summer 1982): 63–75.

Bodnar, John. *Immigration and Industrialization: Ethnicity in an American Mill Town, 1870–1940.* Pittsburgh: University of Pittsburgh Press, 1977.

Borchardt, Knut. "The Industrial Revolution in Germany, 1700–1914." In *The Emergence of Industrial Societies*, edited by Carlo M. Cipolla, 76–160. Vol. 1 of *The Fontana Economic History of Europe.* London: Collins/Fontana, 1973.

Boyer, George R. and Timothy J. Hatton. "Migration and Labour Market Integration in Late Nineteenth-Century England and Wales." *Economic History Review* 50, no. 4 (November 1997): 697–734.

Brandfon, Robert L. "The End of Immigration in the Cotton Fields." *Mississippi Valley Historical Review* 50, no. 4 (March 1964): 591–611.

Braverman, Harry. *Labor and Monopoly Capitalism: The Degradation of Work in the Twentieth Century.* New York: Monthly Review Press, 1974.

Briggs, Asa. *A Social History of England.* London: Book Club Associates, 1983.

Broadberry, Stephen N. and Douglas Irwin. *Labour Productivity in the US and the UK During the 19th Century.* London: Centre for Economic Policy Research, 2004.

Brody, David. *Steelworkers in America: The Nonunion Era.* Chicago: University of Illinois Press, 1998.

Brown, M. Craig and Charles N. Halaby. "Machine Politics in America, 1870–1945." *Journal of Interdisciplinary History* 17, no. 3 (Winter 1987): 587–612.

Bruce, Robert V. *1877: Year of Violence.* New York: Quadrangle, 1970.

Brundage, David. *The Making of Western Labor Radicalism: Denver's Organized Workers, 1878–1905.* Urbana: University of Illinois Press, 1994.

Bryce, James. *The American Commonwealth.* Vol. 2. Indianapolis: Liberty Fund, 1995.

Buchanan, Joseph. *The Story of a Labor Agitator.* New York: Outlook, 1903.

Burnham, Walter Dean. "The Changing Shape of the American Political Universe." *American Political Science Review* 59 (March 1965): 7–28.

Burnham, Walter Dean. *Critical Elections and the Wellsprings of American Politics.* New York: W. W. Norton, 1970.

Cairncross, A. K., *Home and Foreign Investment, 1870–1913.* Cambridge: Cambridge University Press, 1953.

Chandler, Alfred D., Jr. *The Visible Hand: The Managerial Revolution in American Business.* Cambridge, MA: Harvard University Press, 1977.

Charlton, John. *"It Just Went Like Tinder": The Mass Movement and New Unionism in Britain, 1889.* London: Redwords, 1999.

Chudacoff, Howard P. *Mobile Americans: Residential and Social Mobility in Omaha, 1880–1920.* New York: Oxford University Press, 1972.

———. "Success and Security: The Meaning of Social Mobility in America." *Reviews in American History* 10, no. 4 (December 1982): 101–112.

Cipolla, Carlo M., ed. *The Fontana Economic History of Europe: The Emergence of Industrial Societies.* Vol. 1. London: Collins/Fontana, 1973.

Clawson, Mary Ann. "Fraternal Orders and Class Formation in the Nineteenth-Century United States." *Comparative Studies in Society and History* 27, no. 2 (October 1985): 672–695.

Coates, Ken and Tony Topham, *The Making of the Labour Movement: The Formation of the Transport and General Workers' Union, 1870–1922.* Nottingham: Spokesman, 1994.

Cochran, Thomas C. and William Miller, *The Age of Enterprise: A Social History of Industrial America*. New York: Harper & Row, 1961.

Cole, G. D. H. *British Working Class Politics, 1832–1914*. London: George Routledge & Sons, 1941.

Commons, John R. "Labor Conditions in Slaughtering and Meat Packing." In *Trade Unionism and Labor Problems*, edited by John R. Commons, 222–249. New York: Augustus M. Kelley, 1967, originally 1905.

———, ed. *Trade Unionism and Labor Problems*. New York: Augustus M. Kelley, 1967.

Commons, John R. and John B. Andrews, eds. *A Documentary History of American Industrial Society*. Vol. 9. Cleveland: Arthur H. Clark, 1910.

Commons, John R. et al. *History of the Labour Movement in the United States*. Vol. 2. New York: Macmillan, 1936.

Conzen, Michael F. "Local Migration Systems in Nineteenth Century Iowa." *Geographical Review* 64, no. 3 (July 1974): 339–361.

Cooper, Jerry M. *The Army and Civil Disorder: Federal Military Intervention in Labor Disputes, 1877–1900*. Westport, CT: Greenwood Press, 1980.

———. "The Army and Industrial Workers: Strikebreaking in the Late 19th Century." In *Soldiers and Civilians: The US Army and the American People*, edited by Garry D. Ryan and Timothy K. Nenninger, 136–152. Washington, DC: National Archives and Record Administration, 1987.

Cooper, Patricia A. "The 'Traveling Fraternity': Union Cigar Makers and Geographic Mobility, 1900–1919." *Journal of Social History* 17, no. 1 (Autumn 1983): 127–138.

Couvares, Francis G. "The Triumph of Commerce: Class Culture and Mass Culture in Pittsburgh." In *Working Class America: Essays on Labor, Community, and American Society*, edited by Michael H. Frisch and Daniel J. Walkowitz, 123–152. Urbana: University of Illinois Press, 1983.

Cresswell, Tim. "Embodiment, Power and the Politics of Mobility: The Case of Female Tramps and Hobos." *Transaction of the Institute of British Geographers*, n.s., 24, no. 2 (1999): 175–192.

Cullen, Jim. *The Art of Democracy: A Concise History of Popular Culture in the United States*. New York: Monthly Review Press, 1996.

Currarino, Rosanne. *The Labor Question in America: Economic Democracy in the Gilded Age*. Urbana: University of Illinois Press, 2011.

Currie, Janet and Joseph Ferrie. "The Law and Labor Strife in the United States, 1881–1894." *Journal of Economic History* 60, no. 1 (March 2000): 42–66.

Danhoff, Clarence H. "Farm-Making Costs and the 'Safety-Valve': 1850–1860." *Journal of Political Economy* 49, no. 3 (June 1941): 317–359.

Davis, Graham. *In Search of a Better Life: British and Irish Migration*. Brimscombe

Port, Stroud, UK: History Press, 2011.

Davis, Graham and Matthew Goulding. "Irish Hard-Rock Miners in Ireland, Britain, and the United States." In *In Search of a Better Life: British and Irish Migration,* edited by Graham Davis, 179–195. Brimscombe Port, Stroud, UK: History Press, 2011.

Davis, Mary. *Comrade or Brother?: A History of the British Labour Movement.* 2nd ed. London: Pluto Press, 2009.

d'Eramo, Marco. *The Pig and the Skyscrapper, Chicago: A History of Our Future.* London: Verso, 2002.

Destler, Chester McA. "Consummation of a Labor-Populist Alliance in Illinois, 1894." *Mississippi Valley Historical Review* 27, no. 4 (March 1941): 589–602.

DeVault, Ileen A. "'To Sit Among Men': Skill, Gender, and Craft Unionism in the Early American Federation of Labor." In *Labor Histories: Class, Politics and the Working-Class Experience,* edited by Eric Arnesen, Julie Green, and Bruce Laurie, 259–283. Urbana: University of Illinois Press, 1998.

Dick, Everett. "Going Beyond the Ninety-Fifth Meridian." *Agricultural History* 17, no. 2 (April 1943): 105–111.

Dorigo, Guido and Waldo Tobler. "Push-Pull Migration Laws." *Annals of the Association of American Geographers* 73, no. 1 (March 1983): 1–17.

Doucet, Michael J. and John C. Weaver. "Material Culture and the North American House: The Era of the Common Man, 1870–1920." *Journal of American History* 72, no. 3 (December 1985): 568–575.

Douglas, Paul. "The Problem of Labor Turnover." *American Economic Review* 8, no. 2 (June 1918): 306–316.

———. "An Analysis of Strike Statistics, 1881–1921." *Journal of the American Statistical Association* 18, no. 143 (September 1923): 866–877.

Dubofsky, Melvyn. "The Federal Judiciary, Free Labor, and Equal Rights." In *The Pullman Strike and the Crisis of the 1890s: Essays on Labor and Politics,* edited by Richard Schneirov, Shelton Stromquist, and Nick Salvatore, 159–178. Urbana: University of Illinois Press, 1999.

———. *Hard Work: The Making of Labor History.* Urbana: University of Illinois Press, 2000.

———. *The State and Labor in Modern America.* Chapel Hill: University of North Carolina Press, 1994.

Dubofsky, Melvyn and Warren Van Tine. *John L. Lewis: A Biography.* New York: New York Times Book Co., 1977.

DuBois, W. E. Burghardt, ed. *The Negro Artisan: A Social Study.* Atlanta: University of Atlanta Press, 1902.

Ely, Richard T. *The Labor Movement in America.* New York: Thomas Y. Crowell, 1886.

Engels, Friedrich. *The Condition of the Working Class in England*. Stanford, CA: Stanford University Press, 1968.

Erie, Steven P. *Rainbow's End: Irish-Americans and the Dilemma of Urban Machine Politics, 1840–1985*. Berkeley: University of California Press, 1988.

Ferrie, Joseph P. "The End of American Exceptionalism? Mobility in the United States Since 1850." *Journal of Economic Perspectives* 19, no. 3 (Summer 2005): 199–215.

Fine, Nathan. *Labor and Farmer Parties in the United States, 1828–1928*. New York: Russell & Russell, 1961.

Fink, Leon. "Labor, Liberty, and the Law: Trade Unionism and the Problem of the American Constitutional Order." *Journal of American History* 74, no. 3 (December 1987): 904–925.

——. *The Long Gilded Age: American Capitalism and the Lessons of a New World Order*. Philadelphia: University of Pennsylvania Press, 2015.

——. "The New Labor History and the Powers of Pessimism: Consensus, Hegemony, and the Case of the Knights of Labor." *Journal of American History* 75, no. 1 (June 1988): 115–136.

——. *Workingmen's Democracy: The Knights of Labor and American Politics*. Urbana: University of Illinois Press, 1983.

Finn, J. F. "AF of L Leaders and the Question of Politics in the Early 1890s." *Journal of American Studies* 7, no. 3 (December 1973): 243–265.

Flagg, John, Matthew Pethers, and Robin Vandome. "Introduction: Networks and the Nineteenth-Century Periodical." *American Periodical: A Journal of History, Criticism, and Bibliography* 23, no. 2 (2013): 93–104.

Flynt, Josiah. *Tramping with Tramps: Studies and Sketches of Vagabond Life*. New York: Century Co., 1901.

Fohlen, Claude. "The Industrial Revolution in France, 1700–1914." In *The Fontana Economic History of Europe: The Emergence of Industrial Societies*. Vol. 1., edited by Carlo M. Cipolla, 7–71. London: Collins/Fontana, 1973.

Foner, Eric. *Give Me Liberty: An American History*. New York: W. W. Norton, 2012.

——. *Reconstruction: America's Unfinished Revolution, 1863–1877*. New York: Harper & Row, 1988.

Foner, Philip. *History of the Labor Movement in the United States*. Vol. 2. New York: International Publishers, 1975.

——. *Organized Labor and the Black Workers, 1619–1973*. New York: International Publishers, 1976.

Foster, Jim. "The Ten Day Tramps." *Labor History* 23 (Fall 1982): 608–623.

Friedlander, Dov. "Occupational Structure, Wages, and Migration in Late Nineteenth Century England and Wales." *Economic Development and Cultural*

Change 40, no. 2 (January 1992): 295–318.

Friedman, Gerald. "The State and the Making of the Working Class: France and the United States, 1880–1914." *Theory and Society* 17, no. 3 (May 1988): 403–430.

———. "Success and Failure in Third Party Politics: The Knights of Labor and the Union Labor Coalition in Massachusetts, 1884–1888." *International Labor and Working Class History* 62 (Fall 2002): 164–188.

———. "US Historical Statistics: New Estimates of Union Membership, the United States, 1880–1914." *Historical Methods: A Journal of Quantitative and Interdisciplinary History* 32 , no. 2 (Spring 1999): 75–86.

———. "Worker Militancy and Its Consequences: Political Responses to Labor Unrest in the United States, 1877–1914." *International Labor and Working Class History* 40 (Fall 1991): 5–17.

Frisch, Michael H. and Daniel Walkowitz. *Working Class America: Essays on Labor, Community, and American Society.* Urbana: University of Illinois Press.

Gabler, Edwin. *The American Telegrapher: A Social History, 1860–1900.* New Brunswick, NJ: Rutgers University Press, 1988.

Garlock, Jonathan. *Guide to the Local Assemblies of the Knights of Labor.* Westport, CT: Greenwood, 1982.

Gay, Peter. *The Dilemma of Democratic Socialism: Eduard Bernstein's Challenge to Marx.* New York: Collier, 1962.

George, Henry. "The New Party." *North American Review* 145, no. 368 (July 1887), 1–7.

Gerstle, Gary. *Liberty and Coercion: The Paradox of American Government from the Founding to the Present.* Princeton, NJ: Princeton University Press, 2015.

———. "The Resilient Power of the States Across the Long Nineteenth Century." In *The Unsustainable American State,* edited by Lawrence Jacobs and Desmond King, 61–87. Oxford: Oxford University Press, 2009.

Gerteis, Joseph. *Class and the Color Line: Interracial Class Coalition in the Knights of Labor and the Populist Movement.* Durham, NC: Duke University Press, 2007.

Gitelman, H. M. "Adolph Strasser and the Origins of Pure and Simple Unionism." In *The Labor History Reader,* edited by Daniel J. Leab, 153–165. Ithaca, NY: Cornell University Press, 1985.

Goldfield, Michael. *The Color of Politics: Race and the Mainsprings of American Politics.* New York: New Press, 1997.

Goldstein, Robert Justin. "*Labor History* Symposium: Political Repression of the American Labor Movement During Its Formative Years—a Comparative Perspective." *Labor History* 51, no. 2 (May 2010): 271–293.

Goodwyn, Lawrence. *Democratic Promise: The Populist Movement in America.* New York: Oxford University Press. 1976.

Graham, Keith. *Karl Marx, Our Contemporary: Social Theory for a Post-Leninist World*. Toronto: University of Toronto Press, 1992.

Gramsci, Antonio. *Selections from the Prison Notebooks*. New York: International Publishers, 1971.

Green, James. *Death in the Haymarket: A Story of Chicago, the First Labor Movement and the Bombing That Divided America*. New York: Anchor, 2006.

Griffen, Clyde. "Occupational Mobility in Nineteenth-Century America: Problems and Possibilities." *Journal of Social History* 5, no. 3 (Spring 1972): 310–330.

Grob, Gerald. "The Knights of Labor and the Trade Unions, 1878–1886." *Journal of Economic History* 18, no. 2 (June 1958): 176–192.

Grossman, James R. *Land of Hope: Chicago, Black Southerners, and the Great Migration*. Chicago: University of Chicago Press, 1989.

Gutman, Herbert. *Work, Culture and Society in Industrializing America: Essays in American Working Class and Social History*. New York: Vintage, 1977.

Hahn, Steven and Joseph Prude, eds. *The Countryside in the Age of Capitalist Transformation*. Chapel Hill: University of North Carolina Press, 1985.

Handlin, Oscar. *The Uprooted: The Epic Story of the Great Migrations That Made the American People*. Boston: Little, Brown, 1951.

Harring, Sidney L. "Class Conflict and the Suppression of Tramps in Buffalo, 1892–1894." *Law & Society* 11 (Summer 1977): 873–911.

Haydu, Jeffrey. *Between Craft and Class: Skilled Workers and Factory Politics in the United States and Britain, 1890–1922*. Berkeley: University of California, 1988.

Haywood, William D. *Bill Haywood's Book: The Autobiography of William D. Haywood*. New York: International Publishers, 1929.

Heilbroner, Robert L. and Aaron Singer. *The Economic Transformation of America: 1600 to the Present*. New York: Harcourt Brace Jovanovich, 1984.

Hicks, James D. "The Third Party Tradition in American Politics." *Mississippi Valley Historical Review* 20, no. 1 (June 1933): 3–28.

Higbie, Frank Tobias. *Indispensable Outcasts: Hobo Workers and Community in the American West*. Urbana: University of Illinois Press, 2003.

Higgs, Robert. *The Transformation of the American Economy, 1865–1914: An Essay in Interpretation*. New York: John Wiley & Sons, 1971.

Hilbert, F. W. "Trade-Union Agreements in the Iron Molders' Union." In *Studies in American Trade Unionism*, edited by Jacob H. Hollander and George E. Barnett, 221–260. New York: Henry Holt, 1912.

Hild, Matthew. "The Knights of Labor and the Third-Party Movement in Texas, 1886–1896." *Southwestern Historical Quarterly* 119 , no. 1 (July 2015): 24–43.

Hine, Robert V. and Marc Faragher. *The American West: A New Interpretive History*. New Haven, CT: Yale University Press, 2000.

Hinton, Richard J. "American Labor Organizations." *North American Review* 140, no. 338 (January 1885): 48–62.

Hirsch, Susan E. "The Search for Unity Among Railroad Workers: The Pullman Strike in Perspective." In *The Pullman Strike and the Crisis of the 1890s,* edited by Richard Schneirov, Shelton Stromquist, and Nick Salvatore, 430–464. Urbana: University of Illinois Press,1999.

Hobsbawm, E. J. "Economic Fluctuations and Some Social Movements Since 1800." *Economic History Review*, 2nd ser., vol. 1 (1952): 1–25.

Hobsbawm, Eric. *The Age of Empire, 1875–1914*. New York: Vintage Books, 1989.

———. *The Age of Revolution, 1789–1848*. New York: Vintage Books, 1996.

———. *Labouring Men: Studies in the History of Labour*. London: Weidenfeld and Nicolson, 1964.

———. *Workers: Worlds of Labour*. London: Weidenfeld and Nicolson, 1984.

Hollander, Jacob H. and George E. Barnett. *Studies in American Trade Unionism.* New York: Henry Holt, 1912.

Holt, James. "Trade Unionism in the British and US Steel Industries, 1880–1914: A Comparative Study." In *The Labor History Reader,* edited by Daniel J. Leab, 166–196. Chicago: University of Illinois Press, 1985.

Hunt, E. H. *British Labour History, 1815–1914*. London: Weidenfeld and Nicolson, 1981.

Hutt, Allen. *British Trade Unionism: A Short History, 1800–1961.* London: Lawrence and Wishart, 1962.

Ignatiev, Noel. *How the Irish Became White.* New York: Routledge, 1995.

International Trade Union Confederation. *Union Growth: Draft Framework for Action.* Berlin: Third ITUC World Congress, Berlin, May 18–23, 2014.

Jacoby, Sanford M. *Employing Bureaucracy: Managers, Unions, and the Transformation of Work in the Twentieth Century.* New York: Psychology Press, 2004.

———. "Industrial Labor Mobility in Historical Perspective." *Industrial Relations* 22, no. 2 (Spring 1983): 261–282.

———, ed. *Masters to Managers: Historical and Comparative Perspectives on American Employers.* New York: Columbia University Press, 1991.

Jacoby, Sanford M. and Sunil Sharma. "Employment Duration and Industrial Labor Mobility in the United States, 1880–1980." *Journal of Economic History* 52, no. 1 (March 1992): 161–177.

James, John A. and Mark Thomas. "A Golden Age?: Unemployment and the American Labor Market, 1880–1910." *Journal of Economic History* 63, no. 4 (December 2003): 959–994.

Jones, Jacqueline. *American Work: Four Centuries of Black and White Labor.* New York: W. W. Norton, 1998.

Jones, Maldwyn Allen. *American Immigration.* Chicago: University of Chicago Press, 1960.

Josephson, Matthew. *The Politicos.* New York: Harcourt, Brace & World, 1938.

———. *The Robber Barons: The Great American Capitalists, 1861–1901.* New York: Harcourt, Brace & World, 1934.

Judd, Dennis R. and Todd Swanstrom. *City Politics: Private Power and Public Policy.* New York: Pearson Longman, 2004.

Jun, Helen H. "Black Orientalism: Nineteenth-Century Narratives of Race and US Citizenship." *American Quarterly* 58, no. 4 (December 2006): 1047–1066.

Katz, Michael B. "Occupational Classification in History." *Journal of Interdisciplinary History* 3, no. 1 (Summer 1972): 63–88.

Katznelson, Ira. *City Trenches: Urban Politics and the Patterning of Class in the United States.* Chicago: University of Chicago Press, 1981.

Katznelson, Ira and Aristide R. Zolberg. *Working-Class Formation: Nineteenth-Century Patterns in Western Europe and the United States.* Princeton, NJ: Princeton University Press, 1986.

Kazin, Michael. *American Dreamers: How the Left Changed a Nation.* New York: Alfred A. Knopf, 2011.

Kelley, Robin G. D. *Hammer and Hoe: Alabama Communists During the Great Depression.* Chapel Hill: University of North Carolina Press, 1990.

Kindleberger, Charles P. *World Economic Primacy, 1500–1990.* New York: Oxford University Press,1996.

Kipnis, Ira. *The American Socialist Movement, 1897–1912.* Chicago: Haymarket, 2004, originally 1952.

Kirk, Neville. *Comrades and Cousins: Globalization, Workers and Labour Movements in Britain, the USA and Australia from the 1880s to 1914.* London: Merlin, 2003.

Kirkland, Edward. *Industry Comes of Age: Business, Labor and Public Policy, 1860–1897.* Chicago: Quadrangle, 1967.

Kuznets, Simon and Ernest Rubin. *Immigration and the Foreign Born.* National Bureau of Economic Research, 1954.

Labor Research Department. *American Labor Press Directory.* New York: Rand School of Social Science, 1925.

Laslett, John. *Labor and the Left: A Study of Socialist and Radical Influences in the American Labor Movement, 1881–1924.* New York: Basic Books, 1970.

Laurie, Bruce. *Artisans into Workers: Labor in Nineteenth Century America.* Urbana: University of Illinois Press, 1997.

Lebergott, Stanley. *Manpower in Economic Growth: The American Record Since 1800.* New York: McGraw-Hill, 1964.

Le Blanc, Paul. "Radical Labor Subculture: Key to Past and Future Insurgencies." *WorkingUSA: The Journal of Labor and Society* 13 (September 2010), 367–385.

Lee, Everett S. "A Theory of Migration." *Demography* 3, no. 1 (1966): 47–57.

Lee, Susan Previant and Peter Passell. *A New Economic View of American History.* New York: W. W. Norton, 1979.

Leonard, Henry B. "Ethnic Cleavage and Industrial Conflict in Late Nineteenth Century America: The Cleveland Rolling Mill Company Strikes of 1882 and 1885." *Labor History* 20, no. 4 (Fall 1979): 524–548.

Letwin, Daniel. *The Challenge of Interracial Unionism: Alabama Coal Miners, 1878–1921.* Chapel Hill: University of North Carolina, 1998.

Lewis, O. F. "The Tramp Problem." *Annals of the American Academy of Political and Social Science* 40 (March 1912): 217–227.

Lewis, Ronald L. "From Peasant to Proletarian: The Migration of Southern Blacks to the Central Appalachian Coalfields." *Journal of Southern History* 55, no. 1 (February 1989): 77–102.

Lichtenstein, Nelson. *State of the Union: A Century of American Labor.* Princeton, NJ: Princeton University Press, 2002.

Limerick, Patricia Nelson. *The Legacy of Conquest: The Unbroken Past of the American West.* New York: W. W. Norton, 1987.

London, Jack. *The Road.* New York: Macmillan, 1907.

Long, Jason. "Rural-Urban Migration and Socioeconomic Mobility in Victorian Britain." *Journal of Economic History* 65, no. 1 (March 2005): 1–35.

Marlatt, Gene Rona. *Joseph R. Buchanan: Spokesman for Labor During the Populist and Progressive Era.* PhD thesis, Boulder: University of Colorado, 1975.

Marx, Eleanor and Edward Aveling. *The Working-Class Movement in America.* Amherst, NY: Humanity, 2000.

Marx, Karl. *Capital.* Vol. 1. London: Penguin, 1990.

———. *The Poverty of Philosophy.* Amherst, NY: Prometheus, 1995.

McNeill, George, ed. *The Labor Movement: The Problem of Today.* Boston: A. M. Bridgman, 1887.

McVicar, John. *Origins and Progress of the Typographical Union: Its Proceedings as a National and International Organization, 1850–1891.* Lansing, MI: Darius D. Thorp, Printer and Binder, 1891.

Meyer, David R. *The Roots of American Industrialization.* Baltimore: Johns Hopkins University Press, 2003.

Montgomery, David. *Beyond Equality: Labor and the Radical Republicans, 1862–1872.* Urbana: University of Illinois Press, 1981.

———. *1865–1925.* Cambridge: Cambridge University Press, 1989.

———. "Labor in the Industrial Era." In *A History of the American Worker,* edited by Richard B. Morris, 79–113. Princeton, NJ: Princeton University Press, 1983.

———. "Strikes in Nineteenth-Century America." *Social Science History* 4, no. 1 (Winter 1980): 81–104.

———. "Wage Labor, Bondage, and Citizenship in Nineteenth-Century America."

International Labor and Working Class History 48 (Fall 1995): 6–27.

Moody, Kim. *In Solidarity: Essays in Working-Class Organization in the United States.* Chicago: Haymarket, 2014.

Morris, Richard B. *A Labor History of the American Worker.* Princeton, NJ: Princeton University Press, 1983.

Murphy, George G. S. and Arnold Zellner. "Sequential Growth, the Labor-Safety-Valve Doctrine and the Development of American Unionism." *Journal of Economic History* 19, no. 3 (September 1959): 402–421.

Myers, Donald James. "Birth and Establishment of the Labor Press in the United States." Master's diss., University of Wisconsin, 1950.

National Bureau of Economic Research. *US Business Cycle Expansions and Contractions.* Cambridge, MA: National Bureau of Economic Research, 2010. http://data.nber.org/cycles/cyclesmain.html.

Nelson, Bruce C. *Beyond the Martyrs: A Social History of Chicago's Anarchists, 1870– 1900.* New Brunswick, NJ: Rutgers University Press, 1988.

Oestreicher, Richard. "A Note on Knights of Labor Membership Statistics." *Labor History* 25, no. 1 (Winter 1984): 102–108.

———. *Solidarity and Fragmentation: Working People and Class Consciousness in Detroit, 1875–1900.* Urbana: University of Illinois Press, 1986.

Ostrogorski, M. *Democracy and the Organization of Political Parties.* London: Macmillan, 1902.

Nugent, Walter. *Into the West: The Story of Its People.* New York: Vintage, 2001.

Painter, Nell Irvin. *Standing at Armageddon: A Grassroots History of the Progressive Era.* New York: W. W. Norton, 2008.

Paul, Rodman. *The Far West and the Great Plains in Transition.* Norman: University of Oklahoma Press, 1998.

Peck, Gunther. "Mobilizing Community: Migrant Workers and the Politics of Labor Mobility in the North American West, 1900–1920." In *Labor Histories: Class, Politics, and the Working Class Experience,* edited by Eric Arnesen, Julie Green, and Bruce Laurie, 175–200. Urbana: University of Illinois Press, 1998.

Pelling, Henry. *A History of British Trade Unionism.* Harmondsworth, UK: Penguin, 1963.

Perlman, Selig. *A History of Trade Unionism in the United States.* New York: Macmillan, 1922.

———. *A Theory of the Labor Movement.* New York: Augustus M. Kelley, 1949, originally 1928.

Perlman, Selig and Philip Taft. *History of Labor in the United States, 1896–1920.* New York: Macmillan, 1935.

Perrot, Michelle. "On the Formation of the French Working Class." In *Working-Class Formation: Nineteenth Century Patterns in Western Europe and the United States,* edited by Ira Katznelson and Aristide R. Zolberg, 71–110. Princeton, NJ: Princeton University Press, 1986.

Pierenkemper, Toni and Richard Tilly. *The German Economy During the Nineteenth Century.* New York: Berghahn, 2004.

Pinkerton, Allan. *Strikers, Communists, Tramps and Detectives.* New York: G. W. Carleton, 1878.

Piven, Frances Fox and Richard Cloward. *Why Americans Don't Vote.* New York: Pantheon, 1989.

Powderly, Terence V. *The Path I Trod: The Autobiography of Terence V. Powderly.* New York: Columbia University Press.

Pred, Allan R. *The Spatial Dynamics of US Urban-Industrial Growth, 1800–1914.* Cambridge, MA: MIT Press, 1966.

Rachleff, Peter. *Black Labor in Richmond, 1865–1890.* Urbana: University of Illinois Press, 1989.

Ravenstein, E. G. "The Laws of Migration." *Journal of the Statistical Society of London* 48, no. 2 (June 1885): 167–235.

——. "The Laws of Migration." *Journal of the Royal Statistical Society* 52, no. 2 (June 1889): 241–305.

Reuter, Frank T. "John Swinton's Paper." *Labor History* 1, no. 3 (1960): 298–307.

Rezneck, Samuel. "Distress, Relief, and Discontent in the United States During the Depression of 1873–78." *Journal of Political Economy* 58, no. 6 (December 1950): 494–512.

——. "Unemployment, Unrest, and Relief in the United States During the Depression of 1893–97." *Journal of Political Economy* 61, no. 4 (August 1953): 324–345.

Robinson, Jesse S. *The Amalgamated Association of Iron, Steel and Tin Workers.* Baltimore: Johns Hopkins Press, 1920.

Rodgers, Daniel T. *The Work Ethic in Industrial America, 1850–1920.* Chicago: University of Chicago, 1978.

Rodriguez, Marc. *Repositioning North American Migration History.* Rochester, NY: University of Rochester Press, 2004.

Roediger, David. *How Race Survived US History: From Settlement and Slavery to the Obama Phenomenon.* London: Verso, 2010.

——. *The Wages of Whiteness: Race and the Making of the American Working Class.* Rev. ed. London: Verso, 1999.

Roediger, David R. and Elizabeth D. Esch. *The Production of Difference: Race and the Management of Labor in US History.* New York: Oxford University Press, 2012.

Roediger, David R. and Philip S. Foner. *Our Own Time: A History of American Labor and the Working Day.* London: Verso, 1989.

Ross, Steven J. "The Politicization of the Working Class: Production, Ideology, Culture and Politics in Late Nineteenth-Century Cincinnati." *Social History* 11, no. 2 (May 1986): 171–195.

———. *Workers on the Edge: Work, Leisure, and Politics in Industrializing Cincinnati, 1788–1890*. New York: Columbia University Press, 1985.

Ryan, Garry D. and Timothy K. Nenninger, eds. *Soldiers and Civilians: The US Army and the American People*. Washington, DC: National Archives and Records Administration, 1987.

Sakolski, A. M. "The Finances of the Iron Molders' Union." In *Studies in American Trade Unionism*, edited by Jacob H. Hollander and George E. Barnett, 81–107. New York: Henry Holt, 1912.

Saposs, David J. *Left Wing Unionism: A Study of Radical Policies and Tactics*. New York: International Publishers, 1926.

Schlereth, Thomas J. *Victorian America: Transformations in Everyday Life, 1876–1915*. New York: Harper Collins, 1991.

Schneirov, Richard. *Labor and Urban Politics: Class Conflict and the Origins of Modern Liberalism in Chicago, 1864–97*. Urbana: University of Illinois Press, 1998.

———. "Thoughts on Periodizing the Gilded Age: Capital Accumulation, Society and Politics, 1873–1898." *Journal of the Gilded Age and Progressive Era* 5, no. 3 (July 2006): 189–224.

Schneirov, Richard, Shelton Stromquist, and Nick Salvatore, eds. *The Pullman Strike and the Crisis of the 1890s, Essays on Labor and Politics*. Urbana: University of Illinois Press, 1999.

Searle, G. R. *A New England: Peace and War, 1880–1918*. Oxford: Clarendon, 2004.

Shaikh, Anwar. *Capitalism: Competition, Conflict, Crises*. New York: Oxford University Press, 2016.

Shannon, Fred A. *The Farmer's Last Frontier: Agriculture, 1860–1897*. White Plains, NY: M. E. Sharpe, 1945.

———. "The Homestead Act and the Land Surplus." *American Historical Review* 41, no. 4 (1936): 637–651.

———. "A Post Mortem on the Labor-Safety-Valve Theory." *Agricultural History* 19, no. 1 (January 1945): 31–37.

Shefter, Martin. *Political Parties and the State: The American Historical Experience*. Princeton, NJ: Princeton University Press, 1994.

Skocpol, Theda. *Protecting Soldiers and Mothers: The Political Origins of Social Policy in the United States*. Cambridge, MA: Harvard University Press, 1992.

Spence, Clark C. "Knights of the Tie and Rail—Tramps and Hoboes in the West." *Western Historical Quarterly* 2, no. 1 (January 1971) 4–19.

Spero, Sterling D. and Abram L. Harris. *The Black Worker: The Negro and the*

Labor Movement. New York: Atheneum, 1969, originally 1931.

Staley, Eugene. *History of the Illinois State Federation of Labor.* Chicago: University of Chicago Press, 1930.

Stephenson, Charles. "'There's Plenty Waitin' at the Gates': Mobility, Opportunity and the American Worker." In *Life and Labor: Dimensions of American Working-Class History,* edited by Charles Stephenson and Robert Asher, 72–91. Albany: State University of New York Press, 1986.

Stephenson, Charles and Robert Asher, eds. *Life and Labor: Dimensions of American Working-Class History.* Albany: State University of New York Press, 1986.

Stevens, George A. *New York Typographical Union No. 6: Study of a Modern Trade Union and Its Predecessors.* Albany, NY: J. B. Lyon Company, State Printers, 1913.

Stevenson, Robert Louis. *Across the Plains with Other Memories and Essays.* London: Chatto & Windus, 1892.

Stockton, Frank T. *The International Molders' Union of North America.* Baltimore: Johns Hopkins University Press, 1921.

Stromquist, Shelton. *A Generation of Boomers: The Pattern of Railroad Labor Conflict in Nineteenth-Century America.* Urbana: University of Illinois Press, 1993.

Strong, D. D. Rev. Josiah. *Our Country: Its Possible Future and Its Present Crisis.* New York: Baker & Taylor, 1885.

Sumner, Helen L. "The Benefit System of the Cigar Makers' Union." In *Trade Unionism and Labor Problems,* edited by John R. Commons, 527–545. New York: Augustus M. Kelley, 1967, originally 1905.

Sundquist, James L. *Dynamics of the Party System: Alignment and Realignment of Political Parties in the United States.* Washington, DC: Brookings Institution, 1983.

Swinton, John. *Striking for Life: Labor's Side of the Labor Question; The Right of the Workingman to a Fair Living.* Western W. Wilson, 1894.

Taeuber, Conrad. "Rural-Urban Migration." *Agricultural History* 15, no. 3 (July 1941): 151–160.

Taft, Philip. *The A. F. of L. in the Time of Gompers.* New York: Harper & Brothers, 1957.

Tank, Robert. "Mobility and Occupational Structure on the Late Nineteenth-Century Urban Frontier: The Case of Denver, Colorado." *Pacific Historical Review* 47, no. 2 (May 1978): 189–216.

Thernstrom, Stephan. *The Other Bostonians: Poverty and Progress in the American Metropolis, 1880–1970.* Cambridge, MA: Harvard University Press, 1973.

———. *Poverty and Progress: Social Mobility in a Nineteenth Century City.* New York: Atheneum, 1974.

Thernstrom, Stephan and Peter R. Knights. "Men in Motion: Some Data and

Speculations About Urban Population Mobility in Nineteenth-Century America." *Journal of Interdisciplinary History* 1, no. 1 (Autumn 1970): 7–35.

Thompson, E. P. *The Making of the English Working Class*. New York: Vintage, 1966.

———. *The Poverty of Theory and Other Essays*. New York: Monthly Review Press, 1978.

Tomlins, Christopher L. *The State and the Unions: Labor Relations, Law, and the Organized Labor Movement in America, 1880–1960* (Cambridge: Cambridge University Press, 1985.

Trachtenberg, Alan. *The Incorporation of America: Culture & Society in the Gilded Age*. New York: Hill and Wang, 1982.

Tracy, George A. *History of the Typographical Union: Its Beginnings, Progress and Development, Its Beneficial and Educational Features, Together with a Chapter on the Early Organizations of Printers*. Indianapolis: International Typographers Union, 1913.

Traynor, John. *Mastering Modern German History*. New York: Palgrave Macmillan, 2008.

Trent, Alexander, J. and Annemarie Steidl, "Gender and the 'Laws of Migration.'" *Social Science History* 36, no. 2 (Summer 2012): 223–241.

Turner, Frederick Jackson. *The Frontier in American History*. New York: Barnes & Noble, 2009, originally 1920.

Twain, Mark and Charles Dudley Warner. *The Gilded Age: A Tale of Today*. New York: New American Library, 1969, originally 1873.

Tygiel, Jules. "Tramping Artisans: The Case of the Carpenters in Industrial America." *Labor History* 22, no. 3 (Summer 1981): 348–376.

Ulman, Lloyd. *The Rise of the National Trade Union: The Development and Significance of Its Structure, Governing Institutions, and Economic Policies*. Cambridge, MA: Harvard University Press, 1955.

Vandome, Robin. "The Advancement of *Science*: James McKeen Cattell and the Networks of Prestige and Authority, 1895–1915." *American Periodicals* 23, no. 2 (2013): 172–187.

Voss, Kim. *The Making of American Exceptionalism: The Knights of Labor and Class Formation in the Nineteenth Century*. Ithaca, NY: Cornell University Press, 1993.

Voss-Hubbard, Mark. "The 'Third Party Tradition' Reconsidered: Third Parties and American Public Life, 1830–1900." *Journal of American History* 86, no. 1 (June 1999): 124–150.

Walkowitz, Daniel J. *Worker City, Company Town: Iron and Cotton-Worker Protest in Troy and Cohoes, New York, 1855–84*. Urbana: University of Illinois Press, 1981.

Ward, David. *Cities and Immigrants*. New York: Oxford University Press, 1971.

Ware, Norman J. *The Labor Movement in the United States, 1860–1890*. New York: Vintage, 1964.

Warne, Frank Julian. *The Coal-Mine Workers: A Study in Labor Organization*. New York: Longmans, Green, 1905.

Watts, Sarah Lyons. *Order Against Chaos: Business Culture and Labor Ideology in America, 1880–1915*. New York: Greenwood, 1991.

Weber, Adna Ferrin. *The Growth of Cities in the Nineteenth Century: A Study in Statistics*. Ithaca, NY: Cornell University Press, 1965, originally 1899.

Weir, Robert E. *Beyond Labor's Veil: The Culture of the Knights of Labor*. University Park: Pennsylvania State University Press, 1996.

———. "Blind in One Eye: Western and Eastern Knights of Labor View the Chinese Question." *Labor History* 41, no. 4 (2000): 421–436.

———. "A Fragile Alliance: Henry George and the Knights of Labor." *American Journal of Economics and Sociology* 56, no. 4 (October 1997): 421–439.

———. *Knights Unhorsed: Internal Conflict in a Gilded Age Social Movement*. Detroit: Wayne State University Press, 2000.

Wells, David A. "How Shall the Nation Regain Prosperity?" *North American Review* 125, no. 257 (July–August 1877): 110–132.

Wertheimer, Barbara Mayer. *We Were There: The Story of Working Women in America*. New York: Pantheon, 1977.

Wiener, John. "Class Structure and Economic Development in the American South, 1865–1955." *American Historical Review* 84, no. 4 (October 1979): 970–992.

Wilentz, Sean. "Against Exceptionalism: Class Consciousness and the American Labor Movement, 1790–1920." *International Labor and Working-Class History*. 26 (Fall 1984): 1–24.

Willcox, Walter F. "The Decrease of Interstate Migration." *Political Science Quarterly* 10, no. 4 (December 1895): 603–614.

Willett, Mabel Hurd. "Women in the Clothing Industry." In *Trade Unionism and Labor Problems,* edited by John R. Commons, 371–395. New York: Augustus M. Kelley, 1967, originally 1903.

Williams, R. Hal. *Realigning America: McKinley, Bryan, and the Remarkable Election of 1896*. Lawrence: University of Kansas Press, 2010.

Winder, Robert. *Bloody Foreigners: The Story of Immigration to Britain*. London: Abacus, 2004.

Witte, Edwin E. *The Government in Labor Disputes*. New York: McGraw-Hill, 1932.

Woodward, C. Vann. *Origins of the New South, 1877–1913*. Baton Rouge: Louisiana State University Press, 1971.

———. *Reunion and Reaction: The Compromise of 1877 and the End of Reconstruction*. New York: Doubleday Anchor, 1956.

Wright, Carroll D. "The Amalgamated Association of Iron and Steel Workers." *Quarterly Journal of Economics* 7, no. 4 (July 1893): 400–432.

———. "The National Amalgamated Association of Iron, Steel, and Tin Workers, 1892–1901." *Quarterly Journal of Economics* 16, no. 1 (November 1901): 37–68.

Wright, Gavin. *Old South, New South: Revolutions in the Southern Economy Since the Civil War*. Baton Rouge: Louisiana State University, 1996.

———. "The Origins of American Industrial Success, 1879–1940." *American Economic Review* 80, no. 4 (1990): 651–668.

Wyman, Mark. *Hard Rock Epic: Western Miners and the Industrial Revolution, 1860– 1910*. Berkeley: University of California Press, 1979.

———. *Hoboes, Bindlestiffs, Fruit Tramps and the Harvesting of the West*. New York: Hill and Wang, 2010.

———. *Round-Trip to America: The Immigrants Return to Europe. 1880–1930*. Ithaca, NY: Cornell University Press, 1993.

Zieger, Robert H. *For Jobs and Freedom: Race and Labor in America Since 1865*. Lexington: University of Kentucky Press, 2007.

Zieren, Gregory. "The Labor Boycott and Class consciousness in Toledo, Ohio." In *Life and Labor: Dimensions of American Working Class History,* edited by Charles Stephenson and Robert Asher, 131–146. Albany: State University of New York Press, 1986.

Zolberg, Aristide. "How Many Exceptionalisms?" In *Working-Class Formation: Nineteenth-Century Patterns in Western Europe and the United States*, edited by Ira Katznelson and Aristide R. Zolberg, 397–455. Princeton, NJ: Princeton University Press, 1986.

Zunz, Olivier. *The Changing Face of Inequality: Urbanization, Industrial Development, and Immigration in Detroit, 1880–1920*. Chicago: University of Chicago Press, 1982.

Government Publications

Bureau of Statistics. *Statistical Abstract of the United States, 1891*. Washington, DC: US Government Printing Office, 1892.

Bureau of Statistics. *Statistical Abstract of the United States, 1893*. Washington, DC: US Government Printing Office, 1894.

Bureau of Statistics. *Statistical Abstract of the United States, 1896*. Washington, DC: US Government Printing Office, 1897.

Bureau of Statistics. *Statistical Abstract of the United States, 1898*. Washington, DC: US Government Printing Office, 1899.

Bureau of Statistics. *Statistical Abstract of the United States, 1899*. New York, Johnson Reprint Corporation, 1900.

Bureau of Statistics. *Statistical Abstract of the United States, 1900*. Washington, DC: US Government Printing Office, 1901.

Bureau of the Census. *Compendium of the Ninth Census, 1870*. Washington, DC: US Government Printing Office, 1872.

Bureau of the Census. *Compendium of the Tenth Census,* June 1, 1880. Washington, DC: US Government Printing Office, 1883.

Bureau of the Census. *Abstract of the Eleventh Census: 1890*. 2nd ed. Washington, DC: US Government Printing Office, 1896.

Bureau of the Census. *Abstract of the Twelfth Census of the United States, 1900*. Washington, DC: US Government Printing Office, 1904.

Bureau of the Census. *Historical Statistics of the United States: Colonial Times to 1970*. Pts. 1 and 2. Washington, DC: US Government Printing Office, 1975.

Commission on Industrial Relations. *Final Report and Testimony Submitted to Congress by the Commission on Industrial Relations*. Vol. 5. Washington, DC: US Government Printing Office, 1916.

Commission on Industrial Relations. *Final Report and Testimony Submitted to Congress by the US Commission on Industrial Relations*. Vol. 11. Washington, DC: US Government Printing Office, 1916.

Commissioner of Labor. *The First Annual Report of the Commissioner of Labor, March 1886*. Washington, DC: US Government Printing Office, 1886.

Commissioner of Labor. *Third Annual Report of the Commissioner of Labor, 1887*. Washington, DC: US Government Printing Office, 1888.

Commissioner of Labor. *Tenth Annual Report of the Commissioner of Labor, 1894*. Washington, DC: US Government Printing Office, 1896.

Commissioner of Labor. *Sixteenth Annual Report of the Commissioner of Labor, 1901*. Washington, DC: US Government Printing Office, 1901.

Commissioner of Labor. *Twenty-First Annual Report of the Commissioner of Labor, 1906*. Washington, DC: US Government Printing Office, 1907.

Department of the Interior. *Abstract of the Eleventh Census: 1890*. 3rd ed. Washington, DC: US Government Printing Office, 1896.

Illinois Bureau of Labor Statistics. *Fourth Biennial Report of the Bureau of Labor Statistics of Illinois, 1886*. Springfield, IL: H.W. Roeker, Printer and Binder.

Industrial Commission. *Reports of the Industrial Commission on Labor Organizations, Labor Disputes, and Arbitration, and on Railway Labor*. Vol. 17. Washington, DC: US Government Printing Office, 1901.

Industrial Commission. *Report of the Industrial Commission on the Chicago Labor Disputes of 1900*. Vol. 8. Washington, DC: US Government Printing Office, 1901.

Industrial Commission. *Reports of the Industrial Commission on the Relations and Conditions of Capital and Labor Employed in Manufactures and General Business.* Vol. 7. Washington, DC: US Government Printing Office, 1901.

Industrial Commission. *Reports of the Industrial Commission on the Relations and Conditions of Capital and Labor Employed in Manufactures and General Business.* Vol. 14. Washington, DC: US Government Printing Office, 1901.

Industrial Commission. *Reports of the Industrial Commission on the Relations and Conditions of Capital and Labor Employed in the Mining Industry.* Vol. 12. Washington, DC: US Government Printing Office, 1901.

US Senate. *Report of the Committee of the Senate Upon the Relations of Labor and Capital.* Vol. 1. Washington, DC: US Government Printing Office, 1885.

US Senate. *Report of the Committee of the Senate Upon the Relations Between Labor and Capital.* Vol. 2. Washington, DC: US Government Printing Office, 1885.

US Senate. *Report of the Committee of the Senate Upon the Relations Between Labor and Capital.* Vol. 3. Washington, DC: US Government Printing Office, 1885.

Industry Reports and Periodicals

American Iron and Steel Association. *Statistics of the American and Foreign Iron Trade for 1885.* Philadelphia: American Iron and Steel Association, 1886.

American Iron and Steel Association. *Statistics of the American and Foreign Iron Trade for 1895.* Philadelphia: American Iron and Steel Association, 1896.

Labor Periodicals

American Federationist. New York, 1893–1894.

Boycotter. New York, 1884.

Chicago Boycotter. Chicago, 1886.

Cigar Makers' Official Journal. Chicago, 1880–1904.

Commercial Telegraphers' Journal. Chicago, vol. 16, January 1918.

Detroit Unionist. Detroit, 1882–1883.

Haverhill Laborer. Haverhill, MA, 1884–1885.

Irish World and American Industrial Liberator. New York, 1890.

Iron Molders' Journal. Cincinnati, 1874–1899.

John Swinton's Paper. New York, 1884, 1886, 1887.

Journal of United Labor. Philadelphia and Boston, 1879–1888.

Labor Enquirer. Denver, 1882–1887.

Labor Leader. Boston, 1893–1894.

Labor Leaf. Detroit, 1884–1886.

Laborer. Haverhill, Brocton, and Marlboro, MA, 1885–1886.

Machinists' Monthly Journal. Chicago, 1897, 1899.

Miners' Magazine. Western Federation of Miners, Butte, MT, 1900.

National Labor Tribune. Pittsburgh, 1884–1887.

Patterson Labor Standard. Patterson, NJ, 1882.

Progressive Age. Chicago, 1881–1882.

Pueblo Courier. Pueblo, CO, 1898.

Railroad Telegrapher. Saint Louis, vol. 21, January 1904.

Standard. New York, 1887.

Typographical Journal. Indianapolis, 1899–1900.

Union Convention Proceedings, Records, and Reports

American Federation of Labor. *An Interesting Discussion on a Political Programme at the 1894 Denver Convention of the American Federation of Labor* (verbatim transcription). New York: Freytag Printing, 1895.

Chicago Trades and Labor Assembly. *Ledger and Minute Book,* 1887–1891.

Forty-Fourth Annual Report of the President and Secretary of the Bricklayers and Masons' International Union of America. December 1, 1909. Indianapolis: Cheltenham, 1909.

Labadie, Joseph A. *Report of Joseph A. Labadie Delegate to the General Assembly, K. of L., Minneapolis, 1887.* Detroit: Printed by John R. Burton, 1887.

Proceedings of the Thirty-Fifth Annual Convention of the Bricklayers and Masons' International Union of America. Milwaukee, January 14–26, 1901.

Proceedings of the Eleventh General Convention of the United Brotherhood of Carpenters and Joiners of America. Scranton, PA, September 17–28, 1900.

Proceedings of the Sixteenth Biennial Convention of the United Brotherhood of Carpenters and Joiners of America. Des Moines, IA, September 19, 1910.

Proceedings of the Fifteenth Session of the Cigar Makers' International Union of America. Toronto, Ontario, September 17, 1883, in supplement to the *Cigar Makers' Official Journal.* September–October 1883.

Proceedings of the Sixteenth Session of the Cigar Makers' International Union of America. Cincinnati, October 1885.

Proceedings of the Seventeenth Session of the Cigar Makers' International Union. Buffalo, NY, October 1887.

Proceedings of the Eighteenth Session of the Cigar Makers' International Union of America. Buffalo, NY, October 1889.

Proceedings of the Sixth Convention of the International Association of Machinists. Cincinnati, May 6–14, 1895.

Proceedings of the Twelfth Session of the Iron Molders' Union of North America. Richmond, VA, July 8, 1874.

Proceedings of the Thirteenth Session of the Iron Molders' Union of North America. Cincinnati, July 1, 1876.

Proceedings of the Fourteenth Session of the Iron Molders' Union of North America. Louisville, KY: July 10, 1878.

Proceedings of the Sixteenth Session of the Iron Molders' Union of North America. Brooklyn, NY, July 10, 1882.

Proceedings of the Eighteenth Session of the Iron Molders' Union of North America. Saint Louis, July 11, 1888.

Proceedings of the Third Annual Session of District Assembly No. 82 (Union Pacific Employes') *Knights of Labor.* Denver, January 2–7, 1887.

Proceedings of the First Convention of Delegates, United Machinists and Mechanical Engineers of America. Atlanta, May 6–10, 1889.

Proceedings of the Sixth Convention of the International Association of Machinists. Cincinnati, May 6–14, 1895.

Proceedings of the First Convention of the Western Federation of Miners. Butte, MT, May 15–19, 1893.

Proceedings of the Third Convention of the Western Federation of Miners. May 1895.

Proceedings of the Thirty-Fourth Annual Report of the President and Secretary of the Bricklayers and Masons' International Union of America. Indianapolis, December 1, 1909.

Proceedings of the Thirty-Fifth Annual Convention of the Bricklayers and Masons' International Union. Milwaukee, January 14–26, 1901.

Record of the Proceedings of the Regular Sessions of the General Assembly, Knights of Labor. 1879–1887.

Record of the Proceedings of the Special Session of the General Assembly, Knights of Labor. Cleveland, May 25–June 3, 1886.

Report of the Proceedings of the Thirteenth Annual Convention of the American Federation of Labor. Chicago, December 11–19, 1893.

Report of the Proceedings of the Fourteenth Annual Convention of the American Federation of Labor. Denver, December 10–18, 1894.

Report of the Sixth Annual Session of the Federation of Organized Trades and Labor Unions of the United States and Canada, Also the Proceedings of the First Annual Convention of the American Federation of Labor. Columbus, OH, December 8–12, 1886.

Report of the Proceedings of the Twenty-Seventh Annual Convention of the American Federation of Labor. Norfolk, VA, November 11–23, 1907.

Report of the Proceedings of the Nineteenth Annual Session of the International Typographical Union, Baltimore, June 5–9, 1871.

Report of the Thirty-Third Annual Session of the International Typographical Union. New York, June 1885.

Report of the Thirty-Fifth Session of the International Typographical Union. Detroit, August 14, 1888.

Report of the Proceedings of the Thirty-Eighth Annual Session of the International Typographical Union. Atlanta, June 1890.

To the Officers and Members of the Thirteenth Session of the Iron Molders' International Union, in Convention Assembled. Cincinnati, July 1, 1876.

Western Federation of Miners. *Executive Board Ledger, 1894–1905.*

NOTES

Chapter 1

1. Thomas J. Schlereth, *Victorian America: Transformations in Everyday Life, 1876–1915* (New York: Harper Collins, 1991), 7.
2. Robert Louis Stevenson, *Across the Plains with Other Memories and Essays* (London: Chatto & Windus, 1892), 54–61.
3. Mark Twain and Charles Dudley Warner, *The Gilded Age: A Tale of Tragedy* (New York: New American Library, 1969, originally 1873), passim.
4. David Roediger and Elizabeth D. Esch, *The Production of Difference: Race and the Management of Labor in US History* (Oxford: Oxford University Press, 2012), 140, 165; Sanford M. Jacoby, *Masters to Managers: Historical and Comparative Perspectives on American Employers* (New York: Columbia University Press, 1991), 13–16.
5. Ken Coates and Tony Topham, *The Making of the Labour Movement: The Formation of the Transport and General Workers Union, 1870–1922* (Nottingham: Spokesman, 1994), 127; Peter Gay, *The Dilemma of Democratic Socialism: Eduard Bernstein's Challenge to Marx* (New York: Collier, 1962), 60–62.
6. Howard P. Chudacoff, *Mobile Americans: Residential and Social Mobility in Omaha, 1880–1920* (New York: Oxford University Press, 1972), 3.
7. Aristide R. Zolberg, "How Many Exceptionalisms?," in *Working-Class Formation: Nineteenth-Century Patterns in Western Europe and the United States*, ed. Ira Katznelson and Aristide R. Zolberg (Princeton, NJ: Princeton University Press, 1986), 399.
8. Robin Archer, *Why Is There No Labor Party in the United States?* (Princeton, NJ: Princeton University Press, 2007), 79.
9. Gary Gerstle, "The Resilient Power of the States Across the Long Nineteenth Century," in *The Unsustainable American State, ed.* Lawrence Jacobs and Desmond King (Oxford: Oxford University Press, 2009), 61–87; Gary Gerstle, *Liberty and Coercion: The Paradox of American Government from the Founding to the Present* (Princeton, NJ: Princeton University Press, 2015), 55–86.
10. Selig Perlman, *A History of Trade Unionism in the United States* (New York: Macmillan, 1922), 119.
11. Neville Kirk, *Comrades and Cousins: Globalization, Workers and Labour Movements in Britain, the USA and Australia from the 1880s to 1914* (London: Merlin, 2003), 46.
12. Eugene Staley, *History of the Illinois State Federation of Labor* Chicago: University of Chicago Press, 1930), 12–13, 47.
13. Theda Skocpol, *Protecting Soldiers and Mothers: The Political Origins of Social Policy*

in the United States (Cambridge, MA: Harvard University Press, 1992), 233–336.

14. Gerald Friedman, "Worker Militancy and Its Consequences: Political Responses to Labor Unrest in the United States, 1877–1914," *International Labor and Working-Class History* 40 (Fall 1991): 8.

15. Richard Jules Oestreicher, *Solidarity and Fragmentation: Working People and Class Consciousness in Detroit, 1875–1900* (Urbana: University of Illinois Press, 1986), 78–79.

16. Daniel J. Walkowitz, *Worker City, Company Town: Iron and Cotton-Worker Protest in Troy and Cohoes, New York, 1855–84* (Urbana: University of Illinois Press, 1981), 235.

17. Staley, *History*, 77.

18. Archer, *No Labor Party*, 87–88. These labor-party efforts in the US will be discussed in detail in a later chapter.

19. *Labor Leader*, November 3, 1894.

20. Archer, *No Labor Party*, 87–89.

21. Werner Sombart, *Why Is There No Socialism in the United States?* (London: Macmillan, 1976, originally 1906), 44, 119.

22. John D. Hicks, "The Third Party Tradition in American Politics," *Mississippi Valley Historical Review* 20, no. 1 (June 1933): 3–4.

23. Mark Voss-Hubbard, "The 'Third Party Tradition' Reconsidered: Third Parties and American Public Life, 1830–1900," *Journal of American History* 86, no. 1 (June 1999): 124–141.

24. Archer, *No Labor Party*, 24–26, 219–225.

25. Stanley Lebergott, *Manpower in Economic Growth: The American Record Since 1800* (New York: McGraw-Hill, 1964), 528–529; these figures were the official statistics used by the Census Bureau. US Census Bureau, *Historical Statistics of the United States: Colonial Times to 1970*, pt. 1 (Washington, DC: US Government Printing Office, 1975), 146–149, 165.

26. US Census Bureau, *Historical Statistics*, pt. 1, 12, 127.

27. Fred A. Shannon, *The Farmer's Last Frontier: Agriculture, 1860–1897* (White Plains, NY: M. E. Sharpe, 1945), 356–357.

28. Fred Shannon, "The Homestead Act and the Land Surplus," *American Historical Review* 41, no. 4 (1936): 637–638; Fred Shannon, "A Post Mortem on the Safety-Valve Theory," *Agricultural History* 19, no. 1 (January 1945): 34–36.

29. *Iron Molders' Journal*, September 10, 1877, 451.

30. *Report on the Proceedings of the Ninth Regular Session of the General Assembly, Knights of Labor*, Hamilton, Ontario, October 5–13, 1885, 13–14.

31. US Census Bureau, *Historical Statistics*, 93–95.

32. John Swinton, *Striking for Life: Labor's Side of the Labor Question: The Right of the Workingman to a Fair Living* (New York: Western W. Wilson, 1894), 53–54.

33. Sombart, *No Socialism*, 115, passim.

34. David Montgomery, *Beyond Equality: Labor and the Radical Republicans, 1862–1872* (Urbana: University of Illinois Press, 1981), 204–205.

35. Stephan Thernstrom, *The Other Bostonians: Poverty and Progress in the American Metropolis, 1880–1970* (Cambridge, MA: Harvard University Press, 1999), passim.

36. Chudacoff, *Mobile Americans,* 89–99.
37. Michael B. Katz, "Occupational Classification in History," *Journal of Interdisciplinary History* 3, no. 1 (Summer 1972): 63.
38. See, for example, testimony from congressional hearing cited in chapter 1. Also see Edwin Gabler, *The American Telegrapher: A Social History, 1860–1900* (New Brunswick, NJ: Rutgers University Press, 1988), passim, and Barbara Mayer Wertheimer, *We Were There: The Story of Working Women in America* (New York: Pantheon, 1977), 242–243.
39. John Bodnar, *Immigration and Industrialization: Ethnicity in an American Mill Town* (Pittsburgh: University of Pittsburgh Press, 1977), xv.
40. Howard P. Chudacoff, "Success and Security: The Meaning of Social Mobility in America," *Reviews in American History* 10, no. 4 (December 1982): 104–106.
41. Perlman, *A Theory of the Labor Movement* (New York: Augustus M. Kelley, 1949, originally 1928), 6–7.
42. Perlman, *Theory,* 146.
43. Ibid., 316.
44. Ibid., 155.
45. Ibid., 242.
46. Sean Wilentz, "Against Exceptionalism: Class Consciousness and the American Labor Movement, 1790–1920," *International Labor and Working-Class History* 26 (Fall 1984): 3.
47. Robert Justin Goldstein, "*Labor History* symposium: Political Repression of the American Labor Movement During Its Formative Years—a Comparative Perspective," *Labor History* 51, no. 2 (May 2010): 283.
48. Jerry M. Cooper, *The Army and Civil Disorder: Federal Military Intervention in Labor Disputes, 1877–1900* (Westport, CT: Greenwood, 1980), 13; David Montgomery, "Strikes in Nineteenth-Century America," *Social Science History* 4, no. 1 (Winter 1980): 92.
49. David Montgomery, *Citizen Worker: The Experience of Workers in the United States with Democracy and the Free Market During the Nineteenth Century* (Cambridge: Cambridge University Press, 1993), 89–104.
50. Jerry M. Cooper, "The Army and Industrial Workers: Strikebreaking in the Late 19th Century," in *Soldiers and Civilians: The US Army and the American People,* ed. Garry D. Ryan and Timothy K. Nenninger (Washington, DC: National Archives and Records Administration, 1987), 136.
51. A notable exception to this being the effective suppression of rural labor unrest by local authorities and unofficial white mobs in the Deep South. Eric Foner, *Reconstruction: America's Unfinished Revolution, 1863–1877* (New York: Harper & Row, 1988), 587–598.
52. See, for example, Melvyn Dubofsky, "The Federal Judiciary, Free Labor, and Equal Rights," in Richard Schneirov, Shelton Stromquist, and Nick Salvatore, *The Pullman Strike and the Crisis of the 1890s: Essays on Labor and Politics* (Urbana: University of Illinois Press, 1999), 159–178; Janet Currie and Joseph Ferrie, "The Law and Labor Strife in the United States, 1881–1894," *Journal of Economic History* 60, no. 1 (March

2000): 42–66; and Leon Fink, "Labor, Liberty, and the Law: Trade Unionism and the Problem of the American Constitutional Order," *Journal of American History* 74, no. 3 (December 1987): 904–925.

53. Edwin E. Witte, *The Government in Labor Disputes* (New York: McGraw-Hill, 1932), 84; William E. Forbath, *Law and the Shaping of the American Labor Movement* (Cambridge, MA: Harvard University Press, 1991), 193.

54. Paul Douglas, "An Analysis of Strike Statistics, 1881–1921," *Journal of the American Statistical Association* 18, no. 143 (September 1923): 868–870.

55. Currie and Ferrie, "The Law," 50–57; Witte, *The Government*, 111–125.

56. Leon Fink, "Labor, Liberty," 904–925; Forbath, *Law*, 128–173.

57. Nelson Lichtenstein, *State of the Union: A Century of American Labor* (Princeton, NJ: Princeton University Press, 2002), 106.

58. US Census Bureau, *Historical Statistics of the Union States: From Colonial Times to 1970*, pt. 2 (Washington, DC: US Government Printing Office, 1975), 1142; John Traynor, *Mastering German History* (New York: Palgrave Macmillan, 2008), 88.

59. Alfred D. Chandler, *The Visible Hand: The Managerial Revolution in American Business* (Cambridge, MA: Harvard University Press, 1977), 204–205.

60. Quoted in Matthew Josephson, *The Robber Barons: The Great American Capitalists, 1861–1901* (New York: Harcourt, Brace & World, 1934), 448.

61. John R. Commons et al., *History of Labour in the United States* (New York: Macmillan, 1936), 105–109.

62. Gerald Friedman, "Worker Militancy and Its Consequences: Political Responses to Labor Unrest in the United States, 1877–1914," *International Labor and Working Class History* 40 (Fall 1991): 8–9.

63. Leon Fink, *The Long Gilded Age: American Capitalism and the Lessons of a New World Order* (Philadelphia: University of Pennsylvania Press, 2015), 103–119.

64. Edwin Gabler, *The American Telegrapher: A Social History, 1860–1900* (New Brunswick, NJ: Rutgers University Press, 1988), 163–167.

65. US Commissioner of Labor, *Twenty-First Annual Report of the Commissioner of Labor, 1906* (Washington, DC: US Government Printing Office, 1907), 764–768.

66. Herbert Gutman, *Work, Culture and Society in Industrializing America* (New York: Vintage, 1977), 260–292.

67. Ileen A. DeVault, "'To Sit Among Men': Skill, Gender, and Craft Unionism in the Early American Federation of Labor," in *Labor Histories: Class, Politics, and the Working-Class Experience,* ed. Eric Arnesen , Julie Green, and Bruce Laurie (Urbana: University of Illinois Press, 1998), 259–283.

68. US Census Bureau, *Historical Statistics of the Union States: From Colonial Times to 1970*, pt. 1 (Washington, DC: US Government Printing Office, 1975), 132–140.

69. United States Industrial Commission, *Reports of the Industrial Commission on Labor Organizations, Labor Disputes, and Arbitration,* vol. 17 (Washington, DC: US Government Printing Office, 1901), 95.

70. Barbara Mayer Wertheimer, *We Were There: The Story of Working Women in America* (New York: Pantheon, 1977), 180–191.

71. Mabel Hurd Willett, "Women in the Clothing Trade," in *Trade Unionism and Labor*

Problems, ed. John R. Commons (New York: Augustus M. Kelley, 1967, originally 1905), 371–395.

72. Wertheimer, *We Were There,* 205; *Report of the Proceedings of the Thirteenth Annual Convention of the American Federation of Labor,* Chicago, December 11–19, 1893, 6–8.

73. Mary Davis, *Comrade or Brother? A History of the British Labour Movement,* 2nd ed. (London: Pluto, 2009), 102, 121–122.

74. Claude Fohlen, "The Industrial Revolution in France, 1700–1914," in Carlo M. Cipolla, *The Fontana Economic History of Europe: The Emergence of Industrial Societies,* vol. 1 (London: Collins/Fontana, 1973), 25; Knut Borchardt, "The Industrial Revolution in Germany, 1700–1914," in Cipolla, *Economic History,* 123–124.

75. US Census Bureau, *Historical Statistics of the United States: Colonial Times to 1970,* pt. 1 (Washington, DC: US Government Printing Office, 1975), 23; Robert Winder, *Bloody Foreigners: The Story of Immigration to Britain* (London: Abacus, 2004), 195–196.

76. Roediger and Esch, *The Production of Difference,* 16, 139–169; Sanford M. Jacoby, *Employing Bureaucracy: Managers, Unions, and the Transformation of Work in the 20th Century* (New York: Psychology Press, 2004), 13–16.

77. David R. Roediger, *How Race Survived US History: From Settlement and Slavery to the Obama Phenomenon* (London: Verso, 2010), 119–120, 99–135; Roediger and Esch, *Difference,* 153.

78. Sterling D. Spero and Abram L. Harris, *The Black Worker: The Negro and the Labor Movement* (New York: Atheneum, 1969, originally 1931), 87–115.

79. W. E. Burghardt Du Bois, ed., *The Negro Artisan: A Social Study* (Atlanta: Atlanta University Press, 1902), 167, 176; Philip Foner, *Organized Labor and the Black Worker, 1619–1973* (New York: International Publishers, 1976), 74.

80. C. Vann Woodward, *Origins of the New South, 1877–1913* (Baton Rouge: Louisiana State University Press, 1971), 139, 311.

81. Woodward, *Origins,* 312–320.

82. Wright, *Old South,* 7–50.

83. John Wiener, "Class Structure and Economic Development in the American South, 1865–1955," *American Historical Review* 84, no. 4 (October 1979): 979.

84. Wright, *Old South,* 97–98.

85. Robert H. Zieger, *For Jobs and Freedom: Race and Labor in America Since 1865* (Lexington: University of Kentucky Press, 2007), 34–35.

86. Wiener, "Class Structure," 984.

87. Robert L. Brandon, "The End of Immigrants to the Cotton Fields," *Mississippi Valley Historical Review* 50, no. 4 (March 1964): 591–611.

88. US Census Bureau, *Historical Statistics,* pt. 1, 22.

89. US Bureau of the Census, *Twelfth Census,* 103–105.

90. Forbath, *Law,* 193; Currie and Ferrie, "The Law," 50–57; Witte, *The Government,* 111–125.

91. Cooper, *The Army,* 13; Jerry M. Cooper, "The Army and Industrial Workers," 136; David Montgomery, "Strikes," 92; Montgomery, *Citizen Worker,* 89–104.

92. Sombart, *No Socialism,* 29–32; Martin Shefter, *Political Parties and the State: The American Historical Experience* (Princeton, NJ: Princeton University Press, 1994), 101–168; Ira Katznelson, *City Trenches: Urban Politics and the Patterning of Class in the United States* (Chicago: University of Chicago Press, 1981), passim.

93. Steven P. Erie, *Rainbow's End: Irish-Americans and the Dilemma of Urban Machine Politics, 1840–1985* (Berkeley: University of California Press, 1988), 1–106.

94. M. Craig Brown and Charles N. Halaby, "Machine Politics in America, 1870–1945," *Journal of Interdisciplinary History* 17, no. 3 (Winter 1987): 595.

95. E. G. Ravenstein, "The Laws of Migration," *Journal of the Statistical Society of London* 48, no. 2 (June 1885): 167–235; E. G. Ravenstein, "The Laws of Migration," *Journal of the Royal Statistical Society* 52, no. 2 (June 1889): 241–305; Guido Dorigo and Waldo Tobler, "Push-Pull Migration Laws," *Annals of the Association of American Geographers* 73, no. 1 (March 1983): 1–17; Everett S. Lee, "A Theory of Migration," *Demography* 3, no. 1 (1966): 47–57.

96. US Census Bureau, *Historical Statistics of the United States: Colonial Times to 1970* (Washington, DC: US Government Printing Office, 1975), 105–106; Simon Kuznets and Ernest Rubin, *Immigration and the Foreign Born* (New York: National Bureau of Economic Research, 1954), 47.

97. See, for example, Olivier Zunz, *The Changing Face of Inequality: Urbanization, Industrial Development, and Immigrants in Detroit, 1880–1920* (Chicago: University of Chicago Press, 1982), passim.

98. Oscar Handlin, *The Uprooted: The Epic Story of the Great Migrations That Made the American People* (Boston: Little, Brown, 1951), 170.

99. See David Montgomery, "Labor in the Industrial Era," in Richard B. Morris ed., *A History of the American Worker* (Princeton, NJ: Princeton University Press, 1983), 87, 101, and David Brundage, *The Making of Western Labor Radicalism: Denver's Organized Workers, 1878–1905* (Urbana: University of Illinois Press, 1994), 38–39.

100. Illinois Bureau of Labor Statistics, *Fourth Biennial Report of the Bureau of Labor Statistics of Illinois, 1886* (Springfield: H. W. Rocker, 1886), 226–227; US Census Bureau, *Historical Statistics,* 23.

101. Karl Marx, *Capital, vol. 1* (London: Penguin, 1990), 271–275, 301, 450, 874.

102. Roediger and Esch, *Difference,* 140.

103. E. P. Thompson, *The Making of the English Working Class* (New York: Vintage, 1966), 9, 728–729.

104. Stephan Thernstrom, "Reflections on the New Urban History," *Daedalus* 100, no. 2 (Spring 1971): 362.

105. See, for example, such pioneering works as David Roediger, *The Wages of Whiteness: Race and the Making of the American Working Class,* rev. ed. (London: Verso, 1999); Noel Ignatiev, *How the Irish Became White* (New York: Routledge, 1995); Jacqueline Jones, *American Work: Four Centuries of Black and White Labor* (New York: W. W. Norton, 1998); and Robin G. D. Kelley, *Hammer and Hoe: Alabama Communists During the Great Depression* (Chapel Hill: University of North Carolina Press, 1990).

106. E. G. Ravenstein, "The Laws of Migration," (June 1885): 167–235; E. G. Ravenstein, "The Laws of Migration," (June 1889): 241–305; Everett Lee, "A Theory of

Migration," *Demography* 3, no. 1 (1966): 47–57; Guido Dorigo and Waldo Tobler, "Push-Pull Migration Laws," *Annals of the Association of American Geographers* 73, no. 1 (March 1983): 1–17; J. Trent Alexander and Annemarie Steidl, "Gender and the 'Laws of Migration,'" *Social Science History* 36, no. 2 (Summer 2012):223–241.

107. E. P. Thompson, *The Poverty of Theory and Other Essays* (New York: Monthly Review Press, 1978), 40.

Chapter 2

1. Michelle Perrot, "On the Formation of the French Working Class," in *Working-Class Formation: Nineteenth Century Patterns in Western Europe and the United States,* ed. Ira Katznelson and Aristide R. Zolberg (Princeton, NJ: Princeton University Press, 1986), 71.

2. *Fifth Biennial Report of the Bureau of Labor Statistics of the State of California for the Years 1891–1892* (Sacramento: A. J. Johnson, Supt. State Printing, 1893), 29.

3. *Report of the Sixth Annual Session of the Federation of Organized Trades and Labor Union of the United States and Canada, Also the Proceedings of the First Annual Convention of the American Federation of Labor,* published by direction of both organizations (Columbus: December 8–12, 1886), 3.

4. Despite its familiarity, the "in itself" formulation is not Marx's. Rather, in *The Poverty of Philosophy,* he writes, "thus, this mass is already a class, as opposed to capital, but not yet for itself." Karl Marx, *The Poverty of Philosophy* (Amherst, NY: Prometheus, 1995), 189. See also Keith Graham, *Karl Marx Our Contemporary: Social Theory for a Post-Leninist World* (Toronto: University of Toronto Press, 1992), 62.

5. E. P. Thompson, *The Making of the English Working Class* (New York: Vintage, 1966), 10.

6. Thompson, *The Making,* 9. The equation of "men" with the class is an unfortunate remnant of pre-feminist thinking.

7. E. P. Thompson, *The Poverty of Theory and Other Essays* (New York: Monthly Review Press, 1978), 98.

8. Richard Schneirov, "Thoughts on Periodizing the Gilded Age: Capital Accumulation, Society, and Politics, 1873–1898," *Journal of the Gilded Age and Progressive Era* 5, no. 3 (July 2006): 196.

9. Antonio Gramsci, *Selections form the Prison Notebooks*, (New York: International Publishers, 1971), 196–197. See also Sarah Lyons Watts, *Order Against Chaos: Business Culture and Labor Ideology in America, 1880–1915* (New York: Greenwood, 1991), 25–27.

10. Gramsci, *Notebooks,* 12.

11. Leon Fink, "The New Labor History and the Powers of Historical Pessimism: Consensus, Hegemony, and the Case of the Knights of Labor," *Journal of American History* 75, no. 1 (June 1988): 131.

12. Fink, "New Labor History," 128–131.

13. Bruce Laurie, *Artisans into Workers: Labor in Nineteenth-Century America* (Urbana:

University of Illinois Press, 1997), 113.

14. Sarah Lyons Watts, *Order Against Chaos: Business Culture and Labor Ideology in America, 1880–1915* (New York: Greenwood, 1991), 7.

15. Michael Kazin, *American Dreamers: How the Left Changed a Nation* (New York: Alfred A. Knopf, 2011), 91.

16. Reprinted in *Labor Enquirer*, March 17, 1883, 7.

17. United States Senate, *Report of the Committee of the Senate upon the Relations Between Labor and Capital*, vol. 1 (Washington, DC: US Government Printing Office, 1885), 4.

18. *Journal of United Labor*, August 1883, 539.

19. Robert E. Weir, *Beyond Labor's Veil: The Culture of the Knights of Labor* (University Park, PA: Pennsylvania State University Press, 1996), 114; *Journal of United Labor*, October 1, 1887, 2497.

20. Rosanne Currarino, *The Labor Question in America: Economic Democracy in the Gilded Age* (Urbana: University of Illinois Press, 2011), 2, 39–40.

21. Daniel T. Rodgers, *The Work Ethic in Industrial America, 1850–1920* (Chicago: University of Chicago Press, 1978), 37.

22. David A. Wells, "How Shall the Nation Regain Prosperity," *North American Review* 125, no. 257: 128–130.

23. Steven J. Ross, *Workers on the Edge: Work, Leisure, and Politics in Industrializing Cincinnati, 1788–1890* (New York: Columbia University Press, 1985), 220.

24. Quoted in Rodgers, *Work Ethic*, 36.

25. Currarino, *Labor Question*, 19–20.

26. United States Senate, *Report of the Committee of the Senate upon the Relations Between Labor and Capital*, vol. 2 (Washington, DC: US Government Printing Office, 1885), 552.

27. United States Senate, *Report*, vol. 1, 255.

28. United States Senate, *Report*, vol. 2, 21.

29. David Montgomery, *The Fall of the House of Labor: The Workplace, the State, and American Labor Activism, 1865–1925* (Cambridge: Cambridge University Press, 1989), 2.

30. George E. McNeill, ed., *The Labor Movement: The Problem of Today* (Boston: A. M. Bridgman, 1887), 464–465.

31. United States Senate, *Report*, vol. 2, 391.

32. United States Senate, *Report*, vol. 1, 743.

33. Ibid., 217, 416.

34. Ibid., 49.

35. Ibid., 84, 217, 416.

36. Ibid., 8.

37. Ibid., 576.

38. Ibid., 135–137.

39. Ibid., 1123.

40. *Iron Molders' Journal*, July 1, 1878, 209.

41. *Iron Molders' Journal*, month ending November 30, 1884, 2.

42. *Iron Molders' Journal*, month ending October 31, 1886, 1.

43. *Journal of United Labor*, April 25, 1885, 970.

44. *Record of the Proceedings of the Sixth Regular Session of the General Assembly* (New York: September 5–12, 1882), 289–290.

45. *Journal of United Labor*, September 25, 1886, 2173.

46. *Progressive Age*, April 30, 1881, 5.

47. *Labor Enquirer*, March 17, 1883, 7.

48. *Labor Leaf*, February 4, 1885, 1; November 11, 1885, 1.

49. *Labor Leaf*, November 8, 1884, 4.

50. *Patterson Labor Standard*, May 27, 1882, 4; *Report of the Sixth Annual Session of the Federation of Organized Trades and Labor Unions, Also the Proceedings of the First Annual Convention of the American Federation of Labor*, 3, 17.

51. Terence V. Powderly, *The Autobiography of Terence V. Powderly* (New York: Columbia University Press, 1940), 425.

52. Thompson, *The Making*, 423.

53. Montgomery, *The Fall*, 2.

54. Thompson, *The Making*, 727.

55. David Montgomery, *Citizen Worker: The Experience of Workers in the United States with Democracy and the Free Market During the Nineteenth Century* (Cambridge: Cambridge University Press, 1993), 249–260.

56. Currarino, *The Labor Question*, 73–79.

57. J. F. Finn, "AF of L Leaders and the Question of Politics in the Early 1890s," *Journal of American Studies* 7, no. 3 (December 1973): 245.

58. Montgomery, *Citizen Worker*, 104–114.

59. Francis G. Couvares, "The Triumph of Commerce: Class Culture and Mass Culture in Pittsburgh," in *Working Class America: Essays in Labor, Community, and American Society*, ed. Michael H. Frisch and Daniel J. Walkowitz (Urbana: University of Illinois Press, 1983), 123–152.

60. For more detail, see Watts, *Order*, 1–36, for a hegemonist account; Ross, *Workers*, 73–79 on workers' "law and order"; Rodgers, *Work Ethic*, passim, for a wide-ranging discussion of contending views on work; and Weir, *Labor's Veil*, 67–80, and Gutman, *Work, Culture*, 79–117, on religion and morality.

61. Richard Oestreicher, *Solidarity and Fragmentation: Working People and Class Consciousness in Detroit, 1875–1900* (Urbana: University of Illinois Press, 1986), 132.

62. Ibid., 129.

63. Ibid., 130.

64. Ibid., 131–132, passim.

65. Ibid., 65.

66. Ibid., 62.

67. Joseph R. Buchanan, *The Story of a Labor Agitator* (New York: Outlook, 1903), passim.

68. David Brundage, *The Making of Western Labor Radicalism: Denver's Organized Workers, 1878–1905* (Urbana: University of Illinois Press, 1994), 37–39.

69. Richard Schneirov, *Labor and Urban Politics: Class Conflict and the Origins of*

Modern Liberalism in Chicago, 1864–97 (Urbana: University of Illinois Press, 1998), 150, 183.

70. Peter Rachleff, *Black Labor in Richmond, 1865–1890* (Urbana: University of Illinois Press, 1989), 109–191.
71. Laurie, *Artisans*, 142.
72. Oestreicher, *Solidarity*, 108–109.
73. David R. Roediger and Philip S. Foner, *Our Own Time: A History of American Labor and the Working Day* (London: Verso, 1989), 81–82.
74. John R. Commons and John B. Andrews, eds., *A Documentary History of American Industrial Society,* vol. 9 (Cleveland: Arthur H. Clark, 1910), 24–25, 30–32, 292.
75. David Montgomery, *Beyond Equality: Labor and the Radical Republicans, 1862–1872* (Urbana: University of Illinois Press, 1981), 249.
76. Thompson, *The Making,* 711–832; United States Industrial Commission, *Report of the Industrial Commission on the Relations and Conditions of Capital and Labor,* vol. 7 (Washington, DC: US Government Printing Office, 1901), 624; Montgomery, *Beyond Equality,* 249–260.
77. United States Senate, *Report,* vol. 1, 88.
78. Roediger and Foner, *Our Own Time,* 138–140.
79. Laurie, *Artisans,* 187; Roediger and Foner, *Our Own Time,* 159–160.
80. United States Industrial Commission, *Report of the Industrial Commission on the Relations of Capital and Labor Employed in the Mining Industry,* vol. 12 (Washington, DC: US Government Printing Office, 1901), 30–58.
81. Roediger and Foner, *Our Own Time,* 160–161.
82. United States Industrial Commission, *Report,* vol. 7, 745.
83. Ibid., 623.
84. United States Industrial Commission, *Reports of the Industrial Commission on Labor Organizations, Labor Disputes, and Arbitration, and on Railway Labor,* vol. 17 (Washington, DC: US Government Printing Office, 1901), xlvi.
85. Thompson, *The Making,* 726–729, 762–779.
86. Benedict Anderson, *Imagined Communities: Reflections on the Origin and Spread of Nationalism,* rev. ed. (London: Vero, 2006), 61–65.
87. John Flagg, Matthew Pethers and Robin Vandome, "Introduction: Networks and the Nineteenth- Century Periodical," *American Periodicals: A Journal of History, Criticism, and Bibliography* 23, no. 2 (2013): 93–104.
88. National Center for Education Statistics, *120 Years of Literacy* (NCES, 1992), http://nces.ed.gov/naal/lit_history.asp.
89. *Progressive Age,* November 12, 1881, 2.
90. John R. Commons et al., *History of Labour in the United States,* vol. 2 (New York: Macmillan, 1936), 15.
91. Richard J. Hinton, "American Labor Organizations," *North American Review* 140, no. 338 (January 1885): 61.
92. *Iron Molders' Journal,* December 31, 1885, 11.
93. *Standard,* January 8, 1887, 8.
94. For example, *Journal of United Labor,* May 7, 1887, 2384.

95. *Patterson Labor Standard,* December 15, 1888, 2.

96. Eleanor Marx and Edward Aveling, *The Working-Class Movement in America* (Amherst, NY: Humanity Books, 2000, 70–72.

97. *Chicago Boycotter,* February 1886, 2.

98. Richard T. Ely, The Labor Movement in America (New York: Thomas Y. Crowell, 1886), 115.

99. *Haverhill Laborer,* February 28, 1885, 3.

100. *Laborer,* October 16, 1886, 1.

101. *Chicago Boycotter,* February 1886, 2; *Boycotter,* April 26, 1884, 2.

102. Richard Schneirov, *Labor and Urban Politics: Class Conflict and the Origins of Modern Liberalism in Chicago, 1864–97* (Urbana: University of Illinois Press,1998), 150; Richard Jules Oestreicher, *Solidarity and Fragmentation: Working People and Class Consciousness in Detroit, 1875–1900* (Urbana: University of Illinois Press, 1986), 130.

103. *Laborer,* November 14, 1885, 3.

104. Buchanan, *Labor Agitator,* 52.

105. Robin Vandome, "The Advancement of *Science*: James McKeen Cattell and the Networks of Prestige and Authority, 1895–1915," *American Periodicals* 23, no. 2 (2013): 172n184.

106. Commons and Andrews, *A Documentary History,* 23.

107. *John Swinton's Paper,* August 21, 1887, 1, 3.

108. *Patterson Labor Standard,* December 15, 1888, 2.

109. *Labor Leader,* September 9, 1893, 1.

110. *Pueblo Courier,* September 9, 1898, 2.

111. Herbert G. Gutman, *Work, Culture and Society In Industrializing America* (New York: Vintage, 1977), 253; Rand School of Social Science, *American Labor Press Directory* (New York: Rand School of Social Science, 1925), 56.

112. *American Federationist,* February 1895, 271–272.

113. *Report of the Proceedings of the Twenty-Seventh Annual Convention of the American Federation of Labor,* Norfolk, VA, November 11–23, 1907, 48.

114. For example see, Laurie, *Artisans,* 176–210, and Roediger and Foner, *Our Own Time,* 145.

115. Oestreicher, *Solidarity,* 214, 249; Chicago Trades and Labor Assembly, *Minutes,* September 2, 1888, 222–223; October 6, 1888, 237–238; Frank T. Reuter, "John Swinton's Paper," *Labor History* 1, no. 3 (1960): 306–307.

116. Richard Schneirov, Shelton Stromquist, and Nick Salvatore, *The Pullman Strike and the Crisis of the 1890s: Essays on Labor and Politics* (Urbana: University of Illinois Press,1999), 1–19.

117. Melvyn Dubofsky, *Hard Work: The Making of Labor History* (Urbana: University of Illinois Press, 2000), 46–47; Commons et al., *History of Labour,* 486–487; John Laslett, *Labor and the Left: A Study of Socialist and Radical Influences in the American Labor Movement, 1881–1924* (New York: Basic Books, 1970), 10–13.

118. Laurie, *Artisans,* 191–192.

119. Gregory Zieren, "The Labor Boycott and Class consciousness in Toledo, Ohio" in *Life and Labor: Dimensions of American Working Class History,* Charles Stephenson

and Robert Asher, eds. (Albany, NY: State University of New York Press, 1986), 131–146.

120. Ibid., 132, 144–146.

121. Laurie, *Artisans,* 201–203.

122. Susan E. Hirsch, "The Search for Unity Among Railroad Workers: The Pullman Strike in Perspective," in *The Pullman Strike and the Crisis of the 1890s,* ed. Richard Schneirov, Shelton Stromquist, and Nick Salvatore (Urbana: University of Illinois Press, 1999), 48–49.

123. David Montgomery, "Strikes in Nineteenth-Century America," *Social Science History* 4, no. 1 (Winter 1980), 92.

124. Montgomery, "Strikes," 92; Schneirov, Stromquist, and Salvtore, *Pullman Strike,* 187–189, 236.

125. Laurie, *Artisans,* 187. Also see John Laslett, *Labor and the Left,* passim.

126. Melvyn Dubofsky, *The State and Labor in Modern America* (Chapel Hill: University of North Carolina Press, 1994), 49.

127. Ira Kipnis, *The American Socialist Movement, 1897–1912* (Chicago: Haymarket, 2004, originally 1952), 123, 247.

128. W. E. Burghardt DuBois, ed., *The Negro Artisan: A Social Study* (Atlanta: Atlanta University Press, 1902), 167, 176.

129. Bruce C. Nelson, *Beyond the Martyrs: A Social History of Chicago's Anarchists, 1870–1900* (New Brunswick, NJ: Rutgers University Press, 1988), 233–234.

130. Leon Fink, The *Long Gilded Age: American Capitalism and the Lessons of a New World Order* (Philadelphia: University of Pennsylvania Press, 2015), 125–127.

131. Kipnis, *American Socialist Movement,* 272–276.

132. Montgomery, *The Fall,* 1–3; Watts, *Order,* 24; Paul Le Blanc, "Radical Labor Subculture: Key to Past and Future Insurgencies," *WorkingUSA: The Journal of Labor and Society* 13 (September 2010): 367–385.

133. United States Industrial Commission, *Report of the Industrial Commission on the Relations and Conditions of Capital and Labor,* vol. 7 (Washington, DC: US Government Printing Office, 1901), 442.

134. Ibid., 755.

135. Ibid., 374.

136. Jeffrey Haydu, *Between Craft and Class: Skilled Workers and Factory Politics in the United States and Britain, 1890–1922* (Berkeley: University of California Press, 1988), 85.

137. Commons et al., *History of Labour,* 535.

138. Melvyn Dubofsky, "The Federal Judiciary, Free Labor, and Equal Rights," in Schneirov, Stromquist, and Salvatore, *Pullman Strike,* 168.

139. Roediger and Foner, *Our Own Time,* 146–147; Jim Cullen, *The Art of Democracy: A Concise History of Popular Culture in the United States* (New York: Monthly Review Press, 1996), 111–134; Francis G. Couvares, "The Triumph of Commerce: Class Culture and Mass Culture in Pittsburgh," in *Working Class America: Essays on Labor, Community, and American Society,* ed. Michael H. Frisch and Daniel Walkowitz (Urbana: University of Illinois Press, 1983), 142–147; Eric Hobsbawm,

Worlds of Labour: Further Studies in the History of Labour (London: Weidenfeld and Nicolson,1984), 185–186.

140. Thompson, *The Making*, 194, 807.

141. R. Hal Williams, *Realigning America: McKinley, Bryan, and the Remarkable Election of 1896* (Lawrence: University Press of Kansas, 2010), 8–9; Josephson, *Politicos*, 349–365.

142. Schneirov, Stromquist, and Salvatore, *Pullman Strike*, 4–6.

143. Ibid., 197.

144. Friedman, "New Estimates," 83; Montgomery, "Strikes," 92.

145. E. G. Ravenstein, "The Laws of Migration," *Journal of the Royal Statistical Society* 52, no. 2 (June 1889): 280.

146. Ibid., 278, 280.

147. E. G. Ravenstein, "The Laws of Migration," *Journal of the Statistical Society of London* 48, no. 2 (June 1885): 181.

148. Alexander J. Trent and Annemarie Steidl, "Gender and the 'Laws of Migration,'" *Social Science History* 36, no. 2 (Summer 2012): 223–241.

149. John R. Commons et al., *History of Labour in the United States*, vol. 1 (New York: Macmillan, 1936), 3.

150. Ibid., 21.

151. Selig Perlman, *A Theory of the Labor Movement* (New York: Augustus M. Kelley, 1949, originally 1928), 165.

152. Norman J. Ware, *The Labor Movement in the United States, 1860–1890: A Study in Democracy* (New York: Vintage, 1964); passim.

153. Selig Perlman and Philip Taft, *History of Labor in the United States, 1896–1932* (New York: Macmillan, 1935), 13; Philip Taft, *The A.F. of L. in the Time of Gompers* (New York: Harper & Brothers, 1957), passim.

154. Lloyd Ulman, *The Rise of the National Trade Union: The Development and Significance of Its Structure, Governing Institutions, and Economic Policies* (Cambridge, MA: Harvard University Press, 1955), 4, 19, passim.

155. David Montgomery, *The Fall of the House of Labor: The Workplace, the State, and American Labor Activism, 1865–1925* (Cambridge: Cambridge University Press, 1989), 48.

156. Melvyn Dubofsky and Warren Van Tine, *John L. Lewis: A Biography* (New York: New York Times Book Co., 1977), 11.

157. Herbert G. Gutman, *Work, Culture and Society in Industrializing America: Essays in Working-Class and Social History* (New York: Vintage, 1977), 29–30.

158. Mark Wyman, *Round-Trip to America: The Immigrants Return to Europe, 1880–1930* (Ithaca, NY: Cornell University Press, 1993), 3–14, 99–124.

159. Simon Kuznets and Ernest Rubin, *Immigration and the Foreign Born* (New York: National Bureau of Economic Research, 1954), 26. This figure is adjusted for "nonimmigrants," such a tourists or businesspeople who departed.

160. Wyman, *Round-Trip*, 11.

161. John Bodnar, *Immigration and Industrialization: Ethnicity in an American Mill Town, 1870–1940* (Pittsburgh: University of Pittsburgh Press, 1977), 28, 51–75, 88.

162. Maldwyn Allen Jones, *American Immigration* (Chicago: University of Chicago Press, 1960), 221-223.
163. Wyman, *Round-Trip,* 153–154. Wyman's chapter on the impact of returning immigrants presents a good deal of intriguing evidence about the impact those who had participated in the labor and socialist movements in the US had on the politics of their native lands.
164. Gutman, *Work,* 30–31; David Brody, *Steelworkers in America: The Non-Union Era* (Urbana: University of Illinois Press, 1998), passim.
165. Kuznets and Rubin, *Immigration,* 39; US Census Bureau, *Historical Statistics,* pt. 1, 93.
166. Bruce Laurie, *Artisans into Workers: Labor in Nineteenth-Century America* (Urbana: University of Illinois Press,1997), passim, 124.
167. Shelton Stromquist, *A Generation of Boomers: The Pattern of Railroad Labor Conflict in Nineteenth- Century America* (Urbana: University of Illinois Press, 1993), passim.
168. Stephan Thernstrom, *Poverty and Progress: Social Mobility in a Nineteenth Century City* (New York: Atheneum, 1974), 159.
169. See, for example, Steven Hahn and Joseph Prude, eds. *The Countryside in the Age of Capitalist Transformation* (Chapel Hill: University of North Carolina Press, 1985); Patricia Nelson Limerick, *The Legacy of Conquest: The Unbroken Past of the American West* (New York: W. W. Norton, 1987); Rodman W. Paul, *The Far West and the Great Plains in Transition, 1859–*1900 (Norman: University of Oklahoma Press, 1998); Marc Rodriguez, *Repositioning North American Migration History* (Rochester, NY: University of Rochester Press, 2004); and Mark Wyman, *Hoboes: Bindlestiffs, Fruit Tramps, and the Harvesting of the West* (New York: Hill and Wang, 2010).
170. Limerick, *Legacy of Conquest,* 117–124.
171. Mark Wyman, *Hard Rock Epic: Western Miners and the Industrial Revolution, 1860–1910* (Berkeley: University of California Press, 1979), 252–253.
172. Mark Wyman, *Hoboes,* 237–254.
173. Paul, *Far West,* 280.
174. Eric Hobsbawm, *The Age of Empire, 1875–1814* (New York: Vintage, 1989), 36.
175. US Census Bureau, *Historical Statistics of the United States: Colonial Times to 1970,* pt. 1 (Washington, DC: US Government Printing Office, 1975), 108. Between 1886 and 1893 no count of those entering from Mexico was made.
176. Kuznets and Rubin, *Immigration,* 39.
177. Ibid., 9, 39.
178. Eric Foner, *Reconstruction: America's Unfinished Revolution, 1863–1877* (New York: Harper & Row, 1988), 81–82.
179. Ronald L. Lewis, "From Peasant to Proletarian: The Migration of Southern Blacks to the Central Appalachian Coalfields," *Journal of Southern History* 55, no. 1 (February 1989): 77–102.
180. Gavin Wright, *Old South, New South: Revolutions in the Southern Economy Since the Civil War* (Baton Rouge: Louisiana State University Press, 1996), 64–66; US Census Bureau, *Historical Statistics of the United States: Colonial Times to 1970* (Washington, DC: US Government Printing Office, 1975), 95.

181. Fred A. Shannon, *The Farmer's Last Frontier: Agriculture, 1860–1897* (White Plains, NY: M. E. Sharpe, 1945), 307–309.
182. US Census Bureau, *Historical Statistics*, pt. 1, 93–95; Robert Higgs, *The Transformation of the American Economy, 1865–1914: An Essay in Interpretation* (New York: John Wiley & Sons, 1971), 23; Robert V. Hine and John Mack Faragher, *The American West: A New Interpretive History* (New Haven, CT: Yale University Press, 2000), 339–340.
183. US Census Bureau, *Historical Statistics*, pt. 1, 12.
184. Conrad Taeuber, "Rural-Urban Migration," *Agricultural History* 15, no. 3 (July 1941): 153–155.
185. Stromquist, *Boomers*, 5.
186. Edward Chase Kirkland, *Industry Comes of Age: Business, Labor and Public Policy, 1860–1897* (Chicago: Quadrangle, 1961), 237.
187. Stephan Thernstrom, *The Other Bostonians: Poverty and Progress in the American Metropolis, 1880–1970* (Cambridge, MA: Harvard University Press, 1973), 222.
188. Olivier Zunz, *The Changing Face of Inequality: Urbanization, Industrial Development, and Immigrants in Detroit, 1880–1920* (Chicago: University of Chicago Press, 1982), 185.
189. Robert Tank, "Mobility and Occupational Structure on the Late Nineteenth-Century Urban Frontier: The Case of Denver, Colorado," *Pacific Historical Review* 47, no. 2 (May 1978): 211.
190. Bodnar, *Immigration*, 56.
191. Stephan Thernstrom, *Poverty and Progress: Social Mobility in a Nineteenth Century City* (New York: Atheneum, 1974), 84–90. For a critique of this view and my answer to it, see the appendix.
192. Thernstrom, *Bostonians*, 221–223.
193. Stephan Thernstrom and Peter R. Knights, "Men in Motion: Some Data and Speculations About Urban Population Mobility in Nineteenth-Century America," *Journal of Interdisciplinary History* 1, no. 1 (Autumn 1970): 22.
194. Clarence H. Danhoff, "Farm-Making Costs and the 'Safety-Valve': 1850–1860," *Journal of Political Economy* 49, no. 3 (1941): 318.
195. Robert Higgs, *The Transformation*, 61–63.
196. Daniel T. Rodgers, *The Work Ethic in Industrial America, 1850–1920* (Chicago: University of Chicago Press, 1978), 163–170.
197. Sanford M. Jacoby and Sunil Sharma, "Employment Duration and Industrial Labor Mobility in the United States, 1880–1980," *Journal of Economic History* 52, no. 1 (March 1992): 161–177.
198. Brody, *Steelworkers*, 39–40; Rodgers, *Work Ethic,* 169.
199. Jeremy Atack, Fred Bateman, and Robert A. Margo, "Part-Year Operation in Nineteenth Century American Manufacturing: Evidence from the 1870 and 1880 Census," *Journal of Economic History* 62, no. 3 (September 2002): 793–800; Richard Schneirov, *Labor and Urban Politics: Class Conflict and the Origins of Modern Liberalism in Chicago, 1864–97* (Urbana: University of Illinois Press, 1998), 188.
200. John A. James and Mark Thomas, "A Golden Age? Unemployment and the American

Labor Market, 1880–1910," *Journal of Economic History* 63, no. 4 (December 2003):
960.

201. E. P. Thompson, *The Making of the English Working Class* (New York: Vintage,
1966), 248–249.

202. US Commissioner of Labor, *Fifth Annual Report of the Commissioner of Labor, 1889*
(Washington, DC: US Government Printing Office, 1890), 160–161.

203. John R. Commons, "Labor Conditions in Slaughtering and Meat Packing," in *Trade
Unionism and Labor Problems,* John R. Commons, ed. (New York: Augustus M.
Kelley Publishers, 1967, originally 1905), 30- 31.

204. *Labor Enquirer*, Denver, August 11, 1883, 2.

205. Sanford Jacoby, "Industrial Labor Mobility in Historical Perspective," *Industrial
Relations* 22, no. 2 (March 1983): 262–268.

206. United States Senate, *Report of the Committee of the Senate upon the Relations Between
Labor and Capital*, vol. 3 (Washington, DC: US Government Printing Office, 1885), 7.

207. Cited in Montgomery, *Fall*, 134.

208. Terence V. Powderly, *The Path I Trod: The Autobiography of Terence V. Powderly* (New
York: Columbia University Press, 1940), 280.

209. Quoted in Montgomery, *Fall*, 134.

210. Thompson, *The Making*, 260–261.

211. H. M. Gitelman, "Adolph Strasser and the Origins of Pure and Simple Unionism,"
in *The Labor History Reader,* ed. Daniel J. Leab (Urbana: University of Illinois Press,
1985), 153–165.

212. Allen Hutt, *British Trade Unionism: A Short History, 1800–1961* (London:
Lawrence and Wishart, 1962), 34–47; Henry Pelling, *A History of British Trade
Unionism* (Harmondsworth, UK: Penguin Books, 1963), 93–127.

213. See chapter 4 for a discussion of the causes of the Knights' decline.

214. Eric Hobsbawm, *Labouring Men: Studies in the History of Labour* (London:
Weidenfeld and Nicolson, 1964), 319.

215. Eric Hobsbawm, *The Age of Revolution, 1789–1848* (New York: Vintage, 1996),
28–29.

216. Charles P. Kindleberger, *World Economic Primacy, 1500–1990* (New York: Oxford
University Press, 1996), 137–141.

217. George G. S. Murphy and Arnold Zellner, "Sequential Growth, the Labor-Safety-
Valve Doctrine and the Development of American Unionism," *Journal of Economic
History* 19, no. 3 (September 1959): 411.

218. David Ward, *Cities and Immigrants* (New York: Oxford University Press, 1971), 57.

219. Adna Ferrin Weber, *The Growth of Cities in the Nineteenth Century: A Study in
Statistics* (Ithaca: Cornell University Press, 1965, originally 1899), 249–251.

220. Ravenstein, "The Laws of Migration" (June 1889): 280; Toni Pierenkemper and
Richard Tilly, *The German Economy During the Nineteenth Century* (New York:
Berghahn, 2004), 98–101.

221. Eric Hobsbawm, *Labouring Men: Studies in the History of Labour* (London:
Weidenfeld and Nicolson, 1964), 37, 41–43.

222. E. H. Hunt, *British Labour History, 1815–1914* (London: Weidenfeld and Nicolson,

1981), 150–152; Pelling, *A History*, 56–57.

223. E. G. Ravenstein, "The Laws of Migration" (June 1889): 288.

224. Dov Friedlander, "Occupational Structure, Wages, and Migration in Late Nineteenth Century England and Wales," *Economic Development and Cultural Change* 40, no. 2 (January 1992): 303; Jason Long, "Rural- Urban Migration and Socioeconomic Mobility in Victorian Britain," *Journal of Economic History* 65, no. 1 (March 2005): 2–3.

225. A. K. Cairncross, *Home and Foreign Investment, 1870–1913* (Cambridge: Cambridge University Press, 1953), 68–71.

226. G. R. Searle, *A New England: Peace and War, 1886–1918* (Oxford: Clarendon, 2004), 87; Conrad Taeuber, "Rural-Urban Migration," *Agricultural History* 5, no. 3 (July 1941): 154–155.

227. A. K. Cairncross, *Home and Foreign Investment, 1870–1913* (Cambridge: Cambridge University Press, 1953), 68–70.

228. George R. Boyer and Timothy J. Hatton, "Migration and Labour Market Integration in Late Nineteenth- Century England and Wales," *Economic History Review* 50, no. 4 (November 1997): 706–708.

229. Bureau of the Census, *Abstract of the Twelfth Census of the United States*, 3rd ed. (Washington, DC: US Government Printing Office, 1904), 100; Richard Schneirov, *Labor and Urban Politics: Class Conflict and the Origins of Modern Liberalism in Chicago, 1864–97* (Urbana: University of Illinois Press, 1998), 19; Asa Briggs, *A Social History of England* (London: Book Club Associates, 1983), 194.

230. Michael P. Conzen, "Local Migration Systems in Nineteenth Century Iowa," *Geographical Review* 64, no. 3 (July 1974): 346; Census Bureau, *Historical Statistics*, pt. 1, 93.

231. Joseph P. Ferrie, "The End of American Exceptionalism: Mobility in the United States Since 1850," *Journal of Economic Perspectives* 19, no. 3 (Summer 2005): 212.

232. E. G. Ravenstein, "The Laws of Migration" (June 1889): 286; Everett Lee, "A Theory of Migration," *Demography* 3, no. 1 (1966): 48.

233. David Ward, *Cities and Immigrants* (New York: Oxford University Press, 1971), 58.

234. Allan R. Pred, *The Spatial Dynamics of US Urban-Industrial Development: Interpretive and Theoretical Essays* (Cambridge, MA: MIT Press, 1966), 61–65.

235. Walter F. Willcox, "The Decrease of Interstate Migration," *Political Science Quarterly* 10, no. 4 (December 1895): 614.

236. John Charlton, *It Just Went Like Tinder: The Mass Movement and the New Unionism in Britain 1889* (London: Redwords, 1999), 89.

237. *Iron Molders' Journal*, March 10, 1877, 258–259.

238. Stromquist, *Boomers*, 127, 268–269.

239. Ravenstein, "The Laws of Migration" (June 1889): 288.

240. Friedlander, "Occupational Structure," 295–296.

241. Ravenstein, "The Laws of Migration" (June 1885): 198.

242. Stanley Lebergott, *Manpower in Economic Growth: The American Record Since 1800* (New York: McGraw-Hill, 1964), 40–45.

243. Samuel Rezneck, "Distress, Relief, and Discontent in the United States During the Depression of 1873–78," *Journal of Political Economy* 58, no. 6 (December 1950):

498–500.

244. *John Swinton's Paper,* January 20, 1884, 1.

245. Samuel Rezneck, "Unemployment, Unrest, and Relief in the United States During the Depression of 1893–97," *Journal of Political Economy* 61, no. 4 (August 1953): 328.

246. Rezneck, "Distress," 500.

247. Stromquist, *Boomers*, xiv–xv, 268–269.

248. For these figures, see tables 10 and 11 below.

249. Pred, *Spatial Dynamics*, 59–67.

250. Richard Schneirov, "Thoughts on Periodizing the Gilded Age: Capital Accumulation, Society, and Politics, 1873–1898," *Journal of the Gilded Age and Progressive Era* 5, no. 3 (July 2006): 196.

251. Henry Nash Smith, *Virgin Land: The American West as Symbol and Myth* (Cambridge, MA: Harvard University Press, 1970), 169, 201–210.

252. Anwar Shaikh, *Capitalism: Competition, Conflict, Crises* (New York: Oxford University Press, 2016), 56–59.

253. Thomas C. Cochran and William Miller, *The Age of Enterprise: A Social History of Industrial America* (New York: Harper & Row, 1961); Alfred D. Chandler Jr., *The Visible Hand: The Managerial Revolution in American Business* (Cambridge, MA: Harvard University Press, 1977); Alan Trachtenberg, *The Incorporation of America: Culture and Society in the Gilded Age* (New York: Hill and Wang, 1982).

254. Kirkland, *Industry*, 210, 214–215.

255. Robert L. Heilbroner and Aaron Singer, *The Economic Transformation of America: 1600 to the Present* (New York: Harcourt Brace Jovanovich, 1984), 182–183.

256. Schneirov, "Periodizing," 189–224.

257. Bureau of the Census, *A Compendium of the Ninth Census, 1870* (Washington, DC: US Government Printing Office, 1872), 796–797; Bureau of the Census, *Abstract of the Twelfth Census of the United States, 1900* (Washington, DC: US Government Printing Office, 1904), 331.

258. David Montgomery, *Beyond Equality: Labor and the Radical Republicans, 1862–1872* (Urbana: University of Illinois Press, 1981), 5–6; Stromquist, *Boomers*, 142–163.

259. Bureau of the Census, *Ninth Census, 1870*, 796–797; Bureau of the Census, *Twelfth Census,* 331.

260. Limerick, *Conquest*, 21.

261. Gavin Wright, "The Origins of American Industrial Success, 1879–1940," *American Economic Review* 80, no. 4 (1990): 661.

262. US Census Bureau, *Historical Statistics of the United States: Colonial Times to 1970,* pt. 1 (Washington, DC: US Government Printing Office, 1975) 602, 604.

263. Wyman, *Hard Rock*, 202.

264. Bureau of the Census, *Twelfth Census,* 331, 352–358.

265. Pred, *Spatial Dynamics,* 61.

266. Ibid., 59–67.

267. Susan Previant Lee and Peter Passell, *A New Economic View of American History* (New York: W. W. Norton, 1979), 268; Ulman, *The Rise*, 10.

268. Kirkland, *Industry*, 164.
269. US Commissioner of Labor, *The First Annual Report of the Commissioner of Labor* (Washington, DC: US Government Printing Office, March 1886), 84.
270. David Brody, *Steelworkers in America: The Nonunion Era* (Urbana: University of Illinois Press, 1998), 32.
271. United States Industrial Commission, *Reports to the Industrial Commission on the Relations and Conditions of Capital and Labor*, vol. 7 (Washington, DC: US Government Printing Office, 1901), 278.
272. United States Senate, *Report of the Committee of the Senate upon the Relations Between Labor and Capital*, vol. 1 (Washington, DC: US Government Printing Office, 1885), 642.
273. US Commissioner of Labor, *First Annual Report of the Commissioner of Labor: Industrial Depressions* (Washington, DC: US Government Printing Office, 1886), 65–66; US Census Bureau, *Historical Statistics*, pt. 1, 127, 135; Robert Higgs, *The Transformation of the American Economy, 1865–1914* (New York: John Wiley & Sons, 1971), 124.
274. US Census Bureau, *Historical Statistics of the United States: Colonial Times to 1970*, pt. 2 (Washington, DC: US Government Printing Office, 1975), 912–913. These figures do not include banks, insurance and real estate firms, railroads, farmers, or professionals.
275. Bureau of Statistics, *Statistical Abstract of the United States* (Washington, DC: US Government Printing Office, 1891, 1893, 1896, 1898, 1900).
276. Trachtenberg, *Incorporation*, 5, 8, 57.
277. Brody, *Steelworkers*, 5, 8.
278. See, for example, United States Senate, *Report of the Committee of the Senate upon the Relations Between Labor and Capital*, vol. 7 (Washington, DC: US Government Printing Office, 1901), 657–674; Mabel Hurd Willett, "Women in the Clothing Industry," in *Trade Unionism and Labor Problems*, John R. Commons, ed. (New York: Augustus M. Kelley, 1967, originally 1903), 371–395; and Jacqueline Jones, *American Work: Four Centuries of Black and White Labor* (New York: W. W. Norton, 1998), 301–336. Space prohibits a detailed discussion of the development of the South. For its distinct course of development, see C. Vann Woodward, *Origins of the New South, 1877–1913* (Baton Rouge: Louisiana State University, 1971) and Gavin Wright, *Old South / New South: Revolutions in the Southern Economy Since the Civil War* (Baton Rouge: Louisiana State University, 1986).
279. Robert V. Bruce, *1877: Year of Violence* (Chicago: Quadrangle, 1970), 20.

Chapter 3

1. E. G. Ravenstein, "The Laws of Migration," *Journal of the Statistical Society of London* 48, no. 2 (June 1885): 181.
2. *Alarm* was a Chicago anarchist paper edited by Albert Parsons.
3. Eric Hobsbawm, *Labouring Men: Studies in the History of Labour* (London:

Weidenfeld and Nicolson, 1964), 34–63.

4. Tim Cresswell, "Embodiment, Power and the Politics of Mobility: The Case of Female Tramps and Hobos," *Transaction of the Institute of British Geographers*, n.s., 24, no. 2 (1999): 180.

5. Ibid., 180–185.

6. Frank Tobias Higbie, *Indispensable Outcasts: Hobo Workers and Community in the American Midwest, 1880–1930* (Urbana: University of Illinois Press, 2003), 25.

7. Cresswell, "Female Tramps," 181; David Montgomery, "Wage Labor, Bondage, and Citizenship in Nineteenth-Century America," *International Labor and Working Class History* 48 (Fall 1995): 19.

8. Jim Cullen, *The Art of Democracy: A Concise History of Popular Culture in the United States* (New York: Monthly Review Press, 1996), 148–151.

9. Allan Pinkerton, *Strikers, Communists, Tramps and Detectives* (New York: G. W. Carleton, 1878), 29–30, 51–52, passim.

10. Josiah Flynt, *Tramping with Tramps: Studies and Sketches of Vagabond Life* (New York: Century Co., 1901), ix, passim.

11. Jack London, *The Road* (New York: Macmillan, 1907), passim.

12. O. F. Lewis, "The Tramp Problem," *Annals of the American Academy of Political and Social Science* 40 (March 1912): 217.

13. Clark C. Spence, "Knights of the Tie and Rail—Tramps and Hoboes in the West," *Western History Quarterly* 2, no. 1 (January 1971): 4–19.

14. See, for example, Frank Tobias Higbie, *Indispensable Outcasts: Hobo Workers and Community in the American Midwest, 1880–1930* (Urbana: University of Illinois Press, 2003); Marc S. Rodriguez, ed., *Repositioning North American Migration History: New Directions in Modern Continental Migration, Citizenship and Community* (Rochester, NY: University of Rochester Press, 2004); and Mark Wyman, *Hoboes, Bindlestiffs, Fruit Tramps and the Harvesting of the West* (New York: Hill and Wang, 2010).

15. Cited in Mark Wyman, *Hoboes*, 36–37.

16. United States Industrial Commission, *Report of the Industrial Commission on the Relations and Conditions of Capital and Labor*, vol. 7 (Washington, DC: US Government Printing Office, 1901), 206.

17. United States Senate, *Report of the Committee of the Senate upon the Relations Between Labor and Capital*, vol. 4 (Washington, DC: US Government Printing Office, 1885), 548.

18. Shelton Stromquist, *A Generation of Boomers: The Pattern of Railroad Labor Conflict in Nineteenth-Century America* (Urbana: University of Illinois Press, 1993), xiv–xv, 268–269.

19. Philip Foner, *History of the Labor Movement in the United States*, vol. 2 (New York: International Publishers, 1975), 29–30.

20. E. P. Thompson, *The Making of the English Working Class* (New York: Vintage, 1966), 191–194.

21. Alfred D. Chandler, *The Visible Hand: The Managerial Revolution in American Business* (Cambridge, MA: Harvard University Press, 1977), 79.

22. John R. Commons et al., *History of Labour in the United States* (New York: Macmillan, 1936), 191.

23. Michael A. Bellesiles, *1877: America's Year of Living Violently* (New York: New Press, 2010), 184–190.

24. Robert V. Bruce, *1877: Year of Violence* (Chicago: Quadrangle, 1970), 292–321; Edwin Gabler, *The American Telegrapher: A Social History, 1860–1900* (New Brunswick, NJ: Rutgers University Press, 1988), 163–168.

25. Frederick Jackson Turner, *The Frontier in American History* (New York: Barnes & Noble, 2009, originally 1920), passim.

26. Rev. Josiah Strong, DD, *Our Country: Its Possible Future and Its Present Crisis* (New York: Baker & Taylor, 1885), 157.

27. Stromquist, *Boomers*, 17.

28. Ibid., xiii.

29. United States Industrial Commission, *Reports of the Industrial Commission on Labor Organizations, Labor Disputes, and Arbitration*, vol. 17 (Washington, DC: US Government Printing Office, 1901), 723.

30. Stromquist, *Boomers,* 127–128.

31. Ibid., xiv, xiii, 16–19, passim.

32. US Commissioner of Labor, *Fifth Annual Report of the Commissioner of Labor, 1889* (Washington, DC: US Government Printing Office, 1890), 160–161.

33. Stromquist, *Boomers*, 120–121; Commissioner of Labor, *Fifth Annual Report*, 161.

34. Gerald Friedman, "US Historical Statistics: New Estimates of Union Membership in the United States, 1880–1914," *Historical Methods: A Journal of Quantitative and Interdisciplinary History* 32, no. 2 (1999): 83; Stromquist, *Boomers*, 13. 19.

35. Gabler, *American Telegrapher*, 39.

36. United States Senate, *Report of the Committee of the Senate upon the Relations Between Labor and Capital*, vol. 2 (Washington, DC: US Government Printing Office, 1885), 185–186; US Census Bureau, *Historical Statistics,* pt. 2, 787.

37. Gabler, *American Telegrapher*, 58.

38. United States Senate, *Report of the Committee of the Senate upon the Relations Between Labor and Capital*, vol. 1 (Washington, DC: US Government Printing Office, 1885), 151.

39. United States Senate, *Report*, vol. 1, 223–224.

40. Ibid., 224–225.

41. Gabler, *American Telegrapher,* 83.

42. United States Senate, *Report*, vol. 1, 149.

43. United States Senate, *Report*, vol. 1, 225–227; Gabler, *American Telegrapher*, 95.

44. Gabler, *American Telegrapher*, 74, 77.

45. This is to judge by the publishing dates of the *Railroad Telegrapher* 21 (January 1904): 1; *Commercial Telegraphers Journal* 16 (January 1918): 1; and United States Commission on Industrial Relations, *Final Report and Testimony Submitted to Congress by the US Commission on Industrial Relations* (Washington, DC: US Government Printing Office, 1916), 10069–10071.

46. Lloyd Ulman, *The Rise of the National Trade Union: The Development and*

Significance of Its Structure, Governing Institutions, and Economic Policies (Cambridge, MA: Harvard University Press, 1955), 65.

47. United States Senate, *Report*, vol. 1, 43.

48. George E. Barnett, "The Government of the Typographical Union," in *Studies in American Trade Unionism,* ed. Jacob H. Hollander and George E. Barnett (New York: Henry Holt, 1912), 29.

49. Jim Cullen, *The Art of Democracy: A Concise History of Popular Culture in the United States* (New York: Monthly Review Press, 1996), 115.

50. *Typographical Journal,* September 1, 1900, 205.

51. George E. Barnett, *The Printers: A Study in American Trade Unionism* (Cambridge, MA: American Economic Association, 1909), 212–215.

52. Allan R. Pred, *The Spatial Dynamics of US Urban-Industrial Growth, 1800–1914* (MIT Press, 1966), 61–65.

53. United States Industrial Commission, *Reports of the Industrial Commission on the Relations and Conditions of Capital and Labor Employed in Manufactures and General Business,* vol. 7 (Washington, DC: US Government Printing Office, 1901), 291.

54. *Detroit Unionist,* September 18, 1882, 1.

55. *Report of the Proceedings of the Thirty-Eighth Annual Session of the International Typographical Union,* Atlanta, June 1890 (Indianapolis: Carlon & Hollenback, 1890), 34.

56. *Typographical Journal,* August 15, 1900, 139.

57. Norman Ware, *The Labor Movement in the United States, 1860–1890* (New York: Vintage, 1964), 135–136.

58. David Montgomery, *The Fall of the House of Labor: The Workplace, the State, and American Labor Activism, 1865–1925* (Cambridge: Cambridge University Press, 1989), 185–191.

59. Terence V. Powderly, *The Path I Trod: The Autobiography of Terence V. Powderly* (New York: Columbia University Press, 1940), 28.

60. Powderly, *The Path I Trod*, 27.

61. Frank T. Stockton, *The International Molders' Union of North America* (Baltimore: Johns Hopkins University Press, 1921), 94.

62. *Iron Molders' Journal,* month ending August 31, 1880, 6.

63. *Iron Molders' Journal,* August 10, 1877, 429.

64. *Iron Molders' Journal,* month ending January 31, 1885, 3.

65. *Iron Molders' Journal,* November 10, 1877.

66. *Iron Molders' Journal,* February 10, 1977, 238.

67. Jeremy Atack, Fred Bateman, and Robert Margo, "Part-Year Operation in Nineteenth Century American Manufacturing: Evidence from the 1870 and 1880 Census," *Journal of Economic History* 62, no. 3 (September 2002): 807.

68. *Iron Molders' Journal,* January 1886, 3.

69. *Iron Molders' Journal* March 10, 1877, 260–261.

70. Ibid., 261.

71. Patricia A. Cooper, "The 'Travelling Fraternity': Union Cigar Makers and Geographic Mobility, 1900–1919," *Journal of Social History* 17, no. 1 (Autumn

    1983): 127.
72. United State Industrial Commission, *Report*, vol. 17, xxxix.
73. Ibid., 280–292.
74. *Cigar Makers' Official Journal*, June 1898, 9.
75. Cooper, "'Travelling Fraternity,'" 129.
76. For example, see *Cigar Makers' Official Journal*, January 1897, 18; July 1897, 14; and May 1898, 10.
77. United States Industrial Commission, *Report*, vol. 7, 257.
78. Ibid., 260.
79. United States Industrial Commission, *Report*, vol. 17, 280–281.
80. Edward Kirkland, *Industry Comes of Age: Business, Labor and Public Policy* (Chicago: Quadrangle, 1967) 46–51, 138–138, 158–159.
81. Department of the Interior, *Abstract of the Eleventh Census: 1890*, 2nd ed. (Washington, DC: US Government Printing Office, 1896), 170.
82. Frank Julian Warne, *The Coal-Mine Workers: A Study in Labor Organization* (New York: Longmans, Green, 1905), 196–200.
83. George McNeill, *The Labor Movement: The Problem of Today* (Boston: A. M. Bridgman, 1887), 241.
84. Ibid., 241–242.
85. Daniel T. Rodgers, *The Work Ethic in Industrial America, 1850–1920* (Chicago: University of Chicago Press, 1978), 163–170.
86. United States Industrial Commission, *Report of the Industrial Commission on the Relations and Conditions of Capital and Labor*, vol. 12, 30–58, 322–338.
87. E. A. Allen, *Labor and Capital: Containing an Account of the Various Organizations of Farmers, Planters, and Mechanics, for Mutual Improvement and Protection Against Monopoly* (Cincinnati: Central Publishing House, 1891) 226.
88. Allen, *Labor and Capital*, 229–230.
89. United States Industrial Commission, *Report*, vol. 12, 700.
90. United States Industrial Commission, *Report of the Industrial Commission on the Relations of Capital and Labor Employed in Manufacture and General Business*, vol. 14 (Washington, DC: US Government Printing Office, 1901) 415.
91. United States Industrial Commission, *Report*, vol. 12, 138–151.
92. United States Industrial Commission, *Report*, vol. 12, 138–151.
93. United States Senate, *Report of the Committee of the Senate upon the Relations of Labor and Capital*, vol. 1 (Washington, DC: US Government Printing Office, 1885), 1163.
94. *Pueblo Courier*, August 19, 1898, 4.
95. Cited in Paul, *The Far West*, 279.
96. Jim Foster, "The Ten Day Tramps," *Labor History* 23 (Fall 1982): 609.
97. William D. Haywood, *Bill Haywood's Book: The Autobiography of William D. Haywood* (New York: International Publishers, 1929), 65.
98. *Miners' Magazine*, January 1900, 1.
99. Haywood, *Bill Haywood's Book*, 90–94.
100. Mark Wyman, *Hard Rock Epic: Western Miners and the Industrial Revolution*,

1860–1910 (Berkeley: University of California Press, 1979), 43.

101. Graham Davis and Matthew Goulding, "Irish Hard-Rocker Miners in Ireland, Britain and the United States," in *In Search of a Better Life: British and Irish Migration,* Graham Davis ed. (Brimscombe Port Stroud, UK: History Press, 2011), 179–193.

102. Wyman, *Hard Rock,* 43, 153.

103. David Montgomery, *The Fall of the House of Labor: The Workplace, the State, and American Labor Activism, 1865–1925* (Cambridge: Cambridge University Press, 1987), 176.

104. Edward Chase Kirkland, *Industry Comes of Age: Business, Labor and Public Policy, 1860–1897* (Chicago: Quadrangle, 1961), 238; US Census Bureau, *Historical Statistics,* 627.

105. *Proceedings of the Eleventh General Convention of the United Brotherhood of Carpenters and Joiners of America, Scranton, Pennsylvania,* September 17–28, 1900, 48.

106. Jules Tygiel, "Tramping Artisans: The Case of the Carpenters in Industrial America," *Labor History* 22, no. 3 (Summer 1981): 350.

107. Quoted in Tygiel, "Tramping Artisans," 355.

108. Ibid., 365.

109. Cited in Ulman, *The Rise,* 52–53.

110. Friedman, "New Estimates," 83.

111. Frank Tobias Higbie, *Indispensable Outcasts: Hobo Workers and Community in the Midwest, 1880–1930* (Urbana: University of Illinois Press, 2003), 33.

112. Mark Wyman, *Hoboes, Bindlestiffs, Fruit Tramps and the Harvesting of the West* (New York: Hill and Wang, 2010), 30.

113. Higbie, *Outcasts,* 25.

114. Higbie, *Outcasts,* 2–3.

115. Gavin Wright, "The Origins of American Industrial Success, 1879–1940," *American Economic Review* 80, no. 4 (1990): 651–668.

116. Gunther Peck, "Mobilizing Community: Migrant Workers and the Politics of Labor Mobility in the North American West, 1900–1920," in *Labor Histories: Class, Politics, and the Working Class Experience,* ed. Eric Arnesen, Julie Green, and Bruce Laurie (Urbana: University of Illinois Press, 1998), 175.

117. Ibid., 25–33.

118. Marco d'Eramo, *The Pig and the Skyscraper, Chicago: A History of Our Future* (London: Verso, 2002), 36–38.

119. Marc S. Rodriguez, "Introduction: Reconsidering Modern Continental Migration, Community, and Citizenship," in *Repositioning North American Migration History: New Directions in Modern Continental Migration, Citizenship, and Community,* ed. Marc S. Rodriguez (Rochester: University of Rochester Press, 2004), xv.

120. Paul Douglas, "The Problem of Labor Turnover," *American Economic Review* 8, no. 2 (June 1918): 310.

121. United States Commission on Industrial Relations, *Final Report and Testimony Submitted to Congress by the Commission on Industrial Relations* (Washington, DC: US Government Printing Office, 1916), 4972–4974.

122. Melvyn Dubofsky, *We Shall Be All: A History of the Industrial Workers of the World,*

abr. ed. (Urbana: University of Illinois Press, 2000), 184–199, 256; Patrick Renshaw, *The Wobblies: The Story of Syndicalism in the United States* (Garden City, NY: Doubleday, 1967), 174–181.

123. US Census Bureau, *Historical Statistics*, pt. 1, 139.

124. David Montgomery, *The Fall of the House of Labor: The Workplace, the State, and American Labor Activism, 1865–1924* (New York: Cambridge University Press, 1989), 58–59.

125. Edith Abbott, "The Wages of Unskilled Labor in the United States, 1850–1900," *Journal of Political Economy* 13, no. 3 (June 1905): 322–323.

126. US Census Bureau, *Historical Statistics*, pt. 1, 165.

127. Richard Schneirov, *Labor and Urban Politics: Class Conflict and the Origins of Modern Liberalism in Chicago, 1864–97* (Urbana: University of Illinois Press, 1998), 23.

128. Schneirov, *Labor,* 100–101.

129. Montgomery, *The Fall,* 94.

130. Quoted in Abbott, "Unskilled Labor," 323.

131. Quoted in Harry Braverman, *Labor and Monopoly Capitalism: The Degradation of Work in the Twentieth Century* (New York: Monthly Review Press, 1974), 64.

132. Richard T. Ely, *The Labor Movement in America* (New York: Thomas Y. Crowell, 1886), 114–115.

133. Stromquist, *Boomers,* 123–124.

134. *Iron Molders' Journal,* month ending March 31, 1884, 13.

135. *Miners' Magazine* 1, no. 2 (February 1900): 1; *Iron Molders' Journal,* March 31, 1884, 13; Ulman, *The Rise,* 57.

136. *Typographical Journal,* August 1, 1900, 97.

137. *Journal of United Labor,* May 25, 1885, 992.

138. *Labor Leaf,* December 10, 1884, 1.

139. *Labor Leaf,* December 3, 1884, 1.

140. *National Labor Tribune,* January 5, 1884, 4.

141. *Labor Leaf,* December 10, 1884, 1.

142. *Labor Leaf,* December 24, 1884, 1.

143. *Labor Enquirer,* May 5, 1883, 4.

144. *Labor Enquirer,* July 7, 1883, 1.

145. *Patterson Labor Standard,* May 20, 1882, 1.

146. *Labor Leaf,* November 4, 1885, 1.

147. *Detroit Unionist,* October 16, 1882, 3.

148. *Labor Enquirer,* April 21, 1883, 4.

149. *Labor Enquirer,* May 5, 1883, 4.

150. *Detroit Unionist,* January 22, 1885, 4.

151. Joseph R. Buchanan, *The Story of a Labor Agitator* (New York: Outlook, 1903), 193–198.

152. *Detroit Unionist,* March 19, 1883, 3.

153. Ely, *Labor Movement,* 115.

154. Robert Louis Stevenson, *Across the Plains with Other Memories and Essays* (London: Chatto & Windus, 1892), 54–61.

Chapter 4

1. On the anti-Chinese issue, see Rob Weir, "Blind in One Eye Only: Western and Eastern Knights of Labor View the Chinese Question," *Labor History* 41, no. 4 (2000): 421–436.
2. Eleanor Marx and Edward Aveling, *The Working Class Movement in America* (Amherst, NY: Humanity Books, 2000), 143.
3. Marx and Aveling, *Working Class Movement*, 143.
4. For general accounts of the Knights' rise and fall, see Leon Fink, *Workingman's Democracy: The Knights of Labor and American Politics* (Urbana: University of Illinois Press, 1983); Kim Voss, *The Making of American Exceptionalism: The Knights of Labor and Class Formation in the Nineteenth Century* (Ithaca, NY: Cornell University Press, 1993); Norman Ware, *The Labor Movement in the United States, 1860–1890* (New York: Vintage, 1964); and Robert Weir, *Knights Unhorsed: Internal Conflict in a Gilded Age Social Movement* (Detroit: Wayne State University, 2000).
5. Richard Schneirov, *Labor and Urban Politics: Class Conflict and the Origins of Modern Liberalism in Chicago, 1864–97* (Urbana: University of Illinois Press, 1998), 307–343; Shelton Stromquist, *A Generation of Boomers: The Pattern of Railroad Labor Conflict in Nineteenth-Century America* (Urbana: University of Illinois Press, 1993), 229–266.
6. Eric Hobsbawm, *Labouring Men: Studies in the History of Labour* (London: Weidenfeld and Nicolson, 1964), 139.
7. Montgomery, "Strikes in Nineteenth-Century America," *Social Science History* 4, no. 1 (Winter 1980): 92; John R. Commons et al., *History of Labour in the United States,* vol. 2 (New York: Macmillan, 1936), 373–374; James Green, *Death in the Haymarket: A Story of Chicago, the First Labor Movement and the Bombing that Divided Gilded Age America* (New York: Anchor, 2006), 150; Ware, *Labor Movement*, 139–145. While it is often said the May 1 date was set by the AFL, the AFL was not actually formed until December 1886.
8. Green, *Haymarket*, 154.
9. Ware, *Labor Movement*, 135–136; Commons et al., *History of Labour,* 366–368.
10. Ware, *Labor Movement*, 66.
11. Gerald Friedman, "US Historical Statistics: New Estimates of Union Membership in the United States, 1880–1914," *Historical Methods: A Journal of Quantitative and Interdisciplinary History* 32, no. 2 (1999): 78; David Montgomery, "Strikes," 92; Ware, *Labor Movement*, 66.
12. Janet Currie and Joseph Ferrie, "The Law and Labor Strife in the United States, 1881–1894," *Journal of Economic History* 60, no. 1 (March 2000): 48, 50. Also see Christopher L. Tomlins, *The State and the Unions: Labor Relations, Law, and the Organized Labor Movement in America, 1880–1960* (Cambridge: Cambridge University Press, 1985), 61; Edwin E. Witte, *The Government in Labor Disputes* (New York: McGraw-Hill, 1932), 84.
13. Commons et al., *History of Labour,* 482–489.
14. Ware, *Labor Movement*, 69, 373.

15. Robert Weir, *Knights Unhorsed: Internal Conflict in a Gilded Age Social Movement* (Detroit: Wayne State University Press, 2000), 19–20.

16. Voss, *Exceptionalism*, 189.

17. Gene Rona Marlatt, *Jospeh R. Buchanan: Spokesman for Labor During the Populist and Progressive Eras* (unpublished PhD thesis, Boulder: University of Colorado, 1975), 259–266; Weir, *Knights Unhorsed*, 63.

18. Richard Oestreicher, "A Note on Knights of Labor Membership Statistics," *Labor History* 25, no. 1 (Winter 1984): 102–108.

19. *Record of the Proceedings of the General Assembly of the Knights of Labor of America,* vol. 4, Richmond, VA, October 4–20, 1886, 8–12; *Proceedings of the General Assembly of the Knights of Labor, Eleventh Regular Session,* Minneapolis, October 4–19, 1887, 1477–1540.

20. Joseph A. Labadie, *Report of Joseph A. Labadie, Delegate to the General Assembly* (Detroit: printed by John R. Burton, November 14, 1887), 8–9.

21. Ware, *Labor Movement,* 262–265.

22. United States Industrial Commission, *Report of the Industrial Commission on the Relations of Capital and Labor,* vol. 7 (Washington, DC: US Government Printing Office, 1901), 623.

23. Richard Schneirov, *Labor and Urban Politics: Class Conflict and the Origins of Modern Liberalism in Chicago, 1864–97* (Urbana: University of Illinois Press, 1998), 202.

24. Montgomery, *Strikes,* 92.

25. Commons et al., *History of Labour,* 416.

26. Friedman, *New Estimates,* 78; Ware, *Labor Movement,* 66.

27. Richard Oestreicher, *Solidarity and Fragmentation: Working People and Class Consciousness in Detroit, 1875–1900* (Urbana: University of Illinois Press, 1986), 188–191.

28. Chicago Trades and Labor Assembly, *Minute Book,* regular meetings, August 7, 1887, and March 18 to May 20, 1888; Schneirov, *Labor,* 240–252.

29. Commons et al., *History of Labour,* 413–414.

30. Schneirov, 248.

31. Weir, *Knights Unhorsed,* 19–20.

32. Voss, *Exceptionalism,* 4.

33. Friedman, "New Estimates," 78.

34. Commons et al., *History of Labour,* 358.

35. US Census Bureau, *Historical Statistics of the United States: Colonial Times to 1970* (Washington, DC: US Government Printing Office, 1975), pt. 1 129, pt. 2, 224; Bureau of the Census, *A Compendium of the Ninth Census, 1870* (Washington, DC: US Government Printing Office, 1972), 796–797; Bureau of the Census, *Abstract of the Twelfth Census of the United States, 1900* (Washington, DC: US Government Printing Office, 1904), 331.

36. David Montgomery, *The Fall of the House of Labor: The Workplace, the State, and American Labor Activism, 1865–1925* (Cambridge: Cambridge University Press, 1989), 293–294.

37. Michael J. Doucet and John C. Weaver, "Material Culture and the North American

House: The Era of the Common Man, 1870–1920," *Journal of American History* 72, no. 3 (December 1985): 568–575.

38. US Census Bureau, *Historical Statistics*, pt. 1, 93–95.

39. National Bureau of Economic Research, *US Business Cycle Expansions and Contractions* (Cambridge, MA: National Bureau of Economic Research, 2010), http://data.nber.org/cycles/cyclesmain.html; Robert Higgs, *The Transformation of the American Economy, 1865–1914: An Essay in Interpretation* (New York: John Wiley & Sons, 1971), 124.

40. US Commissioner of Labor, *The First Annual Report of the Commissioner of Labor* (Washington, DC: US Government Printing Office, March 1886), 84. See chapter 3 for more details.

41. United States Senate, *Report of the Committee of the Senate upon the Relations Between Labor and Capital,* vol. 1 (Washington, DC: US Government Printing Office, 1885), 756.

42. US Census Bureau, *Historical Statistics,* pt. 1, 912–913.

43. US Commissioner of Labor, *Sixteenth Annual Report of the Commissioner of Labor*, 1901 (Washington, DC: US Government Printing Office, 1901), 343.

44. US Commissioner of Labor, *Twenty-First Annual Report of the Commissioner of Labor* (Washington, DC: US Government Printing Office, 1906), 15, 32, 36, 37.

45. Currie and Ferrie, "The Law," 51–53.

46. US Commissioner of Labor, *Third Annual Report of the Commissioner of Labor, 1887* (Washington, DC: US Government Printing Office, 1888), 14.

47. Ibid., 690–705.

48. US Commissioner of Labor, *Sixteenth Annual Report of the Commissioner of Labor*, 1901 (Washington, DC: US Government Printing Office, 1901, 342–343.

49. US Commissioner of Labor, *Third Annual Report of the Commissioner of Labor, 1887* (Washington, DC: US Government Printing Office, 1888), 140–146.

50. John R. Commons, ed., *Trade Unionism and Labor Problems* (New York: Augustus M. Kelley, 1967, originally 1905), 222.

51. Voss, *Exceptionalism*, 222.

52. Joseph R. Buchanan, *The Story of a Labor Agitator* (New York: Outlook, 1903), 109–116.

53. E. A. Allen, *Labor and Capital: Containing an Account of the Various Organizations of Farmers, Planters and Mechanics, for Mutual Improvement and Protection Against Monopoly* (Cincinnati: Central Publishing House, 1891), 226–230.

54. Daniel J. Walkowitz, *Worker City, Company Town: Iron and Cotton-Worker Protests in Troy and Cohoes, New York, 1855–84* (Urbana: University of Illinois Press, 1981), 225–226.

55. Compiled from *Journal of United Labor,* January 1881–December 1884.

56. *Report of the Proceedings of the Second Regular Session of the General Assembly,* Saint Louis, January 14–17, 1879, 108.

57. Jonathan Garlock, *Guide to the Local Assemblies of the Knights of Labor* (Westport, CT: Greenwood, 1982), xvii.

58. Compiled from *Journal of United Labor,* January 1881–December 1884.

59. *Report of the Proceedings of the Sixth Regular Session of the General Assembly,* New York, September 5–12, 1882, 294.

60. *Report of the Proceedings of the Seventh Regular Session of the General Assembly,* Cincinnati, September 4–11, 1883, 418.

61. Compiled from *Report of the Proceedings of the General Assembly,* 1879–1884.

62. US Commissioner of Labor, *Sixteenth Annual Report of the Commissioner of Labor, 1901* (Washington, DC: US Government Printing Office, 1901), 343.

63. *Record of the Proceedings of the Fourth Regular Session of the General Assembly,* Pittsburgh, September 7–11, 1880, 198.

64. See Selig Perlman, *A History of Trade Unionism in the United States* (New York: Macmillan, 1922), 33.

65. Stephan Thernstrom, *The Other Bostonians: Poverty and Progress in the American Metropolis, 1880–1970* (Cambridge, MA: Harvard University Press, 1973), 231–232.

66. Lloyd Ulman, *The Rise of the National Trade Union: The Development and Significance of Its Structure, Governing Institutions, and Economic Policies* (Cambridge, MA: Harvard University Press, 1955), 4.

67. *Journal of United Labor,* May 10, 1886, 2066; *Record of the Proceedings of the Special Session of the General Assembly,* Cleveland, May 25–June 3, 1886, 1, 20–23.

68. *Journal of United Labor,* January 1885–January 1887; Ware, *Labor Movement,* 69.

69. *Record of the Proceedings of the Knights of Labor of America, Eleventh Regular Session,* Minneapolis, October 4–19, 1887, 1547.

70. Ware, *Labor Movement,* 67.

71. David Montgomery, *Citizen Worker: The Experience of Workers in the United States with Democracy and the Free Market During the Nineteenth Century* (Cambridge: Cambridge University Press, 1993), 93.

72. For different views on the impact of such voluntary associations, see David Montgomery, "Labor in the Industrial Era," in *A History of the American Worker,* ed. Richard B. Morris (Princeton, NJ: Princeton University Press, 1983), 101–102; Mary Ann Clawson, "Fraternal Orders and Class Formation in the Nineteenth-Century United States," *Comparative Studies in Society and History* 27, no. 4 (October 1985): 672–695; Peter Rachleff, *Black Labor in Richmond, 1865–1890* (Urbana: University of Illinois Press, 1989), passim; and David Brundage, *The Making of Western Labor Radicalism: Denver's Organized Workers, 1878–1905* (Urbana: University of Illinois Press, 1995, 38–54.

73. Montgomery, "Strikes," 92; Friedman, "New Estimates," 79.

74. Ware, *Labor Movement,* 158–160.

75. Commons et al., *History of Labour,* 422.

76. Sari Bennett and Carville Earle, "The Geography of Strikes in the United States, 1881–1894," *Journal of Interdisciplinary History* 13, no. 1 (Summer 1982): 63–75.

77. Ware, *Labor Movement,* 160–161.

78. Garlock, *Guide,* 65–73, 225–228; Illinois Bureau of Labor Statistics, *Fourth Biennial Report,* 234–240.

79. Friedman, "New Estimates," 92.

80. Ware, *Labor Movement*, 280.

81. United States Industrial Commission, *Report*, vol. 7, 172, 179.

82. Friedman, "New Estimates," 83.

83. United States Industrial Commission, *Report*, vol. 7, 98.

84. Carroll D. Wright, "The National Amalgamated Association of Iron, Steel, and Tin Workers, 1892–1901," *Quarterly Journal of Economics* 16, no. 1 (November 1901): 40.

85. David Brody, *Steelworkers in America: The Nonunion Era* (Urbana: University of Illinois Press, 1998), 50–58; Jesse S. Robinson, *The Amalgamated Association of Iron, Steel and Tin Workers* (Baltimore: Johns Hopkins Press, 1920), 124.

86. Frank T. Stockton, *The International Molders' Union of North America* (Baltimore: Johns Hopkins University Press, 1921), 576.

87. United States Industrial Commission, *Report*, vol. 7, 278.

88. United States Senate, *Report of the Committee of the Senate upon the Relations of Labor and Capital*, vol. 1 (Washington, DC: US Government Printing Office, 1885), 755.

89. Ibid., 359.

90. *Iron Molders' Journal*, December 10, 1876, 179.

91. United States Senate, *Report*, vol. 1, 1140–1141.

92. United States Industrial Commission, *Report*, vol. 7, 97.

93. David R. Meyer, *The Roots of American Industrialization* (Baltimore: Johns Hopkins University Press, 2003) , 283; Pred, *Spatial Dynamics*, 66–67.

94. American Iron and Steel Association, *Statistics of the American and Foreign Iron Trades for 1885* (Philadelphia: American Iron and Steel Association, 1886), 46; American Iron and Steel Association, *Statistics of the American and Foreign Iron Trades for 1895* (Philadelphia: American Iron and Steel Association, 1896), 62.

95. Meyer, *American Industrialization*, 283; Allan R. Pred, *Spatial Dynamics*, 66–67.

96. Wright, "National Amalgamated Association," 58; Robinson, *The Amalgamated Association*, 20.

97. Wright, "National Amalgamated Association," 40.

98. Bruce Laurie, *Artisans into Workers: Labor in Nineteenth-Century America* (Urbana: University of Illinois Press, 1997), 136; *Iron Molders' Journal*, January 1896, 24.

99. *Iron Molders' Journal*, month ending January 31, 1886, 3.

100. *To the Officers and Members of the Thirteenth Session of the Iron Molders' International Union, in Convention Assembled*, Cincinnati, July 1, 1876, 1; *Sixteenth Session of the Iron Molders' Union of North America*, Brooklyn, NY, July 10, 1882, 7.

101. *Proceedings of the Eighteenth Session of the Iron Molders' Union of North America*, Saint Louis, July 11, 1888, 19–20.

102. David Montgomery, *The Fall of the House of Labor: The Workplace, the State, and American Labor Activism, 1865–1925* (Cambridge: Cambridge University Press, 1989), 203–204; John Laslett, *Labor and the Left: A Study of Socialist and Radical Influences in the American Labor Movement, 1881–1924* (New York: Basic Books, 1970), 144–146; Ware, *Labor Movement*, 187.

103. *Proceedings of the Fifth Annual Convention of the International Machinists*, Indianapolis, May 1–10, 1893.

104. Jeffrey Haydu, *Between Craft and Class: Skilled Workers and Factory Politics in the*

United States and Britain, 1890–1922 (Berkeley: University of California Press, 1988), 76.

105. Daniel Letwin, *The Challenge of Interracial Unionism: Alabama Coal Miners, 1878–1921* (Chapel Hill: University of North Carolina Press, 1998), 25.

106. McNeill, *The Labor Movement*, 241, 250.

107. Ibid., 241–242.

108. E. A. Allen, *Labor and Capital* (Cincinnati: Central Publishing House, 1891), 223–231.

109. Gutman, *Work*, 330–339.

110. Report *of the Proceedings of the Thirty-Third Annual Session of the International Typographical Union*, New York, June 1885, 12.

111. John McVicar, *Origin and Progress of the Typographical Union: Its Proceedings as a National and International Organization, 1850–1891* (Lansing, MI: Darius D. Thorpe, Printer and Binder, 1891), 93, 104–105; George A. Tracy, *History of the Typographical Union: Its Beginnings, Progress and Development, Its Beneficial and Educational Features, Together with a Chapter on the Early Organizations of Printers* (International Typographers Union, 1913), 396, 413, 439; Ulman *The Rise*, 65.

112. Supplement to the *Cigar Makers' Official Journal*, September–October 1883, 2.

113. Jim Foster, "The Ten Day Tramps," *Labor History* 23 (Fall 1982): 619, 620, 622.

114. Western Federation of Miners, *Executive Board Ledger*, 1894–1905, 1–11.

115. Lloyd Ulman, *The Rise of the National Trade Union: The Development and Significance of Its Structure, Governing Institutions, and Economic Policies* (Cambridge, MA: Harvard University Press, 1955), 49–107.

116. United States Industrial Commission, *Final Report*, vol. 17, xxvii–xxxi.

117. Ulman, *The Rise*, 68–84.

118. Ulman, *The Rise*, 65.

119. *Cigar Makers' Official Journal* (May 1904), 7; *Proceedings of the Sixteenth Session of the Cigar Makers' International Union* (Cincinnati: October 1885), 3; *Proceedings of the Seventeenth Session of the Cigar Makers' International Union* (Buffalo, NY: October 1887), 3–4; *Proceedings of the Eighteenth Session of the Cigar Makers International Union* (Buffalo, NY: October 1889), 3.

120. *Cigar Makers' Official Journal* (May 1904), 7.

121. US Commissioner of Labor, *Fifth Annual Report of the Commissioner of Labor, 1889, Railroad Labor* (Washington, DC: US Government Printing Office, 1890), 161–162.

122. Freidman, "New Estimates," 78; George Edwin McNeill, *The Labor Movement: The Problem of Today* (Boston: A. M. Bridgman, 1887), 320–327. The figure for average total trade-union membership does not include the average of approximately 180,000 who belonged to unaffiliated local unions. While their members may have traveled, they would not have had traveling cards.

123. Stockton, *Molders' Union*, 94.

124. *Proceedings of the Twelfth Session of the Iron Molders' Union of North America*, Richmond, VA, July 8, 1874, 25; Stockton, *Molders' Union*, 23.

125. *Proceedings of the Thirteenth Session of the Iron Molders' Union of North America*,

Cincinnati, July 1, 1876, 16.

126. Quoted in Ulman, *The Rise,* 79.

127. *Proceedings of the Thirty-Fifth Annual Convention of the Bricklayers and Masons' International Union of America,* Milwaukee, January 14–26, 1901, 22.

128. *Proceedings of the Sixth Convention of the International Association of Machinists,* Cincinnati, May 6–14, 1895, XII.

129. Tygiel, "Tramping Artisans," 366–367.

130. Ulman, *The Rise,* 80–81.

131. Foster, "Ten Day Tramps," 612.

132. *Cigar Makers' Official Journal,* July 10, 1881, 1; *Proceedings of the Seventeenth Session of the Cigar Makers' International Union of America,* Buffalo, NY, October 1887, 5.

133. Ibid., February–October 1881.

134. United States Industrial Commission, *Report,* vol. 7, 170.

135. Helen L. Sumner, "The Benefit System of the Cigar Makers' Union," in *Trade Unionism and Labor Problems,* ed. John R. Commons (New York: Augustus M. Kelley, 1967, originally 1905), 543.

136. Patricia A. Cooper, "The 'Traveling Fraternity': Union Cigar Makers and Geographic Mobility, 1900–1919," *Journal of Social History* 17, no. 1 (Autumn 1983): 133.

137. Melvyn Dubofsky, *Hard Work: The Making of Labor History* (Urbana: University of Illinois Press, 2000), 42–45; US Census Bureau, *Historical Statistics,* pt. 1, 602–603.

138. Foster, "Ten Day Tramps," 612.

139. Foster, "Ten Day Tramps," 619; *Proceedings of the First Convention of the Western Federation of Miners,* Butte, MT, May 15–19,1893, 1; *Proceedings of the Third Convention of the Western Federation of Miners,* May 1895, 1–2; *Miners' Magazine,* June 1900, 4–5.

140. Some of these would have been the same individuals who drifted from local to local, but the impact of turnover on growth was huge nonetheless.

141. Foster, "Ten Day Tramps," 621.

142. United States Industrial Commission, *Report,* vol. 7, 260.

143. Commons, ed., *Trade Unionism,* 534.

144. Cooper, "Traveling Fraternity," 129.

145. Friedman, "New Estimates," 81–82.

146. National Bureau of Economic Research, "US Business Cycle Expansions and Contractions," September 12, 2012, http://data.nber.org/cycles/cyclesmain.html; US Census Bureau, *Historical Statistics of the United States: Colonial Times to 1970,* pt. 2 (Washington, DC: US Government Printing Office, 1975), 224, 232, 889, 912; US Census Bureau, *Historical Statistics,* pt. 1, 238–239.

147. Eric Hobsbawm, *Labouring Men: Studies in the History of Labour* (London: Weidenfeld and Nicolson, 1964), 126–148.

148. Montgomery, "Strikes," 91–92.

149. US Commissioner of Labor, *Sixteenth Annual Report of the Commissioner of Labor, 1901* (Washington, DC: US Government Printing Office, 1901), 340–341.

150. Friedman, "New Estimates," 78.

151. US Census Bureau, *Historical Statistics of the United States: Colonial Times to 1970,*

pt. 2 (Washington, DC: US Government Printing Office, 1975), 914.

152. Alfred D. Chandler, Jr., *The Visible Hand: The Managerial Revolution in American Business* (Cambridge, MA: Harvard University Press, 1977) passim.; Sanford M. Jacoby, *Employing Bureaucracy: Managers, Unions, and the Transformation of Work in the Twentieth Century* (New York: Psychology Press, 2004) passim.

153. Matthew Josephson, *The Robber Barons: The Great American Capitalists, 1861–1901* (New York: Harcourt, Brace & World, 1934), 452.

154. R. Hal Williams, *Realigning America: McKinley, Bryan, and the Remarkable Election of 1896* (Lawrence: University of Kansas Press, 2010), 136–137, passim; Matthew Josephson, *The Politicos* (New York: Harcourt, Brace & World, 1938), 637–661.

155. Michael Goldfield, *The Color of Politics: Race and the Mainsprings of American Politics* (New York: New Press, 1997), 162–167.

156. Stromquist, *Boomers*, 229–266.

157. Schneirov, *Labor and Urban Politics*, 352–353.

158. United States Industrial Commission, *Report,* vol. 17, 17, 217–221, 247–251, 325–339; F. W. Hilbert, "Trade-Union Agreements in the Iron Molders' Union," in Jacob H. Hollander and George E. Barnett, *Studies in American Trade Unionism* (New York: Henry Holt, 1912), 23; Frank Julian Warne, *The Coal-Mine Workers: A Study in Labor Organization* (New York: Longmans, Green, 1905), 204–209, 220–224; *Machinists' Monthly Journal,* June 1899, 343–345.

159. George Barnett, "Collective Bargaining in the Typographical Union," in ed. Hollander and Barnett, *Studies,* 182.

160. Commons, ed. *Trade Unionism,* 1–12.

161. Commons, *History of Labour,* 520.

162. Tygiel, "Tramping Artisans," 369, 372.

163. Ulman, *The Rise,* 611–613.

164. Stockton, *Molders' Union,* 96.

165. United States Industrial Commission, *Report,* vol. 7, 279; *Report of the Proceedings of the Forty-Fifth Session of the International Typographical Union,* Detroit: August 14–19, 1899, 64.

166. Friedman, "New Estimates," 78.

167. Leon Fink, *The Long Gilded Age: American Capitalism and the Lessons of a New World Order* (Philadelphia: University of Pennsylvania Press, 2015), 58.

Chapter 5

1. Leon Fink, *Workingmen's Democracy: The Knights of Labor and American Politics* (Urbana: University of Illinois Press, 1983), 219.

2. John Laslett, *Labor and the Left: A study of Socialist and Radical Influences in the American Labor Movement, 1881–1924* (New York: Basic Books, 1970), 6.

3. G. D. H. Cole, *British Working Class Politics, 1832–1914* (London: George Routledge & Sons, 1941), 127–128.

4. Selig Perlman, *A History of Trade Unionism in the United States* (New York:

Macmillan, 1922), 84.

5. See, for example, Walter Dean Burnham, *Critical Elections and the Wellsprings of American Politics* (New York: W. W. Norton, 1970), 20–21, and R. Hall Williams, *Realigning America: McKinley, Bryan, and the Remarkable Election of 1896* (Lawrence: University of Kansas Press, 2010), 8–9.

6. David Montgomery, *Citizen Worker: The Experience of Workers in the United States with Democracy and the Free Market During the Nineteenth Century* Cambridge: Cambridge University Press, 1993), 24.

7. US Census Bureau, *Historical Statistics of the United States: Colonial Times to 1970*, pt. 2 (Washington, DC: US Government Printing Office, 1975), 1071–1072; Women had voting rights in the territories of Wyoming and Utah by the 1880s, but territorial votes did not count in presidential elections, Williams, *Realigning*, 8–9.

8. Montgomery, *Citizen Worker*, 24.

9. Frances Fox Piven and Richard Cloward, *Why Americans Don't Vote* (New York: Pantheon, 1989), 86–87.

10. US Census Bureau, *Historical Statistics*, pt. 2, 1068; Burnham, *Critical Elections*, 77n10.

11. Steven P. Erie, *Rainbow's End: Irish-Americans and the Dilemma of Urban Machine Politics, 1840-1985* (Berkeley: University of California Press, 1988), 34; Richard Oestreicher, *Solidarity and Fragmentation: Working People and Class Consciousness in Detroit, 1875–1900* (Urbana: University of Illinois Press, 1986), 84.

12. Leon Fink, *Workingmen's Democracy*, xi.

13. Williams, *Realigning*, 4, 9; Burnham, *Critical Elections*, 73.

14. John D. Hicks, "The Third Party Tradition in American Politics," *Mississippi Valley Historical Review* 20, no. 1 (June 1933): 3–4; Mark Voss-Hubbard, "The 'Third Party Tradition' Reconsidered: Third Parties and American Public Life, 1830–1900," *Journal of American History* 68, no. 1 (June 1999): 121–150.

15. Eric Foner, *Free Soil, Free Labor, Free Men: The Ideology of the Republican Party Before the Civil War* (London: Oxford University Press, 1970), 153–154.

16. Matthew Josephson, *The Politicos* (New York: Harcourt, Brace & World, 1938), 158–170.

17. C. Vann Woodward, *Reunion and Reaction: The Compromise of 1877 and the End of Reconstruction* (New York: Doubleday Anchor, 1956), passim.

18. Nathan Fine, *Labor and Farmer Parties in the United States, 1828-1928* (New York: Russell & Russell, 1961), 64–65.

19. Lawrence Goodwyn, *Democratic Promise: The Populist Moment in America* (New York: Oxford University Press, 1976), 429.

20. Williams, *Realigning*, 121–156.

21. James L. Sundquist, *Dynamics of the Party System: Alignment and Realignment of Political Parties in the United States*, new ed. (Washington, DC: Brookings Institution, 1983), 148.

22. Sombart, *No Socialism*, 29–32; Erie, *Rainbow's End*, 52.

23. Martin Shefter, *Political Parties and the State: The American Historical Experience* (Princeton, NJ: Princeton University Press, 1994), 101–103, passim; Ira Katznelson,

City Trenches: Urban Politics and the Patterning of Class in the United States (Chicago: The University of Chicago Press, 1981), 1–72.

24. M. Craig Brown and Charles N. Halaby, "Machine Politics in America, 1870–1945," *Journal of Interdisciplinary History* 17, no. 3 (Winter 1987): 595; Dennis R. Judd and Todd Swanstrom, *City Politics: Private Power and Public Policy,* 4th ed. (New York: Pearson Longman, 2004), 45–49.

25. Judd and Swanstrom, *City Politics,* 57.

26. Richard Schneirov, *Labor and Urban Politics: Class Conflict and the Origins of Modern Liberalism in Chicago, 1864–97* (Urbana: University of Illinois Press,1998), 140–141, passim; Erie, *Rainbow's End,* 46.

27. Schneirov, "Periodizing," 210–211.

28. Bruce C. Nelson, *Beyond the Martyrs: A Social History of Chicago's Anarchists, 1870–1900* (New Brunswick, NJ: Rutgers University Press, 1988), 22–23.

29. Judd and Swanstrom, *City Politics,* 57; Erie, *Rainbow's End,* 32, 64–65.

30. Olivier Zunz, *The Changing Face of Inequality: Urbanization, Industrial Development, and Immigrants in Detroit, 1880–1920* (Chicago: University of Chicago Press, 1982), 105–113.

31. Brown and Halaby, "Machine Politics," 598; Erie, *Rainbow's End,* 80, passim.

32. Shefter, *Political Parties,* 160–164.

33. Ibid., 237–238; Eric Foner, *Reconstruction: America's Unfinished Revolution, 1863–1877* (New York: Harper & Row, 1988), 470.

34. Josephson, *Politicos,* 377–379.

35. Davis Montgomery, *Citizen Worker: The Experience of Workers in the United States with Democracy and the Free Market During the Nineteenth Century* (Cambridge: Cambridge University Press, 1993), 142–143.

36. Erie, *Rainbow's End,* 67.

37. M. Ostrogorski, *Democracy and the Organization of Political Parties,* vol. 2 (London: Macmillan, 1902), 285.

38. Erie, *Rainbow's End,* 79–80.

39. Ostrogorski, *Democracy,* 288.

40. James Bryce, *The American Commonwealth,* vol. 2 (Indianapolis: Liberty Fund, 1995), 788–789.

41. Bruce, *American Commonwealth,* 1041.

42. Ostrogorski, *Democracy,* 285, 289–290.

43. For the figures, see Sundquist, *Dynamics of the Party System,* 148.

44. Steven J. Ross, "The Politicalization of the Working Class: Production, Ideology, Culture and Politics in Late Nineteenth-Century Cincinnati," *Social History* 11, no. 2 (May 1986): 172–174.

45. Richard Schneirov, *Labor and Urban Politics: Class Conflict and the Origins of Modern Liberalism in Chicago, 1864–97* (Urbana: University of Illinois Press, 1998), 211.

46. Fink, *Workingmen's Democracy,* 219–221.

47. Quoted in Donald James Myers, "Birth and Establishment of the Labor Press in the United States" (master's diss., University of Wisconsin, 1950), 153.

48. Oestreicher, *Solidarity,* 119–120; *Labor Enquirer,* March 24, 1883, 4; David

Brundage, *The Making of Western Labor Radicalism: Denver's Organized Workers, 1878–1905* (Urbana: University of Illinois Press, 1994), 76–77.

49. John R. Commons and John B. Andrews, *A Documentary History of American Industrial Society,* vol. 9 (Cleveland: Arthur H. Clark Company, 1910), 23.

50. Shelton Stromquist, *A Generation of Boomers: The Pattern of Railroad Labor Conflict in Nineteenth- Century America* (Urbana: University of Illinois Press, 1993), 24.

51. John R. Commons et al., *History of Labour in the United States,* vol. 2 (New York: Macmillan, 1936), 240.

52. Michael Bellesiles, *1877: America's Year of Living Violently* (New York: New Press, 2010), 188.

53. Nathan Fine, *Labor and Farmer Parties,* 64–65; Commons et al., *History of Labour,* 240–251; Bellesiles, *1877,* 188–189.

54. Lloyd Ulman, *The Rise of the National Trade Union: The Development and Significance of Its Structure, Governing Institutions, and Economic Policies* (Cambridge, MA: Harvard University Press, 1955), 4.

55. *Report of the Proceedings of the Second Regular Session of the General Assembly,* Saint Louis, January 14–17, 1879, 117; Commons et al., *History of Labour,* 47; Gerald Friedman, "US Historical Statistics: New Estimates of Union Membership in the United States, 1880–1914," *Historical Methods: A Journal of Quantitative and Interdisciplinary History* 32, no. 2 (1999): 78.

56. Friedman, "New Estimates," 78; Norman J. Ware, *The Labor Movement in the United States, 1860–1890* (New York: Vintage, 1964), 66.

57. Fink, *Workingmen's Democracy,* xiii.

58. Ware, *Labor Movement,* 362.

59. Commons et al., *History of Labour,* 462, 466.

60. Both quotes in Robert Weir, "A Fragile Alliance: Henry George and the Knights of Labor," *American Journal of Economics and Sociology* 56, no. 4 (October 1997): 427.

61. *Proceedings of the Third Annual Session of District Assembly No. 82* (Union Pacific Employes'), Denver: January 2–7, 1887, 6.

62. Reported in *Iron Molders' Journal,* month ending December 31, 1886, 9. Also see Philip Foner, *History of the Labor Movement in the United States,* vol. 2 (New York: International Publishers, 1955), 130–131, and Commons et al., *History of Labour,* 463–464.

63. Fink, *Workingmen's Democracy,* 225.

64. Ibid., 53, 96–97, 200; Brundage, *The Making,* 97; Schneirov, *Labor,* 228.

65. *John Swinton's Paper,* November 7, 1886; Fink, *Workingmen's Democracy,* 27.

66. *Iron Molders' Journal,* month ending June 30, 1887, 3.

67. Henry George, "The New Party," *North American Review* 145, no. 368 (July 1887): 1–2.

68. Commons et al., *History of Labour,* 467.

69. Weir, "Fragile Alliance," 428.

70. Frank T. Reuter, "John Swinton's Paper," *Labor History* 1, no. 3 (1960): 307; *Patterson Labor Standard,* December 15, 1888, 2; Chicago Trades and Labor Assembly, *Ledger and Minutes Book, 1887–1897,* 222–223; Oestreicher, *Solidarity,* 214.

71. Foner, *History of the Labor Movement*, vol. 2, 145–153.

72. Schneirov, *Labor*, 218–225.

73. Commons et al., *History of Labour*, 467–469.

74. Fink, *Workingmen's Democracy*, 58.

75. US Commissioner of Labor, *Sixteenth Annual Report of the Commissioner of Labor* (Washington, DC: US Government Printing Office, 1901), 139.

76. Fink, *Workingmen's Democracy*, 97.

77. Ibid., 209.

78. Steven J. Ross, *Workers on the Edge: Work Leisure, and Politics in Industrializing Cincinnati, 1788–1890* (New York: Columbia University Press, 1985), 316.

79. Ibid., 211.

80. Jonathan Garlock, *Guide to the Local Assemblies of the Knights of Labor* (Westport, CT: Greenwood Press, 1982), 68–73; Knights of Labor, *Proceedings of the Ninth Regular Session of the General Assembly*, Hamilton, Ontario, October 5–13, 1885, 174; Knights of Labor, *Proceedings of the Tenth Regular Session of the General Assembly, Knights of Labor*, Richmond, VA, October 4–20, 1886, 326–328; Knights of Labor, *Proceedings of the Eleventh Regular Session of the General* Assembly, Knights of Labor, Minneapolis, October 4–19, 1887, 1847–1850; Illinois Bureau of Labor Statistics, *Fourth Biennial Report of the Bureau of Labor Statistics of Illinois* (Springfield, IL: H. W. Roeker, Printer and Binder, 1886), 221.

81. Goodwyn, *Democratic Promise*, 411–421.

82. Chester McA. Destler, "Consummation of a Labor-Populist Alliance in Illinois, 1894," *Mississippi Valley Historical Review* 27, no. 4 (March 1941): 589; Melvyn Dubofsky, *Hard Work: The Making of Labor History* (Urbana: University of Illinois Press, 2000), 46–47.

83. American Federation of Labor, *An Interesting Discussion of a Political Programme at the Denver Convention of the American Federation of Labor* (verbatim transcription) (New York: Freytag Printing, 1895), 55.

84. Matthew Hild, "The Knights of Labor and the Third-Party Movement in Texas, 1886–1896," *Southwestern Historical Quarterly* 119, no. 1 (July 2015): 39–43.

85. *American Federationist*, November 1894, 205–206.

86. David J. Saposs, *Left Wing Unionism: A Study of Radical Policies and Tactics* (New York: International Publishers, 1926), 25; Commons et al., *History of Labour*, 512.

87. *Report of the Proceedings of the Thirteenth Annual Convention of the American Federation of Labor*, Chicago, December 11–19, 1893, 37–38; J. F. Finn, "AF of L Leaders and the Question of Politics in the Early 1890s," *Journal of American Studies* 7, no. 3 (December 1973): 243; Foner, *History of the Labor Movement*, vol. 2, 287–288.

88. *American Federationist*, March 1894, 5–7.

89. Finn, "AF of L Leaders," 261–265; Commons et al., *History of Labour*, 511.

90. Foner, *History of the Labor Movement*, 289–290.

91. Finn, "AF of L Leaders," 244–245.

92. American Federation of Labor, *An Interesting Discussion*, 41.

93. *American Federationist*, February 1895, 285.

94. *Report of the Proceedings of the Fourteenth Annual Convention of the American*

Federation of Labor, Denver, December 10–18, 1894, 40–42; Foner, *History of the Labor Movement,* 290–294.

95. Robin Archer, *Why Is There No Labor Party in the United States?* (Princeton, NJ: Princeton University Press, 2007), 219–225; American Federation of Labor, *An Interesting Discussion,* passim.

96. *Labor Leader,* January 20, 1894; February 17, 1894; October 20, 1894; and November 3, 1894.

97. Finn, "AF of L Leaders," 254–256; *Report of the Proceedings,* 1894, 7–8; American Federation of Labor, *An Interesting Discussion,* 8. Foster was not present at the 1894 convention, but he was still an influential leader through his paper, the *Labor Leader,* which supported Populism as a national political movement.

98. *Report of the Proceedings,* 1894, 7–8; American Federation of Labor, *An Interesting Discussion,* 40, 55.

99. Commons et al., *History of Labour,* 513–514.

100. Philip Taft, *The A. F. of L. in the Time of Gompers* (New York: Harper & Bothers, 1957), 73.

101. Neville Kirk, *Comrades and Cousins: Globalization, Workers and Labour Movements in Britain, the USA and Australia from the 1880s to 1914* (London: Merlin, 2003), 37.

102. Friedman, "New Estimates," 78.

103. *Report of the Proceedings of the Fourteenth Annual Convention of the American Federation of Labor,* Denver, December 10–18, 1894, 14.

104. Eleanor Marx and Edward Aveling, *The Working Class Movement in America* (Amherst, NY: Humanity Books, 2000), 76–77, 149–151; Frederick Engels, *The Condition of the Working Class in England* (Stanford, CA: Stanford University Press, 1968), 352–359.

Conclusion

1. Joseph R. Buchanan, *The Story of a Labor Agitator* (New York: Outlook, 1903), 319.

2. Joseph A. Labadie, *Report of Joseph Labadie, Delegate to the General Assembly, K. of L.,* Minneapolis, 1887 (Detroit: John R. Burton, 1887), 4.

3. Robert E. Weir, *Knights Unhorsed: Internal Conflict in a Gilded Age Social Movement* (Detroit: Wayne State University Press, 2000), 38–39.

4. *Fifth Biennial Report of the Bureau of Labor Statistics of Illinois, 1888* (Springfield, IL: Springfield Printing, 1888), 211.

5. US Commissioner of Labor, *Sixteenth Annual Report of the Commissioner of Labor, 1901* (Washington, DC: US Government Printing Office, 1901), 343.

6. Norman Ware, *The Labor Movement in the United States, 1860–1890* (New York: Vintage, 1964), 117.

7. Ware, *Labor Movement,* 129–130.

8. Ibid., 131.

9. Ibid., 135.

10. Ibid., 134, 162, 179–190; Weir, *Knights Unhorsed,* 51–52; Gerald N. Gob, "The

Knights of Labor and the Trade Unions, 1878–1886," *Journal of Economic History* 18, no. 2 (June 1958): 179–180.

11. Jonathan Garlock, *Guide to the Local Assemblies of the Knights of Labor* (Westport, CT: Greenwood Press, 1982), xviii–xix.

12. Eric Foner, *Reconstruction: America's Unfinished Revolution, 1863–1877* (New York: Harper & Row, 1988), 603.

13. See, for example, Eric Foner, *Reconstruction*, 81–82, and James R. Grossman, *Land of Hope: Chicago, Black Southerners, and the Great Migration* (Chicago: University of Chicago Press, 1989), passim.

14. International Trade Union Confederation, *Union Growth: Draft Framework for Action* (Berlin: Third ITUC World Congress, May 18–23, 2014), 2.

15. US Census Bureau, *Statistical Abstract of the United States: 2012* (Washington, DC: US Government Printing Office, 2011), 45–46.

16. Kim Moody, *In Solidarity: Essays in Working-Class Organization in the United States* (Chicago: Haymarket, 2014), 283–298.

17. See, for example, Moody, *In Solidarity*, 55–61.

18. Susan B. Carter and Elizabeth Savoca, "Labor Mobility and Lengthy Jobs in Nineteenth Century America," *Journal of Economic History* 50, no. 1 (March 1990): 1–16.

19. Stephan Thernstrom, *Poverty and Progress: Social Mobility in a Nineteenth Century City* (New York: Atheneum, 1974); Sanford M. Jacoby, *Employing Bureaucracy: Managers, Unions, and the Transformation of Work in the 20th Century*, rev. ed. (New York: Psychology Press, 2004).

20. The tabulated tables containing this data are in California Bureau of Labor Statistics, *Fifth Biennial Report of the Bureau of Labor Statistics of the State of California for the Years 1891–1892* (Sacramento: State Printing, 1893), 246–466.

21. Carter and Savoca, "Labor Mobility," 14.

22. US Census Bureau, *Statistical Abstract of the United States 2012* (Washington, DC: US Government Printing Office, 2011), 391.

23. Sanford M. Jacoby and Sunil Sharma, "Employment Duration and Industrial Labor Mobility in the United States, 1880–1980," *Journal of Economic History* 52, no. 1 (March 1992): 166–168.

24. California Bureau of Labor Statistics, *Fifth Biennial Report*, 246–466; Carter and Savoca, "Labor Mobility," 6.

25. Jacoby and Sharma, "Employment Duration," 167.

26. National Bureau of Economic Research, *US Business Cycle Expansions and Contractions*, http://data.nber.org/cycles/cyclesmain.html.

27. Jacoby and Sharma, "Employment Duration," 167.

28. Carter and Savoca, "Labor Mobility," 10.

29. California Bureau of Labor Statistics, *Fifth Biennial Report*, 246–466.

INDEX

America, 136, 150
International Trunk Makers Union, 179
International Typographical Union
    (ITU), 33, 97–98, 135–36, 141, 139,
    150
International Working People's Association
    (IWPA), 50
Iowa, 73, 89
Ireland, 107
Irish Democratic Party, 158
Irish Home Rule Party, 5
Iron and Steel Workers Union, 35, 49
Iron Molders' Journal, 7, 34, 44, 74, 79,
    100–101, 136–37, 167
Iron Molders' Union, 100–101, 142
Iron Ship Builders Union, 16
Irving Hall, 160
Italians, 58, 106, 155
Italy, 105

J
Jackson era, 154
James, Benjamin, 105
Japan, 182
Jarrett, John, 34, 136
Jevons, William Stanley, 37
John Swinton's Paper, 44–45, 76, 166, 167
Journal of United Labor, 30, 34–35, 44, 113,
    131, 166, 167

K
Kansas, 63, 110, 113
Kansas City, 108, 110, 115
Katznelson, Ira, 20, 158, 161
Kelley, Florence, 50
Kelly, John, 159
Kennedy, D.F., 42, 51
Kentucky, 17, 63, 138, 164
Kirkland, Edward, 64, 80, 84
Knights of Labor
    assemblies of metal and hard-rock
        miners, 144
    Brotherhood of Telegraphers strike, 178
    culture of opposition, 48

District Assembly 50, 122
District Assembly 92, 39
Journal of United Labor, 30, 34, 44, 113
leadership, 120
limited unionization, and, 124
Local Assemblies representatives, 122
Local Assembly, 128
machinists, and, 138
members, 129–30, 133, 165
organizers, 179
trade unionists, and, 132
trade unions, and, 121
union membership, and, 168

L
Labadie, Joseph, 37, 43, 120, 177, 178
Labor and Capital, 105
Labor and Urban Politics, 158
Labor Enquirer, 35, 39, 44–45, 66, 114–15,
    167
Labor History, 10
Labor Leaf, 35, 38, 45, 114, 117, 167
Labor Movement in America, 113
Land and Labor Clubs, 168
Lassallean socialism, 51
Lasters, 171
Layton, Robert, 30, 33
Legacy of Conquest, The, 59
Lennon, John B., 173, 175
Lewis, John L., 57
Lewis, O.F., 90
Lichtenstein, Nelson, 12
Litchman, Charles, 128
Lithuanians, 105
Livermore, Thomas, 66
Louisville, Kentucky, 164

M
MacArthur, W., 170, 172–73
Machinists and Blacksmiths International
    Union, 100
Machinists' International Union, 170
Maguire, P.J., 119
Malthusian orthodoxy, 37

ABOUT THE AUTHOR

Kim Moody was a founder of *Labor Notes* in the United States and the author of several books on labour and politics. His most recent is *On New Terrain: How Capital is Reshaping the Battleground of Class War* (Haymarket Books, 2017). He is currently a Visiting Scholar at Centre for the Study of the Production of the Built Environment of the University of Westminster in London, and a member of the National Union of Journalist, University and College Union, the British Universities Industrial Relations Association, the Labor and Working Class History Association, and the Working Class Studies Association.